THE ULTIMATE
WEB
MARKETING
GUIDE

Michael Miller

que®   800 East 96th Street,
Indianapolis, Indiana 46240

The Ultimate Web Marketing Guide
Copyright © 2011 by Pearson Education, Inc.

ISBN-13: 978-0-7897-4100-4

ISBN-10: 0-7897-4100-8

Library of Congress Cataloging-in-Publication data is on file.

Printed in the United States on America

Second Printing: September 2011

Trademarks

Warning and Disclaimer

Bulk Sales

Que Publishing offers excellent discounts on this book when ordered in quantity for bulk purchases or special sales. For more information, please contact

U.S. Corporate and Government Sales
1-800-382-3419
corpsales@pearsontechgroup.com

For sales outside of the U.S., please contact

International Sales
international@pearsoned.com

Associate Publisher
Greg Wiegand

Acquisitions Editor
Rick Kughen

Development Editor
Rick Kughen

Technical Editor
Rebecca Lieb

Managing Editor
Kristy Hart

Project Editor
Betsy Harris

Copy Editor
Language Logistics, LLC

Indexer
Lisa Stumpf

Proofreader
Kathy Ruiz

Publishing Coordinator
Cindy Teeters

Book Designer
Anne Jones

Reviewers
Kevin Lee
Rebecca Lieb
Simms Jenkins

Compositor
Nonie Ratcliff

Contents at a Glance

Table of Contents

About the Author

Michael Miller has written more than 100 nonfiction how-to books over the past 20 years, including Que's *YouTube for Business, Using Google AdWords and AdSense,* and *The Absolute Beginner's Guide to Computer Basics.* His other best-selling online marketing books include *The Complete Idiot's Guide to Search Engine Optimization* (Alpha Books), *Sams Teach Yourself Google Analytics in 10 Minutes* (Sams), and *Online Marketing Heroes* (Wiley).

Mr. Miller has established a reputation for clearly explaining technical topics to nontechnical readers, and for offering useful real-world advice about complicated topics. More information can be found at the author's website, located at www.molehillgroup.com.

Dedication

To Sherry—the ultimate.

Acknowledgments

Thanks to all the usual suspects at Que who helped to turn my manuscript into a printed book, including but not limited to Rick Kughen, Greg Wiegand, Betsy Harris, Chrissy White, and technical editor Rebecca Lieb.

We Want to Hear from You!

As the reader of this book, *you* are our most important critic and commentator. We value your opinion and want to know what we're doing right, what we could do better, what areas you'd like to see us publish in, and any other words of wisdom you're willing to pass our way.

As an associate publisher for Que Publishing, I welcome your comments. You can email or write me directly to let me know what you did or didn't like about this book—as well as what we can do to make our books better.

Please note that I cannot help you with technical problems related to the topic of this book. We do have a User Services group, however, where I will forward specific technical questions related to the book.

When you write, please be sure to include this book's title and author as well as your name, email address, and phone number. I will carefully review your comments and share them with the author and editors who worked on the book.

Email: feedback@quepublishing.com

Mail: Greg Wiegand
           Associate Publisher
           Que Publishing
           800 East 96th Street
           Indianapolis, IN 46240 USA

Reader Services

Visit our website and register this book at www.quepublishing.com/register for convenient access to any updates, downloads, or errata that might be available for this book.

Introduction

Marketing isn't as simple as it used to be. A decade or so ago all you had to do was put together an advertising plan, do a few direct mail pieces, and have your publicist put out a regular series of press releases. Piece of cake, that.

Today, it's a lot more complex. In addition to those traditional marketing activities, you have to do whatever it takes to market your company or your products online. In fact, for many businesses web marketing drives more business than does traditional marketing; it's certainly a different (and in some ways, more effective) way of communicating with current and potential customers.

For a traditional marketer, the whole online thing can be a little daunting. I mean, there's just so many things to deal with—search engines, email, blogs, social networks, you name it. And that's before you get into the whole mobile marketing thing, which adds another layer of complexity.

It's not just the number of activities, either. Web marketing is...well, it's *different* from traditional marketing. Marketing in print and over the air is pretty much a mass market, broadcast way of talking to your customers. Online, there's a lot of narrowcasting, focused communication to distinct customer groups. In some instances, it's not even a one-way communication; when you're talking Facebook and MySpace and the like, your customers get to talk back to you. That may be nice in theory, but it's way different from what you're used to out there in the physical world.

What do you need to know to market online? How do you develop an effective web marketing strategy? Which activities do you need to focus on, and how do you do what you need to do? And what about Twitter and Facebook and the iPhone and all the new media that keep popping up?

Whether you're new to this web marketing thing or just trying to keep your head above water, you need a little help. In fact, you might need a lot of help. Don't be ashamed of that.

Not to worry—help is at hand, in the form of the book you hold in your hands. *The Ultimate Web Marketing Guide* is your ultimate guide to anything and everything there is to know about web marketing. Whether you don't know a keyword from a tweet or if you're not sure how to optimize your mobile site for local search, this book will help. I promise. There's a lot to learn, but if you approach it logically, it'll make sense.

What's in This Book

So what can you expect to find in this book? Well, the title rather immodestly describes what's inside.

This is *The Ultimate Web Marketing Guide*, after all, which means I cover everything you need to know about web marketing. It doesn't matter how inexperienced you are, I'll get you up to speed—and help you move on through the newest and most advanced activities.

I start with research and planning and budgets (that includes writing a marketing plan, no surprise) and work through all the possible components of a web marketing strategy. That includes website development, search engine marketing, online advertising, email marketing, blog marketing, social media marketing, online PR, multimedia marketing (podcasts and videos), and the newest big thing, mobile marketing.

For each activity, I present a basic overview of what's involved, get down into key operational details, show you how to implement that activity in your own plan, and describe how to track your performance. It's kind of Web Marketing 101—you learn a little bit about a lot of stuff, with an emphasis on mastering the basics.

And here's the deal: Everything I talk about, I do so in plain English. No convoluted techno-speak here—nor, for that matter, are there many (if any) overused marketing clichés. I try to present things in a conversational manner, that an average person can understand. No insider knowledge necessary.

Who This Book Is For

It would be easy to say that this book is written for anybody doing marketing on the Web, but that isn't necessarily the case—although I think all web marketers can find something of value here.

First, I assume that you have a little bit of marketing knowledge. In other words, I'm writing for marketers, even if you're just starting out in marketing in general or web marketing in particular. So if you don't know what demographics are, or any of the rest of that Marketing 101 stuff, you might be a little lost in places.

Second, if you're working for a Fortune 100 company in a marketing department so large that every keyword you choose has its own staff member assigned, you might find some of what's covered in this book a bit basic. I don't cover a lot of advanced or esoteric topics but pretty much stick to the basics because I believe the basics matter.

With those caveats in place, I don't assume that you have a lot of experience in web marketing. That's what this book is about, after all, showing you the web marketing ropes. So if you've never optimized a web page or written a blog post, don't worry; I'll walk you through everything you need to know.

How This Book Is Organized

The Ultimate Web Marketing Guide is meant to be both a tutorial and reference, which means you can read it from front to back if you like (and that's certainly the way I wrote it), or put it on your shelf and reference individual chapters as necessary. Read it as a whole or out of order, whatever works best for you.

This is a long book, as befits the general topic of web marketing. To make it a little easier to navigate, the book is organized into twelve main parts, each focused on a particular marketing topic:

- **Part I, "Web Marketing 101,"** provides an introduction to web marketing and discusses the marketing fundamentals you need to participate.

- **Part II, "Planning Your Online Activities,"** is all about what you do before you start marketing—research, planning, budgeting, and the like. Read these chapters before you start working on the individual components of your strategy.

- **Part III, "Website Presence,"** addresses the first and most important component of your web marketing, your website. Learn how to design an effective website, integrate ecommerce functionality, and track performance with web analytics.

- **Part IV, "Search Engine Marketing,"** builds on the previous chapters to discuss how to optimize your website to rank higher in the search results for Google and other search engines. You learn all about basic search engine optimization (SEO), advanced optimization techniques, and how to track your search performance.

- **Part V, "Online Advertising,"** covers all different types of web advertising, from pay-per-click (PPC) to display advertising, as well as how to track your online advertising performance.

- **Part VI, "Email Marketing,"** delves into the details of using email as part of your web marketing strategy. You learn how to build email mailing lists, develop an email marketing campaign, and track the performance of your email marketing activities.

- **Part VII, "Blog Marketing,"** helps you get involved in the blogosphere. You learn why and how to create your own company or product blog, as well as how to influence other bloggers to mention your products.

- **Part VIII, "Social Media Marketing,"** shows you how to utilize social networks like Facebook and Twitter in your web marketing plan. You learn how to participate in social media, market on the various social media sites, and track your social media marketing performance.

- **Part IX, "Online PR,"** helps you move your public relations efforts online. You learn how to develop new sources and techniques, create an online press room, and track your online PR performance. (Yes, you can actually track direct results online!)

- **Part X, "Multimedia Marketing,"** is all about using podcasts and videos—especially YouTube videos—in your web marketing mix.

- **Part XI, "Mobile Marketing,"** explains why you need to adapt your web marketing plans to embrace iPhones and other mobile devices. You learn how to design a mobile-friendly website, advertise on mobile devices, market via mobile applications, and track your mobile performance.

- **Part XII, "Online Marketing Management,"** wraps things up by showing you how to manage your web marketing activities and prepare for upcoming changes in technology and communications.

By the end of the book you should have a basic understanding of all the different activities involved in web marketing and should be able to develop and implement your own web marketing strategy.

Conventions Used in This Book

I hope that this book is easy enough to figure out on its own without requiring its own instruction manual. As you read through the pages, however, it helps to know precisely how I've presented specific types of information.

As you read through this book you'll note several special elements, presented in what we in the publishing business call "margin notes." These note present additional information and advice beyond what you find in the regular text.

note This is a note that presents some interesting information, even if it isn't wholly relevant to the discussion in the main text.

Beyond the main text, I end each chapter with a kind of sidebar observation. These sections aren't necessarily factual, as the rest of the text is supposed to be; they're more opinion, looking at web marketing from my personal viewpoint. Take 'em or leave 'em—that's up to you.

Prepare to Market—Online

Now that you know how to use this book, it's time to get to the heart of the matter. But when you're ready to take a break from marketing online, browse over to my personal website, located at www.molehillgroup.com. Here you'll find more information on this book and other books I've written—including any necessary corrections and clarifications, in the inevitable event that an error or two creeps into this text.

In addition, know that I love to hear from readers of my books. If you want to contact me, feel free to email me at webmarketinguide@molehillgroup.com. I can't promise that I'll answer every message, but I do promise that I'll read each one!

With these preliminaries out of the way, it's time to start learning more about web marketing. Turn the page and let's get to it.

Revisiting Marketing Fundamentals

Before you do web marketing, you have to know traditional marketing because when it comes right down to it, web marketing is just traditional marketing done online. Or is it?

Back to Basics: What Is Marketing?

It's important to know what you're doing before you go out and do it. So let's take a few moments and examine just what this thing called "marketing" really is. (Yeah, I know that all you marketing majors learned this back in business school, but not everyone reading this book went to b-school—and even those of us who did don't always remember things properly—so bear with me.)

The American Marketing Association (AMA) is as good a source as any to define the term "marketing," which it does as follows:

> Marketing is the activity, set of institutions, and processes for creating, communicating, delivering, and exchanging offerings that have value for customers, clients, partners, and society at large.[1]

That's a mouthful, to be sure; to me, it sounds like a politically correct definition assembled by committee. It covers all the bases but is less than concise; it really doesn't get down to the real-world core of what marketing is.

---

1. American Marketing Association, January, 2008.

Another definition comes from marketer and economist Philip Kotler, author of *Marketing Management: Analysis, Planning, and Control*, the seminal textbook on the subject. Kotler's definition is as follows:

> Marketing is the social process by which individuals and groups obtain what they need and want through creating and exchanging products and value with others.[2]

Okay, that's a little clearer, if not much shorter. To me, though, it still doesn't convey the essence of what we do as marketers. To that end, I offer my own definition of marketing:

> Marketing is the act of presenting something to someone else.

I don't pretend to be on Kotler's level, but I do like this shorter definition. It conveys in just ten words everything that marketing does.

First, this definition says that marketing is the act of *presenting*. That's pretty wide open. How can we present something? There are lots of ways. We can describe it. (That's a print ad.) We can show it. (That's a TV ad or a live demonstration.) We can even tell someone about it. (That's public relations.) It doesn't matter how we present it; it only matters that we get the word out.

Next, this definition says that we present *something*. It doesn't say what. We can present a product or service. We can present a store or company. We can present a brand or idea. We can even present ourselves.

Finally, there's who we present this thing to—*someone else*. We can present to individuals. We can present to groups. Of course, we can target whom we present to, in various ways—by gender or age or income level, for example. (That's demographic targeting.) And whomever we present to is a potential customer of whatever it is we're presenting.

By this definition, a lot of different activities fall under the guise of "marketing." Most certainly, advertising is a marketing activity, as are PR, direct mail, packaging, copywriting, and trade shows—the mainstays of the traditional marketing department. In essence, marketing is the public face of your company, product, or brand.

---

2. Philip Kotler and Gary Armstrong, *Principles of Marketing* (Prentice Hall, 1980).

But the simple act of presenting oneself to another person is also marketing. If you don't believe me, look at any personals or dating service; these people are marketing themselves to potential mates. Heck, anytime you get all dressed up for special occasion or even for a job interview or important meeting, you're marketing yourself; you're taking special effort to present yourself to other people in the best light possible.

You see, marketing is everywhere. It isn't just something that big businesses do. It's something we all do, every day. And it isn't limited to traditional media or the physical world.

The New Basics: What Is Web Marketing?

If traditional marketing is the act of presenting something to someone else, what is web marketing? Well, all you have to do is add a single word to the original definition, and you get this:

> Web marketing is the act of presenting something to someone else *online.*

That's right, web marketing is traditional marketing done online. It's that simple—and that complex.

So what changes with web marketing? Nothing general, of course, but quite a few particulars.

The first particular that changes is the act of *presenting*. On the Web, the ways in which we present our somethings are much different—and in some ways more varied—than what we're used to. We can present via email. We can present via websites. We can present via podcasts and videos. We can present via blogs and social networks. We can even, if we stretch the definition of the Web, present via mobile phones that connect to the Internet. In short, there are a lot of ways to present things online, and we have to consider them all.

note Web marketing is also referred to as *online marketing, Internet marketing,* and *digital marketing.* These are just different terms for the same set of activities; there's no fundamental difference between one or the other.

The next particular that changes is the *something* that we present. Yes, we can still present ourselves, our companies, our brands, and our products. But we can also present our *websites*. (Though you could argue that your website is an extension of yourself, your company, or your product, it's really a unique entity on its own.)

Finally, there's the *someone else* to whom we present online. While the people we reach probably aren't much different from those we reach via traditional marketing, web marketing lets us target these people in new and more refined ways. In other words, the Web lets us fine-tune our targeting in ways that aren't possible with traditional marketing; we can define our customers quite narrowly if we like.

So web marketing differs from traditional marketing mainly in the ways in which we do things. We still present something to someone; we just do it using the various media and channels available online. That might require us to change some of the ways we do things—different media have their own personalities and quirks, after all. But it shouldn't change what we do. We still have to present those important somethings to those relevant someones—we just do it online.

Essential Web Marketing Skills

Knowing that web marketing is just traditional marketing done online, what skills do you need to do your online marketing?

Well, the most important thing you need to know is that marketing online requires the same basic skills you use for traditional marketing. Marketing is marketing, after all, and key marketing skills are necessary no matter what type of marketing you're doing. So don't worry—all that stuff you learned in b-school still applies.

That said, there are some skills that are more necessary than others when marketing online. And there are some new skills you need to master because what you do online differs somewhat from what you do in traditional media.

So let's look at those marketing skills most important to web marketers. And don't worry if you aren't equally proficient in each; this book will help you learn those things you don't yet know.

Research Skills

Learning about who your customers are, what they do, and why they do what they do is essential no matter what type of marketing you do. It's also important to know what your competitors are up to and to understand a little bit about the dynamics of your particular market. Getting smart about all this stuff requires research.

Fortunately, there's a lot of research available online. That is, it's fairly easy to track what people do online; website analytics help you track what all the visitors to a given website do, even if they can't supply the why. A few clicks of the mouse and you can find out what sites drove people to your website, how long they stayed on your site, what pages they were on when they left, and so forth. That's a lot of built-in data that would be almost impossible to research in the real world outside of the Web.

You need this research—and much, much more—to make intelligent decisions about things such as the design of your website or the construction of your online advertising program. Of course, you also need research for all the traditional reasons—to determine what types of products to sell, how to package and present those products, what prices to set, and the like.

To all our benefit, even traditional research gets easier online. That is, you can use Google and other search tools to find information that might not otherwise be easy to find. You'd be surprised how much raw data is available *somewhere* on the Internet if you just know where and how to look for it. The Internet is a researcher's dream—which is also good for any marketer.

With all this raw data available, however, it's easy to get lost in the numbers. That's where analytical research skills come in. You need to be able to sort the wheat from the considerable chaff and determine what all those numbers really mean. You also need to be able to determine when raw numbers aren't enough—that is, when you need to go beyond the numbers into the whys and wherefores of customer behavior. Even with all the data available on the Internet, there's still no substitute for getting inside the minds of your customers—which is the ultimate research skill you can possess.

Planning Skills

Research helps you decide what to do. Planning skills help you determine how to do it. And trust me, when it comes to web marketing, there's a lot of planning involved.

That's because there's so much to plan. If you take advantage of all the different ways you can market online, you may find yourself simultaneously planning an email campaign, designing a new website, optimizing that website for search engines, creating both pay-per-click and web display ads, recording a series of podcasts, recording a series of videos, running a company blog, courting the attention of other bloggers and webmasters, putting up pages on (and participating in) Facebook and MySpace, feeding the daily demands of a

Twitter feed, trying to translate some or all of this activity for customers with mobile phones...should I stop there?

No matter how you look at it, that's a lot of planning, and it is continual. That is, things never stop. Yes, one ad campaign will stop on a given date, but a new one will start up shortly after. And all that blogging and podcasting and social networking doesn't stop at all—it goes on and on, day after day after ever-lovin' day. If you aren't good at planning, you'll be in way over your head when you actually move on to the Web.

Budgeting Skills

Concurrent with all that planning is budgeting—deciding how much money you spend on which components of your plan. Just because you have more marketing activities available doesn't mean you get a correspondingly larger budget to play with. A lot of budgeting for web marketers is about determining how to slice up the pie. How much money do you spend on search engine optimization versus pay-per-click advertising versus social networking versus all the other things you could (or should) be doing?

Your online budget will work a little differently from your traditional marketing budget, too. In particular, you have to get used to paying by the click for your advertising, as opposed to (or in addition to) paying for impressions. It's a more honest accounting of how your advertising works, but it's done to some degree after the fact rather than beforehand; that is, you pay when people click your ads, rather than paying for a set number of impressions upfront. That makes budgeting not necessarily more difficult, just different.

Project Management Skills

After you do all your planning and budgeting, you get to run all those myriad projects you planned. That's a lot of balls to keep in the air and, as I mentioned earlier, most of them just keep bouncing, bouncing, bouncing with no set end in sight.

Keeping all your online projects straight—and coordinated—will tax even the most organized marketer out there. If you yourself aren't that organized or detail-oriented, you'll want to hire someone who is.

Copywriting Skills

When it comes to web marketing, there's a lot of copy needed. Your website needs content, as does your blog, as do all your ads and emails and Twitter posts. That's a lot of copywriting, and you need it on a continual basis; the Internet is a virtual content machine.

And here's the thing—online copy is different from traditional copy. Online copy is shorter, with Twitter's 140-charcter limit a bit extreme, but other forums almost as limited. It's also written not just for the people who read it, but also for the search engines that search it; you have to keep search engine optimization in mind when writing every piece of copy on the Web. That's a new skill for most and a difficult one for many. Concise and searchable is what web copywriting is all about.

Analytical Skills

We talked earlier about research analysis. You also need to analyze the performance of all the online marketing you do. How do you know when something is working and when it's not? How do you know which activity is delivering the most bang for the buck? When your budget is tight, how do you know which activities to keep and which to slice?

It's all about developing analytical skills. It's not just about raw numbers, how many visitors this activity generated versus how many that one did; it's about taking those raw numbers and translating them into relative value and return on investment. If you can't properly analyze your activities, your web marketing is bound to be inefficient and possibly ineffective—neither of which is exactly desirable.

Communications Skills

This one is kind of obvious, unless you think that nobody really communicates face-to-face online. Well, not all communication is face-to-face, but every tweet you make, every email you send, every comment you contribute in an online forum is a form of communication.

This means, of course, that you're going to be doing a lot of communicating online. Not only do you have the formal stuff (which probably falls under the category of copywriting, as previously described), but you'll also be faced with a ton of informal communication. We're talking private emails to important bloggers and webmasters, Twitter tweets and Facebook posts, replies to blog comments, and answers to a lot of emails from current and potential customers. The reality is that the Internet makes it much easier for people to contact you than they could have in the pen-and-paper days; be prepared for a ton of new interactions with your customer base.

Technical Skills

Most of the skills we've been discussing have analogs in the nondigital world. But there's one new set of skills you'll need to master when you go online, which fall under the general heading of "technical" skills.

What kinds of tech skills are we talking about? It all depends on the kind of support you have; the smaller your team, the more likely you'll need to get your hands dirty in the technical area.

Getting your hands dirty might mean mastering search engine optimization techniques. It might mean learning basic HTML coding. It might mean figuring out how to create a blog and make blog posts. It might even mean getting familiar with audio and video production techniques.

All these technical skills are necessary because just about everything you do online is made possible by one or another technology. Yes, you still have to put together marketing plans and write copy and such, but then those things you do get plugged into the proper technological framework to make their way onto the Internet. If you don't do the technical work, you'll have to hire someone else to do it for you. (And even if you hire it out, it's still good to know a little bit about what's going on so you can communicate what you want to those doing the work.)

The Most Important Skill: Think Like the Customer

Of all the marketing skills, both old and new, you need to master, the most important one remains perhaps the most difficult for many. This skill, essential for any type of marketing success, involves getting inside your customers' heads to discover what they're thinking—why they do what they do and what they want you to do.

I call this skill "thinking like the customer," and it's the only way to know what you should be providing to your current and potential customers. To know what they want and how they'll respond in a given situation, you have to get inside their heads and *think like the customer*.

Some might call this marketing with a customer orientation. I suppose that's a good enough description, although it kind of implies you can have marketing *without* a customer orientation, which I don't think is possible. Not that a lot of companies don't do it; I can cite numerous examples of companies performing marketing activities with no regard at all as to how they'll play with their customer bases. That's marketing blind, in terms of connecting with the customer, and it's a sure-fire recipe for disaster. It happens when you focus too much on internal politics and processes ("my boss said that this is what he wants to see") and not enough on serving your customers' needs and wants.

I'm sure some of you are thinking that *of course* you think like the customer— you have the market research to prove it! That is, you think that because you do a lot of customer surveys and focus groups, you know how your customers think. I would argue that this type of market research provides only second-hand insight into how your customers think. Market research is better than not knowing anything at all about your customers, but even the most focused focus group is a poor substitute for hanging out with actual customers in the real world and getting inside their heads. Research, after all, only tells you what people have done or say they'll do; it really doesn't predict what happens in the ever-changing real world in which we live.

When it comes to web marketing, thinking like the customer can sometimes be defined as thinking like a site visitor, or thinking like a blog reader, or thinking like a Facebook member. You want to think like whomever it is you're trying to connect to; only then will you discover the best ways to connect. Your customers might not read blogs, or they might not have fast-enough connections for viewing videos—you need to know where they go to for the information they want and then put yourself directly in front of them there.

If you don't think like the online customer, you run the real risk of doing lots of stuff you don't need to be doing—as well as not doing lots of stuff you should be. You need to know what your customers do online and what kinds of information and services they're looking for—and then give them what they want.

This *think like the customer* philosophy permeates everything you do online. It determines what kind of website you design and what content you offer. It also determines what other online activities you engage in, whether that be blogs or social networking or whatever. It determines how you interact with your online customers and what products and services you offer online. It determines your entire web marketing strategy.

You still need all your other marketing skills, of course, as well as a certain level of technical skills. But when you learn how to think like your online customer, the rest of what you do will be just filling in the blanks.

The Bottom Line

Web marketing is just like traditional marketing, only you use the tools available online. Similar skills are necessary for web marketing as for traditional marketing, including research, planning, budgeting, project management, copywriting, and analytical and communications skills. In addition, marketing online requires some degree of technical skill, or at least the ability to interface with technical staff.

Equally if not more important is the ability to think like the customer—to get inside your customers' heads and figure out why they do what they do. This insight should inform all your marketing activities, from website design to advertisement creation. It's the best way, if not the only way, to give your customers what they want and nothing less.

B2B V. B2C MARKETING

Throughout this chapter—and throughout this book—I typically refer to people you connect with as "customers." These customers can be retail customers or they can be business customers. It doesn't matter whether you're a business-to-consumer (B2C) or business-to-business (B2B) company—the same marketing skills apply.

That said, some of the individual strategies and tactics you employ will be different in the B2B and B2C worlds. If you're dealing in B2B, for example, you'll probably do less social networking than would a comparable B2C company, if only because companies are less likely to be monitoring Twitter and Facebook feeds than an individual might.

But these strategies and tactics, as important as they are, are just details when it comes to the overall marketing skills you need to bring to the table. Put another way, you need to carry a bag filled with all the available golf clubs (and learn how to use each of them); which club you use on a given hole is determined by the needs of that hole and your individual approach to it.

Throughout this book, then, you learn about all the different skills, strategies, and tactics necessary for all types of web marketing. You have to decide which of these to employ in your own particular business. You need to learn them all but then use the ones that work best for you.

Understanding the Components of Web Marketing

Web marketing isn't just one thing; it's a collection of many different activities. It's a bit of cliché, but I like to think of web marketing as like a golf bag filled with different clubs. You need to learn how to use each of the clubs and then decide which clubs to use on the various holes you play. The clubs in your web marketing bag range from search engine optimization to social networking to blog marketing to...well, pretty much everything covered in this book.

To that end, this chapter provides a general overview of all the different components of web marketing. This is a good place to start if you're not yet sure what's involved—or if you want to brush up on all those clubs in your bag.

Web Marketing Is Your Online Presence

While not every marketer will utilize all the clubs in the web marketing bag, there's one component common to virtually every business. I'm talking about your online presence, as exemplified by your primary website.

Now, it's true that not every entity has or needs a website; you can get by, I suppose, with just a blog or a Facebook page these days. But chances are you have or want a website, which serves as the hub of all your online activities, marketing and otherwise. Everything else you do—your blog, your Facebook/MySpace pages, your Twitter feed, your YouTube videos—builds on what you do on your website. They are all subsidiary components to your website presence.

As such, your website is the most important thing you do online. This is certainly true for marketers in that your website dictates the style and approach of all your other marketing activities. Everything else builds from your website and leads back to it.

Your website is the online face of your company, organization, brand, or product. It must reflect what you are, what you do, and how you do it; it is how current and potential customers view you and, in many cases, interface with you. A bad website will turn customers off to your brand or company, while an outstanding website will create new and more loyal customers. It's something you can't take for granted.

Building an effective website, then, is key. Both the content and design of your site should work toward establishing or supporting your brand and products. In addition, both content and design should fit in holistically with all your other marketing activities.

> **note** Learn more about web marketing via your website in Part III of this book, "Website Presence."

Your customers should find a similar experience when they visit your site as they do when they view an advertisement or read a direct mail piece. Everything should work in concert, while also exploiting the specific nature of each medium.

If you plan to sell merchandise on your website, the entire process of ecommerce needs to be factored into the equation. Not only do you have to support your brand and products on your site, you also have to facilitate the sale of those products via order-

> **note** Learn more about ecommerce marketing in Chapter 8, "Creating an Ecommerce Website."

ing pages, a shopping cart, and checkout system. It's an added wrinkle—but a potentially profitable one if you're in the business of selling things online.

Web Marketing Is Search Engine Marketing

Your website also serves as a vehicle for attracting new customers via search. That is, your site needs to rank high in the search results when customers search for topics related to your business. For most sites, the majority of new visitors come directly from Google and other search engines, so the ability to rank highly in these search results is a critical component of your web marketing efforts.

To gain a higher position on search results pages, you have to optimize your site for Google and other search engines. This is called *search engine optimization* (SEO) and is a major factor in website design and content creation. That is, you have to design your site and create its content in ways that the search engines find attractive. The better optimized your site, the higher it will appear in those search results.

Why is it so important that Google's users see your site in the search results when they search for a related topic? It's simple: The higher your site is in the search results, the more it will be clicked. That's because most searchers only look at the first few sites on a search results page. In fact, to get any clicks at all, your site needs to be on the first page of those search results, and it's even better to be near the top of that first page.

The nice thing about search engine marketing is that it's relatively free; you don't have to (and in fact can't) pay for placement on most search engines' search results pages. Your placement on a search results page is entirely organic; the results you get are a direct result of how relevant your site's content is to the query being placed. The better your site matches the query, the higher it ranks in the search results—and the more visitors are sent to your site.

note Search engine marketing is effective because it's relatively simple to translate a search query into the ultimate intentions and desires of the customer. Customers essentially state in their queries what they're interested in; nothing is hidden, and nothing has to be guessed.

It's that simple—and that difficult. Because you can't buy your way to the top of the search results, you have to obtain your ranking via hard work, smarts, and skill. That's good news for smaller competitors because all the money of a big competitor is useless against a site that does better SEO. Of course, a big company can spend big bucks on SEO services, but a smaller company can get similar results by doing effective SEO in-house. This is one instance where a bigger budget doesn't guarantee better results.

Because most companies get so many visitors from the major search engines and because it's a relatively low-cost activity, search engine marketing is a major component of most web marketing plans. It's also an ongoing component; you have to constantly tinker with your site to maintain a high search ranking. That makes search engine marketing a bit time-consuming but well worth the effort.

note Learn more about search engine marketing in Part IV of this book, "Search Engine Marketing."

Web Marketing Is Online Advertising

There's another way to get your name in front of web searchers, of course, and that's by purchasing ad space on those very same search results pages. For this reason, most marketers consider search engine advertising to be part of search engine marketing. It's certainly an important component of most web marketing plans.

To advertise with Google, Yahoo!, Bing, and other major search engines, you typically create a *pay-per-click* (PPC) advertisement. A PPC ad is so-named because you pay only when the ad is clicked by a customer; you don't pay for the placement itself. It's true results-oriented advertising, unlike most traditional advertising in the offline world.

PPC advertising is also different in that you have to bid on those keywords that people are searching for. If you're a high bidder, your ad gets prominently displayed on the search results page for that particular keyword; if you're outbid, your ad gets displayed lower in the search results or not at all.

This sort of keyword bidding makes PPC advertising challenging for those used to traditional cost-per-thousand (CPM) advertising. Not only do you have to write compelling ad copy (but not a lot of it—PPC text ads are typically very short), you also have to figure out the right keywords and how much to bid on each one. It's tricky, but it's the way the advertising game is played on the Web.

Or rather, that's the way some of the advertising game is played on the Web. More traditional display advertising also exists, typically in the form of graphical banner ads found on the top or the sides of pages on some websites. These ads are typically paid for on a CPM impressions basis, although some banner ads are also sold as part of a PPC program. In any instance, there's a lot of ad inventory available on the Web, so you'll definitely want to consider some form of online advertising as part of your web marketing plan.

> **note** Learn more about PPC and other forms of online advertising in Part V of this book, "Online Advertising."

Web Marketing Is Email Marketing

I've always viewed advertising, even PPC advertising, as a kind of passive marketing. You put your ads in front of customers, most of whom choose to ignore them. It's not intrusive, and as such has a relatively low rate of effectiveness. (On the Web, click-through rates are typically in the low single digits.)

Email marketing, on the other hand, is both more intrusive and typically more effective. This is true "push" advertising; you push your message via email directly to consumers' inboxes. It's a lot harder to ignore a targeted email message than it is a web page ad.

Because of this, email marketing appeals to many types of companies, especially those with aggressive direct sales operations. Compared to other parts of the marketing mix, email marketing has several advantages, including

- **It's low-cost**—It costs next to nothing to send 100,000 emails, compared to the tens of thousands of dollars it would take to send an equivalent number of traditional pieces of mail.
- **It's fast**—You can get an email into the hands of a customer within seconds, compared to the days or weeks it might take to place an offer with traditional media.
- **It's easily trackable**—All you have to do is create a distinct landing page for the URL in the email and then track traffic coming to that page.
- **It's proactive**—Compared to search engine marketing, which waits for a user to find you, you're pushing your message to your customer base.
- **It's targeted**—You can send email promotions to specified customers in your company's database.

So how do you use email marketing? It depends on the company. Some companies send out regular emails announcing weekly promotions; others send out emails only when new products or other important news is at hand. For example, I personally look forward to the weekly emails from Ticketmaster, which announce upcoming shows in my area; it's how I keep informed of artists I like who are coming to town. Other people I know like to receive the regular promotional emails from their favored airlines or hotel chains, announcing current deals they might like to take part in. If you send out emails with

note Don't confuse true email marketing with its bastard cousin, spam or junk email. Email marketing is *opt-in* marketing; that is, recipients have to actively agree to receive your email marketing messages. Spam, on the other hand, requires no prior approval and is in virtually all instances an unwanted intrusion. People ignore spam; many people actually look forward to opt-in email messages from their favorite companies.

information that directly benefits your customer base, you have a winning proposition—and an important component of your web marketing plan.

> **note** Learn more about email marketing in Part VI of this book, "Email Marketing."

Web Marketing Is Blog Marketing

A website is just one kind of online presence. Many companies also host their own blogs, which they use to announce new products, promotions, and the like. You can also use a blog to establish a more direct connection with your most loyal customers. In this instance, you use blog posts to take readers behind the scenes to see how your company works and to get to know your company's employees. It's a great way to put a human face on an otherwise faceless entity.

You can include a blog as part of your normal website or as a freestanding presence. The key is to update your blog regularly and frequently; customers have to have a reason to keep coming back, which they won't do if they keep seeing the same old posts over and over. That means spending the requisite amount of time to maintain and post to your blog—more work, I know, but necessary.

Blogs—other blogs, that is—also represent a new promotional channel for your company. There are lots of blogs out there that act as de facto authorities on a given topic or for a given region, and readers look to these blogs when making related purchasing decisions. If you can gain the endorsement of these influential bloggers, new customers will follow.

This argues in favor of adding key bloggers to your online public relations mix. You should actively court the support of influential bloggers. In some instances, you can buy your way into their good graces by providing them with free products to review. Whether they actually review your goods or just mention them kindly in their blogs, it's welcome exposure.

> **note** Learn more about the various types of blog marketing in Part VII of this book, "Blog Marketing."

Web Marketing Is Social Media Marketing

In a way, blog marketing is a form of social media marketing. That is, some bloggers develop their own lively blog communities that resemble the topic-oriented communities that are part and parcel of many social networks.

Social networking, of course, is the latest and greatest thing online. (Or at least it is now; something later and greater will come along soon, I'm sure.) A social network is a website or service that lets users of various types connect with each other to share what they're doing. People create groups of "friends" or "followers" that they connect with; this connection is typically in the form of short messages or status updates.

Today, Facebook is the preeminent social networking site; it's de rigueur for a company or organization to create its own page on Facebook and sign up loyal customers as fans. You can then update your customers on new products, promotions, and other activities by posting status updates to your Facebook page.

Twitter is also a big deal, although it's more of a micro-blogging service than a social network. That is, you really don't have a company page, as you do on Facebook; all you do is post short (140-character) updates, or "tweets," that are then received by those customers who choose to follow you. You use these tweets to keep your customers updated on what you're doing and what you have to offer.

The other big social networking site is MySpace, although it's not as important as it used to be—unless you're an entertainer. For musicians, comics, actors, and the like, MySpace is the place to be. (Musicians can even sell their music directly from their MySpace pages, which makes it a blend of social networking and online music store.) Depending on the type of business you're in, MySpace may or may not make sense for your web marketing mix.

Then there are the big multi-player videogames that create their own virtual worlds online. Second Life, in particular, has its own virtual economy; you can set up shop in the Second Life world to advertise or even sell your products. It sounds odd, but this sort of immersive reality is more than just a graphical version of the old-fashioned chat room; it's a valid and viable marketing vehicle for many businesses.

The key with any type of social marketing, however, whether on Facebook, Twitter, or Second Life, is participation. These sites are really nothing more than large online communities, and you need to be an active participant if you're going to make it work for you. You just can't put up a static page

note There are also social media that let users share the things they like online, via bookmarks or references. These social bookmarking services, such as Digg and Delicious, are a great way to encourage your customers to spread the word across the Web; one satisfied user can beget dozens or hundreds of bookmarks to your site or blog.

and expect that to do the job; you have to constantly post updates and other information of interest to community members. You also need to interact with members of the community by visiting and posting to their pages and discussions. People will follow you on these social networks, but only if you also follow them. It's a give and take sort of thing, just like life in a real-world community.

> **note** Learn more about marketing via Facebook and other social networking sites in Part VIII of this book, "Social Media Marketing."

Web Marketing Is Online Public Relations

Some marketers regard social marketing as a form of public relations. Certainly, enlisting the support of sympathetic bloggers is a public relations activity. In fact, a lot of what you do online falls under the category of online PR. There are a lot of influencers online—websites, blogs, you name it.

In fact, many of the old media people you deal with now prefer to be contacted online. Instead of sending out physical press releases via postal mail, you send out virtual press releases (and accompanying media) via email. It's a lot faster—and lower cost.

Many companies also find that supporting media of all types is made easier by putting key marketing materials in a press room on their websites. It's actually easier to put all your product images, press releases, management bios, or whatever on your website, where all media can access them, than it is to supply these materials via traditional methods. A well-stocked and easy to use online press room will actually get you more placements than you would have had otherwise.

For these reasons, you really need to think of online PR as a new activity in your marketing bag. And unlike traditional PR, it's something you can measure; while you might never know what a mention in a traditional print magazine got you, it's easy enough to track those visitors to your website that resulted from an online press release or mention in a particular blog. Old-time PR people might not like this new accountability, but it puts the PR part of your program in the same league as your other measurable marketing activities.

> **note** Learn more about web-based public relations in Part IX of this book, "Online PR."

Web Marketing Is Multimedia Marketing

The Internet isn't all text, of course. Much web-based communication is done with sight and sound via digital videos and audios.

Audio marketing takes the form of *podcasts*, which are short audio broadcasts that can be streamed or downloaded from your website or from a third-party provider, such as Apple's iTunes Store. Think of a podcast as your own little radio show, which you can use to promote your company or products.

Video marketing takes the form of digital videos. You're familiar with YouTube, of course, which is the Internet's largest video sharing community. While YouTube is a haven for user-generated videos of all shapes and sizes, it's also a place where savvy businesses market themselves via videos that somehow promote their products and brands. Many companies produce self-help videos or infomercial-like videos that offer true value to viewers, who are then encouraged to click over to their main websites for more information. It's not a place for blatant commercials, but rather a subtle sell that builds brand and product loyalty.

You can also include videos and podcasts on your own website, of course. Many companies and organizations like to create video blogs, where the president or other company representative does the talking-head thing to keep viewers informed of new company, product, or industry developments. Lots of people prefer to view something rather than to read it in text format; for that reason, it's important to include video as part of your web marketing strategy.

> **note** Learn more about podcast and video marketing in Part X of this book, "Multimedia Marketing."

Web Marketing Is Mobile Marketing

Most people are used to accessing the Internet from a computer, using a web browser. But that's not the only way to go online; in fact, within a few years it might not even be the dominant way.

That's because more and people are accessing the Internet from their smartphones. I'm talking the Apple iPhone, Google Nexus One, and just about any phone that offers Internet connectivity and a mobile web browser. Connecting to the Web via a mobile phone puts a whole new spin on things; not only do you need to rethink your web page design (to offer a version that looks good on and works well with mobile screens), but you also have to consider how you can connect with these mobile users.

Mobile marketing is particularly important for local businesses. People use their phones while they're out and about, and you need to get in front of these potential customers and lead them directly to your local store. That means mobile SEO, of course, to improve your ranking with mobile searches, but it also means purchasing mobile ads for display on these devices. What you're doing on the computer-based Internet probably needs to be at least tweaked, if not totally overhauled, for the growing millions of mobile users.

In other words, mobile marketing is one more club you need in your web marketing bag. That bag keeps getting bigger as more opportunities arise online, and you need to keep developing new skills to keep up with the latest web marketing developments.

> **note** Learn more about mobile marketing in Part XI of this book, "Mobile Marketing."

The Bottom Line

Web marketing is a series of activities that present your product, company, or message to potential customers online. These activities include website creation, search engine marketing and search engine optimization, pay-per-click and display advertising, email marketing, blog marketing, social media marketing, online public relations, and audio and video marketing. Web marketing also includes mobile marketing to people who access the Internet via iPhones and other mobile devices.

HOW MANY PEOPLE DOES IT TAKE TO EXECUTE A MARKETING PLAN?

As you ponder all the different possible components of your web marketing plan, you're probably asking yourself, who does all this stuff? As in—do I have to do it all myself?

The answer, of course, is no. Or maybe it's yes. It all depends on the size of your organization, your marketing staff, and your budget.

In a small company or organization, it's likely most or all of these activities will be handled by a single individual. That might sound daunting, but it's not so bad. Many of these activities only take a little bit of your time each day, and it's easy enough to multi-task such activities as ad campaign maintenance, blog posting, and monitoring your Facebook page. Other activities, such as website SEO, are less regular and can be fit in when you have time. (And you can always hire out those activities you can't do to qualified freelancers or consultants.)

If you're in a large organization, however, you'll want to divide these activities among multiple individuals. Have one person handle your advertising; another your blog posts, tweets, and Facebook updates; and another your email campaigns. Let each person concentrate on a single area of expertise so you don't have everyone trying to do everything. Just make sure someone coordinates all these activities; you don't want anyone going rogue on you.

Basically, there's more than enough here to keep a large team quite busy. Or if your organization doesn't have the resources, you can scale back on some activities to make things more manageable for a smaller staff or even a single individual to do. You'd be surprised how many small companies can achieve the same presence as their larger and more established competitors with just one or two people running the show. On the Web, it's relatively easy for a little fish to look like a big fish—if a company's smart about it.

2

Balancing and Budgeting Online Activities

Given all the different vehicles available for web marketing, it's imperative that you give careful consideration to which elements you use to market your business online. There's no set formula; what works for one business might be a total failure for another.

In short, you need to construct a marketing mix that utilizes those components that best fit your marketing needs. You also need to allocate your budget accordingly—figuring out how much to spend on which online activities is a challenge for any marketer today.

Creating an Effective Web Marketing Mix

Marketing your business or organization online is not a simple proposition. You can't just put up a website and hope that potential customers will trip over it. No, you have to reach deep into your bag of marketing tricks to attract customers online, sway them in your direction, and persuade them to do whatever it is you want them to do—to become aware of your brand, purchase what you're selling, and so on.

As you learned in Chapter 2, "Understanding the Components of Web Marketing," there are many tools you can utilize when planning your online marketing activities. I won't repeat all that information here, but instead compare the different vehicles available and how they're typically incorporated in a marketing mix.

Search Engine Marketing

Search engine marketing is the act of optimizing your website to rank higher in the search results from Google and other search engines. This is the most common and undoubtedly the most important component of most companies' online marketing mixes.

Why is search engine marketing so important? It's simple: Most websites get at least half of their new visitors directly from search engine results pages. You need to optimize your website so that it appears as high as possible in the search engine rankings; the higher your site ranks, the more traffic you get.

The key to search engine marketing, then, is ensuring that your site ranks high enough in the search results to get noticed by potential customers—higher, most certainly than your competitors. Because you can't directly buy your way to the top of the results, you have to improve your rankings organically, by utilizing tried-and-true search engine optimization techniques.

So for most web marketers, search engine marketing and the attending SEO represent a major component of their online marketing mix. It's not the only thing you should do to market your business online, but it may be the most important.

PPC Advertising

The second most important web marketing vehicle for most sites is also related to search engines. Pay-per-click advertising buys placement on those same search results pages for your text and image ads. You purchase a specific keyword, and your ad appears whenever someone searches for that keyword.

While PPC advertising probably won't drive as much traffic to your site as will organic search results, it can still be an effective part of your mix. There will always be some percentage of searchers who either confuse paid results with organic results, thus benefiting PPC advertisers, or who trust the paid results much the same way they trust display ads in traditional Yellow Pages directories. Either way, you benefit by placing your ad on the relevant search results page.

PPC advertising can also be beneficial if you compete in a niche with some very influential targeted websites. That's because most PPC ad networks also place your ads on third-party websites that contain relevant content. Identify those sites where you'd like to place your ads, find out which ad networks those sites use, and place your ads with those networks. Purchasing the right keywords will almost guarantee placement for your ads on those sites, which should generate some very targeted traffic.

Display Advertising

Display advertising is usually less a factor than PPC advertising, at least for companies desiring direct click-through results. The problem is that display ads, when compared to search engine marketing or PPC ads, have much, much lower click-through rates. Many people see a display ad and move right past it. Even if the ad registers, they don't bother to click through, which results in click-through rates in the low single digits.

That doesn't mean that display ads have no place in your online marketing plan. If you purchase space on enough high-traffic websites, even a low click-through rate can generate significant traffic. And let us not forget, users can still receive your ad message even if they don't click the ad.

Because of this, display ads on web pages are most often used for brand-building purposes or to reinforce aspects of a larger marketing campaign. Of course, you can use display ads to drive traffic directly to your website; you just have to design your display ads in such a way to encourage clicking, and the link has to be quite obvious within the ad. In fact, display advertising is one of the fastest-growing parts of online marketing, especially as big national advertisers slowly but surely move onto the Internet. If you have a message for a mass audience and the corresponding budget, this might be a way to go.

note Even though online display ads are less efficient than online text ads, they're so much less expensive than offline ads that the inefficiencies are effectively offset.

Email Marketing

If you offer goods or services for sale over the Web, email marketing should be an essential part of your marketing mix. That's because email marketing is a form of direct marketing in that you're using the emails not to increase brand awareness or simply drive traffic to your website, but rather to solicit direct sales of a particular product or service.

An email marketing campaign involves sending targeted email messages to a company's existing customer base; these emails can advertise upcoming promotions, new products, and the like. As such, you use email marketing to entice more sales from your existing customer base. And as all marketers know, it costs a lot less to get more sales from a current customer than it does to create a new customer.

Blog Marketing

Blogs are becoming more important to savvy online marketers—especially those that recognize that a company blog can be an effective channel of communication between a company and its customers. In this regard, blogs let companies talk to and with their customer bases, and they can use the blog to convey the company's message or to solicit input from interested customers. It's a great way to research what's on the minds of your most active customers.

Because hosting and posting to a blog are relatively inexpensive (the biggest expense is the time to manage the blog), company blogs can be especially valuable to small and budget-conscious organizations. As such, an internal blog can be a valuable component of a company's overall online marketing plan.

It's also important, of course, to court attention from other bloggers. When a well-read blogger mentions your company or product, that's like free advertising to all of that blogger's readers. In fact, it can be even better than that; in some readers' eyes, it's tantamount to a celebrity endorsement.

You influence these influencers using traditional public relations techniques adapted for the Web and work them much as you'd work reviewers at traditional print newspapers and magazines. But there are also some blogs that let you pay for a mention or review. This sort of paid placement is similar to product placement in movies or TV shows and is becoming more common in the blogosphere.

Social Media Marketing

Social networking, which is the biggest subset of all the social media, is the new big thing on the Web, and most of the hype is justified. A surprising number of consumers sign up to follow their favorite companies (and celebrities, of course) on Twitter, Facebook, and the like.

As such, it's important to establish your own presence on these social networks. It's becoming a big enough part of the mix that many larger companies have at least one individual devoted solely to social media marketing—making the daily tweets and status updates and posting product information and photos on a regular basis.

You should also create the appropriate profile page for your company and use that page to announce upcoming products, promotions, and events. Naturally, your profile page should include links back to your company's website—or, even better, a landing page customized for your "friends" on that social network.

In addition, Facebook and MySpace (not Twitter, though) let you advertise on their sites. These ads are typically PPCs, where you specify a particular demographic profile and your ad is served to members who match those demographics. It's probably too early in the game to know just how effective these ads can be, but they're probably worth considering as a supplement to your mainstream social networking activities.

Online Public Relations

Public relations is always a key component of your marketing strategy, whether you're talking traditional or web marketing. In some aspects, online PR is no different from traditional PR; you're trying to get as many outlets as possible to mention your latest product or service. But online PR involves many new and different channels you need to address, from blogs and social networks to topic-oriented communities and message boards. It's not as simple as sending out a hardcopy press release.

Another way that online PR differs from traditional PR is that results are more easily tracked. With traditional PR, about the only thing you can track is actual mentions in the media. With online PR, however, you can track actual sales that result from mentions on various websites; all you have to do is provide the solicited media with their own dedicated URLs to link back to your site.

Multimedia Marketing

If you want to cover all bases with your online marketing, you need to create both audio and video components in the form of podcasts and online videos. Done right, these elements can bring in lots of new customers—and help support your existing customer base.

Podcasts are like short web-based radio broadcasts. Many people listen to podcasts on their computers; many more download podcasts to their iPods and listen on the go. In either case, if you offer informative content in a podcast, you'll get listeners—and those listeners will translate into new customers.

Online videos can both attract new customers and support existing ones. Most videos today are served via YouTube and similar video sharing sites; if you produce a YouTube video that goes viral, it can be seen by a potential audience of millions—some subset of which can then be persuaded to visit your website for more information or to purchase whatever it is that you're selling.

Of course, the most effective podcasts and videos aren't overt advertisements; online users don't waste their time listening to or watching online what they tend to skip over when they're listening to traditional radio or watching traditional television. Instead, you need to create a podcast or video that people really want to listen to or watch—something entertaining, educational, or informative. That might be a funny video promoting your brand or product, a how-to video demonstrating how to do something that people really need to do, or a podcast packed with useful news or information. In fact, the most effective podcasts and videos are more like infomercials; they use a light sell to get their message across and entice viewers to ask for more.

The good thing about this type of multimedia marketing is that it's relatively cost-effective. You can produce a podcast with a low-cost USB microphone and your existing computer; most YouTube videos are shot with standard consumer-grade camcorders and edited with video editing software included for free on most computers. That results in a big bang for your marketing bucks, which is why podcasts and videos are so attractive—especially to smaller marketers.

Mobile Marketing

The last component of your online marketing mix has nothing to do with computers. Mobile marketing involves those activities targeted at users accessing the Web from their smartphones. There's a big market of just iPhone users; factor in all the other mobile phones with Internet access, and you can see how large this market is.

It's also a growing market, as web-enabled phones become more and more common. You'll need to adapt some of your marketing efforts to target these mobile users; this means creating mobile-friendly web pages and ads and even devising mobile-only marketing campaigns. Don't ignore this one; given time, the mobile web will be bigger than the computer-based Internet.

Website Marketing

Of course, all these elements revolve around yet another key marketing vehicle—your website. You need to design your website so that it ties in to all your other marketing efforts, as well as serve as a home base for everything you're doing online.

That means creating a website that's rich in content and that mirrors your ongoing image and branding efforts. As we've previously discussed, it should also be search engine friendly—that is, optimized for search engine marketing. And it needs to include separate landing pages for all the ads and links that drive traffic to the site.

All that's a tall order, but it's vitally important. In fact, your website is the most important part of your web marketing strategy. Everything you do starts with your site, and everything you do leads to your site. It's the hub of all your web marketing activities.

Coordinating Your Web Marketing Activities

Most companies will include several if not all of these vehicles in their web marketing plans. As such, it's important that all these components mesh with one another. They should all carry the same message; you don't want to present one image to the search engines, another to customers viewing display ads, and yet another to blogs and social networks. Your message should be consistent, no matter where customers encounter that message.

What does that mean, in reality?

First, it means that the way you define your business has to be consistent. The keywords you choose as part of your search engine optimization should also be the keywords you purchase for your PPC advertising, should also be keywords in the copy for your display ads, should also be highlighted in the promotional emails you send to customers, should also be talking points when you communicate with influential bloggers, should also be present in the electronic press releases you send to online news organizations, should also be featured in the copy on your web pages, and so on. You can't describe your business one way in press releases, another way in advertisements, and yet another way to the search engines—you must have a consistent message.

That extends to using themes and images from your display advertising on your website—especially in the landing pages you create for your search engine and email marketing campaigns. When someone clicks the URL in a promotional email, he or she should land on a page that not only repeats the message of the email, but also mirrors the look and feel of your display advertising. Again, consistency is the key.

That doesn't mean, however, that you can't adapt the message for the medium. PPC and display ads, for example, demand much less copy than do promotional emails and landing web pages. Your message and image have to reflect how they're being delivered. Given the unique qualities of each online medium, you can't be a slave to consistency.

You should also strive to exploit the unique features of each channel. Granted, there's not a whole lot you can do with a three-line text PPC ad, but most online channels have qualities that reward creativity. For example, you can put together a contest on YouTube that encourages viewers to submit their own videos for your newest product; this is not a campaign that is easily mirrored in other online media. (That contest, of course, should not conflict with the main image and message you convey in other media.)

The point is, all of your online channels need to work together. They have to convey a consistent message and image and should not send conflicting messages to your customer base. Your online marketing mix should be a consistent whole that is greater than the sum of its parts.

And driving your consistent message is your intimate knowledge of the market and your customers—your ability to *think like the customer*. This insight helps you select the right keywords for your search engine marketing and PPC advertising, as well as informs the messages and images you send in your display advertising and public relations efforts.

Setting Your Web Marketing Budget

Part and parcel of concocting the proper web marketing strategy is budgeting for those activities. That includes setting a total web marketing budget, as well as allocating that budget to individual activities.

Setting the Total Budget

How much money should you budget for your web marketing activities? If you have any marketing experience at all, you should know better than to expect an exact dollar answer to this question. Your budget depends on the size of your company, the available funds, the competitive landscape, and what you hope to accomplish.

That said, I can offer some general guidelines.

Looking at things from the top down, you should consider allocating anywhere from 15% to 50% of your total marketing budget to online activities.

These are rough guidelines, I know, but they get you in the ballpark. If you're a smaller company, you should probably lean toward the larger percentage; larger companies will typically spend a little less percentage-wise but still expend a large dollar amount.

Let's look at a couple of examples. Let's say you're a company with a revenue of $1 million in an industry that typically spends about 5% of revenue on marketing. This puts your total marketing budget at $50,000. If you allocate half your total marketing budget to online activities, you'll spend $25,000 yearly.

In contrast, let's say you're a company with $10 million in revenue in an industry that typically spends 15% of revenue on marketing. This puts your total marketing budget at $1.5 million. If you allocate 15% of that budget to online activities, you'll spend $225,000 yearly.

Beyond raw percentages, there are other factors to keep in mind when setting your marketing budget. These include the following:

> **note** Marketing expenditures as a percent of total revenue varies wildly from industry to industry and company to company. In the B2B market, 5% of revenue is a good average; in the B2C market, some companies budget upward of 15% of revenue for marketing. (Retailers typically spend more than any other market segment on marketing.) Look to the appropriate industry trade group to determine what your competition is likely spending.

- **What is your competition spending?** If your primary competitor is spending seven figures a year on web marketing, you can't spend a few hundred thousand dollars and expect to keep up. To compete effectively in the online space, you need to match what the competition is spending or at least get close and try to spend more wisely. If you can't match the competition dollar-for-dollar in similar activities get used to seeing your site rank lower than the competition in Google's search results.

- **How behind the curve are you?** If you're just now getting into web marketing, you have a lot of catch-up to do. There's a bit of a start-up curve when it comes to marketing online in that it costs money to launch a website, hire staff, build an email mailing list, and the like. Your first-year expenditures will be higher than average but should normalize in subsequent years.

- **What new opportunities are coming?** That last bit about decreasing spending in subsequent years? That may or may not be true. When it comes to web marketing, there's always something new that needs to be added to your mix; developing a static mix or budget is like shooting at a moving target. (For example, social networking didn't even exist a few years ago; now it's a major part of overall web marketing.) You need to be prepared to jump on the next big thing—which means either shifting funds allocated to other activities, keeping some spare funds available for such eventualities, going over budget, or missing these new opportunities.

- **What's important?** It's probably wise to budget online marketing in such a way that increases as a percentage of your total marketing budget over time; there's no arguing web marketing is becoming more important year after year.

- **What does it really cost?** We've been talking top-down percentages, which is how many companies budget. But there's benefit in doing a bottom-up budget, where you look at each activity separately and what it will cost over the budgeted time period. You might find that you don't need to spend as much as you thought—or that your original budget was woefully low.

- **What can you afford?** Percentages are great, but you spend real dollars. There's no point budgeting a big percentage if you don't have the real cash to back it up. Be realistic as to what you can afford and budget accordingly.

So there are some guidelines and some questions to ask. Take it from there.

Allocating the Budget

Once you have a total web marketing budget, you need to divvy it up among the various online marketing activities you wish to undertake. Knowing this, what's the best way to slice up the pie?

While you can always do a bottom-up budget for each activity you'd like to undertake, that might not provide the best overview of where you want to put your marketing muscle. I prefer top-down guidance, especially if you look at things from the right perspective.

I like to organize web marketing activities into three categories:

- **Home base**—The central hub of all your online activities.

- **Outbound communication**—Activities designed to attract new customers.

■ **Two-way communication**—Activities that encourage communication between you and existing customers.

You then assign different marketing activities to each category, as detailed in Table 3.1.

Table 3.1   Online Marketing Categories

Category	Activities
Home base	Website and blog, including search engine marketing and SEO
Outbound communication	PPC and direct advertising, email marketing, online PR
Community outreach	Social networking, podcasts, videos

With your activities thus categorized, you can pretty safely allocate a third of your web marketing budget to each category. That's a rough guideline but one that works—and ensures an equal focus on your home base, new customer acquisition, and customer networking.

So for example, if you have a $100,000 budget for your online marketing activities, budget $33,333 for your website and blog; $33,333 for advertising, email marketing, and PR; and $33,333 for social marketing, podcasts, and videos.

This allocation, by the way, should apply to more than just the dollars you spend. It should also affect your staff assignments and, most importantly, the amount of time you devote to each type of activity. That's right—you probably should spend a third of your time dealing with your website and blog, a third creating advertising and email campaigns, and a third managing your social networking activity. That should give you a good balance across the board.

note Some activities cross categories. For example, mobile marketing has both home base and new customer outreach components. You should divvy up your budget accordingly.

note Naturally, expected or historical results should also figure into your marketing budget allocations. You should almost always fund activities with a higher return on investment (ROI) at higher levels than those with a lower ROI—unless it's an activity that has a greater strategic importance going forward, of course.

3

The Bottom Line

Not all web marketing activities are equal—or have equal impact. You need to design a web marketing mix that reflects the goals and needs of your organization, picking and choosing which activities you engage in accordingly. For most companies that means placing primary focus on search engine marketing and SEO, with other activities assuming a subsidiary importance (although every company is different).

Whatever your mix, you need to coordinate your marketing activities so that they present a uniform image to your customers. In addition, your online activities need to be of a whole with your traditional marketing; customers need to come away with the same impression, no matter how they come into contact with you.

This all feeds into the setting of your web marketing budget. Most companies spend between 15% and 50% of their total marketing budget on web-based activities. You then need to allocate your web marketing funds across all the different activities you engage in; spend a third on your home base (website and blog), a third on attracting new customers, and a third on social networking with existing customers.

CONTINGENCY PLANS

Here's a truism when you're first getting started online: You're going to spend a lot more than you thought. Budgets expand and break, and things always cost more than you anticipated. You need to plan for that or at least set your budget a little higher than the bottom-up forecasts indicate.

It also wouldn't hurt to have a little slack in your budget for both unexpected expenditures and for taking advantage of unforeseen opportunities. Let's say, for example, that a major competitor goes out of business. You'll want to aggressively pursue that company's former customers, which means spending some bucks for advertising and email marketing. Or maybe something interesting and relevant to your business happens out in the real world; a big PR push can gain a lot of media attention during the short term. You need to have the spare funds necessary to take advantage of these opportunities.

How you plan for these unplanned contingencies is up to you. Maybe you have an "unassigned" category in your budget, or maybe you just budget everything 5% higher than you actually expect to spend and use that excess as you see fit. Some marketers prefer to leave their budgeting a bit vague, not necessarily assigning tight category allocation, so that they have the freedom to spend where it makes sense at the time. However you approach it, however, you need to expect the unexpected—and be prepared to take advantage of it.

3

Integrating Online and Traditional Marketing

Web marketing is just part of your total marketing mix. Granted, it's an important part and a growing part, but you can't (at least not yet) abandon your other marketing activities and rely solely on the Web.

To that end, you have to make your online and traditional marketing activities work together for best effect. How do you get the most out of all the media you use?

Splitting Your Budget

Just how much of your existing marketing budget do you have to allocate for online activities? We discussed this in depth in the previous chapter, but in general you'll want to spend anywhere from 15% to 50% of your marketing budget for online activities. Whichever end of this range you embrace, that's a big shift.

You can spend closer to the lower number if you're a bigger company with a bigger overall budget. That's because a lot of online activities have a fixed cost that's the same no matter the size of the company. For example, the cost of setting up a basic website is pretty much the same for a small company or a big one—although you can always can spend a lot more for a fancier site, if you want. And if a small company wants the same online social presence as a larger one, it'll have to spend the same amount of time blogging and social networking.

A smaller company, then, will probably devote a larger percentage of its budget to online activities than a larger one will. If that describes your situation, you have some hard choices to make—especially if you need to shift half your budget from traditional activities to online ones. In this instance, you may want to consider increasing your overall budget to help compensate—and to avoid killing still-useful traditional marketing activities.

note Some activities, however, do scale upward with size—advertising, for example. A big company can have a much bigger advertising budget (and run a lot more ads in a lot more places) than a smaller company might.

Online and Traditional Analogs

Even though online marketing activities appear to be much different from traditional marketing activities, in reality some of these new activities are quite similar to the older ones you're used to. As such, the skills you've already acquired may translate, to some degree, to the new media.

Which new activities are analogous to traditional activities? Let's take a look.

Online Advertising: Print Advertising

This first one is somewhat obvious—to some degree, advertising is advertising. So the print advertising skills you've learned apply to some degree to the new online advertising you'll be doing.

Probably the biggest advertising skill that carries forward is that of copywriting. You have to write copy for your online ads just as you do for your traditional print ads, after all. There's always a need for copy.

Online ads, however, typically use much less copy than you're used to seeing in print. A typical PPC ad, for example, only has three or four lines to work with—and one of them is your website's URL. So that's a few short lines of text compared to the several paragraphs you typically have in a newspaper or magazine advertisement.

The upshot is that your online copywriting has to be much more concise than your print copywriting. Every word counts; there's no room for wasted words. This doesn't necessarily lead to elegant wordsmithing, but if done right does result in some very efficient and effective copy.

Another essential difference between online and print advertising is that with print ads, when they're printed, they're done. With online ads, there's a lot of tweaking and rewriting on-the-fly, based on the real-time results you receive from your campaign. It's easy, almost *too* easy, to change online ad content while an ad is running. You just can't do that with print advertising.

As to art direction…well, most web ads are text ads, no images at all. That, sorry to say, doesn't translate into much work for the art guys. That said, some PPC ads are image ads, and display advertising is a small but growing segment of the online advertising category, which means that there's still some art direction needed. Otherwise, art and design skills can be applied to website design, which has plenty of room for both words and pictures.

Ecommerce: Catalog/Direct Marketing

If you currently sell merchandise via catalogs and other direct marketing vehicles, those skills translate almost exactly to ecommerce marketing—that is, to creating an effective ecommerce website. All those product pages in your catalog become product pages on your website; in fact, on the Web you have space for even more copy and pictures than you do in print. If you're good at catalog marketing, you should be equally good at ecommerce. The same copywriting, art design, and related skills apply.

It's not just your marketing skills that translate; the entire backend operation you set up for your catalog/direct marketing operation should be able to function intact for your online operation. It's true. Some of the most effective ecommerce players, such as L.L. Bean and Lands End, were catalog merchants in the past. (And remain so today—in addition to their online sales.) While upstart ecommerce sites struggled to set up workable warehouses and shipping operations, the catalog guys just plugged their websites into their existing backends and were good to go—complete with top-notch customer service—from day one. It's an almost exact translation of skills.

Email Marketing: Direct Mail

Similarly, if you're currently doing direct mail marketing, you can apply most of those skills to email marketing. An email solicitation is quite similar to one made via postal mail. It's the same words and pictures, just without the paper and return envelop. If you can write effective direct mail copy, you should be good to go for email marketing campaigns.

And as with catalog marketing, the fulfillment operation you have set up for direct mail should be able to transition fairly easily to email fulfillment. An order is an order, in any case. You just have to retrain the backend folks to receive orders electronically instead of via the phone or mail, and the rest follows.

Video Marketing: Television Advertising

If you decide to dip your toes into online video marketing via YouTube or other sites, then you can apply some of the skills learned producing television commercials to the new medium. Notice that I said *some* of the skills—not necessarily all.

In particular, you can use the writing and production skills you learned in commercial production to help you produce your new online videos. Online videos need storyboards and dialogs, just as traditional commercials do, so those skills translate very well. In addition, whatever you know about video production will translate, to some degree, to the new medium.

What's different about online video is that it doesn't typically have the same production values as do television commercials. You don't need to rent a studio and hire a crew of professionals; most of the videos you see on YouTube are produced in the field, using consumer-grade webcams. You'll need to adjust to that.

You'll also need to adjust to the fact that you can't just put a commercial online. The online videos you create have to be more like infomercials, providing a modicum of useful information or advice, rather than blatant promotional messages. The online viewer simply won't sit through commercials; you have to offer something of real value to attract eyeballs on the Web. So that means moving from a strict promotional approach to something more value-added; it's a different application of your skills.

Online PR: Traditional PR

Another obvious analog between traditional and online marketing is public relations. In many ways, it doesn't matter where you're doing it; PR is PR. You're still trying to influence people and publications to provide free mention of your company or products.

In the traditional world, you're trying to influence magazine and newspaper editors, television and radio producers, reviewers, and so on. Online, you're trying to influence bloggers and webmasters, as well as online reviewers. In fact, it may be many of the same people just doing slightly different jobs.

You can also use online media to reach your traditional PR contacts. Instead of sending out a paper press release via postal mail, you send out an electronic press release via email. The techniques are much the same, just using a different delivery method.

What Activities Don't Translate?

For all those traditional marketing activities that have exact or similar analogs in the online world, there are many new activities that don't compare to anything you've done before. These new activities require new skill sets and perhaps new staff to successfully master.

What are these new nontraditional activities? Here's a short list:

- **Search engine marketing**—There's probably not much you've done previously that prepares you for optimizing your website or blog to rank higher in web search engine results. This activity requires a modicum of technical skills paired to a marketing mindset but is truly unlike anything you've done in the past.

- **Podcasting**—Okay, so creating a podcast is kind of like producing a radio show. But how many of you have produced radio shows as part of your traditional marketing? If you've done full-length radio, you have a head-start, but chances are the only radio you've done are 30-second commercials—which have little to do with longer podcasts. So this is probably going to require new skills for most of you.

- **Social networking**—It would be nice if it were otherwise, but most traditional marketers don't have a lot of daily interaction with their customers. That's what's different about social networking; it's a constant interaction with customers online. Maybe you apply some PR skills, but it's still a kind of face-to-face communication that we just haven't had the opportunity to do before. When you move to Facebook and Twitter and the like, you'll really get your hands dirty and learn how to deal, as politely as possible, with people who have very strong opinions about you and what you do. Social networking may have more in common with customer support than it does with traditional marketing—which means you'll probably be learning as you go along.

Which Activities Can You Eliminate?

When it comes to working with both online and traditional media, then, you have some tough choices to make. You have to slice off some of your existing marketing budget to fund your online activities; few organizations will provide funds over and above the existing marketing budget to go online. And since you'll probably have to divert some of your existing funds to pay for what you want to do online, you'll have to cut back on something.

What, then, has to go? There are some tough choices ahead.

Eliminating Duplicative Activities

The easiest activities to cut or cut back on are those that duplicate new online activities—that is, activities that reach the same or similar audience with the same general goals.

For example, if you're in the direct marketing business, you probably spend a lot of money sending out print catalogs and flyers. That's the way it's always been done, after all. But with the advent of the Web, a certain number of customers who previously perused your catalogs are now shopping directly at your website. That's a good thing, as it costs a lot less to put up a web page than it does to print multiple catalog pages. It also means you can divert some of your budget for print catalogs to your website. You don't have to print as many catalogs each year, send them to as many people, or make them quite so fancy. Cut back on your catalog budget and instead spend the money making a better website.

The same thing goes if you do a lot of direct mail. Traditional postal mail is being replaced by electronic mail, and the same should be the case with your promotional efforts. Cut back on your direct mail budget and funnel those funds into email marketing instead—piece of cake.

Other decisions might be less easy to make. Do you cut your print advertising budget to pay for your PPC web ads? How much of your PR activity shifts to the Web? Do you need to go to as many trade shows now that you're reaching the same customers via Facebook and Twitter? You'll need to make these decisions on a case-by-case basis, but know that the decisions will have to be made.

Cutting Ineffective Activities

Budget cutting is easier when there's a clear example of something not working. If you see declining results for a particular activity quarter after quarter, you need to take a closer look—and possibly cut that activity completely.

What sorts of activities are ripe for cutting? Perhaps you're a car dealer that used to do a lot of classified advertising. It's no secret that newspaper audiences are getting smaller, with fewer readers hitting the classifieds each day.

If your classified ads are resulting in significantly fewer sales, why continue funding that activity at previous levels?

This approach to budget cutting requires a totally objective look at the data. You can't let your emotions or your attachment to certain activities get in the way of your decision making. If something's not working, you need to be dispassionate about cutting it. It doesn't matter that you've always done things this way or that there's a long company tradition of this or that; you need to be able to let go of the past and make decisions based on what's happening today.

That doesn't mean that you should make these decisions rashly or without reason. You need to look at the data for several time periods and see where the trends are heading. You also need to look for any extraneous circumstances that might be affecting the results in the short term; some declining performers come back naturally over time.

In other words, do your homework. Find those activities that are truly declining in effectiveness and then direct those funds to other activities—presumably online ones—that are more effective. It's really quite simple if you can be objective about it.

Coordinating Web Marketing and Traditional Marketing

Once you achieve the ideal mix of traditional and web-based marketing activities, you now need to coordinate those activities. How then, exactly, do your online and traditional marketing efforts mix?

The answer is surprisingly simple. Your online and traditional marketing activities should work together in the same way as the components of your web marketing plan do. Online and traditional activities should complement each other while delivering a consistent message, while at the same time exploiting the unique features of each medium.

This means that all of your activities should have a similar look and feel and deliver a similar message and image. It shouldn't matter where customers see you; what they see should be similar. After all, your company isn't different online than in the real world, and your marketing should be likewise similar.

This doesn't mean, however, that all you have to do is move your existing marketing activities to the Web. It's not *that* simple. Uploading an existing television commercial to YouTube will result in sure-fire failure. Likewise, you can't expect your current print advertising to translate well into a web page banner.

No, you need to think of your activities holistically, while at the same time tailoring each activity for its specific medium. Web-based advertising is a much different beast than traditional print advertising, and you have to approach it differently. You can do this while still maintaining a consistent company or brand image, of course, which is what you need to do. It'll take some work, but you can do it.

It gets easier when what you do is driven by your knowledge of what your customers want. Customer research—my old "think like the customer" mantra—not only informs the keywords that drive your search engine marketing, but it also determines what traditional media you use and the words and images you use in each media.

The end result is that all your potential customers, however you reach them, receive a powerful and consistent message—even if that message is fine-tuned for the particular aspects of that media. So you should use similar images in your television and online video ads, as well as similar copy in your print and online ads—and, of course, that copy should include many of the keywords you use in your search engine marketing and PPC advertising. One medium relates to and feeds the next, and the consistency of your message increases its power and effectiveness.

The Bottom Line

As you ramp up your online marketing activities, your overall marketing budget will start to shift from traditional to web-based activities. Depending on your organization, you may allocate 15% to 50% of your total marketing budget to online activities.

To pay for your online marketing, you'll need to cut or cut back on some of your traditional marketing activities. That means eliminating duplicative activities as well as cutting those activities that are no longer productive.

As you develop your total marketing mix, make sure that you coordinate all your activities, online and traditional. You need to present a unified image and message to your customers, no matter which media they see you in. It's all about holistic marketing across multiple media—while still tailoring each activity to the specific medium.

WHO DOES WHAT?

You can't create a holistic marketing plan across multiple media if you separate your online and traditional marketing staffs. You can't have one department responsible for the one and not for the other, and you can't employ two different ad agencies that might work at cross purposes.

The sort of cross-pollination necessary for a successful marketing mix argues for a centralized marketing effort, all working from the same customer data and with the same drivers and keywords. Your thinking should be holistic, while employing specialists to implement your message and plan for each specific medium.

It's also important to assign to a single individual some sort of oversight over all your various marketing activities. You can't have groups going off on their own without considering other ongoing activities. Someone has to make sure that all your activities, online and off, have a similar look and feel—and that someone may be you. Coordination is essential, and so is doing a little planning in advance. If everyone knows what to accomplish ahead of time, devising and executing a holistic marketing campaign will be much easier.

4

5

Online Research and Analysis

Before you put together your web marketing plan, you have to do a little homework. You need to know a bit about your customers and your competition—in short, you need to conduct some rudimentary market research.

As you'll soon learn, this market research will become a continuing thing as you need to track and analyze the performance of the online marketing activities you undertake. So you'll be constantly collecting and collating data, with the aim of making your marketing more effective and more efficient.

Fortunately, there's a lot of research you can do online—more than you're used to with traditional offline marketing. Even better, much of this online research is free.

Quantitative Versus Qualitative Research

Let's start by discussing different types of research. While there are lots of ways to look at research, most marketers divide it into two basic types: quantitative and qualitative.

The differences between the two types of research are obvious. *Quantitative research* is all about measurement; it tracks something that's already happened. *Qualitative research*, on the other hand, is *not* about numbers; it's more about *why* and *how* things happened, with the aim of using that knowledge to predict future behavior. Both types of research are useful, although quantitative research is far and away the most common type you'll encounter—especially on the Web.

Quantitative Research

When you perform quantitative research, you're collecting data. Through this data collection, quantitative research describes something that has happened in numerically precise terms. It's an historical measurement.

As such, quantitative research is perhaps the easiest type of research to do. All you have to do is somehow track customer behavior.

In the physical world, you can do this by counting customers who walk through a door or by tracking sales of a particular item. Any data that describes what people did is quantitative.

On the Web, there's a veritable goldmine of quantitative data to be had. It's relatively easy to track the actions of every visitor to your website or blog—where they came from, what they do when they get to your site, how long they spend there, what pages they view, and where they leave from. It's also easy to measure the performance of your web advertising. It's all a matter of tracking clicks—who clicks your ad, what they do when they get to your site, and so forth.

You can even find out some interesting information about the people who click your ads or visit your site. By analyzing the tracks their computers leave, you can determine where each visitor lives, what type of operating system and web browser they use, and so forth. Unfortunately, you can't track gender, age, schooling, or similar demographics, but you can find out all sorts of technical data.

The nice thing about this sort of quantitative research is that it's totally objective. Numbers are numbers, after all. If the data says that 65% of visitors leave your site without clicking a second page, then that's what happened; there's no arguing with the data. It's the *Dragnet* approach to market research—just the facts, ma'am.

The downside of quantitative research is that you don't really learn why something happened. Yes, you found out that 65% of your site's visitors leave too quickly, but you don't know why this is the case.

So quantitative research is good for describing what's happened in the past, but because you don't discover the reasons behind the actions, this is relatively ineffective in predicting what will happen in the future. (Unless, that is, the future is exactly like the past—with no new or changed variables.)

Qualitative Research

Qualitative research doesn't just describe what has happened; it attempts to go beyond the numbers to determine the root of an observed behavior. As such, it's somewhat more useful in predicting future behavior.

In traditional marketing, qualitative research typically encompasses consumer surveys and focus groups. Both methods are used to gather the impressions and thoughts of consumers, surveys by asking specific questions, and focus groups by observing participants' comments and group dynamics.

Now, I have to say that I'm not a fan of these types of traditional qualitative research. That's because they're both subjective—you're relying on participants to reply truthfully and in the case of focus groups, to react naturally. I don't think either expectation is realistic.

In the case of surveys, people often tell you what they think you want to hear. It's also common for people to respond in a politically correct fashion, especially with controversial questions. As such, the responses you receive do not necessarily reflect that person's behavior in the real world. It's an idealized response, not an accurate measurement—and therefore can't be used to accurately predict future behavior.

In the case of focus groups, you have all the issues common with surveys (people responding how they think they should as opposed to how they really should), with the added problem of group dynamics. If you've ever observed or participated in a focus group, you know exactly what I mean. It's easy for one or two people to dominate the group, consciously or unconsciously, which leads to herd behavior. It's not a natural environment by any means.

Of course, the most qualitative of qualitative research is observational research. This is where you put a guinea pig (sorry, "research subject") in a small room filled with cameras, microphones, and/or two-way mirrors and watch him do what he does, much as you'd watch a mouse in a cage. This is the type of research Microsoft does to determine the usability of its Windows operating system. You might think this type of usability research would be effective...they are watching people do something, after all. But it isn't that simple.

The problem with observational research is due to something called the *Hawthorne Effect*. This describes how the process of observing someone actually changes the behavior of the person being observed. That is, when people know they're being observed, they subtly change what they're doing, often to become more productive or to give the observers what the subjects think they want to see. It's the Hawthorne Effect that makes all observational studies at least somewhat suspect.

But that's qualitative research in the so-called real world. Moving online, web-based qualitative research consists of online surveys and focus groups—the online equivalent of what you have in the real world. And as with traditional qualitative research, there are no guarantees that what you get will be accurate or useful.

Take the example of web-based surveys. First of all, you have the traditional issue of people answering untruthfully; people can misrepresent themselves just as well online as they can when surveyed over the phone or via postal mail. Even worse, most online surveys are "opt-in," meaning someone has to make a conscious effort to go to a website and fill in the form. In today's time-pressured world, who does this sort of thing? What you end up with are surveys completed by people at the extremes—people who either really love or really hate what you do. There won't be a lot of responses in the middle.

Online focus groups, typically conducted using instant messaging or teleconferencing technology, suffer from many of the same issues as real-world focus groups, though it might not be quite as bad for single-leader herd behavior because it's more difficult to influence others when they're not physically face to face. But all the other issues remain.

Like I said, I'm not a huge fan of this type of qualitative research. Better to stick to the raw numbers of quantitative research—of which there are plenty on the Web.

Researching Traffic Patterns with Web Analytics

Here's the good news. Just about anything that any visitor to your website does can be tracked, via a set of tools collectively called *web analytics*; this is how you'll do the bulk of your online research.

Understanding Web Analytics

Web analytics is quantitative research; it's the collection and analysis of data relating to website visitors. As such, web analytics presents a way to measure the traffic to your website and then find out what visitors are doing during their visits.

Web analytics can help you discover

- How many visitors your site attracts
- Where your visitors came from—which sites directed the most traffic to your site, as well as where geographically your visitors are located
- How long visitors are staying on your site
- Which pages visitors visit first and which they visit last before they leave
- If visitors came to your site from a search engine, what keywords they searched for that brought up your site in their search results

■ If visitors came to your site from an advertisement, where that ad was placed and what percentage of visitors who saw your ad clicked it to go to your site

■ What types of web browsers your visitors are using—so you can better design your site to look good with those browsers

There are many firms that offer web analytics tools and services. One of the most popular is Google Analytics (www.google.com/analytics/), part of the vast Google empire. Google Analytics is unusually comprehensive in the metrics it tracks; it's powerful enough to track traffic at large websites, but easy enough for smaller sites to implement. It's also relatively easy to use and completely free.

note Learn more about web analytics in Chapter 9, "Tracking Website Analytics."

Beyond Data Collection: Using Web Analytic Data

While it may be interesting to know how many people visit your site each month, as well as what sites drove the most traffic to yours, but how can you put this data to good use?

The key is to analyze the data about what happened in the past to both predict and influence what happens in the future. That is, you can use web analytic data to make informed decisions about your website strategy.

Examine the data to determine what is and isn't working on your site and then use that information to play up your site's strengths and improve its weaknesses. If you know, for example, that a particular page is pulling a lot of traffic from Google and other search engines, you expand on that page's content to attract even more of that traffic. Or if you determine that visitors are leaving too soon after viewing a given page—that is, if there's nothing there to keep them sticking around—you can work to improve that page's content to be more valuable to visitors.

note When examining web analytics data, it's tempting to get engrossed by all the raw data available. While individual numbers are important, it's more important to examine longer-term trends. For example, it's more important to examine how the number of visitors is changing over time than it is to obsess over a single visitor number.

5

Web Analytics and Internet Advertising

Web analytics is also valuable if you're purchasing advertising on the Internet, especially pay-per-click advertising. You can track and analyze which keywords are triggering the most ad displays, which ads have the highest click-through rates, and which campaigns result in the most conversions from clicks to actual sales.

In other words, you can use web analytics to track the effectiveness of each ad you place. With proper analysis, you can learn which ads are driving the most potential customers and which ads aren't pulling their weight. That information will help you better place ads in your next campaign so you can fine-tune your advertising strategy over time.

Without web analytics, you have no idea which ads are working and which aren't. You learn from both your successes and your failures.

Researching Customer Opinions with Polls and Surveys

Online research isn't exclusively quantitative. There are ways to conduct qualitative research online, such as using online polls and surveys.

Web-Based Polls

It's relatively easy to add a poll gadget or widget to your website or blog. This type of poll captures specific responses to your questions by requesting respondents to select one (or more) answers from a pre-selected list. For example, you might ask the question "How did you find this website?" and supply the following possible answers:

a. Google or other search engine

b. Link from another website or blog

c. Link from a news article

d. Link in an email message

e. Friend's recommendation

f. Other

You can include open-ended questions by providing a blank text box for respondents to type into. Including open-ended questions makes data collection more difficult, of course, but can often be revealing—especially if you didn't think of all possible responses when you constructed the survey.

Email Surveys

You can also gather market intelligence through the use of email surveys. These are questions you send to select users via email. You can collect responses via email or, more commonly, direct respondents to your website (via a link in the email message) to complete the survey.

While web-based poll gadgets are easy to embed in a website, conducting a full-fledged email survey is a more involved process. That's because website poll gadgets typically ask a single question at a time; email surveys are usually more involved, asking dozens of questions.

As such, email surveys are more like traditional direct mail surveys and are best created by dedicated market research firms. A good market research firm can not only help you develop the right set of questions, but can also help you assemble a good mailing list to send the survey to. They'll also help you manage the survey from start to finish.

Limitations of Online Surveys

The problem with online polls and surveys, of course, is that people self-select who participates. You can't expose all your customers to the pool, so you start out by limiting respondents to those customers who actually visit your website or blog or to those you send an invitation email to; you exclude all customers who aren't online, don't know about your site, or just don't care to visit your site. Participation is further narrowed to those people who opt to answer the questions, which can greatly skew the results. Don't for a minute think you're getting a representative sample of your total customer base.

That said, you can obtain useful information from online surveys. It's always better to ask than not to ask, after all. But take the results with a grain of salt and don't assume that what you learn from these online respondents is indicative of what everyone thinks.

Researching Customer Behavior with Comment Analysis

Another way to conduct qualitative research is to monitor the customer comments on your website, blog, or Facebook page. What people say about you online can tell you a lot about what they're thinking—and about how you're viewed.

First, of course, you must have a forum that encourages customer comments. Blogs are natural; all you have to do is enable comments beneath all your official posts. Beyond blogs, you can initiate a message forum on your website and encourage customer participation. You can also enable a discussion tab on your Facebook page, to similar effect.

The key here is to observe and analyze what people are talking about on the forums and blogs and translate that into actionable information. What problems are people reporting? What questions are they asking? What products are they most interested in? What do they like—and what do they hate—about your products and your company? If you look closely, the information can be found.

> **note** You don't have to read all the comments yourself; there are many web- and software-based tools available to help collect and analyze customer comments.

You can also get some of this information from emails sent directly to your company, as well as reports from your customer service and technical support departments. Know, however, that you're more likely to hear complaints from these channels; that's what they're set up to take, after all. Don't expect unsolicited emails of praise.

For that matter, you'll also need to take the forum and blog comments with a grain of salt. The people who take the time to participate in a company's blog or Facebook page may not represent the bulk of your customer base. These true fans may be frequent and profitable customers, but they're also people who care enough to bother; most people don't care enough and can't be bothered, so the vocal minority who post may have little in common with the silent majority who don't. Not that there is no value to the comments posted, just that you can't allow the strong opinions of a few sway your service to the many who don't post.

Researching the Competition

Online research isn't limited to learning about your customers. There are also plenty of sources to learn more about your competition.

Website Research

Let's start with competitor's websites. Want to know how much traffic your competitors are attracting? That information is available. Several companies are in the business of reporting or estimating website traffic, and much of this information is available for free. (Some of it you have to pay for, which is the way research goes.)

For example, Alexa (www.alexa.com) offers all manner of data about just about any site on the Web, all for free. Enter the URL of the site you're researching, and Alexa displays the following information:

- Traffic rank (how this site compares to others)
- Pageviews per user
- Bounce rate
- Average time on site
- Number of sites linking to this site
- Percent of global Internet users who visit this site
- Top subdomains within this site
- Percent of visitors who came from a search engine
- Top search queries that find this site
- Audience snapshot—a brief description of the typical site visitor
- Audience demographics—a more detailed demographic overview (age, gender, education level, children, and browsing location) of the site's visitors

That's pretty good information, and it's all free. It certainly will give you a sense of how much traffic is going to a given site, where they're coming from, and who they might be.

note For what it's worth, Alexa is a subsidiary of Amazon.com.

Other sites, such as Compete (www.compete.com), comScore (www.comscore.com), Hitwise (www.hitwise.com), and Nielsen NetRatings (www.nielsen.com), offer similar competitive intelligence, but not all are free. You can also check out the free Google Trends for Websites (www.google.com/trends/); just enter a website's URL and, when the next page appears, click the Websites link.

Company Research

You can also find out about your competitors' companies, in general. Depending on the company, you may be able to view the most recent financials (revenues, profits, expenses, you name it), company news, even the names of key managers. Useful information all.

Where do you look for information about competitors? Here are some tips:

When you're searching for businesses on the Web, consider this advice:

- If all you want is a business' street address or phone number, use Google or one of the major Yellow Pages sites—or just look for that information on the company's own website.

- If you want to get the "official" line about a company *direct from the company itself*, peruse the company's website. Look for an "about us" or "corporate information" link for company-supplied information, typically targeted towards investors.

- If you want detailed and impartial financial information about a public company, check out the free financial reports at the government's EDGAR database (www.sec.gov/edgar.shtml). Additional information and research reports may be available (for a fee) from sites such as Hoovers (www.hoovers.com) and EDGAR Pro (www.edgar-online.com).

- If you're looking for financial information about a private company, there's less out there to find; private businesses are not required to disclose the same level of information as publicly-traded companies are. That said, you can also pay for Dun & Bradstreet reports (www.dnb.com) or search Better Business Bureau reviews (www.bbb.org).

- If you want to look for press releases from or about a company, check out the PR Newswire site (www.prnewswire.com). This site includes both recent press releases and a huge press release archive.

- If you want to look for news about a company, search Google News (news.google.com), then fine-tune your search to cover a specific date range.

Researching Virtually Anything with Web Search

Any overview of online research would be remiss if it didn't mention all the information you can find via Google (www.google.com), Yahoo! (www.yahoo.com), Bing (www.bing.com), and other web search engines. While you can't find *everything* by searching Google, you can find almost anything—if you're a savvy enough searcher. Construct the right query and click through the search results with an avid curiosity, and you'll be surprised what you can find online.

I like Google in particular because of all the interesting little sub-searches it offers. For example, there's Google Book Search (books.google.com), which lets you search the text of hundreds of thousands of books and periodicals;

Google Scholar (scholar.google.com), which lets you search academic journals and papers; Google Blog Search (blogsearch.google.com), which lets you search blogs and blog posts; Google Patent Search (www.google.com/patents/), which lets you search for applicable patents; and Google Groups (groups.google.com), which lets you search (and create) topic-oriented web groups and newsgroups. With all these resources at your fingertips, chances are you can find exactly what it is you're looking for.

Other Sources of Online Research

And that's not all. If you have the budget to pay for it, numerous firms offer all manner of market research conducted over the Web. You can conduct online focus groups, panels, studies, surveys, you name it. Many companies also offer similar *mobile* research, focusing on the burgeoning mobile web market. The best way to find these companies is to go Google and search for "online market research;" do a little homework and you're sure to find what you're looking for.

The Bottom Line

As with traditional market research, online research can be either quantitative or qualitative. There is a wealth of quantitative data available online, chiefly website visitor information provided by web analytics services. More qualitative research is available via website and blog polls and surveys, as well as surveys conducted via email; you can also gain insight into customer behavior by monitoring comments on web forums and blogs. In addition, the Web is a rich source of competitive information, from website traffic to financial metrics. And when in doubt, use Google to find what you're looking for!

HANDS-ON EXPERIENCE

All the research in the world, whether conducted online or via traditional methods, is no substitute for first-hand experience with your customers. Research is for guys in the corner office who can't be bothered to get out from behind the desk and meet consumers face-to-face. It's better than not knowing anything about your customers, but it's still second-hand (or third-hand) information.

Getting to know your customers is hard; it requires a lot of time and effort. It's also difficult, because the minute you walk through that office door you're no longer a part of the marketplace you're observing; you're on the other side of the table. We all lose track of our roots when the workday begins; there's just too much other stuff to do to maintain a consumer perspective.

That said, we all need to try to get out of the office and get a first-hand impression on what's happening in the real world. It's what I call *thinking like the customer*, and the only way to do it is to get your hands dirty. Market research, quantitative qualitative, can only give you the most rudimentary glimpse at what customers are really thinking. Real knowledge of what consumers are thinking comes from putting yourself out there with them.

Fortunately, as more and more consumers move online, it's becoming easier to interface with them electronically. If you simply can't talk with all your customers face-to-face, you can talk with some of them online, via blogs and Facebook pages and the like. Granted, today's blog readers might be the extreme fans and haters, but that's starting to change as the general public becomes more comfortable with social interaction over the Internet. It won't be long until you *can* go face-to-face—virtually, of course—with your core audience on the Web. And that's a major benefit accruing from the growth and acceptance of the Internet.

5

Creating a Web Marketing Plan

Before we get into all the nitty gritty details of web marketing, you need a plan—a web marketing plan. You don't want to go blindly into web marketing. You need to know what you're doing and why and what your goals are. Without a plan, you're just shooting from the hip—which is no way to run a successful business.

Why You Need a Web Marketing Plan

A web marketing plan is much like a traditional marketing plan, just tweaked for the Web. It tells you where you are, where you want to be, and how you're going to get there. The plan's focus should be on those web-based activities that contribute to some web-related goal, such as increasing traffic to your website or increasing web sales.

An effective web marketing plan is a roadmap to success. It forces marketing personnel (and your company's senior management) to embrace a set of common goals, strategies, and tactics; it keeps staff from going rogue or from taking on irrelevant or unwanted activities. It also encourages staff to think in terms of both internal and external goals and to utilize the appropriate marketing vehicles to accomplish those goals.

A web marketing plan is also necessary to achieve internal support for your marketing activities. It's something you can put in front of senior management to let them know what you hope to accomplish and to negotiate for the resources to accomplish those goals.

Finally, a web marketing plan is a tool you can use to measure your accomplishments. A good marketing plan includes quantifiable goals, whether financial (revenue or profit) or market-oriented (market share, website traffic, and so on). How close you come to meeting or exceeding those goals determines how successful your marketing activities have been.

Understanding the Elements of a Marketing Plan

A web marketing plan contains the same elements as a traditional marketing plan, which include the following:

- Executive Summary
- Mission
- Situational Analysis
- Goals and Objectives
- Marketing Strategy
- Action Plan
- Budget

The plan itself should cover a distinct timeframe, typically one year. That is, you plan all your activities one year in advance—and your goal is what you hope to accomplish in the coming twelve months.

Let's look at each section of the plan in more detail.

Executive Summary

The Executive Summary is a one-page overview of the major points in your plan—from your mission all the way through your action plan and budget. Even thought the Executive Summary is the first section of your plan, it's the part you write last, after you've come up with all the details in the other sections.

If the Executive Summary sounds redundant, it probably is—but in a good way. If your audience reads nothing but this one page (which is all some will read), they'll absorb the salient points of what you intend to accomplish with your marketing activities.

Mission

The meat of your web marketing plan begins with the Mission section. This section provides the general rationale for your marketing activities; it explains why you want to do what you want to do.

You can express your mission in the form of a short mission statement or with a longer explanation of why you're producing this plan. This section can be as short as a single sentence but no longer than a paragraph.

The ideal Mission section should meet these criteria:

- It must define a clear direction for your marketing activities.
- It must define specific parameters for your marketing activities.
- It must be achievable.
- It must be measurable in general terms—you either achieve your mission or you don't.

In a web marketing plan, your mission should specifically address the Internet, both as a sales/customer channel and marketing medium. You are doing this because of the Web, after all.

For example, a company revamping its website might create the following mission statement:

"CompanyCo. intends to revise its website for ecommerce activities and optimize the site to improve its search ranking. We aim to rank in the top five search results within three months of the site launch, and to generate $200,000 in online revenues within six months of launch."

Or, for a company moving into social media marketing, the following mission statement:

"CompanyCo. will initiate social media marketing activities by establishing a Facebook page and Twitter feed, both of which will be updated daily with company and product news and announcements. Our goal is to attract a minimum of 10,000 followers of each activity, and to drive an additional 10,000 pageviews per month to our website within the first six months of launch."

As you can see, both of these mission statements define a specific direction, lay out the requisite marketing activities, are measurable, and, hopefully, are achievable.

Situational Analysis

The Situational Analysis section of your plan presents a snapshot of where things stand as the plan is conceived. It sets a baseline against which future action is both dictated and measured.

What sorts of things are we talking about? You should include subsections covering the following situations, tweaked to feature web-related issues:

- **Environment**—The big-picture trends (economic, demographic, social, and technological) that impact your company and its marketing activities. In a web marketing plan, the chief environmental issue is almost always technological in that more and more people are using email, or the Web, or social networks, or other tech tools.

- **Market**—The current size and growth trends for the market in which you compete, including key segments of that market. It's important to break out the Internet as a market segment.

- **Competition**—A description of your major competitors, including their size, market share, key product lines, and (particularly) online activities.

- **Customer base**—A description of your current or target customer, including an analysis of consumer wants and needs and how your customers utilize the new technology.

- **Products**—A description of your company's current products, including unit and dollar sales, pricing, and contribution margin, either by individual product or by major product line. You should highlight those products that have particular promise online or that can most gain from online exposure and promotion.

- **Distribution**—A description of the major distribution channels for your company's products, as well as distribution channels used by your competition. You should break out online sales as a channel for each product.

The Situational Analysis section should be a mix of hard data and qualitative analysis and comment, and you should put it together using internal data (for the internal items) and external market research (for the external items).

Opportunities and Issues

This section of your marketing plan analyzes the following opportunities and threats:

- **External opportunities**—These are market opportunities that your company is poised to take advantage of. Naturally, you should focus on online opportunities.

- **External issues**—These are market factors that present a threat to your company. Special attention should be given to web-related issues.

- **Internal strengths**—These are things that you do well, when compared to the competition, that can help you take advantage of the external opportunities you identify.

- **Internal issues**—These are inside-the-company issues that challenge the success of your marketing opportunities. (If you're not yet fully exploiting the Web, that's an issue. You should examine why this is the case.)

After stating these individual opportunities and issues, you should then identify the *key issues* that need to be addressed by your company. These key issues will help you determine the strategies and tactics you pursue.

Goals and Objectives

This section builds from the key issues identified in the Opportunities and Issues section. Here is where you set quantifiable goals you wish to achieve with your marketing activities.

These goals can be internal (for example, a certain level of sales or a specific number of website visitors) or external (a particular market share or a defined search ranking on Google). What's important is that they be numeric and pegged to a specific timeframe so that you can objectively state whether or not they've been achieved.

For example, if you state as a goal that you want to have "the best website in our industry," well, that's not very quantifiable, is it? What exactly do you mean by "best website?" There's no way to measure success.

On the other hand, if you set as a goal that you want to attract an average of 100,000 visitors per day to your website by June 1, it will be easy to see whether or not you've achieved that goal. When June 1 rolls around, either you're averaging 100,000 visitors per day or you're not. It's a goal that's easy to measure.

This section can contain a single goal or multiple goals. When talking about a website, for example, you might set goals for number of visitors, number of pageviews, average time on site, and search ranking. (Heck, you can even set a goal of when you want your site—or its redesign—to go live.) Product goals can include unit sales, dollar sales, profit margin, and the like. You get the picture.

Just remember to set a timeframe to measure your progress—typically six or twelve months into the future. And make sure your goals are achievable; there's no point in planning for the impossible.

Marketing Strategy

As the title implies, this section of the plan sets forth your company's overall online marketing strategy. It refers to the preceding section and describes how your company will pursue the identified opportunity. This section also typically includes information about the products or services you'll be offering, as well as your sales, distribution, and marketing strategies for those products. It describes the market segments you're competing in, your unique positioning, your product and pricing strategy, and the web marketing activities you expect to engage in.

> **note** The Marketing Strategy section is the strategic section of your plan; it's not where you discuss specific tactics. In other words, this section describes the *what* you're doing, not the *how* you're doing it.

As such, this section should cover the following:

- Define your company—what you are and what you do.
- Define the market in which you compete and determine how you want to compete—as a market leader, follower, challenger, or niche player.
- Identify your target customers.
- Identify the products or services that your company provides, along with the unique characteristics that distinguish them from the competition.
- Describe your pricing model in relation to that of your competitors.
- Identify the distribution channels you use or intend to use.
- Describe the online marketing activities you will use to accomplish your goals.

This section describes what you intend to do to accomplish the goals set in the Goals and Objectives section. It does this by identifying the products or services you'll sell, who you'll sell them to, how they'll be priced and distributed, and how they'll be promoted—in this instance, online.

Action Plan

The Action Plan section describes specific tactics you'll use to implement the marketing strategy set forth in the Marketing Strategy section. This is where you get down to the details of which online marketing activities you'll be undertaking and how much you'll be spending on each one.

Think of the Action Plan as your marching orders, a set of step-by-step instructions you can hand to your staff to implement. It's the most detailed section of your entire marketing plan.

When writing the Action Plan for your web marketing activities, you should devote separate subsections to individual activities. As such, you may want to include some or all of the following:

- Website activities
- Blog activities
- Search engine marketing
- Advertising
- Email marketing
- Podcasts and videos
- Social networking
- Public relations

For each subsection, describe the exact activities you expect to undertake, along with a timeline (typically by month or quarter) for these activities. Describe each event, present its timing, estimate its costs, and then detail the event's goals and objectives (pageviews, visitors, dollar or unit sales, market share gains, and so forth).

You can then roll up all your marketing activities into a master timetable and master budget—the latter of which demands its own section of the plan.

Budget

The final section of your marketing plan is the one that the numbers guys will turn to first, so you have to make sure that everything adds up. This section is your master marketing budget, detailing how much money you expect to spend over the plan period—typically one year. The Budget section should include all the normal financial reports that accounting types like to see, so make sure you work with your finance department accordingly.

Writing Your Marketing Plan

Now that you know what goes into a full-featured online marketing plan, how do you go about writing that plan?

First, the good news: An effective marketing plan doesn't have to be a massive document. I know that there's a lot of information that needs to be presented, but (depending on the needs of your particular organization), you can present a lot of it in bullet points. It's important that your audience (senior management, typically) get the gist of what you're proposing, so presenting them with a novel-length document probably isn't the best way to go about it.

That said, you do need to include all the pertinent information in as much detail as is necessary. That means doing your homework ahead of time—and a lot of it. Then you can decide how best to present each piece of data. Some information should be presented in text format; other information can be presented visually, typically in a table or graph. Use the format that works best for you.

It's easy to get overwhelmed by all these details and lose sight of what you're trying to achieve. To mitigate this, I like to think of a marketing plan as a discussion; writing the plan, then, simply entails documenting that discussion.

Here's how I like to approach it. Imagine that you're sitting in a coffeehouse or bar, talking with a colleague about your marketing activities. You talk your friend through what you're doing and what you'd like to do, and that becomes your marketing plan. In the course of your conversation, you cover the following points:

- Why you're doing what you're doing in just a sentence or two. (This is the Mission section of your plan.)
- What's happening in the market and with your company. (This is your Situational Analysis.)
- What opportunities you think there are in the current market. (This is the Opportunities and Issues section.)
- What you think you can accomplish with your web marketing activities. (These are your Goals and Objectives.)
- How you plan to accomplish these goals. (This is the Marketing Strategy section.)
- What specific activities you want to undertake. (This is your Action Plan.)
- How much money you'll need to spend to accomplish your goals. (This is the Budget section.)

That doesn't sound too daunting, does it? Just a normal conversation, something you can talk through in ten or fifteen minutes or so over a cup of coffee or bottle of beer. That's all you need to do.

Creating your plan, then, is simply writing down what you'd say and then filling in few blanks and making it all look pretty. It doesn't have to be any more difficult than that.

The Bottom Line

A marketing plan serves two purposes. First, it helps you gain approval from senior management for your marketing activities. Second, it serves as a roadmap, a set of instructions that guide you and your staff in the coming months.

A web marketing plan should contain the same sections as a traditional marketing plan: Executive Summary, Mission, Situational Analysis, Goals and Objectives, Marketing Strategy, Action Plan, and Budget. Consider the creation of your marketing plan to be similar to carrying on a conversation about your marketing activities; what you might describe to a colleague becomes your written plan.

USING THE PLAN

It's all too common. You spend a week or a month creating a detailed marketing plan, present it to senior management, and then set the thing on a shelf—where it stays, unread, until the following year, when you start the entire process over again.

Even the best-written marketing plans are worthless if they're not followed. If you don't follow your own action plan, what's the point of planning at all?

The key to a successful marketing plan is not so much the plan itself, but rather what you do with it. If you put it on the shelf and ignore it, you probably won't achieve your goals. (If, in fact, you even remember what your goals are.) On the other hand, if you treat your marketing plan as an active document, a set of instructions for your day-to-day marketing activities, then you stand a good chance of accomplishing what you set out to do.

I like to revisit the marketing plan on a regular basis—at least quarterly, ideally monthly. You can then gauge your progress on an ongoing basis and know when you need to shift gears or reassign priorities. If things aren't going to plan, there's no shame in changing those goals midstream; better to do this after three or six months than to be a year down the road and discover that you're not going to get there.

6

In other words, make your marketing plan a living document. Follow the action plan you set forth, constantly measure your progress to plan, and adapt your plan as necessary throughout the year. This is the way to ensure success—and make the entire planning process worthwhile.

7

Designing an Effective Website

When it comes to marketing your company or yourself online, it's all about creating an effective online presence. This includes just about everything you do online, from the keywords you target to the blog posts you make, but centers around one essential element—your website. Nothing else matters if you don't create an exceptional website experience; all the advertising and promotion you do is wasted if there isn't an effective home to drive customers to.

Developing your online home, then, is where web marketing starts. But what makes for a great website? It's all about giving customers what they want, and in most cases, simpler is better.

Creating Your First Website

Your website is the nexus of all your online activities. Your advertising and promotions point customers to your website, and your blog, Twitter feed, and Facebook page are all offshoots of your website. It is the hub from which all your other activities connect.

Creating an effective website, then, is imperative. And for your website to be effective, it most provide an exceptional experience to your customers. They must find what they're looking for—and a little bit more.

If you already have a website, good for you—you can skip this section and move ahead a few pages. If you don't yet have a website, however, you need to get down to business. And there are a number of ways to do just that.

When it comes to creating a website, you can spend a little money or a lot. Let's start with the low-cost options first and then move on up the money scale.

Prepackaged Websites

If you want a website fast and for not a lot of money, you can essentially purchase one off the shelf. That's right, I'm talking about prepackaged or predesigned websites, where all you have to do is fill out a few forms, make a few choices, and then hand over your credit card information.

Going the prepackaged route is definitely the simplest way to go. It's also the fastest; you can have a site up and running in a matter of minutes, no kidding. But there are, as you might suspect, some drawbacks to this approach.

First, you have to settle for the site designs that are offered. You can't do a fully customized site, and your site is going to look at least a little like all the other sites offered by this particular service. And it won't look completely like what you might like it to look.

In addition, most prepackaged sites are somewhat limited. There might be a limit on the number of pages you can create or on the type of technology you can use on a page. You can be assured that a prepackaged site simply won't be as sophisticated as a site you design from scratch.

Then there's the issue of search engine optimization. Few prepackaged sites are fully optimized for search, and fewer still let you do the fine-tuning necessary for effective search engine optimization. The result is that a prepackaged site is less likely to show up in search results than one that you've fully optimized from the ground up.

That said, some of the prepackaged site services offer some nice looking sites. Many services offer site templates tailored for particular types of businesses or industries, so you start off on the right foot, anyway.

Aside from ease and speed, a prepackaged website should include everything you need as part of the package. For example, if you want to sell products online and take credit card orders, look for a package that includes a shopping cart and online payment service. It should all be included, including domain name registration and web hosting.

Of course, you do have to pay for this convenience—but not much. You can find prepackaged sites for as little as $5 or so per month, which is much cheaper than you'd have to pay to have someone build your site.

Where can you find a prepackaged website? Here are some of the major services:

- Homestead (www.homestead.com)
- Microsoft Office Live Small Business (smallbusiness.officelive.com)
- Web.com (www.web.com)
- Web Piston (www.webpiston.com)
- Yahoo! Small Business (smallbusiness.yahoo.com)

Do-It Yourself Websites

If you have some experience with HTML coding or know someone who does, you can create your own website. This obviously will take more time than filling in the forms for a prepackaged website, but you'll get more of what you want in the final design.

Creating a website from scratch is a lot of work, of course, and you really do need to know what you're doing, both in terms of design and coding. While most HTML editing programs use a WYSIWYG interface, you still need to delve into the raw code to do some of the fancy stuff. I wouldn't recommend it for the technologically inexperienced.

If you do decide to build it yourself, you'll need to invest in a full-featured HTML editing program, such as Adobe Dreamweaver or Microsoft Expression Web. You'll also have to purchase your own domain name and find a web hosting service. And if you want to do any ecommerce transactions, you may need to purchase or subscribe to shopping cart, checkout, and online payment services. Like I said—a lot of work.

Professionally Designed Websites

For larger companies—and many smaller ones, too—the best approach is to hire an outside firm to create your site. You'll need to spec the site in terms of what you want to see and offer, but then you let the web design firm do the rest. They have the staff to handle all the design and technology stuff; some can even help you provide content for the site.

The key thing is, they know what they're doing. They've done it hundreds of times before, so they don't have to reinvent any wheels. You just tell them what you want, and they do it—for a nice fee, of course. But for many companies, this is probably the best way to get the site you want.

7

Enlisting a professional design takes on another meaning, of course, if you have a large staff of design, technical, and content experts already on hand. That's right, if your company is large enough that you can form either a permanent or de facto web design department, then you can create a professional website in house, no consultants or outside firms necessary. Be aware, however, that once you get the site up and running, these staff members won't necessarily be free to return to their previous duties because there's a lot of ongoing work necessary to keep a large website up and running on a daily basis. That temporary web design team may turn into a full-time web hosting department.

Budgeting Your Website

If you decide to go with an outside firm to create your website, how much should you spend to get it built? As with most marketing activities, it all depends.

If you're going low-budget, you can hire a local guy to do the work for you. In this instance, low-budget means a few thousand bucks, although you probably get what you pay for.

If you go to an experienced web design company, you'll get a small group of designers working on your project. You'll also spend at least $10,000. Again, though, you get what you pay for.

Then there are the big agencies that offer womb-to-tomb web services. These folks provide an entire team of experts, nay, a veritable army of designers and copywriters and tech gods. They'll not only design your site, they'll write the copy, provide SEO services, and buff your nails and wax your car at the same time. Though you'll get lots of handholding and pretty project handouts, you'll also spend north of $50,000 for the experience.

You can also design your site in-house, of course, providing you have the staff—designers, copywriters, and the requisite HTML code jockeys—and that these folks don't have anything else to do for a few months. All things considered (and expensed), however, don't expect to spend less in house than you would by going out of house.

However you decide to proceed, know that your initial expenditure won't be your last expenditure. You'll need to keep spending, month after month, to keep your site up and running and to keep it updated for new products and campaigns and such. In fact, you'll probably spend twice as much per year on maintaining the site as you did to build it. That's just the way it goes, so you better plan for it.

Website Design: Keep It Simple

I've been dealing with website design since the advent of the Web in the mid-1990s, and here's something I've come to expect. Call it the Internet equivalent of entropy; over time, web pages and websites become more complicated—and as they become more complex, they become less useful. I'm not sure why this is. Perhaps it's because you keep adding things to an existing design, or maybe it's because multiple masters keep getting their way. In any case, there are numerous examples of once easy-to-use websites becoming overly cluttered—and less easy-to-use—over time. It just happens.

This clutter can take many forms. Sometimes it's multiple content modules, all competing for attention. Sometimes it's an overabundance of design elements, each getting in the way of the others. Sometimes it's technology gone wild with too many moving elements going nowhere. Whatever the cause or causes (and it can be more than one), the result is a web page that many visitors find too confusing to use.

It doesn't have to be this way. In fact, some of the most popular sites on the Web are the most simple. These sites have resisted the temptation to clutter up their home pages and instead present a very simple and clear message to their visitors.

Take, as the best example, Google—by most accounts the most-visited site on the Web. Why is Google so popular? Of course, it's because it's such a useful site, offering the most effective search results on the Web. But it's also because that's pretty much all you find on Google's home page; there's no confusing what it does or how to do it.

And here's something else. Google has made only minimal changes to its home page in the decade or so since its inception. The company has resisted the temptation to dance with the design du jour; it has kept its simple design consistent while its competitors have swung wildly back and forth. That's good branding for you.

Compare Google with its fading competitor, Yahoo!. The Yahoo! home page tries to do so many things that it's easy to miss the fact that it's a search engine. (Yes, the search box is at the top of the page, but there's a lot of stuff beneath it; there's news and services and even advertising!) And the company has responded to the Google competition by changing its site design on a fairly regular basis. You never know what you're going to find when you visit Yahoo!; it's an inconsistent, confusing mess.

7

FIGURE 7.1

Google's simple, easy-to-use home page.

FIGURE 7.2

Yahoo!'s cluttered, inconsistent home page.

Well, you say, Google is trying to do just one thing. Your company, on the other hand, has lots of stuff to present—multiple product lines, technical support, corporate information, you name it. That may, in fact, be the case. But you can still present multiple pieces of information—or multiple pathways—in a simple, easy-to-navigate fashion. It's all a matter of knowing what your customers want to find and how they want to find it.

This might mean foregoing the in-your-face presentation of the promotion or branding message of the season. It could mean presenting one primary item and other items in a subsidiary fashion. It might even mean relegating some items to smaller links or placement on navigational menus. Not everything can take primary position; not everything is of equal importance.

Just remember, the Internet's top sites—Google, Facebook, Wikipedia— have relatively simple gateway pages, and there's a reason for that.

Be Wary of Technology—and Design

While we're on the topic of keeping things simple, let's consider all the fancy technological and design elements that many websites use today. I'm talking Flash animations, videos, and those things that in general exist to "wow" site visitors.

In other words, all the things that visitors hate.

That's right, all those fancy elements your design and technology people love are roundly despised by many web users. People just want to do what they want to do; they don't want to be interrupted in their quests. And trust me, animations and movies and things that go "pop" are interruptions—unwanted and unnecessary interruptions. They get in the way of getting to where you want to go.

As a user, I'm sure you've experienced this. You go to a site, and before you can even visit the home page, you're greeted with some sort of animation or video. You're forced to sit through this thing, which takes several seconds (or more) to load and then just as long to play before you can start looking for the information you want. It's a huge roadblock, one that many visitors simply click away from without ever visiting the site beyond.

Now, why would a website do this? It's the online equivalent of making customers visiting a bricks and mortar store to wait outside while you put on a little play, and you don't let them the front door until the production is finished. If you did this in the real world, most of your customers would just walk away. So why would you do this online?

It's the same thing with other technological and design gimmicks. Yeah, they're fun, and I'm sure you and your design and technology staffs really like them. But do they truly serve your site visitors or merely annoy them? That's

7

the question to ask—and most of the time, the right answer will be to avoid these doodads completely.

As an example of what not to do, consider the Mr. Bottles site (www.mrbottles.com). Not only is the design itself eye-poppingly bad (can anybody read that colored text against the background image?), there's a little "Return to Top" graphic that pops up insistently on the right, pictures that keep changing in front of your eyes, and a guy who I assume is Mr. Bottles talking to me in an animation at the bottom of the page. I don't necessarily want to listen to Mr. Bottles, but I'm forced to—and I'm sure the tech guys thought this was really neat.

FIGURE 7.3
Too many tech gadgets on the page at Mr. Bottles.com.

As Mr. Bottles demonstrates, technology can get in the way of presenting your message. Simple, straightforward text content may be technologically boring, but it provides visitors with the information they're looking for. Don't force anything else on them that they don't want or need.

Content Matters

What really matters when constructing a website is the content. In fact, it's the only thing that matters. You could have the worst-looking website in the world, but if your content is useful and unique, you'll still grab the visitors. Not that design should be totally ignored, but your primary focus should be in providing that content that your customers want.

The Right Content for Your Site's Visitors

What sort of content should you include on your site? Whatever it is that your customers want and need! That probably includes information about the products and services you offer, as well as support for those same products and services. Your website is a great place to offer owner's manuals, how-to videos, and the like—the sorts of things that actually reduce your customer support load. You should also use your site to include all the brochures and catalogs and product pages you offer in an easy-to-navigate format. And if you sell your own products, you definitely need a product ordering/shopping cart/checkout path.

> **note** Want an example of strong content triumphing over weak design? Look no further than Wikipedia, one of the top ten sites on the Web and hardly an example of cutting edge design—it's quite ugly, really. But the content is first-rate, which is why it attracts millions of visitors each day. Wikipedia proves that content matters and design, less so.

In addition, you can add to the customer experience by offering discussion forums, blogs, and the like on your site. Use your site to promote customer feedback and interaction—but then make sure you manage these elements and respond to customer comments.

You can also use your site to broadcast your latest promotions, display your latest commercials, offer corporate information for investors, host press materials for the media, and provide contact information for customers and others. In short, your website can do lots of things for lots of people. It's all about the content.

Content on the Page

When you're putting content on a page, consider that web users don't like to scroll all that much. You might get one or two down-scrolls out of them but not three or four. It's the online equivalent of putting newspaper content above the fold.

To that end, think in terms of short pages—which means short blocks of text. If you have something longer to present, break it up onto multiple pages. Believe it or not, visitors are more likely to click to a second (or third) page than they are to scroll down a single page.

Of course, writing web copy is an acquired skill. Not only should you keep your pages short, but you should also write in short sentences and paragraphs and then introduce each section with a heading or subheading. Website visitors tend to graze more than read, and your copy needs to recognize this.

7

I call it "chunky" content—both on the page and in pages on your site. Don't be wordy, and don't be overly complex. You don't have to insult your audience, just remember that nobody's visiting your site for the deathless prose.

> **note** Copywriting for websites is very similar to direct response copywriting. You have to describe what you're providing in words, not pictures, and if you're selling something, provide a strong "why to buy" message.

Content for Search Engines

One more thing about website content. It's not just your human visitors you need to consider.

That's right, your content is also browsed by robots—software robots, to be exact. These programs, called *spiders* or *crawlers*, are sent out across the Internet by Google and the other search engines in search of relevant pages to add to their search indexes. As such, these programs need to be able to figure out just what a page is about, which they do by examining the content of your copy, especially those *keywords* you include.

It's all in service of what we call search engine optimization, and it means you have to be of two minds when writing your website copy. Yes, you have to provide readable, compelling copy for your visitors but at the same time incorporate all the necessary keywords and phrases that matter to the search engines—and in a fashion that influences how the search engines rank a page. You don't want to sacrifice one for the other; never make your page less readable just to cram in another keyword. Go for readability first and then incorporate the keywords as you can.

It's not that easy to do, which is why some professional web copywriters earn big bucks. And those bucks are well-spent; a well-optimized web page will rank higher in Google's search results, which leads to more new visitors to your site.

> **note** Learn more about copywriting for search engines in Part IV of this book, "Search Engine Marketing."

Navigating Your Site

All the content you provide on your site has to be easily found. That means coming up with some sort of navigational scheme that makes sense to your site's various constituencies. You can't just put it all out there in a list and expect people to find what they need.

Potential customers need to be able to quickly click to product information. Current customers need a quick link to owner's manuals and support resources. The press needs to be able to easily find the photos and press releases they need. And everyone needs immediate access to contact information, whether in the form of a web contact form, clickable email addresses, or honest-to-goodness real-world telephone numbers.

In this respect, consider navigation to be in service to your site's content—and a necessary service.

Devise a Hierarchy

What does this mean in practice? Well, it means some sort of easy-to-understand hierarchy, using the model of directories and subdirectories and even sub-subdirectories.

For example, consider a company that manufacturers yard machinery—lawn mowers, snow blowers, and so on. This company uses its website to present its products, offer customer documentation and support, provide service options, and steer visitors to local dealers. It also offers a press section for media support, a section for investors, and a general "contact us" page.

The first level of organization should probably be by these general areas. As such, the site's main menu system should include the following options:

- Products
- Documentation and Support
- Service
- Find a Local Dealer

The nonconsumer sections (press, investors, and contact us) probably don't belong on the main menu. Instead, they can be accessed via links at the bottom of the home page.

So far, so good. But this company offers a variety of products. So maybe clicking the Products menu displays a Products page, with additional links to the different types of products—lawn mowers, snow blowers, weed whackers, and so forth. But that's two clicks to get to a more specific product line page and then at least another click to view specific product models. Customers don't like to click so much; it's better if there are direct links or submenus to get to the product line pages faster.

The best way to do this is via submenus off the main menu items. In this instance, clicking Product on the main menu would display a series of submenu items—Lawn Mowers, Snow Blowers, and such. Clicking a submenu item then takes the visitor directly to that product line page, without any intermediate pages (and clicks) necessary.

FIGURE 7.4

Submenus at the Crutchfield site (www.crutchfield.com) lead directly to specific product categories.

You can even include sub-submenu items. Let's say this company sells two types of lawn mowers, riding and walking. This would necessitate clicking the Products menu to display the Lawn Mowers submenu; clicking the Lawn Mowers submenu would display the Riding Mowers and Walking Mowers sub-submenu items. Visitors could then click one of these items to display either the riding or walking mower page.

The key is to figure out what visitors are looking for on your site and then make it easy to get there. Minimize the number of clicks that have to be made; it's always better to get there in one click than in two or three.

note It's also a good idea to include a general site search box near the top of your home page. This way serious visitors can search directly for the item they want, rather than clicking through a long series of menus.

7

Be Intuitive

Your navigational system must be easy to find and easy to figure out. That probably means a set of pull-down menus or links across the top of the page or along the left side; that's where most people look for navigation.

Your menus don't have to be fancy, either. In fact, they probably shouldn't be fancy. It's better to use easy-to-understand text instead of impossible-to-comprehend graphics. Don't make it difficult on your visitors—just point them to where they want to go.

As an example of what *not* to do, consider the Phonetics website located at www.phonetics.com. Not only do you get a despised introductory Flash animation, but you also get a set of navigational icons along the left side of the page. Now, I assume the Phonetics folks know what these icons mean, but I certainly don't. Maybe that little icon of a house goes to the home page (it does, in fact), but what about that eyeball thingie, or the telephone, or what I assume is a lightning bolt? What do they mean, and where do they lead to? I guess we can all figure out that clicking one of these icons takes you to a specific part of the site, but which icon leads where? I doubt I'm the only one confused.

FIGURE 7.5

Nonintuitive navigation at Phonetics.com.

You have to make the navigation as intuitive as possible; don't be cute about it. Be clear about what leads where and use wording that mimics how customers describe things, rather than how you might describe them internally.

Think Like the Customer

That last point is important. I recently visited a major consumer electronics site, looking for information about flat-panel TVs. I found the products section easily enough and quickly navigated to the section for LCD TVs. What I encountered next, however, totally confused me. Instead of letting me look at sets by screen size or price or features, I saw options for "G25 Series," "G20 Series," "S2 Series," "U2 Series," "X2 Series," and the like. (The names have not been changed to protect the innocent.) I don't know about you, but I have no idea what any of these series are. I just want to find an appropriate TV set; I don't know whether what I want is a U2 or S2 or X2 or whatever model.

So this particular website lost me, and I didn't buy any of their products. The folks who designed this site were not thinking like the customer; they were following internal product guidelines that, while they might make sense inside the company, don't mean a thing to the average consumer. Don't you fall into this trap; present your content the way your customers think of it, not the way you and your bosses do.

Dynamic Drill-Down Navigation

Another navigational approach is to simplify the menu system as much as possible but then use what is called *dynamic drill-down* or *faceted navigation*. With this approach, all the pages on your site are all essentially on the same level but accessed through different virtual paths. There are no predefined paths or hierarchy, just what a user chooses dynamically.

You typically do this by displaying a large number of products or items on a main category page, but then let the customer drill down through the results by selecting various facets, such as TV type, screen size, and price range. It makes it easy for a visitor to find the particular item he's looking for, using the criteria that matters to him.

One advantage to dynamic drill-down navigation is that it essentially lets each customer define his own navigation. The customer can drill down through the available items in any number of ways, not forcing a navigational design on the him. It's also good for search engine optimization;

because all product pages are essentially at the same level, nothing is buried too deep for the search crawlers to find.

Narrow Your Results by:

TV Type: LCD Flat-Panel
[Remove]

Customer Reviews
Top-Rated (17)

Current Offers
On Sale (40)
Special Offers (37)
Free Shipping (44)
Financing Offers (105)
Outlet Center (17)

Status
Coming Soon (3)
New Arrivals (28)

Price Range
Less than $200 (13)
$200 - $249.99 (11)
$250 - $499.99 (38)
$500 - $749.99 (24)
$750 - $999.99 (16)
$1000 - $1249 (6)
$1250 - $1499 (1)
$1500 - $1999 (6)
$2000 - $2499 (6)
$2500 - $2999 (2)
$3000 and Up (3)

Screen Size
1" to 20" (21)
21" - 29" (26)
30" - 39" (34)
40" - 49" (32)
50" - 59" (7)
60" and Up (4)

FIGURE 7.6

Dynamic drill-down navigation on the Best Buy website (www.bestbuy.com).

Website Look and Feel

Finally, we come to the design of your web pages—how your pages look. This is, of course, a matter for the design team, but as a marketer, you need to have significant input.

First, the design has to be in service of the content—no design for design's sake. Every element on the page has to serve a purpose; the design has to be efficient and make your page more effective. (This may be tough for the designers...sorry.)

Next, and equally important, your site has to present your brand identity. Someone visiting your home page should know at a glance what company or product he's dealing with. Content is important, yes, but visual identity must be maintained.

7

Finally, your site design has to be of a whole with the rest of your corporate and brand image. You don't want a red background on your website if your corporate image is all about blue, for example. You want to include the same branding elements on your site as you do in all your advertising and other materials. It all has to look like it came from the same place; customers will be confused by any inconsistency in identity.

I wish I could offer more specific design advice, but every company and every website is unique. What works for Coca Cola might not work for Pepsi, and definitely won't work for Honda or Sony or for you. Work with your designers to create a site that looks and feels like your product, your company, and your ads and other marketing activities. Keep it as simple as possible and make sure that the design doesn't get in the way of the content or the navigation. It's not easy; you'll devote a lot of discussions to this part of the project. But if you do it right, your customer base will recognize your website as your company's homebase on the Web—which is what it should be, after all.

FIGURE 7.7

Two different but equally effective approaches to website branding: Coca Cola (www.coca-cola.com)…

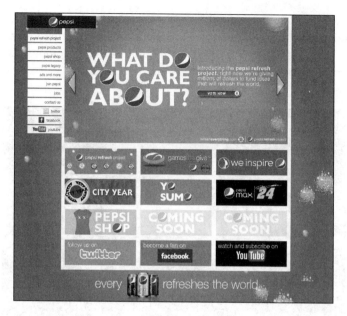

FIGURE 7.8

and Pepsi (www.pepsi.com).

Consider Color

One more thing about page design. I know you want to stick to the colors that your brand is known for. I also know that your designers will be pestering you to accept a particular color palette for your pages. But if you go too wild with color, you can create readability problems—and if you make your site hard to read, people won't visit.

When it comes to readability, nothing beats good old black text on a white background. That's how you're reading this book, after all, and it works pretty well; you get good contrast without hurting your eyes.

Next best is black text on a light neutral background, like beige or light gray. After that, a light color background is probably okay—light yellow, light blue, or light green, for example.

What you want to avoid are dark or brightly colored backgrounds. Black text on an orange background, for example, will be pretty much unreadable. Weird color combinations, such as green text on a purple background, are also bad.

7

For that matter, you should avoid reverse text (white text on a black background), with a few exceptions. You can use reverse text for short text blocks; it's actually effective to convey emphasis. But you shouldn't use reverse text for long blocks of text, as it's very hard on the eyes.

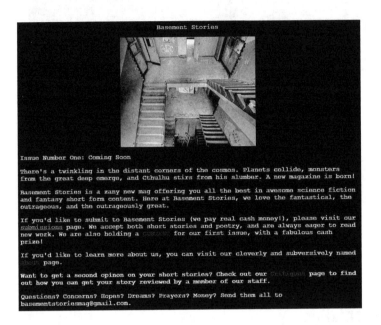

FIGURE 7.9

A full page of reverse text at the Basement Stories site (www.basementstories.org)—very difficult to read. (Also hard to love: Blue links on the black background.)

And, just as you shouldn't put dark text on a dark background, you also shouldn't put light text on a light background. It's all about contrast, and light on light (and dark on dark) doesn't give you enough. If you find it hard to read, your customers will too.

The point is that you want to make it easy and pleasant for visitors to read your content. Make the text pop from the background and consider using a larger font size, especially if you have an older customer base. (You don't want old farts like me to have to squint when reading your pages!)

note Check the contrast ratios on your site by using AccessColor (www.accesskeys.org/tools/color-contrast.html). This is a free tool that analyzes the color contrast and brightness levels on your site and then tells you if there's not enough contrast between your foreground and background elements.

Creating Unique Landing Pages

It's not just your site's home page that's important. You need to design every page on your site with the same intensity of focus.

That's because you don't know on which page a visitor might enter your site. Not everyone types your home page's URL into their browsers; some visitors come via links found elsewhere on the Web.

To that end, you'll need to consider some pages on your site as dedicated *landing pages*—those pages that visitors land on when entering from another site. Some landing pages might be obvious—product pages, for example, or pages devoted to a particular brand. These pages should be treated as if they were home pages.

Other landing pages are devised to serve other web marketing activities. For example, if you create a pay-per-click advertisement, you need to create a unique landing page that customers see when they click that ad. You don't want customers clicking from a product-specific ad to land on your site's general home page; you want them landing on a page that follows directly from the advertisement they just clicked.

Landing pages of this type are all about presenting a consistent image to potential customers. You wouldn't get a lot of sales if someone clicked on an ad for blenders and landed on a page that talks about your company's vast international manufacturing capability. That sort of inconsistent message is a surefire way to get people to click back to someone else's site.

So you need to create a series of activity-specific landing pages on your site. Each landing page has to be product- or service-specific and reference the ad or activity that led to the page. Each landing page must also continue your overall site branding, as every page on your site should. Use the landing page to continue the customer's journey; give her the information she clicked for and provide a path for her to get even more info or purchase the product.

The Bottom Line

When it comes to creating your web presence, it all starts with your website. Construct your website with a marketing focus making sure it's easy for your visitors to find what they're looking for with few unnecessary interruptions. Present this content in small, easily accessible modules and design your pages to reinforce your existing brand or product image. And whatever you do, don't let the design and technology people add lots of useless stuff to the site; keep the focus on your current and potential customers and keep things as simple as possible.

7

WHO DESIGNS—OR REDESIGNS—YOUR WEBSITE?

Here's a simple question: Who designs your website—or helps in its redesign? The answer could determine the success or failure of all your web marketing efforts.

That's because ownership of a company's website is often claimed by multiple parties within an organization. Conflicting organizational ownership is never a good thing; corporate infighting can not only slow down progress, but also result in ineffective compromises.

Even worse is when the wrong party runs the thing. Imagine if your company's finance department ran your website; no doubt it would be extremely cost-effective, but at the expense of meaningful content or attractive design. While that's an extreme example, similarly inappropriate results will occur if site design and management are turned over to parties who don't have an overt customer focus.

In most organizations, website development is a joint effort between the marketing, design, and technology departments. While all three parties have much to contribute, only the marketing department thinks with the customer in mind. Having either the design or technology folks take charge could be disastrous.

Take the designers first. If left to them, your website would be bright and hip, or maybe cool and hip, whichever is today's prevailing style. It would be stylish, full of cute little fleur de lis and other totally useless design elements. It would pop and sizzle and crackle, and it wouldn't matter if there were any substance beyond the style. All eye candy, no real content.

Of course, it wouldn't be much better if the techie guys ran the project. These folks, God bless 'em, just love to throw in all the latest technological doodads, in the form of animations and movies and things that peek out here and pop out there. In fact, a tech-designed website would be so technologically advanced that many, if not most visitors wouldn't be able to view it because it would require the latest browsers and a super-fast broadband connection and who knows what else. Oh, and maybe there'd be some room for real content in there somewhere, providing you could slip it in between the animations.

7

What both these approaches have in common is that they're not thinking about your site's visitors. Designers want to put pretty pictures in front of your visitors, without a thought as to what the visitors actually want to see. Techies want to utilize all the latest technologies, without a thought as to how those technologies are used—or whether they're actually usable.

It's up to the marketing department, then, to consider what your site's visitors want—to *think like the customer*. Most customers want something specific, something meaty, something useful; they want substance, not style, and they want to find what they want quickly and easily. It's about useful content presented in a user-friendly fashion. Design and technology come into play only in the service of these needs.

This means that the marketing department truly needs to research and deliver on these customer needs. You can't just spew forth the latest corporate platitudes and branding guidelines; you have to get beyond what the corporation and its executives like and create a site that focuses exclusively on your current and potential customers.

So you, as the marketing representative, somehow need to take charge of your website project. You need to work with the design and technology people, incorporating their suggestions without letting them run wild. And you have to manage the higher-ups who have their own ideas about how things should look, but not necessarily focus on driving the site in a customer-focused direction. That shouldn't be too difficult, should it?

7

Creating an Ecommerce Website

Most websites share many of the same common features, but there's one type of website that's a bit different. I'm talking about ecommerce sites, those sites that offer products and services for sale to their visitors. An ecommerce site has its own unique features and challenges, especially from a marketing perspective, that are worth evaluating.

Different Ways to Sell

If you're in the online retail business, there are actually a few different ways to do it. It's not a one-size–fits-all situation.

Build It from Scratch

First, you can build your site from scratch. You start with a blank page and go from there, designing your home page and product pages, plugging in navigation and search modules, integrating a shopping cart and checkout, and signing up for an online payment service.

This is the route taken by big companies, of course, although smaller companies can also build from scratch by hiring out the work. Know, however, that this is the most costly and time-consuming approach, primarily because you're reinventing a lot of wheels as you go along. You do, however, get the perfectly designed site of your dreams.

Use a Prepackaged Storefront

For smaller retailers, a better approach may be to go with a prepackaged storefront. When you contract with a storefront design service, you essentially plug your logo and product inventory into a predesigned store template. Everything you need is provided—automatically generated product pages, inventory and customer management, shopping cart and checkout system, and online payment service.

The reason prepackaged storefronts are popular with smaller retailers is that it's relatively easy to do, and you can get your site up and running quite quickly. The downside of this approach is that you pay for it—and keep on paying for it. Most of these services not only charge you an upfront cost (typically quite low) but also an ongoing commission on everything you sell. In other words, you pay for the convenience of a prepackaged storefront.

Utilize Third-Party Ecommerce Services

Between these two extremes is a sort of middle ground. Many third-party services exist that provide the needed features for a quality online storefront, without you having to do the coding from scratch—and without you ceding a portion of your ongoing profits. You simply pick and choose the modules and services you need and plug them into your site.

This approach is great if you already have a website up and running or want a well-designed site without having to reinvent the whole ecommerce process. You can find inventory management modules, shopping cart and checkout modules, and the like. Depending on the provider(s) you use, you may pay a larger upfront cost with no ongoing fees or "rent" the services via a monthly or yearly subscription. And you retain the look and feel you want.

> **note** You're not limited to selling your merchandise on your own website; you can also sell via eBay, the Amazon Marketplace, and other web-based exchanges. Learn more in my companion book, *Selling Online 2.0: Migrating from eBay to Amazon, craigslist, and Your Own E-Commerce Website* (Michael Miller, Que, 2009).

What Goes Into an Ecommerce Website?

Let's be plain about it: Ecommerce means running an online store. What, then, do you need to successfully sell merchandise to customers online?

As you will soon see, there's a lot to think about—and every single item needs marketing input. The checkout process, for example, isn't just a way to take orders; if done properly, you can influence customer satisfaction and maybe make some add-on sales. You need to look at every single part of your ecommerce site from a marketing perspective and do everything needed to ensure satisfied customers.

So what do you need to consider? Let's look at the key elements.

Home Page

Every website needs a home page, of course, but the home page for a retailer's site is even more important than for other types of sites. Your ecommerce home page must not only promote your business, but also profile key products.

Your home page can't be static, either. You need to refresh the featured products on a fairly constant basis so that returning customers always see new deals when they visit. It's easiest if you use some sort of template for the home page design, into which you can easily place the products you're currently promoting. This argues for some sort of home page automation, as opposed to you manually recoding the page each time you change featured products.

> **note** You'll want to establish your brand via design elements, logo placement, and so on. Your entire site, home page and product pages alike, should reflect the look and feel of your brand and business. Remember, your ecommerce website is the online equivalent of a retail storefront—that's Marketing 101.

Navigation and Search

While you may sell some products directly from your site's home page, it's more likely that customers are going to either browse or search for the precise products they're looking for. That means establishing an appropriate navigational structure so that customers can quickly and easily find the products they're looking for.

At the very least, this means organizing your products into logical categories and letting users click a link or menu item to view all products in that category. You may even want to provide dynamic drill-down navigation within a category, as discussed in Chapter 7, "Designing an Effective Website," so that customers can more easily fine-tune their buying choices. For example, if you sell big-screen TVs, you might want to provide drill-down links so that customers can view TVs by size, by type (plasma, LCD, CRT), by brand, by price, and so forth.

You'll also want to integrate a search function across your entire site. That means putting a search box at the top of every page so that visitors can search for the specific items they want.

The key thing is that you need to think through how your customers will use your site before you start building it. It's tough to go back and redesign or reorganize a site after it's up and running; it's much easier to take your time and think it through thoroughly beforehand.

Product Pages

It should go without saying that every product you offer for sale should have its own page on your site. This needs to be a content-rich page, not just a flashy advertisement. You need to include one or more product photos, a detailed description, all relevant dimensions and sizes and colors and such, as well as any other information that a customer might need to place an informed order.

In fact, consider organizing the information on a product page into multiple tabs. You can have one tab for overview information, another for detailed specifications, a third for a gallery of product photos perhaps, maybe a fourth for product support—instruction manuals, downloads, and the like. Give customers all the information they may want, but in a way that isn't too overwhelming.

Customer Reviews

Many sites let their customers rate and review the products offered on the site, typically on a tab on the product page. This provides another key information point for shoppers, as well as offers unique feedback to the seller. While this isn't a necessity, many customers are coming to expect this feature; it's actually a useful marketing tool.

Inventory Management

You don't want to manually update your site's product pages whenever you sell an item. Instead, you'll need some sort of automatic inventory and listing management system, where a product sale automatically updates both your inventory database and your product pages.

Shopping Cart and Checkout System

When a customer purchases a product, that product needs to go into that customer's shopping cart—the online equivalent of a physical shopping cart. The cart holds multiple purchases and then feeds into your site's checkout system, which then interfaces with your online payment service.

Payment Service

When you sell something, you need to get paid. If you have your own merchant credit card account to accept plastic payments, great. If not, you'll want
to sign up with one of the major online payment services—PayPal, Google
Checkout, or Checkout by Amazon—to process credit card payments for you.

Customer Service

Your customers will want to contact you with questions or issues, and you'll
want to contact your customers with purchase confirmation and shipping
information. It's best if you can automate all of these customer communications using web-based forms and email marketing.

Promoting Your Site

Ecommerce isn't like *Field of Dreams*; you can't just build a website and
assume that customers will come. No, you have to promote your site and the
products you sell—which is where web marketing comes in.

Online promotion can take many forms; virtually any component of your web
marketing mix can be used to drum up sales. You may elect to purchase pay-
per-click (PPC) advertising, a la Google AdWords. You may opt to purchase
larger, more expensive display ads on select sites. Or you may choose to promote your site via friendly bloggers or on social networks like Facebook.
You most definitely want to optimize your site so that it ranks high on Google
and other search sites and probably want to submit your site listings to
Shopping.com and other comparison shopping sites. And once you get a few
customers, you'll want to coax additional sales out of them via a targeted
email mailing list.

What's key is that you do *some* form of promotion for your online store. You
can't assume customers will stumble over your site while they're surfing; the
Internet just doesn't work that way anymore. You need to promote your
online store with the same aggressiveness as you'd promote a bricks and mortar retail store; you have to drive customers to your site and push them to buy
what you're selling.

Just as advertising in print and broadcast media is a key part of the traditional retail marketing mix, online advertising should be a major component
of your ecommerce marketing. Probably the most effective type of online
advertising for retailers is PPC advertising; you can drive customers directly

from your ad to a specific product page and only pay when your ad is clicked. It's targeted advertising, as PPC ads only appear on search pages and third-party sites related to the keywords you purchase. This type of advertising isn't about building a brand image; it's about moving units—which PPC advertising does quite well.

However you decide to promote your store, you need to have a plan in place before you open your virtual doors. Knowing how you'll be promoting your site is every bit as important as deciding what products to sell, how your site will look and feel, and what checkout and online payment services you'll use. An un- or under-promoted site is a site with few if any customers. And that's a sure ticket to business failure.

Utilizing Search Engine Marketing and Shopping Directories

Hand-in-hand with PPC advertising is search engine marketing. A lot of potential customers use Google, Yahoo!, and Bing to search for good deals on what they're looking to buy, so if your site appears high in these customers' search results, they'll click to and possibly purchase from you instead of a competitor. So search engine optimization and identifying the best keywords are also key.

You should also submit your site—and your site's inventory—to the major *shopping directories*. These are sites, sometimes called *price comparison sites*, that compare products for sale from multiple online retailers. Consumers use these sites to find the lowest prices on the products they're shopping for; obviously, they can drive a lot of qualified customers directly to your site's product pages.

Most consumers are under the impression that these sites scour the Web for prices from a wide variety of online retailers. That's a false impression; instead, these sites build their price/product databases from product links submitted and paid for by participating retailers. And not only are these product listings submitted by retailers, they're also (in most cases) paid for by retailers.

Fortunately for retailers with large inventories, payment isn't on a per-listing basis; instead, you pay when customers click your product listings. This is the old pay-per-click model, and the individual fee is, of course, a cost per click. CPC charges run anywhere from a nickel to more than a buck, depending on the site and the product category.

So if you run a website that offers products for sale, you can often get more visibility by listing with the major online shopping directories than you would relying on organic search results from Google, Bing, and Yahoo! Even though you pay for the click-throughs, those clicks will likely result in sales.

FIGURE 8.1

Comparing prices at bizrate, a popular online shopping directory.

There are lots of shopping directories out there, but here are the top ones you should focus on first:

- Bing Shopping (www.bing.com/shopping/)
- bizrate (www.bizrate.com)
- Google Product Search (www.google.com/products/)
- MySimon (www.mysimon.com)
- NexTag (www.nextag.com)
- PriceGrabber (www.pricegrabber.com)
- Shopping.com (www.shopping.com)
- Yahoo! Shopping (shopping.yahoo.com)

> **note** Google Product Search doesn't charge for its product listings, which makes it different from the other shopping directories. It offers a mix of organic and submitted results—which means you still should submit a product feed for best results.

Each online shopping directory operates a consumer front end (for shoppers) and a merchant front end (for retailers). You can typically find the link to the merchant page at the bottom of the site's consumer home page.

As noted, you need to submit your active inventory to each shopping directory. Before you do this, however, you have to sign up for the site's merchant program—sometimes called an advertiser program. This is normally a simple process, with no upfront charge. During this process you'll have a chance to review the site's cost per click rates, any additional listing features you can

8

pay for, and the site's data submission process. Make sure you know what you're signing up for before you commit and send your first data file.

You'll submit your inventory listings as some sort of data file; check with each site to get their specs. Many sites also accept your inventory as an RSS or Atom feed, which makes it easier to keep things up to date. How often you update your inventory file depends on the site's requirements and how often your inventory levels change. You may be able to get by uploading a file once a week, or you may need to upload an updated data file daily. Again, check the site's requirements.

The Bottom Line

Building an ecommerce website is more challenging than building a more brand-oriented site. Not only do you have to establish your brand image, you also have to offer your products for sale—which means designing product pages, shopping cart and checkout systems, and a customer support mechanism. You can incorporate all of these elements into an existing website design, either by building from scratch or using third-party ecommerce services, or you can go the prepackaged storefront route—which might be a good idea for smaller retailers.

Once your site is launched, you need to promote the site and the products you sell. For most online retailers, that means some mix of PPC advertising and search engine marketing—with other web marketing activities thrown in as necessary. You have to drive customers to your site—and close the sale once they're there.

CHANNEL CONFLICT

Here's a question you probably haven't asked, although you should have. You can sell your products on your own website—but should you?

This is an important question if you're a manufacturer who uses independent retailers to sell your product out in the real world. If you also offer your products on your own website, you're effectively competing with your own retailers—which they probably don't like. It's channel conflict, pure and simple, and sales you make directly from your site could be cutting into sales that would otherwise flow through your retailer base.

Retailers, of course, don't like manufacturers cutting themselves into the action. Some manufacturers, however, don't really care because they make more money if they cut out the middlemen and book sales themselves. Other manufacturers simply view it as a service to their customers if they can order directly online. Still other manufacturers just haven't thought it through.

But think it through you must. Are you a manufacturer or a retailer? To me, that's a key question. I've seen too many manufacturers try to offer products for sale online, only to stumble in fulfillment and customer service; it's just not what they do well. So they end up with both alienated retailers and dissatisfied customers.

You should also ask whether you want to invest in your retail channel or try to make it obsolete. If you need your retailers and will for the foreseeable future, then don't take their customers away, no matter how tempting that may be. Put some sort of mechanism on your site to drive customers to their local retailers or to those retailers' websites. Don't get greedy and try to steal those customers for yourself.

If, on the other hand, you want to eventually eliminate your retail channel, then by all means have at it. The Internet does let you deal directly with customers, and that may be a good thing. Many companies strive to develop a more direct relationship with their customers, which includes selling directly. It's certainly doable—but only if you're customer-focused. If you're more focused on producing products than thinking like the customer, then you're in for a big surprise.

9

Tracking Website Analytics

When it comes time to determine how well your website is performing, you need to know a few things. It helps to know how many people are visiting your site, of course. It's also nice to know how many pages are viewed, as well as which are your top-performing pages.

That's just the tip of the iceberg, however. There's a lot more you can discover about the people visiting your site—information that provides important insight into the kinds of visitors your site is attracting and how they're finding your site.

To gather this data about your site's performance, you use a *web analytics* tool. Web analytics is the collection and analysis of data relating to website visitors. It's a way to measure the traffic to your website and then find out what visitors are doing during their visits.

Understanding Web Analytics

If you run a website, why might you want to employ website analytics?

It's simple: Website analytics help you better understand your site's visitors by tracking visitor behavior so that you have a better idea what your visitors are doing—and why. With the right analytics package, you can discover not only how many people are visiting your site, but what they're doing there, how long they're staying, and where they came from.

What kind of data is measured? Web analytics track such metrics as unique visitors, pageviews, traffic sources, exit pages, and the like. It also tracks the paths taken by your site's visitors—what sites lead them to your site and what pages they view once they get to your site. There's even information to be had about where your visitors live and what kind of technology they're using.

Web analytics, then, examines both the quantity and quality of visitors to a site. The goal is to better understand how a website is being used; you can then use that information to optimize the site's usage. It's more than just basic data collection—it's an attempt to learn more about how people use a site and why.

Who Uses Web Analytics?

You might think that web analytics is one of those market research tools used only by big companies with big marketing budgets. That isn't true, however. Web analytics is for any size company or website, as a small personal website has access to the same statistics as does a large corporate one.

In fact, any website can benefit from knowing more about their visitors. Websites both large and small can use web analytics to determine where new visitors are coming from and tailor the site's content to those sources. It's valuable data, no matter the size of your site—or the amount of traffic it attracts.

> **note** You can use web analytics to track not just traditional websites, but also blogs, podcasts, online videos, web-based advertisements, and the like.

How Web Analytics Works

When it comes to tracking web visitors, there are two fundamental types of analytics:

- **Onsite analytics** uses site-specific data to track visitors to a specific website.
- **Offsite analytics** uses Internet-wide information to determine which are the most visited sites on the Web.

Offsite analytics are used to compile industry-wide analysis, while onsite analytics are used to report on individual website performance. You're probably most interested in onsite analytics, to better track what's happening with your customers on your website—although offsite analytics is useful for gathering competitive research.

Onsite analytics works by utilizing a technique known as *page tagging*. This technique places a "bug," in the form of a piece of unseen JavaScript code, in the basic HTML code for a web page. This embedded code collects certain information about the page and its visitors, and this information is then passed on to a web analytics service, which collates the data and uses it to create various analytic reports.

Key Web Analytics Metrics

There are many different data points that can be collected via web analytics. Some of these data points, or metrics, might be familiar to you; others may not. Table 9.1 details some of the most important of these metrics and what they measure.

Table 9.1   Key Web Analytics Metrics

Metric	Description
% exit	The percentage of users who exit from a given web page.
Active time (engagement time)	The average amount of time that visitors spend actually interacting with content on a web page, based on mouse moves, clicks, hovers, scrolls, and so on.
Bounce rate	The percentage of visits where the visitor enters and exits on the same page, without visiting any other pages on the site in between.
Click	A single instance of a visitor clicking a link from one page to another on the same site.
Click path	The sequence of clicks that website visitors follow on a given site.
Click-through rate (CTR)	The percentage of people who view an item who then click it; calculated by dividing the number of clicks by the number of impressions.
First visit	The first visit from a visitor who has not previously visited the site.
Frequency	A measurement of how often visitors come to a website, calculated by dividing the total number of sessions or visits by the total number of unique visitors.
Hit	A request for a file from a web server. Note that a hit is *not* the same as a pageview, as a single page can have multiple elements (images, text boxes, and so forth) that need to be individually loaded from the server. For example, a web page that includes four images would result in five hits to the server.
Impression	A single display of an advertisement on a web page.
New visitor	A visitor who has not made any previous visits to a website.
Page depth (pageviews per session)	The average number of pageviews a visitor initiates before ending a session, calculated by dividing total number of pageviews by total number of sessions.

Table 9.1   Key Web Analytics Metrics (continued)

Metric	Description
Pageview	A display of a complete web page. One visitor looking at a single page on your site generates one pageview. (Pageviews typically don't include error pages or those pages viewed by web crawlers or robots.)
Pageview duration (time on page)	The average amount of time that visitors spend on each page of a website.
Repeat visitor	A visitor who has made at least one previous visit to a website.
Session	A series of pageviews from the same visitor with no more than 30 minutes between pageviews—and with no visits to other sites between pageviews. Unlike a visit, a session ends when a visitor opens a page on another site.
Session duration	The average amount of time that visitors spend on a website each time they visit.
Singleton	A visit from a visitor where only a single page is viewed.
Unique visitor	A visitor who visits your site one or more times within a given timeframe, typically a single 24-hour period; a visitor can make multiple visits during that timeframe but counts as just a single unique visitor. For example, a user visiting your site twice in one day is counted as a single unique visitor.
Visibility time	The time (in seconds or minutes) that a single page or element is viewed by a visitor.
Visit	A series of pageviews from the same visitor with no more than 30 minutes between each pageview. Unlike a session, a visit continues (for 30 minutes) even after a visitor leaves your site.
Visitor	A uniquely identified client that views the pages on a website; someone who visits your site.

What to Look For

Okay, that's a lot to digest. Let me point your attention to the most important of these metrics, the ones that truly measure your website's performance.

> **note** When tracking pay-per-click ad performance, additional metrics come into play. These include average cost per click, average position, conversions, conversion rate, and so on.

Visits and Visitors

The first number that most people involved with a website want to know is how many visitors there were to the site. The more visitors you have, the busier your site is.

Now, there are visitors and there are *unique* visitors. While the raw visitor number might be larger, you're actually interested in the latter. That's because the raw visitor data can track the same visitors more than once. When you track unique visitors, you're tracking individual people, even if they make multiple visits to your site within a 24-hour period.

When a visitor views your site, that counts as a *visit*. Obviously, you can have more visits than you have visitors, as people can visit more than once a day. That said, it's nice to know how often your site is being accessed, so the visits number is good for that.

Together, visits and visitors tell you how many people are viewing your site and how many times your site is being accessed during a given time period. These are quantity metrics that let you know just how popular your site is.

Pageviews

Most of us want visitors to view more than just one page on our sites. The pageviews metric is one to look at for this information. A pageview is just as the name describes, a view of a single page by a site visitor. A visitor can view more than one page per visit, of course; in most instances, the more pageviews, the better.

Session Duration

Do you want visitors to get their information quickly and then leave? Or do you want them to stick around a bit and see what you have to offer? In either instance, you're interested in the session duration metric. Session duration measures the average amount of time that visitors spend on your website per visit. A shorter session duration may indicate that visitors don't like what they see and thus leave prematurely; a longer session duration could indicate that visitors are having trouble finding what they want—or that they really like what they find and stick around to read more.

Bounce Rate, % Exit, and Top Exit Pages

The shortest visits are those where someone lands on your site and then clicks away to another site, without ever viewing a second page. This single-page exit is measured by the bounce rate metric, which calculates the percentage of visits where the visitor enters and exits on the same page without visiting any other pages in-between. Obviously, a high bounce rate is a bad thing.

You can measure bounce rate for your entire site and for individual pages. This last approach is recommended if you've created multiple landing pages on your site, for use with PPC advertisements and the like. Identify those pages with a high bounce rate and then try to discover the reason for it and fix the issue.

Related to bounce rate is the % exit metric, which measures the percentage of users who exit from a given web page. This metric is interesting in that a high % exit could indicate people getting frustrated with a given page. (It can also indicate a natural exit point from your site, of course, such as the conclusion page of your checkout process.)

It's also interesting to learn which pages people leave from—that is, the top exit pages on your site. Ideally, these are pages created to be exit pages, such as your "thank you for ordering" pages. You have some investigating to do if you find people are exiting from pages that should be leading them to other pages instead. You typically want visitors to follow one or more specified paths through your site, and any page that isn't propelling visitors further down that path need to be examined.

Top Pages

Okay, so you know that you're getting visitors to your site; what pages are they looking at while they're there?

You can learn which of your site's pages are most popular by looking at the top pages metric. This is simply a list of the pages with the most pageviews, in descending order. You might be surprised—for many sites the top page is *not* the home page.

Top Landing Pages

This leads us to a discussion of your site's top landing pages. A landing page is the first page that a visitor lands on. Some visitors land on your home page, of course, but many don't. A visitor can land on a page buried deep in your site if that page is linked to from another site or if that page pops up in Google's search results.

The top landing pages might be by design (that is, you created them to be linked to from a PPC ad or press release), or they may occur organically. In any case, the top landing pages are arguably the most important pages on your site; they're certainly the first pages that most visitors see. Know what they are and pay attention to them.

Traffic Sources

How are people finding your site? That information is typically available in some sort of traffic sources analysis. A traffic source is the site visited just before a visitor hits your site; presumably, something about that site led them to yours.

Traffic sources can be any of the following:

- **Search engines** such as Google, Yahoo!, and Bing
- **Referring sites** that include links to your site
- **Advertisements** such as PPC ads, where a visitor clicked through to link to your site
- **Direct traffic**, where a visitor manually enters your site's URL

What percentage of visitors you get from each type of traffic source tells you what part of your web marketing plan is most effective. It also provides guidance into where you should direct future activities.

Keywords

For most sites, you'll find that your top traffic source is a search engine. Now it's time to drill down a little deeper and find out what people are searching for that's leading them to your site.

To that end, you want to look at the keywords metric in your web analytics. These are the top terms searched for by visitors who came to your site from a search engine. Knowing what people are searching for helps you determine what keywords to use in your site's SEO, as well as what keywords to purchase in your PPC advertising.

Geographic Data

Some web analytics tools can tell you where visitors live, in terms of countries, states, and even cities. If you're marketing regionally or locally, this is great information. If you run a local restaurant, for example, and find out you're getting a ton of visitors from Kuala Lumpur, you might want to do a little digging to find out why because it's wasted bandwidth. In any case, this is interesting data to look at.

Web Analytics Tools

Here's the deal: Some of the best web analytics tools are free. But while there are any number of companies offering expensive web analytics packages, the data that these tools collect is free for the picking on any website; it's just a matter of collecting and analyzing it. You can get just as smart using a free web analytics tool as you can with an expensive analysis package.

So what are the most popular web analytics tools? Here's a list of vendors to check out:

- ClickTale (www.clicktale.com)
- Google Analytics (www.google.com/analytics/)
- Logaholic (www.logaholic.com)
- MetaTraffic (www.metasun.com)
- Mint (www.haveamint.com)
- Omniture (www.omnigure.com)
- Piwik (www.piwik.org)
- Unica (www.unica.com)
- VisiStat (www.visistat.com)
- WebTrends (www.webtrends.com)
- Woopra (www.woopra.com)
- Yahoo! Web Analytics (web.analytics.yahoo.com)

Getting to Know Google Analytics

Of the tools we've discussed, I personally like and use Google Analytics. I like it for several reasons, not the least of which is that it's completely free. It's also easy to use and unusually comprehensive in the metrics it tracks.

Because of its cost (or lack of), Google Analytics is popular with websites both large and small. It's powerful enough to track traffic at large websites but easy enough for smaller sites to implement. It tracks all the key metrics detailed in Table 9.1 and more, displaying its results in series of "dashboards" and custom reports.

What sorts of data does Google Analytics analyze? On the main dashboard alone you find the following data:

- Site visits per day
- Total number of visits
- Total pageviews
- Average number of pages per visit
- Bounce rate
- Average time on site
- Percent new visits
- Top countries where visitors live
- Top sources of traffic
- Top pages on your site

FIGURE 9.1

The main Google Analytics dashboard.

And that's just what you see on the main dashboard; there's a lot more information available when you start drilling down.

Google Analytics utilizes onsite analytics to track visitor behavior on a specific site. After you register your site with Google Analytics, Google generates a unique piece of JavaScript code for your site. You then copy and paste this code into the underlying HTML of each page on your site you want to track; once embedded, this code tracks visitor behavior and transmits that data back to Google, where it is analyzed and displayed.

Of course, most web analytics tools work the same way; they track the same visitor data, after all. You should feel free to check out a variety of such tools and pick the one that best suits your needs—and your budget.

The Bottom Line

Web analytics tools let you gather and analyze data about your website's visitors. You can find out how many visitors you get in a given period, how many pages they're viewing, which pages they're viewing, and from which sites they're coming. Many web analytics tools, such as Google Analytics, are free; they all work by placing a piece of invisible code on the pages you want to track.

You use web analytics to determine not only how your site is performing, but also who is visiting your site and why. Web analytics can help you fine-tune your site's content and design, as well as the marketing activities you use to drive visitors to your site.

ANALYZING TOP CONTENT

A large website consists of many, many individual pages. When you want to make each page as effective as possible, you need to know which pages are working and which aren't. This is where content analysis comes in.

Content analysis looks at each page of your site and determines which pages are pulling their weight and which aren't. There are lot of different metrics to look at, but in general you want to know which pages attract the most visitors (these are your top *landing pages*—where people enter your site from other sites), as well as which pages people tend to leave from (these are the *top exit pages*—where people decide they don't want to stick around any longer). You also want to know which pages are the most popular on your site, as measured in visitors and pageviews; these are the pages that obviously have the most appeal to visitors.

A page that has a large number of pageviews, or one that is a top landing page, likely is attracting visitors because of its content. The better the content—that is, the more useful, relevant, and unique the content—the more attractive it will be to visitors, whether they're coming from search engines or other sites. A page that doesn't have a lot of pageviews and isn't a big landing page destination is probably one with weak content, which you would need to examine and revamp.

As such, you can use these content metrics to fine-tune your site's content. Identify the strong pages and work to make them even stronger, and find the weak pages and either get rid of them or rework them. The goal is to have a site where almost every page offers unique value that attracts both new and repeat visitors.

9

10

Understanding Search Engine Marketing

Search results rankings are important—they drive a ton of traffic to your website. In fact, most sites get the majority of new visitors from Google and the other major search engines. People find you because they're searching for something, and your site came up in the search results.

So while you can purchase pay-per-click (PPC) ads, seed influential blogs, and work the social networks, you'll get a majority of links from good old-fashioned search engine results. And you can't buy these results. How you rank is a function of the quality of your site, not the size of your web marketing budget.

Search Engine Marketing Explained

Because search engines drive so much traffic to most websites, you want to ensure that your site ranks as high as possible in the results for all the major search engines. This activity is what we call *search engine marketing*, and it involves optimizing your site to rank higher in these search results.

note Most marketers consider search engine marketing to include both search engine optimization and pay-per-click search advertising. I prefer to treat them separately, as the former involves website design and the latter is really just another form of paid advertising. Read my explanations in the "Search Engine Marketing and PPC Advertising" sidebar at the end of this chapter.

Why High Rankings Are Important

Why is a high ranking in the search results important? Don't searchers read the entire page of search results and then go onto the next?

Unfortunately, no. Most people don't read through entire pages of search results; instead, they just graze the top results. That's right, most don't even scroll down to the bottom of the first page of results, let alone click to the second or third results pages.

So if you want to be seen—and get the clicks—you have to rank in the top five or ten sites that pop up when someone searches for a given topic. Any lower, and the number of visitors you attract decreases rapidly.

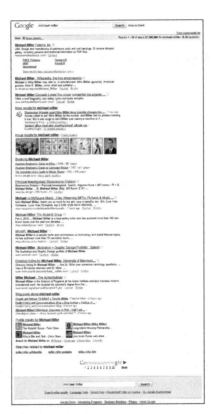

FIGURE 10.1
A full page of Google search results; far more people click the sites at the top than they do those at the bottom.

How Search Engine Marketing and SEO Work

Search results are what we call *organic*. This means they happen naturally; you can't buy them. Google and the other search engines generate their results based on which sites they feel best match a particular query; they don't accept money for placement. You just can't buy your way to the top.

Because search results occur organically, you have to find other ways to affect your ranking. If you have the right content and site design, users searching for a given topic will see your website among the top search results. That results in click-throughs to your site, which you hopefully convert into customers, revenue, and profit. This is what search engine marketing is all about—doing whatever it is you have to do to improve your ranking with Google and the other search engines.

Welcome to Search Engine Optimization

To improve your search engine rankings, then, you need to optimize your site for these very same search engines. This process, not surprisingly, is called *search engine optimization*, or SEO.

What does SEO entail? We go into more detail in the next few chapters, but in general it requires you to focus the content of your site to best match the terms or keywords that your desired customers are searching for. You have to identify the keywords they use in their queries and then feature those keywords throughout your site—in the visible copy and behind the scenes in the appropriate HTML code.

SEO also requires you to organize your site in such a way that search engines can more effectively determine its content. That also affects web page design—there are design techniques that can improve your search ranking and those that can cause the search engines to ignore you completely.

SEO is all about hard work and smart design. It's more about the time and effort you spend rather than the money you spend. A bigger budget doesn't necessarily lead to better results.

Big Bang for Small Bucks

Out of all the tools in your web marketing arsenal, search engine marketing provides the most bang for your buck; it's a relatively low-cost way to increase traffic and generate revenues. Because you can't buy placement in search engine results, your primary cost is the SEO effort itself—and SEO isn't that expensive.

In a way, search engine marketing is a great leveler. A small firm with good SEO skills can rank higher in the search results than larger competitors. It doesn't matter how big the company or its web marketing budget; SEO is more about smart marketing than it is about the money.

So for most online marketers, search engine marketing and the attending SEO represent a major component of their online marketing mix. It's not the only thing you should do to market your business online, but it may be the most important thing.

How Search Engines Work

To better understand how search engine marketing and SEO work, you need to understand how the search engines work—what they search for and how. A short lesson ensues.

How a Typical Search Works

Searching a site like Google, Yahoo!, or Bing is deceptively simple. The user enters a search query, clicks the Search button, and then waits for the site to display a list of matching results.

A typical search of this type takes less than half a second to complete. That's because all the searching takes place on the search engine site's own web servers. That's right; a user may think that he's searching the Web, but in effect he's searching a huge index of websites stored on the search site's servers that was created over a period of time. Because the user is only searching a server, not the entire Web, his searches can be completed in the blink of an eye.

note Google and other search engines are now augmenting the use of compiled search indexes by real-time results from Facebook, Twitter, blogs, and other social media. So you get some real-time results mixed in with the indexed web pages.

Of course, the user is unaware of what happens behind the scenes; he simply types his query into the search box on the search site's main web page, clicks the Search button, and then views the search results page when it appears. Where the results are stored and how they're served is irrelevant.

How a Search Site Builds Its Database—And Assembles Its Index

So searching Google or another search engine really means searching the index to that site's in-house database of web pages—not the Web itself. These databases hold literally billions of individual web pages. That's not necessarily the entire Web, but it is a good portion of it.

How does a search site determine which web pages to index and store on its servers? It's a complex process with several components.

First and foremost, most of the pages in the site's database are found by special *spider* or *crawler* software. This is software that automatically crawls the Web, looking for new and updated web pages. Most spiders not only search for new web pages (by exploring links to other pages on the pages it already knows about), but also periodically recrawl pages already in the database, checking for changes and updates. A complete recrawling of the web pages in a search site's database typically takes place every few weeks, so no individual page is more than a few weeks out of date.

The search engine's spider reads each page it encounters, much like a web browser does. It follows every link on every page until all the links have been followed. This is how new pages are added to the site's database, by following those links the spider hasn't seen before.

> **note** Google's spider software is known as GoogleBot. It's smart enough to crawl more frequently those pages that are frequently updated; it visits static pages less frequently. For example, pages on a news site might be crawled hourly, where more static pages on a reference site might be crawled once every few weeks.

The pages discovered by the spider are copied verbatim into the search site's database—and copied over each time they're updated. These stored web pages are used to compile the page summaries that appear on search results pages.

To search its database, the search site creates an index to all the stored web pages. This search engine index is much like the index found in the back of this book; it contains a list of all the important words used on every stored web page in the database. Once the index has been compiled, it's easy enough to search for a particular word and have returned a list of all the web pages on which that word appears.

And that's exactly how a search index and database work to serve search queries. A user enters one or more words in a query, the search engine searches its index for those words, and then those web pages that contain those words are returned as search results. This is fairly simple in concept but much more complex in execution—especially given that each search engine indexes all the words on several billion web pages.

How Search Results Are Ranked

As a web marketer, you care less about how Google or Yahoo! searches the Web than you do about how high up you appear in that search engine's results pages. What makes a search engine rank a particular site high in its search results and a similar site much lower?

Each search engine has its own particular algorithm for ranking the pages in its search index. In general, though, they follow similar methodology; similar factors are important to all the major search engines. To that end, it's instructional to look at how Google, the Web's largest and most popular search engine, ranks its results.

10

Google, like all the other search engines, attempts to serve its users by ranking the most important or relevant pages listed first and ranking less-relevant pages lower in the results. How does Google determine which web pages are the best match to a given query?

While Google keeps its precise methodology under lock and key, for competitive reasons, we do know that there are three primary components to its results rankings:

- **Text analysis**—Google looks not only for matching words on a web page, but also for how those words are used. That means examining font size, usage, proximity, and more than a hundred other factors to help determine relevance. Google also analyzes the content of neighboring pages on the same website to ensure that the selected page is the best match.

- **Links and link text**—Google then looks at the links (and the text for those links) on the web page, making sure that they link to pages that are relevant to the searcher's query.

- **PageRank**—Finally, Google relies on its own proprietary PageRank technology to give an objective measurement of web page importance and popularity. PageRank determines a page's importance by counting the number of other pages that link to that page. The more pages that link to a page, the higher that page's PageRank—and the higher it will appear in the search results.

Examining PageRank

Of all these factors, Google's PageRank is probably the most interesting. While it's just one factor among many, and actually not as important today as it was just a year or two ago, it's something that distinguishes Google from its competition.

The theory behind PageRank is that the more popular a page is, the higher that page's ultimate value. While this sounds a little like a popularity contest (and it is), it's surprising how often this approach delivers high-quality results.

The precise formula used by PageRank (called the *PageRank Algorithm*) is a tightly

note PageRank is page-specific, not site-specific. This means that the PageRank of the individual pages on a website can (and probably will) vary from page to page. Also note that PageRank is not calculated in real time; Google updates its PageRank figures only a few times a year.

held secret, but we do know that it's calculated using a combination of the quantity and quality of inbound links. That is, the number of inbound links you receive matter, but it's also important *which* pages are linking to your site.

You see, Google figures that links from pages more closely related to your page's topic should mean more than random links from unrelated pages. So, for example, if you're marketing hospital supplies, a link from a hospital website would result in a higher rank than a link from a site about minor-league baseball. With this in mind, it's likely that a page with fewer, higher-ranked pages linking to it will have a higher PageRank than a similar page with more (but lower-ranked) pages linking to it.

Dynamic Pages Are Hard to Index

As big as the databases at Google, Yahoo!, and Bing are, there are still lots of web pages that don't make it into those databases. What kinds of web pages are difficult for the search engines to index and why?

First, know that most search engines today don't do a good job of searching the "deep Web," those web pages generated on the fly from big database-driven websites—that is, pages that are created when a visitor fills in a form or enters a search query on a site. Similarly, search engines also don't always find pages served by the big news sites, pages housed on web forums and discussion groups, pages of blog posts, and so on.

What's the common factor behind these hard-to-index web pages? They all contain "dynamic" content that changes frequently, and the pages themselves don't always have a fixed URL. With most dynamic web pages, the URL—and the page itself—is generated on the fly, typically as a result of a search within the site itself.

This lack of a permanent URL makes these pages difficult, if not impossible, for a search engine spider to find. That's because a spider, unlike a human being, can't enter a query into a site's search box and click the Search button. It has to take those pages that it finds, typically the site's fixed home page. The dynamically generated pages slip through the cracks, so to speak.

This is why it's possible to search for a page that you know exists (you've seen it yourself!) and not find it listed in a search engine's search results. It's not a trivial problem; more and more of the Web is moving to dynamically generated content, leaving at least half the Internet beyond the capability of search engine spiders. This should give you pause if you plan on including dynamic web pages on your own website.

10

Images Are Less Important than Text

In addition to dynamic pages, most search engines have a hard time analyzing—or even recognizing—images and other nontext content on a web page. This may include pictures (without text captions), videos, or those annoying Flash animations that most consumers don't like anyway.

What all these media types have in common is that they don't contain any text. And because text is what search engines index, the search engines don't index these pages. In effect, a web page without text is invisible to the search spiders!

So if your website relies heavily on images, animations, and other media, it may be negatively affecting your search rankings. Better to replace those pretty pictures with boring—but more effective—text content!

> **note** While search engines ignore images, they can and do index the image's file names and anchor text, as well as any text surrounding the images. So if you must include images, make sure they're tagged in the accompanying HTML and have a caption beneath them on the page.

Examining the Major Search Engines

Okay, you're convinced—search engine marketing is important. Which search engines, then, should you target?

Google

The number-one search engine, in terms of searches and users, is Google (www.google.com). In any given month, depending on who's doing the counting, Google is responsible for about 65% of all web searches made in the U.S; its market share is even higher in some other countries (approaching 90% in the U.K, for example). That makes Google an extremely dominant player; no other search engine has half its market share.

Google's audience is as broad a cross-section of web users as you're likely to find. Where some other engines might attract less technical users of various sorts, Google attracts technophiles and technophobes alike. And, given Google ubiquity, you're likely to find it as the default search engine on most new PCs and many web browsers.

In other words, Google should be the number-one target of your search engine marketing efforts. No other search engine comes close.

FIGURE 10.2

Google, the Web's most popular search engine.

When it comes to optimizing your site for Google search, the most important factor is your site's content. Google is better than other search engines at filtering out typical SEO tricks (yes, there are SEO tricks; you learn some in the next few chapters), so your pages need to include genuine informational copy. You need to write naturally and make your copy look more like a news article than a collection of random phrases. Make sure you write grammati-

> **note** Translating percentages into raw numbers, in an average month Google's ~60% market share equals a little over 5 billion discrete searches. In contrast, Yahoo! generates almost 1.5 billion searches per month, and Bing gets about 800,000 searches per month.

cally and don't use sentence fragments. In some instances, using fewer occurrences of a key phrase may result in higher rankings than repeating the phrase more often.

Bottom line: If you have a better organic site than your competitors, you'll rank higher than if you try to force your way into Google's search index.

Yahoo!

Yahoo! (www.yahoo.com) has been around quite a bit longer than Google but long ago lost the number-one position to its chief competitor. Today, Yahoo!'s search market share is in the 17% range and declining slightly, which makes it the number-two player to the Google juggernaut.

Unlike Google, Yahoo! has a fairly busy search page; it looks like a portal than a pure search engine. Because of this, Yahoo! attracts a lot of users who want to do more than search, which results in a slightly less technical user base than that of Google.

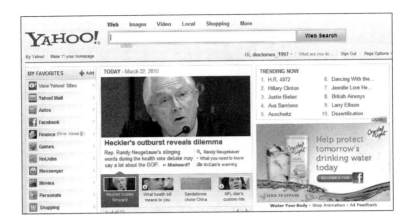

FIGURE 10.3
Yahoo!, the number-two search engine.

When determining search ranking, Yahoo! tends to weigh the page content higher than other factors. This means that using descriptive page titles and text goes a long way to improving your search results. It pays to put your effort into copywriting, making sure to include exact keywords and phrases within your text.

Bing

The number-three search engine today is also the newest—sort of. Bing (www.bing.com) is the latest iteration of Microsoft' search engine; it was formerly known as Live Search, Windows Live Search, and, before that, MSN Search. Fortunately for Microsoft, it looks like the fourth time might be a charm.

Like Google, Bing sports a relatively Spartan Google-like interface, albeit with a pretty picture behind the search box. Microsoft bills Bing not as a search engine but as a "decision engine," whatever that means. From a marketing perspective, it appears that they're focusing on quality over quantity in the search results.

Officially launched in June, 2009, Bing has been gaining market share on a month-by-month basis. Last time I checked (February 2010), Bing's share was approaching 12%. That makes it the number three player (still), but growing.

Bing's success (relative to Microsoft's previous search efforts, in any case) has led to a flood of publicity on how Bing is eating into Google's share of the search market. While it's true that Bing is gaining share, it hasn't necessarily been at Google's expense. The way I read the numbers, Bing is taking share away from Yahoo!, not Google. During Bing's launch, Yahoo!'s share slid down from 20% to 17% or so, while Google has remained fairly steady in the mid-60s. In any case, it's hard to get *too* excited about a number-three player with 12% market share, no matter how effective the spinmeisters are.

FIGURE 10.4
Bing, number-three with a bullet.

In terms of search results, Bing's aren't necessarily as focused as Google's. You can improve your Bing ranking by obtaining several links from other sites to your site and then tweak your page content to include a large number of descriptive phrases and keywords. It's less important that you use your keywords and phrases in an organic manner. You also don't need the high-quality, authoritative content that Google demands. This means that a poor quality site with good SEO might rank higher than a more authoritative site that hasn't been well-optimized.

> **note** Interestingly, Yahoo! has contracted with Microsoft for Bing to power Yahoo! search results. While end users will still see separate interfaces and possibly different search rankings, the search database and index will be the same for both sites.

Other Search Engines

Even though there are dozens of other search engines out there, only two additional engines are worth bothering with: AOL Search and Ask.com, both of which have a 2%–3% market share—not enough to challenge Google or

Yahoo!, but still enough to be statistically significant. The other smaller players in this space, unfortunately for them, don't match Ask.com's combined.

AOL Search (search.aol.com) is typically the number-four player in the search engine market, with less than a third of the users of number-three Bing. The AOL Search engine is basically the Google search engine (they have a business partnership) with a few enhancements and AOL-specific content thrown into the results. As such, optimizing your site for Google search also does a good job of optimizing it for AOL Search.

FIGURE 10.5
AOL Search, powered by Google.

Ask.com (www.ask.com) is the number-five player and, as such, doesn't command a lot of attention, although it's always been a bit of an innovator in how it approaches the search function. It differs from the other search sites in that it looks heavily at topical communities on the Web and uses links from within those communities to determine page relevance. The practical result is that Ask.com becomes important if you're in a vertical market or your site is about a narrowly defined topic. Optimizing for Ask.com, then, is a bit different than optimizing for the traditional search engines; instead of focusing on keywords and HTML tags, it pays attention to getting links from trusted sites in the relevant topical community.

Which Search Engines Should You Target?

Now that you know a little bit about each of the major search engines, which ones should you focus your search engine marketing efforts on?

Obviously, you have to optimize your site for Google. Google is the big dog in search, for good reason, and if you ignore Google, you'll kiss off more than half your potential site traffic. You simply can't do that; you have to optimize your site with Google in mind.

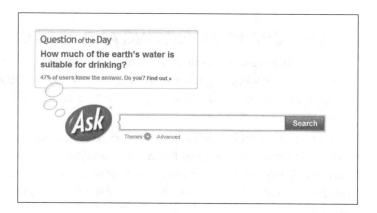

FIGURE 10.6

Ask.com, a slightly different search engine.

Beyond Google, both Yahoo! and Bing probably deserve your attention, if only because their demographics differ a bit from Google's. While Google attracts a more general demographic, Yahoo! and Bing both skew a little older and a little less techno-savvy. The same applies to AOL Search, which benefits from AOL's somewhat-captive audience of oldsters and youngsters.

So it helps if you know who your audience is. If your audience is female and over 50, you might not get as much traffic from Google as you would with a different demographic profile; you might find that you get more queries from Yahoo! and Bing users than you might have expected. Examine your demographics and see if you might benefit from pushing harder with the non-Google search engines.

The Bottom Line

For most web marketers, search engine marketing—in particular, search engine optimization—is the most important part of their online marketing efforts. That's because search engines drive the majority of new traffic to most websites; the higher your site can rank in the search results, the more traffic you'll generate. Most search engines work in the same fashion, sending software agents across the Web to find and index the pages they find. The end result is a giant database, a search index that is then used to fulfill end user search queries. How high a page ranks in a given query ultimately depends on how relevant that page is to the query; search engines look at a variety of factors, including keyword usage, link text, and inbound links, to determine the page's ranking.

10

SEARCH ENGINE MARKETING AND PPC ADVERTISING

Search engine marketing technically includes anything that increases the number of clicks you get from the major search engines. SEO to improve your search ranking is a big part of this, of course, but so is pay-per-click advertising.

That's because most PPC ads appear on search results pages. Yes, Google AdWords and the other PPC ad networks also place ads on relevant third-party websites, but the majority of placements—and resulting clicks—are on the search results pages of the network's host search engine.

So you end up driving traffic from the search engines both organically (via SEO) and via paid placements (via PPC advertising). Of these two methods, organic search results in far more clicks and is less expensive; PPC advertising drives fewer visitors at a higher cost.

Because the approaches are really quite different (save for the common focus on search keywords), I prefer to treat organic search engine marketing as a separate activity. PPC advertising, in my mind, is better grouped with other online advertising activities.

But if you hear a marketer referring to PPC advertising as part of search engine marketing, you now know why. It's really just a matter of classification—each has its place in the mix.

Essential Search Engine Optimization

Successful search engine marketing requires effective search engine optimization. That is, you need to optimize your site so that it appears high in the search results when someone searches for a keyword that matters to you.

How do you perform search engine optimization? You have to know what Google and the other search engines are looking for and then tweak your site's content, code, and design accordingly.

What Search Engines Look For

How do Google and the other search engines decide what pages appear at the top of a search results page? It's all about determining what a page's content is about and how that content relates to the search at hand.

The goal of a search engine is to provide the most accurate results to its users. The search engines don't care so much about the individual websites in their databases; they care about giving their users a more effective and efficient search experience.

When a search engine ranks search results, it's with the intent of delivering the one best answer to that particular user's query. Ideally, then, if someone is searching for a particular topic, those sites that best cover that topic will rise to the top of the search results.

But how do the search engines know what content is on a given page? There are a number of things the search engines look for—which happen to be the very things you'll want to optimize on your site.

Keywords

A search engine doesn't yet have the human capacity to read sentences and paragraphs and understand what it reads. Current technology enables a search engine to pull specific words and phrases from a page's text, but that's about it; the search engine has no way of knowing how well those words and phrases are used.

To determine what's important on a page, search engines look for *keywords*. A keyword is a word or phrase entered as part of a search query; the search engine tries to find the keyword on a web page and then determines how important that keyword is on the page.

The search engine does this by noting where on the page the keyword appears and how many times it's used. A site with a keyword buried near the bottom of a page will rank lower than one with the keyword placed near the top or used repeatedly in the page's text. It's not a foolproof way of determining importance and appropriateness, but it's a good first stab at it.

For example, if someone is searching for "golf" and your web page includes the word "golf" in a prominent position—in the first sentence of the first paragraph, for example—then your page is a good match for that search. If, on the other hand, if you have a page about sports in general that doesn't include the word "golf" at all or only includes it near the bottom of the page, then the search engine will determine that your site *isn't* a good match for that searcher. It doesn't matter if you have a big picture of Arnold Palmer at the top of your page (search engines can't read image, remember); unless you use the keyword prominently and relatively often, you won't rank high for that particular search.

So the major search engines, when they examine your pages, are going to look for the most important words—those words used in the page's title or headings, those words that appear in the opening paragraph on the page, and those words that are repeated throughout the page. The more prominently you include a word on your page, the more important a search engine will think it is to your site.

Conversely, giving prominent placement to the *wrong* words can hurt your search rankings and provide less relevant results. For example, if your site is about sports but you for some reason include the words "dental" and "molar" multiple times on the page, it will likely be viewed as a site about dentistry. This not only drives the wrong visitors to your site, but also lowers your search ranking in general because you're now one of the less useful sports listed.

HTML Tags

A search engine looks not just to the visible text on your site, but also to the page's underlying HTML code—specifically, the *metatdata* in the code. This metadata includes your site's name and keyword "content," which is specified within the <META> tag. This tag appears in the head of your HTML document before the <BODY> tag and its contents.

A typical <META> tag looks something like this:

```
<META NAME="KEYWORDS" CONTENT="keyword1, keyword2, keyword3">
```

It's easy enough for a search engine to locate the <META> tag and read the data contained within. If a site's metadata is properly detailed, this gives the search engine a good first idea as to what content is included on this page.

Beyond the <META> tag, search engines also examine the <TITLE> tag in the code. The search engines figure that the words you use in your page's title define, to some extent, the key content on the page. For this reason, you want to make sure that each page's <TITLE> tag includes two or three important keywords, followed by the page's name.

The search engines also seek out the heading tags in your HTML code—<H1>, <H2>, <H3>, and so forth. For this reason, you should use traditional heading tags (instead of newer Cascading Style Sheet coding) to emphasize key content on your pages.

Inbound Links

Google was the first search engine to realize that web rankings could be somewhat of a popularity contest—that is, if a site got a lot of traffic, there was probably a good reason for it. A useless site wouldn't attract a lot of visitors (at least not long-term), nor would it inspire other sites to link to it.

So if a site has a lot of other sites linking back to it, it's probably because that site offers useful information relevant to the site doing the linking. The more links to a given site, the more useful that probably is.

This is where Google got their PageRank algorithm, if you recall, which is based primarily on the number and quality of sites that link to a particular page. If your site has a hundred sites linking to it, for example, it should rank higher in Google's search results than a similar site with only ten sites linking to it.

And it's not just the quantity of links; it's also the quality. That is, a site that includes content that is relative to your page is more important than just some random site that links to your page. For example, if you have a site about movies, you'll get more oomph with a link from another movie-related site than you would with a link from a site about NASCAR. Relevance matters.

Optimizing Your Site's Content

There are lots of SEO tricks and tools you can employ, but the most effective thing you can do to improve your search ranking is to improve your site's content. Everything else you do is secondary; when it comes to SEO and improving your search ranking, content is king.

What Is Quality Content?

How do the search engines define quality content? Pretty much the same way you and I do. It's content that fills visitors' needs and relates to and answers the questions at hand.

Quality content is useful content. It's informative, and it's accurate. It's grammatically correct, it's punctuated properly, it reads well. It's original, it's lean and mean, and it's on point. It is relevant to the topic at hand and, most important, it is authoritative.

In most cases, quality content is not overtly promotional or commercial in nature. It's content that informs the reader without being self-serving. It answers important questions without leaving more questions unanswered. It serves a useful and practical purpose.

In short, quality content distinguishes your site from competing sites. When a visitor says "I learned something important there," you know you have quality content. If a visitor instead says, "I'm not sure why I bothered visiting that site," you know that your content is lacking on the quality front.

Why Does Quality Content Matter?

As to why quality content matters, it's all about delivering relevant results. All the major search engines want to provide searchers with sites that best answer their users' queries; they don't want to serve up sites that leave their users still asking the same questions.

There are other reasons for improving your site's content, of course. First and foremost, the better your site's content, the more satisfied your users will be. You should want to create the most useful, authoritative site possible on the topic at hand; you should not be willing to settle for offering second-rate content to visitors who can quickly and easily click away from your site to one that offers better content.

In addition, the better the content on your site, the more likely it is that other sites will link to it—and these inbound links are also important to your site's search ranking. If your site's content disappoints, other sites won't link to you; if your content excels, you'll get a lot of links without having to ask for them.

> **note** Experts dub content that attracts links from other quality sites as "linkworthy." If your site is just like all the others out there, it's not linkworthy—that is, there's no reason for other sites to link to yours.

Providing Authoritative Information

All this talk about creating quality content is fine, but just how do you go about doing it? The first thing you need to do is provide authoritative information.

You want your site to have content so complete that users won't have to visit any other site to find out more about your given topic. Include every piece of information that's relevant, make sure that you answer any questions your user base might pose, and you establish your site as the leading authority on the topic.

Then there's the matter of *relevant* content; the longest web page isn't necessarily the most authoritative. If you do a good job figuring out what particular information your target audience is looking for, your page can be more concise than a competing page that throws in everything but the kitchen sink. In other words, offering targeted information is often a better approach than being unnecessarily comprehensive.

So at the core of providing authoritative information is knowing what that information should be—which is a function of knowing what your target visitor is looking for. It all gets back to the concept of *thinking like the customer*. You have to know what the customer wants to know what information he's looking for and how he's looking for it. When you can provide exactly the right information, you become the authority.

Writing Engaging Copy

Now we come to the softer side of authority—how you present the information on your web pages. There's a lot to be said for presenting your information in a grammatically correct, properly punctuated, engaging fashion.

What does this mean? Well, it means utilizing your own copywriting skills or hiring
an experienced copywriter. In fact, there's
a whole army of web-friendly copywriters
out there, and they know how to fine-tune
copy for the particular needs of the web
audience, as well as incorporate SEO techniques into their copy (which we discuss
next). It's just like traditional marketing
copywriting, except different.

Bottom line: Facts alone don't make for
quality content. You have to present your
facts in a way that is readable and easy to
follow—just as you do in any medium.

> **note** Engaging copy
> involves more than
> just including all the keywords
> you've identified—which could
> be viewed as *keyword stuffing*.
> This is a technique wherein the
> site owner inserts multiple
> instances of a keyword onto a
> page, often using hidden, ran-
> dom text, in an effort to increase
> the keyword density and thus
> increase the page's apparent
> relevancy of a page. Most search
> engines today view keyword
> stuffing as a kind of search-
> related spam and employ sophis-
> ticated algorithms to detect the
> technique.

Crafting SEO-Friendly Content

Your site's content not only has to be
authoritative and engaging, but it also has to be presented in such a fashion
that search engines notice it. This means making your content SEO-friendly—
which may be a new skill for you.

Just what is SEO-friendly content? Here's a list of things that can make or
break the way search engines interpret your site's content:

- **Use words, not pictures**—It bears repeating that today's search
  engines only look at the text on a web page, not at a page's images,
  videos, Flash animations, and the like. If you have important content
  to present, present it in the body text on your page.

- **Include keywords in your copy**—When you're presenting your core
  concepts, make sure you work in those keywords and phrases that your
  potential visitors will be searching for. If a keyword doesn't exist in a
  page's copy, search engines won't return that page as part of the relevant search results.

- **Repeat keywords and phrases naturally**—It's not enough to include
  your most important keywords and phrases once on a page. You need
  to repeat those keywords and phrases—but in a natural manner. It
  can't look as if you're keyword stuffing; the words have to flow organically in your text.

- **Make the important stuff more prominent**—Whether we're talking
  keywords or core concepts, the most important information on your
  web page should be placed in more prominent positions on the page

where it will be more easily found by search crawlers. This may mean placing the information in one of the first two or three paragraphs on your page. It may also mean placing key concepts in your page's headings and subheadings.

- **Break up the copy**—It's always a good idea to modularize the content on your page. Instead of presenting a long train-of-thought block of text, break up that block into short chunks, each chunk introduced by its own prominent heading or subheading. Make it easy for readers—and search crawlers—to find the information they want on your page.

- **Length matters**—While I'm an admirer of concise copy, some search engines appear to reward those sites that have more words per page. On average, today's top search engines seem to have a preference for pages with content in the 1,000-word range. But that's just an average. For Google's top ten search results, the average number of words per page is about 950; for Yahoo!, it's closer to 1,300 words per page.

Remember, though, that the way you present your content is secondary to the content itself. You have to start with authoritative content and then work from there.

Optimizing Your Site's Keywords

To some degree, all search optimization revolves around the use of keywords and key phrases. Whether you're talking the content on a page or the code that underlies that content, you use keywords to give your content and code more impact.

It's vital, then, that you learn how to create a list of keywords and key phrases relevant to your site and how to include them in your site's coding and content. It all starts with learning how to *think like the customer*; you need to get inside searchers' heads to determine which words they'll use in their queries.

Performing Keyword Research

The art of determining which keywords to use is called *keyword research*, and it's a key part of SEO. When you know which keywords and phrases that your target customers are likely to use, you can optimize your site for those words and phrases; if you don't know how they're searching, you don't know what to optimize.

While you can conduct extensive (and expensive) market research to determine how your target audience is searching, or even guess as to what the top searches are, there are simpler and more effective ways to get smart about this. Several companies offer keyword research tools that compile and analyze keyword search statistics from all the major search engines. You can use the results from these keyword research tools to determine the most powerful keywords to include on your site.

These keyword research tools work by matching the content of your website with keywords relevant to that content; they've already searched through hundreds of thousands of possible keywords and phrases on the most popular search engines and mapped the results to their own databases. You enter a word or phrase that describes what your site has to offer, and the research tool returns a list of words or phrases related to that description, in descending order of search popularity.

Some of the more popular keyword research tools include the following:

- KeywordDiscovery (www.keyworddiscovery.com)
- Wordtracker (www.wordtracker.com)
- WordZe (www.wordze.com)

These tools don't come cheap; expect to pay $35 to $70 *per month* to subscribe.

Determining the Right Keyword Density

Once you've generated a list of keywords, you now have to use those keywords on your web pages. Let's start by examining how and how often you should include keywords in your page's copy.

First, know that the more often you use a keyword in your body text, the more likely it is that search crawlers will register the keyword—to a point. Include a keyword too many times, and crawlers will think you're artificially "stuffing" the keyword into your phrase, with no regard for the actual content. If you're suspected of keyword stuffing in this fashion, don't be surprised to see your search ranking actually decrease or your page disappear completely from that search engine's search results. (As I've mentioned, search engines don't like keyword stuffing.)

Thus you need to determine the correct keyword density when you're optimizing the content of a web page. What is an optimal keyword density? That depends. If you have a lot of different keywords on a long page, you could have a density of 20% or more and still rank fine. If you only have a

note *Keyword density* is the number of times a keyword or phrase appears compared to the total number of words on a page.

handful of keywords on a short page, a 5% keyword density might be too much. The key is to make sure your page is readable; if it sounds stilted or awkward due to unnecessary keyword repetition, then chances are a search engine will also think that you're overusing your keywords.

Writing Keyword-Oriented Copy

So what's the best way to incorporate keywords into your site's content?

First, know that web copywriting is very similar to direct response copywriting. You have to describe things in words, not pictures, and if you're selling something, provide a strong "why to buy" message. The big difference between direct response copywriting and web copywriting is that with web copywriting, you have two different audiences: the site's visitors and the search engines.

This means you have to provide readable, compelling copy for your visitors, while at the same time incorporate all the necessary keywords and phrases that matter to the search engines. You don't want to sacrifice one for the other; never make your page less readable just to cram in another keyword. Go for readability first and then incorporate the keywords as you can.

One way to improve both readability and search optimization is to break your copy into small sections or chunks of text and then introduce each section with a heading or subheading. As you learn shortly, search crawlers look for keywords in your heading tags; headings also help readers identify important sections on your page. So chunking up your text has benefit for both your audiences.

Two other good places to include keywords are in your page's first and last paragraphs. Not only do search crawlers look more closely at the beginning and end of your page and tend to skip the middle parts, readers look to the first and last paragraphs to introduce key ideas and then summarize your page's content. It's just like in writing a newspaper article; it's the first and last graphs that are most important.

Of course, when you incorporate keywords and phrases into your text, you have to do so in a natural fashion—while using the word or phrase verbatim. So if one of your key phrases is "windmill farm," you have to use that exact phrase and in a way that doesn't sound forced. This is a definite copywriting challenge but one that can be met.

One last thing. On the Web, there's little benefit to short copy. Not only do readers want as much information as possible, longer copy provides more opportunity for you to place your keywords and phrases without overly increasing keyword density. Let's face it, if you have ten keywords to include,

11

it's easier to do so on a 1,000-word page (organized into shorter reader-friendly chunks, of course) than on one that only includes 100 words total. (Put another way, a shorter page is more likely to sound keyword stuffed than a longer one.)

So write more copy if you need to—but make sure you chunk into shorter sections for the reader. As noted previously, some studies say that pages in the 1,000 page range rank best with most search engines; certainly, anything less than 250 words is too little. Use the extra words to add more keywords and phrases to your page—and to provide more useful information to your site's visitors.

Optimizing Your Site's HTML Tags

Another important use of keywords is within your site's HTML code; most search crawlers scan specific HTML tags for information they use in indexing a page. Insert your keywords and phrases into these tags, and you'll improve your site's results for that search engine.

Which HTML tags do you need to focus on? There are a few, but they're relatively easy to work with—assuming you know a little HTML.

<TITLE> Tags

We'll work our way down from the top, starting with your page's title. The title is the text that appears in the title bar of a web browser; the title should present your page's official name and provide a glimpse to its content. It's also an effective place to use your chosen keywords.

That's because the page title is one of the first places that search crawlers look to determine the content of your page. Crawlers figure that the title should accurately reflect what the page is about—for example, if you have a page titled "The Yellow School Bus Page," the page is most likely about yellow school buses. Unless you mistakenly or purposefully mistitle your page, the search crawler will skim off keywords and phrases from the title to use in its search engine index. In addition, when your page appears on a search engine's results page, the title is what the search engine uses as the listing name.

note As with all HTML tags, capitalization is not important. For example, you can enter this tag as either **<TITLE>** or **<title>**; it works the same either way.

For all these reasons, you need to get your most important keywords and phrases into your page's title—which you do via the HTML <TITLE> tag. This tag appears in the head of your document before the body text. It's a simple tag that looks something like this:

```
<TITLE>Insert your title here</TITLE>
```

Just insert your chosen title text between the <TITLE> and </TITLE> tags. Whatever is between the tags is your page's official title and is what appears in the web browser's title bar.

What's the ideal length for a title? Well, a title can't exceed 64 characters; any additional text is truncated. So you have to keep the 64-character limit in mind but aim to include from three to ten words total. This makes the title both readable for users (short enough to scan) and useful for search engines (long enough to include a handful of keywords).

What should you put in your title? Your page's official name, of course, but also one or more of the most important keywords for your site. It's best if the name includes the keywords, but you can always add the keywords after the name, following some sort of divider character—a colon (:) or semi-colon (;) perhaps or a vertical line (|) or dash (-) or even a simple comma (,).

> **note** When counting characters, remember that a space counts as a character, same as a letter or number or special character.

For example, if your site is named New Energy Sources, you might enter the following <TITLE> tag:

```
<TITLE>New Energy Sources: Wind, Solar, Geothermal, Tidal, Biomass</TITLE>
```

That's 59 characters and 8 words, both of which fit within our guidelines. Users will see the name of the site in their title bars and in the search results, and search engines will link this page to queries regarding all types of new energy.

<META> Tags

The <META> tag is actually several tags, each with its own specific attribute that conveys so-called metadata (data about your page) to the search crawlers. You can insert multiple <META> tags (one for each attribute) into the head of your document, like this:

```
<HEAD>
<TITLE>The Big Yellow Schoolbus Page</TITLE>
<META NAME="DESCRIPTION" CONTENT="Everything you need to know about
schoolbuses">
```

```
<META NAME="KEYWORDS" CONTENT="schoolbus, school, bus, yellow,
transportation, education, children, students ">
</HEAD>
```

As you can see from this example, there are two primary **<META>** attributes— **DESCRIPTION** and **KEYWORDS**. (There are actually more than two attributes, but these are the important ones for SEO.) Each attribute is defined by the **NAME** attribute, as in **NAME=***"ATTRIBUTE"*. Then the **CONTENT** attribute is used to define the content for the description or keywords. It's all fairly straightforward.

> **note** The only problem with **<META>** tags is that they've been so overused that many search engines now ignore them (for example, Yahoo! recognizes the **<META> KEYWORDS** attribute, but Google doesn't). That said, you can't ignore **<META>** tags because they do feed information to some search engines.

Let's continue by looking at the **DESCRIPTION** attribute. The text assigned to this attribute is used by some search engines as the description for your web page in their search results. This means you want to think of the **DESCRIPTION** text as a short promotional blurb that describes what your page is about.

The tag works like this:

```
<META NAME="DESCRIPTION" CONTENT="Insert your description here">
```

The variable text is the bit between the quotation marks. It's read as a complete text string—a block of text, as it were. (And it's okay to include commas in the **DESCRIPTION** text because they're treated as-is.) Within this descriptive text, you should make sure to include as many keywords or phrases that fit naturally (avoid keyword stuffing).

The second important **<META>** tag uses the **KEYWORDS** attribute. As you might suspect, this attribute is your opportunity to tell the search engines which keywords your page is targeting.

It's easy to add this tag to your page's HTML code. Just use the following template:

> **note** One good use of the **KEYWORDS** tag is to include common misspellings of legitimate keywords used on your site. For example, if you use the keyword "convertible," you might use the **KEYWORDS** tag to include the misspellings "convertable," "convirtible," and "convertibal." Similarly, you can use the tag to list synonyms for your actual keywords—such as "soft top" and "rag top."

```
<META NAME="KEYWORDS" CONTENT="keyword 1, keyword 2, keyword 3">
```

Separate each keyword or phrase by a comma. You can include as many keywords or phrases as you like, and capitalization doesn't matter. And this is important—the keywords you include in this tag *don't* actually have to appear on the web page.

Header Tags

A header is a heading or subheading within your body text, kind of like a newspaper headline or the headings between sections in this book. The HTML standard lets you use six different levels of headings, from **<H1>** to **<H6>**, in descending order.

Headers are important because most search crawlers look in these tags for content information. They figure that if a topic or keyword is important enough to be included in the header, it probably describes your page's content and that it's important enough to index.

So first of all, you have to organize the information on your page into short chunks of text and then introduce each text block with its own header. Include in the header text as many keywords and phrases as you can that describe the given text in an organic fashion.

> **note** Many cutting-edge web designers have switched from the older **<H1>**-style heading tags to Cascading Style Sheet (CSS) **<DIV>** and **<SPAN>** codes. That's unfortunate, as most search engines look for the traditional heading tags to determine the content of a page. If you want to optimize your ranking in most search indexes, you'll have to include both CSS coding and the traditional **<H1>** and **<H2>** tags.

The form of this HTML code is simple:

```
<H1>This is the header text.</H1>
```

Obviously, insert your own text between the "on" and "off" tags, and use the other header tags (**<H2>**, **<H3>**, **<H4>**, and so on) for lower-level headers.

Anchor Text

Keywords are also important for the *anchor text* on your page—the text that accompanies your web links.

The anchor text is one of the elements that search engines evaluate to determine the value of a link. You can increase the value of an outbound or intra-site link by including keywords in the anchor text. This lets the search crawlers know that the site you're linking to is related to the keyword—and thus a more relevant link.

For example, if one of your top keywords is "microprocessor" and you're linking to the Intel website, the anchor text that links to the website should include the word "microprocessor." In this instance, you might write and link from the following sentence:

> Intel manufactures the majority of the microprocessors found in today's PCs.

While you could limit the link to the phrase "Intel," the anchor text would not include your keyword "microprocessor." Better, then, to format the entire sentence—including the word "microprocessor" as the anchor text for the link.

Obviously, you create the link for the anchor text using basic HTML code. This sort of linking is done automatically by most HTML editing or web page creation programs, or you can code the text manually, like this:

```
<a href="http://www.intel.com">Intel manufactures the majority of the
microprocessors found in today's PCs..</a>
```

The takeaway here is to always include one or more keywords in the anchor text you use to link to related sites.

Optimizing Your Site's Design and Organization

When it comes to SEO, content is king, but design is also important. A good design can help search crawlers identify key content, while a bad design can negatively impact how your site ranks. In fact, some designs can actually make your site *invisible* to search crawlers. Assuming that you want your site seen and indexed, you need to pay attention to a few design basics.

To that end, let me present some tips you can use to optimize the individual pages on your website. These are universal tips that work on any type of page on any type of site.

Put the Most Important Stuff First on the Page

Search crawlers start at the top of a page and then read downward. Like human readers, they may not read the entire page, so it's essential to put the most important elements at the top of your page, in the main headings, and in initial paragraphs. A search crawler will see your leading content and register it as important; content lower on the page will be registered as subsidiary if it's noted at all.

Use Headings and Subheadings

Another way to tell a search engine that something is important is to include it in a heading or subheading on the page. As we've previously discussed, your page's heading tags are singled out by most search crawlers on the assumption they highlight the most important content of your site. So you need to use headings to separate and highlight content on your page and to highlight your most important keywords and phrases.

Use Text, Not Pictures (or Videos or Flash…)

Though I've mentioned this before, it bears repeating: Search crawlers read text and nothing but text. They don't read images, they don't read Flash animations, and they don't read videos. Every element on your page other than text is essentially invisible to search crawlers. It's only the text that matters.

This is important if your website designers (or even the techie guys) insist on presenting important content via nontext elements. The most glaring example of this are sites that use nothing but Flash animation on their introductory pages, which not only annoys many users but causes most search crawlers to skip completely over them—and perhaps the rest of the site.

The reason this is bad is that a complete Flash page is basically a blank page as far as the major search engines are concerned. If the page is completely in Flash, the search engines have no idea what the page is about. They can get some idea of the content from the page's <TITLE> and <META> tags, but that's not nearly as good as reading the site's actual content—which they can't because there's no text to read.

The same thing goes with pages that rely on images or videos for the bulk of their content. A search crawler can't look at an image or view a video; it has no way (short of a file's **ALT** tag) to determine what the image or video is about. Again, the page appears blank to the search crawlers.

So the first thing you need to do is overrule those designers who want to Flash up your site and take a back-to-basics, text-based approach. You don't need to get rid of all images, animations, and videos, but they need to be downplayed on the page—and supplemented by well-written, descriptive text.

Simplify Long URLs

If you use dynamically generated pages on your site, you may want to rethink the practice. One reason for this is that the URLs generated are typically long and complex—which is not ideal for either human users or search crawlers.

11

In this respect, search crawlers are similar to humans; they like URLs that are short and simple and have trouble deciphering overly long URLs, especially those that have values after a "?" character. So the longer your URL, the less likely it is to be indexed by the major search engines.

For that reason, you need to create search engine-friendly URLs. Use short file names for each page and keep the navigation as flat as possible to shorten the file path.

> **note** For those dynamically generated pages with lots of "?" values, consider performing what is called a *URL rewrite*. This essentially creates a URL lookup table for your site. When a server query is generated, it checks the lookup table for the appropriate page and returns a virtual path to the file instead of using dynamically generated values.

Optimizing Inbound Links

As you've learned, Google bases a large part of its search ranking on how many and what kinds of sites link to your pages. It assumes that the more authoritative and relevant your content, the more inbound links you'll have.

It's imperative, then, that you work on increasing the inbound links to your site. You need to work not just on the quantity of these links, but also their quality; the more relevant and authoritative the sites that link to yours, the higher the import that search engines will assign to those links.

There are a number of different ways to build links to your site. These range from the completely "white hat" approach of building quality content and waiting for other sites to notice it and link to you to the questionable practice of buying links to the pure "black hat" approach of building phony websites to link back to your main site. Naturally, I'm a fan of the organic white hat methods—although there's no harm in asking for links if you want.

Creating Linkworthy Content

The most important part of attracting inbound links is having site content that other sites want to link to. It's a matter of building a "linkworthy" site; if you have quality content, websites and blogs will link to you.

The keys to creating linkworthy content are to be authoritative, creative, and add value not found in competing sites. Your site needs to fully address the chosen topic and offer unique content. If related sites find your content to be both valuable and unique, they'll make the links.

Getting the Word Out

Of course, for a website or blog to link to you, it has to know about you. The old adage of "if you build it, they will come" is only viable if they actually hear about what you're doing.

There are many ways to get the word out about your site. Probably the most popular approach is to employ traditional public relations techniques. Issue a press release (paper or electronic), make some phone calls, fire off some emails to relevant blogs and forums—anything you have to do to create a buzz about your site. When other sites and blogs start talking about your site, you'll attract interested visitors, some of whom will find it worthwhile to link to your site.

The nice thing about generating links in this fashion is that they're truly organic.

note When you attract links organically, you should experience a trickle-down effect—that is, other sites will link to your site when they see the link on another respected sites. Quality links beget more links.

The links come from sites and blogs that are interested in your content and are thus highly relevant. They link because they want to, not because they're asked to or paid to. They're quality links—just what Google and the other engines tend to rank high.

Making Link Requests

This isn't to say that you can't ask other sites to link to yours. In fact, making link requests is an important part of any SEO strategy, but sometimes you have to be a bit aggressive in creating new inbound links.

How do you ask another site to link to yours? It's as simple as identifying the site or blog (based on its relevance and quality) and then sending an email to the site's webmaster or author.

Let's start with how you identify a relevant site. Here's where you rely on the quality of the search engines. Query Google, Yahoo!, or Bing for your site topic, and see which other sites appear at the top of the rankings; you can also use Google Blog Search (blogsearch.google.com) to search for blogs on this topic. This should give you a short list of those sites and blogs that might be interested in what your site has to offer.

Now you want to spend a little time on each of these sites. Get to know what the site or blog does and also who does it. It's best if you can identify the webmaster or content provider by name; a personal email works a lot better than one addressed to "Dear Webmaster." If it's a site or blog with a thriving community, make your presence known on the message boards or via blog comments. You'll get a better response to your request if you're a known friend of the site than if you're a random stranger.

The actual request process requires some hands-on work. Compose an email, addressed to the correct person, that describes your site, why it's relevant to his site or blog, and then ask that person to create a link to your site. Make sure you include the URL of the landing page on your site to which you want them to link. You should also include some suggested text to include as the anchor text for the link. (Remember—the anchor text should include one or more keywords or phrases relevant to your site.)

At that point, the targeted site either will or won't make the requested link. If the answer is yes, you're good to go. If the answer is no (or, more likely, if you don't receive an answer), there's no harm in asking again.

Automating Link Requests—or Not

If the entire link request process sounds too tedious to you, you can always send out bulk (and impersonal) emails or engage the service of a link request specialist. The former is easy enough to do, although it smacks of spam; as to the latter, you can find plenty of firms that do this via a simple Google search.

That said, I'm not a big fan of automating the link request process. The quality of any link you get from a "Dear webmaster, please link to our site" request is, in all probability, quite low. You'll almost always generate higher-quality links from personal requests.

Engaging in Link Trading

Then there's the issue of link trading, or reciprocal linking. There are two ways to do this, one of which generates higher quality results than the other.

The best way to trade links is directly with another site. That is, you identify a site or blog that you'd like to have linked to yours and email that site. In your email, you offer to place a link to their site in yours if they reciprocate with a link back to your site. You both benefit from the link exchange.

note I'm not a big fan of automated link exchanges. I am, however, a fan of active link trading. There's no harm at all in exchanging a link on your site for a link from a relevant website. One good turn deserves another, as the saying goes—sometimes it takes a link to get a link.

The more suspect way to trade links is via a link exchange service or program. These services, such as GotLinks (www.gotlinks.com) and LinkMarket (www.linkmarket.net), can provide hundreds of sites to link to your site in exchange for links from your site to theirs. The only problem with these link exchanges is that the linking sites are not necessarily high-quality sites; they're often not even sites relevant to your site's topic. In some instances, the links you get are from obvious link farms—not sites that help you increase your search ranking.

Purchasing Links

Finally, we come to the controversial topic of link purchasing—paying for links back to your site. This could involve sending another site a one-time check or perhaps agreeing to share some portion of your site's ad revenue.

Some marketers view link purchasing as a black hat technique, somehow less pure than trading links or generating links organically. But there are some good reasons to consider this approach.

For example, if the only way you can get a link from a relevant, high-quality site is to pay for it, that may be better than not getting the link at all. And some high-volume sites only sell their links, which means you have to pay to play.

Bottom line? Paying for links shouldn't be your first approach, but you shouldn't rule it out, either. Sometimes it's the only way to get the inbound links you need.

Optimizing Links Between Pages on Your Site

There's one last type of link to deal with—those links from one page on your site to another. These internal links are important for a number of reasons.

First, and perhaps most important, internal links help the individual pages on your site to get noticed by the various search crawlers. Search crawlers actually look for internal links; they use these links to identify further pages on your site. For this reason, you should include links to all your important pages on your site's home page, as well as in your site's menu and navigation system.

Second, using a keyword or phrase in the anchor text accompanying an internal link helps to build the relevancy of the linked-to page. It's a simple thing; search crawlers look to the anchor text for targeted keywords. The more anchor text you create via internal links, the more keywords get noticed.

This also increases the ranking of your site's internal pages with that search engine. The closer a page is from your site's home page, in terms of number of clicks, the higher that page will rank with the search engine. Include a direct link from your site's home page, and you'll ensure a higher ranking for the linked-to internal page.

For all these reasons, you need to pay as much attention to your site's internal links as you do to building inbound links from external sites. There's no getting around it—every link is important, whether it's inbound or internal!

Optimizing Images

As you've hopefully learned by now, search crawlers pretty much ignore images, videos, and other media files on a web page. They crawl a page's text and look at certain HTML tags, but that's about it—which means, of course, that any content on your site that isn't text is essentially invisible to the search engines.

But what do you do if you use a lot of images and videos on your web pages, instead of text? (Some designers are insistent, after all…) Well, there are ways around the crawlers' limitations, as you'll soon learn.

Using the ALT Attribute

Images are inserted into a web page via the following bit of HTML code:

```
<IMG SRC="image.jpg" WIDTH="XXX" HEIGHT="XXX" ALT="description"
TITLE="title" >
```

In decoding the code, the <IMG> tag says that there's an image to insert, the **SRC** attribute defines the location of the image file, and the **WIDTH** and **HEIGHT** attributes define the size of the image (in pixels)—all pretty standard stuff. It's the **ALT** and **TITLE** attributes, however, that deserve closer inspection.

The **ALT** attribute defines what a web browser should display if, for some reason, the image file isn't available or doesn't display on a page. Instead of seeing the chosen image, the user would see the text entered between the quotation marks in the **ALT** attribute.

More important, the **ALT** attribute is what a search crawler reads to determine the content of an image file. Because they can't view the actual content of an image file itself, they rely on the text description in the **ALT** attribute to tell them what the image is about. It's an inexact science, of course; there's no law, unfortunately, prohibiting a site designer from describing an image of a wrinkled old man as a "hot babe."

Limitations noted, the **ALT** attribute is how you get the search engines to recognize your page's images as valid content. This means you need to enter descriptive text into the **ALT** attributes for each and every image on your website. Make sure the attribute text not only describes the image, but also includes (you guessed it!) important keywords and phrases. In other words, use the **ALT** tag to reinforce your site's keyword scheme—while still describing how an image looks.

Using the TITLE Attribute

The final attribute for the <IMG> tag is the **TITLE** attribute. This attribute assigns a title to the image, which is what displays if a user hovers his cursor over an image.

While the **TITLE** attribute isn't crawled as often as the **ALT** attribute, it still represents an opportunity to describe your image in words. Follow the same approach as you do with the **ALT** attribute; use the **TITLE** attribute to hold a description of the image, along with important keywords and phrases.

Optimizing for Image Search

A surprisingly large number of search engine users search not for text, but for images. For this reason, the major search engines have specific algorithms they use to ascertain the content of the images found on the pages in their indexes and to rank those images for relevance.

Knowing this, there are ways you can optimize your images for image search ranking. Employ these techniques:

- Add the **ALT** and **TITLE** attributes to all your image tags and use them to embed keywords and phrases—as well as text that describes the image.

- For the image file itself, create a file name that both describes the image and includes one or more keywords. Use hyphens in the file name to isolate the keywords.

- Add a descriptive caption for each image in the body text of your web page. Don't leave any image standing alone with mention in the text; search crawlers can derive the content of an image by the text that surrounds it.

- Include the **WIDTH** and **HEIGHT** attributes in the <IMG> tag so that Google Image Search can place your image in the right size bracket.

Follow this advice and you can get your site ranked for both traditional searches and the more specialized image searches.

The Bottom Line

Search engine marketing may be—probably is—the most important component of your web marketing plan. That's because most new visitors find your website by searching; the higher your site ranks in the search results, the more potential customers you attract.

To improve your site's search ranking, you have to utilize search engine optimization techniques. SEO improves your site's visibility to the major search crawlers and helps the search engines identify your site as relevant to search queries.

The most effective ways to optimize your site include improving your site's content, identifying and utilizing the keywords that people search for, taking advantage of key HTML tags, and improving the quantity and quality of inbound links to your site. In addition, you need to minimize the use of non-text elements and organize the content on a page efficiently. The result of effective SEO should be higher search ranking—and more traffic to your site.

SEARCHING THE DARK WEB

When we talk about optimizing your site for search, we're talking primarily about Google, Bing, and Yahoo!. But there's a whole other part of the Internet out there that you're probably not aware of—and that could prove detrimental to your company's online plans.

I'm talking about the *dark web*, also known as the *deep web, invisible web,* or *dark net*. This is a part of the Internet that is beyond the reach of traditional search engines—sites and pages that are not found and indexed by Google et al. Now, some of these are simply old, abandoned websites, but the majority have been deliberately designed to avoid detection.

That's right, the dark web is a haven for individuals and organizations that don't want to be found. As you might suspect, it's host to all manner of criminal activity, from spamming to identity theft to worse.

Dark websites employ all manner of tricks to remain invisible to Google and the other search engines. Think of it as SEO in reverse; these sites don't want to be found and indexed. Now, these sites *can* be found, but it's difficult; you pretty much have to be invited in. Once you're in, however, you'll find all sorts of nasty stuff, from stolen credit card numbers to phishing lists to terrorist chat rooms. Really, you don't want to know.

While Google can't find (and really doesn't look for) this stuff, law enforcement agencies and cyberintelligence firms can; that's their job. The main reason you need to be aware of this dark web is in the event your information shows up there—in the form of stolen customer information, lookalike phishing sites, or leaked corporate intelligence. If you happen to be the victim of this sort of criminal activity, report it to the appropriate law enforcement agency or hire yourself a good cyber-intelligence firm. Let the good guys go after the bad guys in the dark web, on your behalf.

12

Advanced SEO Techniques

In the previous chapter you learned basic search engine optimization techniques—the things every marketer needs to do to improve the search ranking of his or her website. But there's even more SEO you can do—and *should* do—if you want to stay one step ahead of the competition.

Submitting Your Site to the Search Engines

We've talked about how the search crawler programs from the major search engines crawl the Web to find websites to index. You can wait for these crawlers to find your site organically, or you can be more proactive and tell the search engines about your site yourself.

Submitting Your Site to Google

The Web's largest search engine is also one of the easiest to submit to. Let me show you.

To submit your site to the Google index, all you have to do is go to www.google.com/addurl/, shown in Figure 12.1. Enter the URL for your home page into the appropriate box (including the http://), add any comments you might have about your site, and then click the Add URL button. That's it; Google will now add your site to the Googlebot crawl list, and your site will appear in appropriate search results.

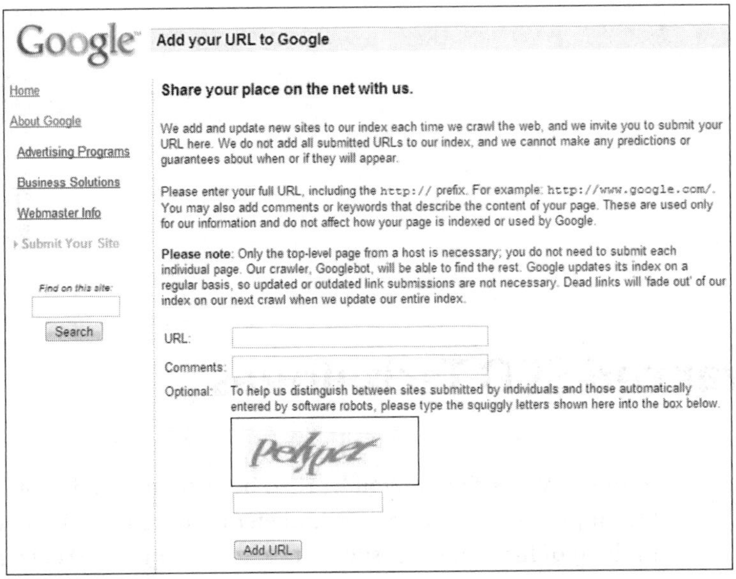

FIGURE 12.1
Submitting your site to Google.

Note that you have to add only the top-level URL for your site; you don't have to add URLs for any subsidiary pages. For example, if your home page is http://www.homepage.com/index.html, enter only http://www.homepage.com. Googlebot will crawl the rest of your site once it finds the main URL.

Submitting Your Site to Yahoo!

Submitting your website to Yahoo! is an equally simple process. Point your web browser to http://siteexplorer.search.yahoo.com/submit/. Here you have the option of submitting the URL for a website or a blog (site feed). You'll choose the first option, of course, which expands the page as shown in Figure 12.2. Enter your website's URL into the Submit a Website or Webpage box; make sure you include the http:// prefix. After entering your URL, click the Submit URL button, and you're done.

FIGURE 12.2

Submitting your site to Yahoo!.

Submitting Your Site to Bing

To submit your site to Microsoft's Bing search engine, go to www.bing.com/webmaster/SubmitSitePage.aspx, shown in Figure 12.3. Enter your entire site URL into the Type the URL of Your Homepage box (including the http://) and then click the Submit URL button. As with the Google and Yahoo! submission services, Bing's search crawler will be instructed to crawl your site and index all the internal pages linked from your home page.

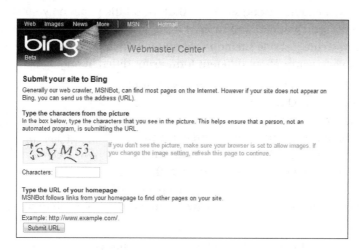

FIGURE 12.3

Submitting your site to Bing.

Creating a Sitemap

When you submit your site to a search engine, you submit the URL for your home page only. This instructs the search engine's crawler to visit your home page and crawl any internal links you have from your home page to other pages on your site—and, often, to other pages linked to from those pages.

However, not all the pages on your site are linked to your home page. When you want all the pages on your site submitted for indexing, you have to create something called a *sitemap*—literally, a hierarchical map of your entire website. You then submit this sitemap to the major search engines, and they use the sitemap to index all the relevant pages on your site.

> **note** As easy as this site submittal process is, some marketers prefer to offload the task to a site submittal service. These services let you enter your URL once, and then they submit your site to multiple search engines and directories. They handle all the details required by each search engine. If you go this route, pick a free service; there's no reason to pay for something that you could have otherwise have done yourself.

Understanding Sitemaps

A sitemap is, quite simply, a method of submitting the pages of your site to search engines, using site feeds that list all the pages on your site. The big three search engines all support a single sitemap standard, which means you can create just one sitemap that all the search engines can use; you don't have to worry about different formats for different engines.

When you create a sitemap, you save it in a separate XML file; this file contains the distinct URLs of all the pages on your website, in simple hierarchical order, along with important information about each page. When a search crawler reads the sitemap file, it learns about all the pages on your website and can then crawl all those pages for submittal to the search engine's index.

> **note** Learn more about sitemaps and the unified sitemap protocol at www.sitemaps.org.

To make sure that all the search crawlers find your sitemap file, you need to specify the file's location in your site's robots.txt file. This is a small text file stored in your site's root directory that is automatically read by search engine crawlers; it contains commands that tell the crawler what to (or what not to) crawl on your site.

Why Sitemaps Matter

Given that search crawlers are supposed to crawl all the links on your site and that you can always manually submit your site for crawling, why bother creating a sitemap? It's simple; sitemaps get more of your site exposed to the search engines—even those pages that are somewhat buried.

In addition, your sitemap contains useful information about each page on your site. You can use it to tell the search engines how important each page is on your site, as well as the freshness of each page. That's very useful when the search engines compile their rankings.

> **note** Sitemaps supplement, rather than replace, the usual methods of adding pages to the search engines' indexes. If you don't utilize a sitemap, your pages may still be discovered by the search engines' crawlers, although there's no guarantee.

Finally, because the sitemap includes the date on which each page on your site was last updated, it's also an excellent way to inform the major search engines of all the new and updated pages on your site. This is a benefit both to you and to each search engine—you get your newer content indexed faster, while they get to provide more fresh, up-to-date pages in their search results.

In other words, creating a sitemap has nothing but upside potential. It's a little more work, yes, but well worth the potential improvement in your site's rankings.

Creating a Sitemap

There are two ways to create a sitemap. The hard way is to manually construct the file by hand. The easy way is to use a dedicated sitemap-creation tool to do the work for you. I prefer the latter method.

To use a sitemap-creation tool, all you have to do is enter the URL for your home page and then press a button. The tool then crawls your website and automatically generates a sitemap file, which typically takes just a few minutes. Once the sitemap file is generated, you can then upload it to the root directory of your website, reference it in your robots.txt file, and, if you like, submit it directly to each of the major search engines.

Some of these sitemap tools are web-based, some are software programs, and most are free. The most popular of these tools include the following:

- AutoMapIt (www.automapit.com)
- AutoSitemap (www.autositemap.com)

- GSiteCrawler (www.gsitecrawler.com)
- SitemapsPal (www.sitemapspal.com)
- SitemapDoc (www.sitemapdoc.com)
- XML-Sitemaps.com (www.xml-sitemaps.com)

In most instances, you should name your sitemaps file sitemaps.xml and place it in the uppermost (root) directory of your website—although you can name and locate it differently, if you like.

Pointing to Your Sitemap

Once you've create your sitemaps file, you now have to let crawlers know where it is. You do this via a reference in the robots.txt file, which should be located in the root directory of your website.

What you need to do is add the following line to your robots.txt file:

```
SITEMAP: www.sitename.com/sitemaps.xml
```

Naturally, you need to include the actual location of your sitemaps file. The example here works only if you have the file in your site's root directory; if it's in another directory, include that full path. Also, if you've named your sitemaps file something other than sitemaps.xml, use the actual name.

The next time a search engine crawls your site, it will read your robots.txt file, learn the location of your sitemaps file, and then read the information in that file. It will then crawl all the pages listed in the file and submit information about each page to the search engine for indexing.

Submitting Your Sitemap to the Search Engines

Most of the major search engines also let you manually submit your sitemaps files. While you don't have to do this (the robots.txt method works just fine), there's no harm in being proactive.

Here's how to submit your sitemap to the big three search sites:

- **Google**—Start by going to the Google Webmaster Tools dashboard (www.google.com/webmasters/tools/dashboard). If your site is not yet added to your Dashboard, do so now and then click the Add a Sitemap link beside your site and enter the URL for your sitemap file.
- **Yahoo!**—Go to siteexplorer.search.yahoo.com/submit/ and click the Submit Site Feed link. Enter the path and filename of your sitemaps file and then click the Submit Feed button.

■ **Bing**—Go to the Bing Webmaster Center (www.bing.com/webmaster/) and log in with a Windows Live account and click the Add a Site button. When the next page appears, enter the URL for your sitemap file into the Sitemap Address box and then click the Submit button.

> **note** The primary advantage to submitting your sitemap directly to Google and the other search engines is that you often get access to specialized monitoring and reporting tools. For example, when you submit your sitemap directly to Google, you get the use of Google's Webmaster Tools Dashboard (www.google.com/webmasters/tools/dashboard), which provides a variety of summary, diagnostic, and statistical information about your site.

Even if you submit a complete sitemap, Google and the other search engines don't guarantee that they will crawl or index all the URLs on your website. However, because the search engines use the data in your sitemap to learn more about your site's structure, this should improve the crawler schedule for your site and ultimately improve the inclusion of your site's pages in the search results.

SEO for Local Search

If you run a local or regional business, you don't necessarily want to attract website visitors from all across the country or the world; instead, you want to attract local customers only. This issue can occur when you do such a good job optimizing your site that you end up appealing to distant visitors that you don't necessarily want. What you need to do is optimize your site for *local search* so that it shows up only in the search results of people searching for businesses in your area.

Optimizing for Local Search

Optimizing your site for local search requires a new angle on established techniques. That is, you do many of the same things as you do for general SEO, while emphasizing local information.

What's key is that you have to explicitly include local information on your site—local addresses, city and state names, store locators, local events and calendars, and so on. You then have to expose this information to the search engines by treating the most important local information as you would traditional keywords and phrases.

Local customers are searching for businesses or products that are nearby. Their keywords will include things like a city name, state name, Zip code, even a street name, address, or neighborhood name. It's important, then, for you to add your local information as keywords and phrases to your site. These keywords can include any or all of the following:

> **note** It's important that your local information, especially store addresses, be in text format. Remember, a map is an image file, and search crawlers can't read or index image files. Maps are good for your human visitors, but they have to be supplemented by text information.

- Street address
- City
- State
- Zip code
- Phone number with local area code
- Neighborhood
- Region
- Native nicknames ("Hoosier," "Gopher," and so on)

You should include these keywords—especially your street name, city, and state—in your site's **<META>** tags. If you have multiple locations, create a page for each one and include that location's address in each page's **<TITLE>** tag. Work the address and other local locators into the first paragraph of text on each page. You should never assume that your visitors know where you're located; even if they do, the search crawlers won't.

And when you're defining your location, think the way your customers are likely to think. People do search within their cities, but they may also search by larger metropolitan area or region. For example, if your business is in San Jose, California, you should definitely include "San Jose" as a key phrase—but you should also use phrases such as "Silicon Valley," "Bay Area," "South Bay," and the like. You want to reach as many possible

> **note** It's also a good idea to include a sitewide page footer with your local address information.

customers as possible; as I continue to stress, you need to *think like the customer* and describe your location the way your customers are likely to.

So optimizing your site for local search is really just a matter of broadening your keyword set. Take into account your location(s), different ways of referring to that location, abbreviations for your region, local nomenclature, and so on. That means more keywords in more places on your site—a little more work, but worth it when you start attracting more local customers.

Submitting for Local Search

When you're optimizing for local search, you need to submit your site to more and different sites than you normally do. That's because there are many different places where people can search for local businesses; they're not limited to just Google, Yahoo!, and Bing.

So after you've optimized your site with local keywords, take the time to list your site with all the important local search engines, directories, and Yellow Pages sites. Most of these sites let you list your business for free; take advantage of this opportunity to put your site in front of as many users as possible.

So which are the most important local directories for you to target? Table 12.1 provides a short list, along with information on how to submit your site to each.

Table 12.1   Local Search Directories

Local Directory	Home Page URL	How to Submit Your Site
AskCity	city.ask.com	Send email to askcitybusiness@help.ask.com with the subject line, "Ask City Feedback—Business." Include the following information in your email: business name, address, phone number, business category, website URL, and email contact address.
Bing Maps	www.bing.com/maps/	Listings provided by Superpages; submit at advertising.superpages.com
Dex	www.dexknows.com	Submit at www.advertisewithdex.com
Google Maps	maps.google.com	Submit at www.google.com/local/add/
Local.com	www.local.com	Submit at advertise.local.com
Superpages	www.superpages.com	Submit at advertising.superpages.com
TrueLocal	www.truelocal.com	Submit at www.truelocal.com/BusinessSuggest.aspx
Yahoo! Local	local.yahoo.com	Submit at listings.local.yahoo.com/csubmit/
YellowPages.com	www.yellowpages.com	Submit at store.yellowpages.com/post/
Yelp	www.yelp.com	Submit at biz.yelp.com

In addition, many cities and localities have their own local websites and directories, often run by local newspapers or television stations. For that matter, many local governments, chambers of commerce, and city convention bureaus host their own local sites. These websites often include directories of local merchants and are great places to list your business. You should search for any local sites or directories for your area and do what you need to get listed on these sites.

Finally, you should list your site information with the three major providers of business information:

- Acxiom (www.acxiom.com)
- InfoUSA (www.infousa.com)
- TARGUSinfo (www.targusinfo.com/industries/dsp/identification/)

These companies consolidate business data (names and addresses) and then sell that information to other companies. Making sure these services have your location and website information ensures that your business will appear in several places, both online and off. Visit their sites and look for the links that let you add or update your business data.

SEO for Mobile Search

Mobile search is, quite simply, search optimized for and performed on a mobile device of some sort, such as an iPhone. Why should you concern yourself with mobile search? It's a matter of size; the market for mobile search is already big—and is going to get much bigger.

Why Mobile Search Matters

According to eMarketer (www.emarketer.com), there are already an estimated 28.8 million mobile searchers in the U.S. (as of 2008). This number is projected to grow to 55.8 million users by 2011. That's about 75% of all mobile Internet users, or 22% of all mobile phone users—a big chunk of the cellular market.

And here's the thing: Most of these mobile searchers are looking for businesses. They use their phones when they're out and about and need to find something—a restaurant, a gas station, a bookstore, whatever. So if you work for a business with a local presence, you don't want to miss out on these millions of mobile

note Even though there are many startups targeting the mobile search market, things appear to be shaking out in favor of the big three (Google, Yahoo!, and Bing), each of which has a mobile-specific search offering. So when you're optimizing your site for mobile search, these are the sites to keep in mind and submit to.

searchers. If you're not appearing in mobile search results, you're missing out an all those customers.

That said, SEO for mobile search is arguably more important than for traditional web-based search. That's because of the small size of most mobile phone screens. Where you might settle for being number 20 in traditional search results because most search engines display 20 results per page, most mobile search engines return just a half-dozen or so results per screen. If you're not in the top five or so, you're on page two (or three or four). And, as we all know, results on the first page perform significantly stronger than those on subsequent pages.

Performing Mobile Search Optimization

Here's the most important thing to know about mobile SEO: Mobile search is local search. That's because most people searching on their mobile phones are looking for local information. They're looking for local businesses and services—in fact, they're looking for places close to their current locations.

So what are the best practices for mobile SEO? They're primarily what you do to optimize your site for local search, including:

- Add your address, city, state, Zip code, and other location identifiers to your keyword list.
- Include your local keywords in each page's <TITLE>, <META>, and heading tags.
- Fold your local keywords into the body text of each page, as appropriate.
- Create a sitemap for your mobile site—and submit that sitemap to the big three search engines.

It's pretty straightforward stuff.

> **note** When you're creating a mobile version of your website, make sure you include your phone number on every page. Many mobile users will want to phone you once they see your site in their search results.

12

SEO for Blogs

If you include a blog as part of your website or just run a freestanding blog, you need to optimize that blog for search. Fortunately, most blogs are structured in a way that is very easy for the search crawlers to crawl. Because of their natural hierarchical structure, search engines like blogs a whole lot.

You see, a blog is nothing more than a database of information—the blog postings themselves. The information in the database is displayed on a static page template, which results in the blog page readers see in their web browsers. You need to optimize both the data in the database and the layout and content of the template.

Optimizing the Blog Template

The first thing to pay attention to is your blog's template, which defines how blog posts are displayed. The template also contains the content that surrounds the blog posts themselves—the blog title and description, as well as everything displayed in the blog's sidebar.

As with traditional websites, keywords are important to optimizing your blog. After you decide on the keywords and phrases that reference the main topics of your blog, you need to insert those keywords within your blog's descriptive text—which, ideally, should appear high on your blog page, probably directly underneath the name of the blog. You should also place important keywords in the template's <TITLE> tag, <META> tags, and in all alternative image text. It's these keywords that search engines look for when they're indexing blogs; the more prominent and relevant the keywords in your blog, the higher your blog will appear in the search engine's results.

You also need to take a look at your blog template to see how it handles the display of your blog posts. In most blogs, the template defines that the title of the blog post links to the full text of the post. You need to make sure that the titles of your posts actually are links so that search engines pick up the link from the title to the post. Not all blog templates do this by default.

Finally, look at the contents of your template's sidebar. To get your blog and blog posts noticed in social media, you want to add "quick add" buttons for major social bookmarking services (Digg, Delicious, and so on) and social networking sites (Facebook, MySpace, and Twitter). If you can, configure your template so that these buttons are automatically added to the bottom of each blog post as well.

Optimizing Blog Posts

You can also optimize each post on your blog. Here you also use traditional SEO techniques.

Start by including important keywords in the title of each blog post. This is even more important than with traditional websites, given that many content syndicators and aggregators only list the title of a post. Because only the title is seen in most new readers, this makes the title much more important than the main text of a post.

Next, focus on the content of each post. Again, it's important to weave keywords into the post text, especially in the first paragraph of longer posts. Consider the first few sentences of a blog post as important as the <META> DESCRIPTION tag on a traditional website; it's what you see when your post is listed on a search engine's results page.

If a post includes links to other blogs or websites, make sure you sprinkle keywords into the links' anchor text. Do the same if you include an internal link to another post on your blog.

Finally, liberally apply labels or tags to each of your posts. These tags are one of the ways that readers find content on your blog, but they're also useful to searchbots trying to determine your blog's content. Assign each keyword or phrase as a separate label; because these labels are internal links to your post, that increases the number of links, which is always a good thing.

Submitting Your Site Feed

Although submitting your blog to the major search engines is very similar to submitting your website, you actually submit your *site feed* instead of the blog's URL. This way the search engines are automatically notified when you add new posts to your blog.

Site feeds are important because Google and the other major search engines have difficulty tracking frequently updated content—in particular, the type of dynamic content generated by blogs. Put simply, search crawlers don't crawl dynamic pages as well as they do static pages.

The solution, as you might suspect, is to publish your blog's content as an RSS or Atom feed. The search engines do a good job digesting feeds to populate their search indexes.

> **note** A site feed is an automatically updated stream of a blog's contents. Site feeds can be in either the RSS (Really Simple Syndication) or Atom formats (they're both variations of the same thing). When a blog has a feed enabled, any updated content is automatically published as a special XML file that contains the feed. The syndicated feed is then picked up by feed reader programs and website aggregators—as well as the major search engines.

12

To submit your site feed to the major search engines, you first need to know the URL of the feed. You can find this by clicking the RSS or Atom button found on your blog; the URL of the next page is your site feed URL. It's typically something like www.yourblogname.com/rss.xml or www.yourblog-name.com/atom.xml, although that varies from service to service.

When you submit your feed to the major search engines, they should be notified via the feed whenever you make a new post to your blog. Here's how to submit to the big three search sites:

- **Google**—Submit your site feed using Google's sitemap submission process. Begin by going to www.google.com/webmasters/tools/dashboard and adding your blog as a new site. Once added, click the Add a Sitemap link and then enter the URL for your site feed.

- **Yahoo!**—Go to http://siteexplorer.search.yahoo.com/submit/, click the Submit Site Feed link, enter the URL of your feed, and then click the Submit Feed button.

- **Bing**—Go to www.bing.com/webmaster/SubmitSitePage.aspx, enter the URL for your feed into the Type the URL of Your Homepage box, and then click the Submit URL button.

SEO Tools

As you get more into advanced SEO, you'll want to perform analyses and activities that are tough to do manually. To help in this, a number of companies offer various types of SEO tools. You use these tools to fine-tune your site's SEO and hopefully improve your search rankings.

Inbound Link Tools

Because Google's PageRank puts a high value on inbound links, it's important to know which sites are linking to yours. Use the following tools to analyze and build your inbound links:

note Inbound links are also called *backlinks*.

- Backlink Anchor Text Analysis (www.webconfs.com/anchor-text-analysis.php)
- Backlink Builder (www.webconfs.com/backlink-builder.php)
- Backlink Summary (www.webconfs.com/backlink-summary.php)

Keyword Tools

Keywords are important to the success of your site. You need to choose the right keywords, get the right keyword density, and then monitor the success of the keywords you've chosen.

In addition to the keyword generation tools described in Chapter 11, "Essential Search Engine Optimization," the following tools should help fine-tune the keywords you use on your site:

- Keyword Density Analyzer (www.keyworddensity.com)
- Keyword Density Checker (www.webconfs.com/keyword-density-checker.php)
- SEODigger (www.seodigger.com)

Other SEO Tools

Some SEO tools just don't fit into any other category. Here are a few of these unique—but uniquely useful—tools:

- Search Engine Spider Emulator (www.webconfs.com/search-engine-spider-simulator.php) displays the spidered text on your site, along with the spidered links and the contents of your site's <META> tags.

> **note** In addition to these individual tools, a handful of sites offer a variety of tools, along with other helpful SEO information and advice. These sites include SEO Chat (www.seochat.com/seo-tools/), SEOmoz (www.seomoz.org), and Webconfs.com (www.webconfs.com).

- Similar Page Checker (www.webconfs.com/similar-page-checker.php) helps to determine how similar one page is to another on your site.
- URL Rewriting Tool (www.webconfs.com/url-rewriting-tool.php) rewrites long dynamic URLs as shorter static ones.
- Link Sleuth (http://home.snafu.de/tilman/xenulink.html) checks your site for broken links.

The Bottom Line

Beyond the basic SEO techniques discussed in the previous chapter, there are a number of more advanced techniques you can employ to improve your site's ranking with the major search engines. These include manually submitting your site to the search engines, creating a sitemap of your site, and optimizing your site for local and mobile search. You should also optimize your blog for search—both the blog template and individual blog posts.

SEO MAINTENANCE

Even if you do a perfect SEO job on your current website, that's not good enough. Just because you rank high today doesn't mean that you'll rank quite as high tomorrow. In fact, given the changing nature of the Web and the constant influx of new websites, chances are your ranking will start to slide over time.

You see, your website doesn't exist in a vacuum. While your site stays the same, everything around it changes—and affects your search ranking. Sometimes your competitors get better at optimizing their own sites; sometimes you get new competitors who take ranking space. Your customers evolve over time too, of course, and sometimes your customer base shrinks. It's even possible (probable, to be frank) that the search engines change how they rank sites; it's not uncommon to wake up one morning and discover that you've dropped several rankings at Google or Bing, even though you've changed nothing on your site.

For these reasons, then, you need to constantly stay on top of your site's search engine performance and make any necessary changes to maintain your ranking. This argues in favor of developing an ongoing SEO maintenance plan for your website. This plan should include performance tracking, competitive analysis, keyword evaluation, content updating, structural analysis, and inbound link development.

What does this mean in practice? For most sites, it means constantly evaluating your search ranking and tweaking your site's SEO. Add new keywords, shake up your site design, write fresher content. Do whatever you have to do to keep pace with what's happening outside your control—and try to maintain the highest search ranking you can.

12

Tracking Search Performance

As you've learned in the previous chapters, search engine optimization is an arduous and continual process. How do you know, then, how effective your SEO has been?

There are lots of ways to track the effectiveness of your SEO efforts, from monitoring site visitors to looking at your ranking at Google, Yahoo!, and Bing. We look at some of the more popular tracking methods in this chapter.

Why It Pays to Improve Your Performance

Obviously, you want your SEO to improve your site's ranking with Google and the other major search engines and, thus, to increase traffic to your site. But how much of an increase can you expect to achieve?

I like the analysis performed by Oneupweb (www.oneupweb.com), a firm offering search engine optimization and marketing solutions. This company analyzed what a bump in Google's search rankings might mean to a website, in terms of increased traffic. The gains are impressive.

The first month a site appears on Google's first page of search results, the number of unique visitors to the site more than triples, increasing 337% from pre-results levels. By the end of the second month, traffic doubles again, for a total increase of 627% from pre-results levels.

That's right, if you successfully employ SEO techniques in a way that places your site in Google's top 20 matching sites, you can expect your site traffic to increase six-fold. That quantifies why SEO is important—and why it pays to analyze your results to maximize your site's performance.

What to Look For

There are lots of data points you can use the measure the effectiveness of your SEO program. We discussed these in depth in Chapter 9, "Tracking Website Analytics," but this is as good a place as any to provide quick look at those metrics that I feel are most important for measuring SEO success. Not that you should ignore all the other data, of course; it's just that these metrics are good indicators of how your search efforts are delivering.

Visitors

Our first key metric is one with which you should be quite familiar—the number of visitors, either on a site-wide or page-specific basis. To measure ongoing SEO success, you want to look at the number of visitors over time instead of on a specific date. A one-time snapshot doesn't really tell you that much, but if you see that the number of visitors per day is increasing over time, you know you're doing something right.

Pageviews

As you should already know, a pageview is how many times a particular page on your site has been viewed. The more pageviews, the more popular the page.

You should look at pageviews for two reasons. The first is to see how the popularity of a page increases over time; an increasing number of pageviews means that you're doing something to attract more traffic to the page. The second reason is to determine the relative popularity of pages on your site— that is, which are your site's most popular pages, as determined by their respective number of pageviews.

Landing Pages

A landing page (sometimes called an *entrance page*) is the page where a visitor enters your site, often via direct link from a search results page. Look at the most popular landing pages on your site and try to determine why these pages attract so many visitors. Is it because they're searched for or because they're linked to? (You can use two of the other metrics—queries and inbound links, which we discuss in short order—to help answer this question.)

13

Referring Sites

Now let's turn our attention to how visitors get to your site. Look for some sort of list or graph that breaks out referring sites by type. These charts typically segment inbound traffic as coming from referring sites (sites with direct inbound links to yours), *search sites* (Google, Yahoo!, and the rest), *direct links* (users entering your site's URL directly into their web browsers), and *other*. Analyzing this data tells you how important search engines and referring sites are to your site traffic.

note If your site shows a low percentage of traffic coming from search engines, don't assume that search engines aren't important. It's just as likely that your site is ranking low with the major search engines, and you need to further beef up your SEO efforts.

Next, take a look at which specific sites are driving the most traffic to your site. Chances are, Google, Yahoo!, and Bing will be among the top traffic drivers. Display this data in descending order and make a note to pay special attention to the top-referring sites; it's also a good idea to find out *why* a lot of traffic is coming from a given site.

Queries

For the portion of traffic coming from the search engines, you want to determine which keywords are generating the most traffic. Take a look at the list of queries or keywords generated by your analytical tool; this will tell you the most important keywords for your site.

If this list matches your own internal keyword list, great. If not, you may want to either rethink which keywords are most important (based on the ranking of actual keyword queries) or rework your site's SEO to better emphasize your desired keywords.

Tracking Site Traffic with Web Analytics

If all you want to do is see whether your SEO efforts have increased traffic to your site, you can use the web analytics tools we discussed in Chapter 9. These tools, such as Google Analytics (www.google.com/analytics/) do a very good job of counting visitors, pageviews, and such.

Obviously, you want to look at this data over time, preferably before your SEO campaign and then in the months after the SEO is implemented. Ideally you'll see a significant bump in all important metrics, and you want to see traffic increase substantially.

The Ultimate Metric: Search Engine Rank

That said, there's one more metric you want to analyze to determine the effectiveness of your SEO activities—raw search engine ranking. It makes sense, really; if you're optimizing your site to rank higher with the search engines, you need to find out whether your ranking actually is improving.

In theory at least, search rank should result in higher visitor and pageview numbers. A high ranking means more people will see and click through to your site; a low ranking means fewer visitors. It's really that simple.

Determining Your Rank

That said, determining your site's search rank is anything but simple. That's because there isn't a single "search rank" metric. You need to determine where your site ranks when someone searches for each of the keywords you've deemed important. You end up with multiple ranking—one for each keyword you target.

To determine your search ranking at Google, Yahoo!, or Bing, you have to query the search site for the keyword in question and then see where your site ranks. You really do have to manually query each search engine for each keyword you select or use a tool that does the querying for you. That's a lot of work.

> **note** Search engine ranking also has to take into account multiple listings for different media. If you play your cards right, you can show up multiple times on a search results page—for your website, a blog post, a video, even a Facebook update or Twitter tweet. It's all about managing multiple media online, any or all of which can show up in search engine results.

What Affects Your Ranking?

Another issue is that your ranking at any given search engine depends on more than just your site; the quality of competing sites also affects how high you rank. This is why your ranking might change from day to day, or even from hour to hour. It may be nothing you're doing; it may, in fact, be the result of changes made to competing sites.

For example, let's say that you typically rank in the middle of the first page of Google's search results for a given keyword. If a new and better site comes online, you could find your ranking decrease—even if you changed nothing about your site. The performance of the new site affects your ratings, knocking you down as the new site takes your place in the rankings.

Search ranking, then, is a dynamic measurement. Don't expect your results to remain static. They can and probably will change over time.

Tracking Individual Search Engine Performance

Web analytics is great for tracking your website's traffic, but it doesn't tell you anything about how your performance at the individual search engines. For that, you have to use their site-specific tools.

Tracking Google Performance

To track your performance at Google, the most popular search engine, you use Google's Webmaster Tools, located at www.google.com/webmasters/tools/. Webmaster Tools, like Google Analytics, is a free service.

The Webmaster Tools Dashboard lists all the websites you've registered with Google to date. You can add websites to the Dashboard via the Add Site box at the top of the page. Once added, Google performs all available analysis.

To view details about a website, click the site's name in the Dashboard. This displays the Webmaster Tools Overview page, which conveys a variety of top-level information, including when Google last crawled your site, whether pages from your site are included in the Google index, and any errors found when crawling your site.

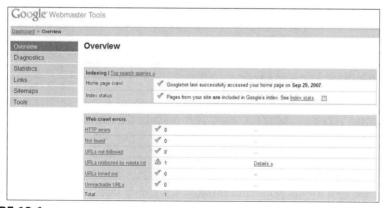

FIGURE 13.1

Google's Webmaster Tools Overview page.

Additional information is available by clicking the links along the left side of this page. These include the following:

- **Diagnostics**—This lists pages on your site that Google had trouble crawling and why.

- **Statistics**—This is probably the most useful information, including Top Search Queries (what queries visitors used to find your site, as well as which of those queries generated the most clicks), Crawl Stats (the average PageRank of the pages on your site), Index Stats (links to data that Google knows about your site), Subscriber Stats (number of users who subscribe to your site feed), and What Googlebot Sees (displays the wording of the anchor text in other sites that link to your site).

- **Links**—Displays lists of which external pages link to your site, as well as which external pages your site links to.

- **Sitemaps**—Use this page to submit your sitemap to Google and to check its status.

- **Tools**—Use this link to access a variety of analytic tools. You can analyze the robots.txt file, generate a new robots.txt file, manage the verification of your site, set the rate your site is crawled, set a geographic target or preferred domain, enhance the image search on your site, remove URLs from Google's index, and generate analytical gadgets for display on your iGoogle home page.

There's a lot of data here, but you get the gist of it. Given how much traffic is probably coming to your site from Google and that Google's Webmaster Tools are free, this is one analytical tool you probably want to become familiar with.

Tracking Yahoo! Performance

Compared to what Google offers in the way of website analysis, both Yahoo! and Microsoft come up short. That said, both of these sites do offer a variety of analytical tools—all of them useful, but just not as many as Google offers.

Yahoo!'s analytical tools are offered as part of Yahoo! Site Explorer (http://siteexplorer.search.yahoo.com). After you've added your site for analysis, you see a Summary page that displays your site's status, number of pages indexed, key terms, and the like.

This page is simple in appearance but offers more in-depth data, if that's what you want. For example, to display a list of pages on your site that are crawled by Yahoo!, with the most popular listed first, click the number link for Number of Pages Indexed. From the resulting page, click the Inlinks button to display all the sites that link back to your site; you can filter this list to show links only from other sites (Except from This Domain) and to show links to either the current URL or your entire site.

Additional data and services are available by clicking the following links in the sidebar of the main page:

- **Feeds**—Use this page to submit sitemaps, RSS feeds, and the like to Yahoo!.

- **Crawl Errors**—Displays errors found while crawling your site, such as pages not found.

- **Top Queries**—Lists the top queries from Yahoo! users that found your site.

- **Statistics**—Displays the number of pages crawled, number of hosts linking to your site, number of hosts linked to from your site, and other interesting data.

- **Authentication**—Tells you whether or not your site has been authenticated for tracking by Yahoo!.

- **Actions**—Use this page to delete pages on your site from the Yahoo! index and to submit dynamic pages on your site.

FIGURE 13.2

Exploring all the external links to a web page with Yahoo! Site Explorer.

Tracking Bing Performance

Let's examine the web tools that Microsoft offers for its Bing search engine. These tools are accessed from the Bing Webmaster Center (www.bing.com/webmaster/). When you first access the tools, you're asked to add your website; this is also where you add your site's sitemap, tell Microsoft how you'll verify that you're the site's owner (via either an XML file or a special <META> tag), and supply your contact email address. However you choose to authenticate your site, Microsoft next displays the text you need to add in either the file or the tag.

When your site is authenticated, you have access to the complete set of tools. Click your site name and you see the Summary tab; other tabs list specific types of information, as follows:

- **Summary**—Displays when your site was last crawled, how many pages on your site are indexed, your site's rough rank, on a scale of 1 to 5 bars (5 is best), and the top five pages on your site.

- **Profile**—Displays the location of your site's sitemap, how your site is verified, and your contact information.

- **Crawl Issues**—Displays any issues Bing discovered while crawling your site, such as missing or blocked pages, malware, and the like.

- **Backlinks**—Displays which external pages link back to your site.

- **Outbound links**—Displays all the external pages linked to from your site.

- **Keywords**—Enter a keyword to display the top pages on your site for that keyword, along with each page's 1-to-5 ranking.

- **Sitemaps**—Use this tab to submit a sitemap of your site to Bing.

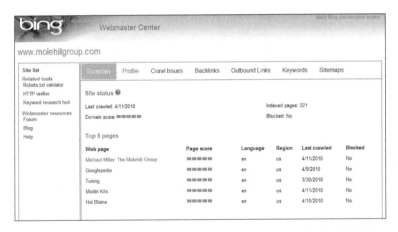

FIGURE 13.3

Viewing summary information about how Bing sees your website.

All in all, Bing's Webmaster Center displays much useful information—not quite as much as you get from Google's Webmaster Tools, but still a lot of good stuff for any marketer.

Third-Party Tracking Tools

In addition to the general web analytic tools and the site-specific search tools just discussed, there are also a handful of third-party tools that help you analyze the search performance of your site. Many of these tools consolidate data from multiple search sites, which is quite useful.

Here are some of the tools you might want to use in your marketing analysis:

- **Google PageRank Prediction Tool** (www.iwebtool.com/ pagerank_prediction)—This tool is useful when you want a good guess of how a page might rank within Google's PageRank system. The PageRank Prediction displays the current and predicted PageRank for any selected page, along with the estimated accuracy of the prediction and the number of inbound links (backlinks) to the page.

- **GoRank Online Keyword Rank Tracking** (www.gorank.com)—This is one of the best tools for tracking where your site ranks at Google for various keywords over time. The free report tracks the ranking of multiple keywords over the day, week, and month. It's a great way to see if your site is increasing or decreasing in search engine popularity.

- **Search Engine Position Tool** (www.iwebtool.com/ search_engine_position)—Use this tool when you want to know where your site places in Google's search results for a particular keyword. Enter your domain and the specific keywords you want to track and then click the Check button. The tool returns your site's position and which page of the results it appears on. It's a manual-entry kind of tool, but it gets the job done.

- **Search Engine Rankings** (http://mikes-marketing-tools.com/ ranking-reports/)—Use this tool to see where your site ranks vis-à-vis specific keywords on the major search engines. This free tool checks your site against a specific keyword for eight different search sites— Google, Bing, Yahoo! Search, AlltheWeb, AOL Search, AltaVista, the Open Directory, and the Yahoo! Directory.

- **SEO Trail** (www.seotrail.com)—This is a free tool that monitors the search rankings, indexed pages, inbound links, and social bookmarks from Alexa, Google, Bing, and Yahoo!— as well as the social bookmarking sites Delicious, Digg, and Technorati.

note Alexa (www.alexa.com), a subsidiary of Amazon.com, compiles traffic data for a large number of public websites.

13

■ **Xinu Returns** (www.xinureturns.com)—This tool displays your site's ranking at Google, Technorati, Alexa, and DMOZ (Open Directory); the number of pages indexed on Google, Bing, and Yahoo!; the number of backlinks (inbound links) listed on numerous sites; the number of social bookmarks for your site at Delicious, Digg, and other sites; and other interesting information. It essentially centralizes a lot of data you can find elsewhere and as such performs a useful function for the busy marketer.

Tracking Your Competitors

Tracking your own site's performance is great, but your site doesn't exist in a vacuum. You also want to see how your site compares with competing sites—which argues for using tools that track your competitors' performance.

Probably the most useful of such tools is Compete's Search Referrals tool (http://searchanalytics.compete.com). Available in both free and paid versions, this tool helps you analyze how competing websites are performing. Start by entering the URL of a competing website or by selecting the general category in which you compete. Search Analytics then displays the top keywords and phrases that drive traffic to that site or sites in that category. This tool also displays the site share (percentage of all site referrals), engagement (a measure of the amount of time spent on the site after entering the keyword), and effectiveness (a measure of the total number of people referred by the keyword and their engagement) for each keyword listed.

The Search Analytics tool can also show you which sites get the most clicks from a keyword. Just select the Keyword Destination tab and enter a keyword or phrase, and the tool displays the top sites for that keyword. You also see the keyword share, site share, and average monthly referrals for each matching site.

In addition, the Search Analysis tool lets you see how two sites (your site and a competing site, for example) compete in the keyword race. Select the Compare Sites tab, enter the URLs for two sites, and click the Go button. The tool now lists the top keywords the two sites share, along with which of the two sites has the advantage for each keyword.

Also useful is Compete's Site Profile tool (http://siteanalytics.compete.com). This is a traditional site-analysis tool, similar to Google Analytics. It displays a variety of web analytic data, such as visitors, pageviews, and the like. It gets interesting when you click the Compare Sites tab; you can now compare stats for up to three competing sites. Just enter the URLs, and Site Analytics displays a series of graphs that compare the number of site visitors, visit length, traffic growth, and other data for the sites.

The Bottom Line

There are a number of ways to measure the success of your SEO efforts. You can track increased traffic to your site by looking at traditional web analytics—pageviews, visitors, and the like. Even better, you can track your search ranking at the major search sites, as well as a variety of other site-specific data. You do this by manually querying each site for each keyword you target, using the search engines' proprietary webmaster tools, and using third-party search performance tools.

At the end of the day, you want to look for increased activity resulting from your SEO efforts. That means tracking each metric over time because looking at a single data point in time won't tell you much.

DEFINING SUCCESS

How do you know when your SEO efforts are successful? There's no standard to compare to—you have to create your own definition of success.

The most obvious measurement of success is an improvement in your search rankings at Google, Yahoo!, and Bing. How much of an improvement is good, however, depends. You can make your goal a set increase in number of positions (improving by ten positions, for example), or to reach a specific position. For example, you might say your goal is to hit the first page of search results or to be in the top ten search results, or even to achieve the number-one ranking for a given keyword.

You can also set your goals in comparison to your competitors. You may say, then, that you're successful when your site ranks above a specific competitor's site for a given keyword or that you rank above all your direct competitors. (This measurement gives you a little cover in case a noncompeting site like Wikipedia bests your ranking.)

13

Ultimately, however, you want to measure what any increased search ranking means to your site. In this instance, success should translate into increased visitors, pageviews, and (if you sell directly on your site) product sales. If better search rankings *don't* bring you more traffic and sales, there's something seriously wrong with either the keywords you're targeting or the performance of your site itself.

Understanding Online Advertising

Search engine marketing is the number-one component of most companies' online marketing plans. But number two is a new version of an old standby—online advertising. That's right, the Web is just a big container for all sorts of ads, just like what you're used to running in print and over the air.

Except that online advertising isn't *quite* the same as traditional print or broadcast advertising. First, customers can act directly on online ads, which they can't on traditional ads. Because of this, it's much, much easier to track the effectiveness of online advertising; you can track not just how many people view an ad, but how many click the ad, go to your website, and then buy something. That introduces a level of accountability unheard of in more than a century of traditional advertising.

How Online Advertising Differs from Traditional Advertising

What is online advertising? Well, like all advertising, it's a paid display of your promotional message—online, in this instance.

With traditional advertising, you pay for space on the printed newspaper or magazine page or you pay for time on radio or television airwaves. With online advertising, you pay for space on a web page.

So the pay for placement thing is pretty much the same. What's different about online advertising is that you have a lot more say over where your ad gets placed and who sees it. You also can track each ad's performance with a level of granularity not possible in traditional advertising—right down to the individual person clicking an ad.

Targeted Placement

Let's tackle the placement part of the equation. When you're advertising online, you place your ad on a web page. In most instances you can dictate both where on the page your ad appears and on what websites.

When you're running a display ad, you typically have the choice of several page placements. Many sites offer advertising along the top of the page (so-called *banner advertising*), along the left or right sides, along the bottom of the page, or in a box somewhere in the middle. Not all sites offer all positions, of course, but you'd be surprised at what's available if you're willing to pay for it.

Page placement is less assured when you're running pay-per-click advertisements. We discuss the mechanics of this type of ad in more detail later in this chapter, but in general know that the higher you bid for a per-click price, the more likely your ad will appear higher on a page. Bid lower, and your ad will likely appear lower on the page. It's a kind of pay for placement deal.

Equally important, you can easily place your ads with just those websites that meet specific targeting requirements. You can choose specific sites where you want to appear or identify sites by their traffic or demographic values. And with pay-per-click ads, you let the ad network determine which sites to use; you identify (and pay for) certain keywords, and your ad appears on sites with content that matches those keywords. You can't get much more targeted than that.

The point is, online advertising is more about narrowcasting than broadcasting your message. Traditional media tend toward the broadcast model, where your message goes out to a large audience with a lot of waste, and you end up overshooting your target audience. In contrast, online media are very targeted. If you only want to reach 45-year-old males who read comic books, you can do it; you don't have to show your ad to everyone and their brother, either.

Improved Tracking

There's an old saying among advertisers that you know that only half of your advertising works, but you don't know which half. Well, with online advertising, you can quickly and easily determine which half of your advertising is working—down to a specific ad on a specific website.

That's because online, you can track when an ad is clicked. That's right, when someone takes action with an ad, you know it. There's no guessing as to whether this ad or that drove a given person into a store to make a purchase; you know precisely which ads delivered the most traffic back to your website. (And from there, you can track further actions—including sales.)

This puts a lot more responsibility on you as an advertiser, of course. There's no more waffling about a given ad enhancing your brand image or planting the seeds of a sale or other happy horse manure. Online, an ad either gets clicked or it doesn't. You know immediately whether your advertising is working by tracking the traffic from the ad to your website. The more clicks you get, the more effective the ad is. If you don't get any or many clicks, then you know a particular ad is in the half that doesn't work.

This ability to track ad results clearly distinguishes online advertising from its offline brethren. With traditional advertising, there's no way to know how effective any single ad is; sure, you can tell if sales go up during the course of a campaign, but you don't know which ads in which media truly drove those sales. With online advertising, there's no way *not* to know how each ad is performing; you get near-real time data that can help you fine tune your future ad content and placement.

Efficiency of Investment

This combination of relevant placement and improved tracking makes online advertising a much more efficient investment than other types of advertising. You don't have to engage in broad placement when you only want to target a narrow audience. You don't have to put up with half your ads not working when you can easily determine which ads are pulling customers and which aren't.

The upshot is that you can typically get better results with less investment online. Now, you may not get the broad reach that you do with traditional media, but you also don't pay for that broad reach. You can create very targeted ads for a very targeted audience, which will likely result in higher response rates. In other words, you can target the exact audience you want, and pay only for those results.

Different Payment Models

All this talk about online advertising makes it sound like there's only one type of ad, which isn't the case. There are lots of different types of ads you can run and several different payment models to choose from for those ads.

Let's look at the payment models first. With online advertising, you can pay for impressions, as with traditional media, but you can also pay for performance. This type of arrangement lets you pay by the click—that is, you pay only when an interested customer clicks your ad. All those people who aren't interested and don't click...you don't have to pay for them. It's not a bad deal.

14

CPM—Cost-per-Thousand

Let's start with the payment model you're probably most familiar with, the good old cost-per-thousand impressions (CPM) model. It's simplicity itself; you pay a certain price to get your ad in front of a thousand eyeballs.

> **note** The "M" in CPM comes from the Latin word *mille*, or thousand. If Latin isn't your thing, know that some people refer to this payment method as CPT, or literally cost-per-thousand.

For example, you might make an ad placement with a $50 CPM. That is, you pay $50 for each 1,000 impressions. This may be measured in terms of 1,000 copies printed of a newspaper or magazine or 1,000 viewers of a television program. In any case, you apply this $50 CPM rate to the total number of impressions—the total print run or the full viewership. So, continuing the example, if you place your ad in a magazine with a 100,000-copy print run, you pay $5,000 total for your ad—that's 100,000 divided by 1,000, times the $50 rate.

With this traditional model, you're paying for exposure, not for results. It doesn't matter if you don't make a single sale from the ad; you still pay the full cost of the ad. The only thing the host medium guarantees is the eyeballs; what the bodies connected to those eyeballs do after viewing your ad is totally up in the air.

While this payment model is not the dominant model on the Web, it is still used for some online advertising. You're most likely to find CPM pricing with online display ads. In this instance, an ad network guarantees placement on a selection of websites that deliver a specified amount of traffic; you apply the CPM rate to the website traffic, and you get how much you pay.

> **note** Cost-per-view (CPV) advertising is a uniquely online version of traditional CPM advertising. Instead of charging for ephemeral "impressions," CPV advertising charges for distinct views of an advertisement or website. It's kind of the same thing but measured with web-specific pageview metrics.

Know, however, that with the online CPM model, there is no guarantee of any sort of driving traffic back to your website. You're paying solely for placement, not for results.

CPC—Cost-per-Click

Instead of paying for impressions or views, most online advertisers opt for a more performance-oriented payment method. The most popular online payment method, then, is cost-per-click (CPC), a hallmark of pay-per-click (PPC) advertising. With CPC/PPC ads, the advertiser pays only when a user clicks an ad. The advertiser does not pay for the placement of the ad itself, so the number of impressions or views is mostly irrelevant.

note Of all the different payment models, CPC is far and away the most prominent in online advertising.

The actual cost-per-click is typically determined by how much the advertiser is willing to bid on a specific keyword. That is, you choose a keyword to associate with your ad, and your ad is displayed on websites that have similar content or on search results pages when someone searches for that keyword on Google, Yahoo!, or other search engine. How often your ad is displayed or how high up on the search results page are factors of how high you bid for that keyword in relation to how high competing advertisers also bid. If you bid more than your competitors, your ad will be seen more often and more visibly. If you're cheap about it (that is, if you get significantly outbid), your ad will be less visible.

As to that CPC bidding, how much you actually end up paying is a factor of what you bid versus what your competitors for that keyword bid. You don't necessarily pay the full bid price; if you outbid the competition, you'll only be charged slightly more than the next-highest bid. So if you bid $2 per click and the next-highest bid is $1 per click, you might only be charged $1.10 per click or so. In any case, you'll never be charged more than your specified bid amount.

And remember, you only pay when someone clicks your ad. Even if your ad gets displayed on a website that has 100,000 visitors per day, if only one of those visitors clicks your ad, you pay just for that single click. (Of course, if you only get one click from a 100,000-visitor site, there's probably something wrong with your ad—or you're advertising on the wrong site.)

Given that you never know in advance how many clicks an ad might receive, how do you know how much you'll spend for CPC advertising? That's simple; you establish a budget up front. The ad network will run your ad until you've hit your budget level and then cease all further display. You're never charged more than what you budgeted.

Most online ad networks work with a daily CPC budget level. So, for example, if you set a $100 daily budget and bid $2 per click, your ad will run each day until you've received 50 clicks. (That's the $100 total budget divided by $2 per click.)

The advantage of CPC payment is that you're truly paying for results. You don't pay if no one takes action on your ad. It's that simple—and that powerful.

14

For this reason, CPC is the dominant payment method for online advertising. Certainly, all the text ads you see on the search sites are CPC in nature; much display advertising is also moving to the CPC model.

CPA—Cost-per-Action

When it comes to affiliate advertising, which we discuss shortly, cost-per-action (CPA) is the dominant payment method. This is more a commission model in that the advertiser pays the host site not when a user clicks an ad, but only when that click results in a sale or other type of customer transaction. Payment is typically in the form of a commission or percentage of the final sales price.

CPO—Cost-per-Order

Cost-per-order (CPO) payment is a form of CPA advertising. Instead of paying a commission on the full dollar value of a sale, you instead pay a set fee for the completion of a customer order resulting from a click to your ad.

CPL—Cost-per-Lead

Cost-per-lead (CPL) advertising is a form of CPA advertising, geared more to customer or lead acquisition than dollar sales. That is, you pay the host site for the acquisition of customer names or contact information, typically a set dollar amount per lead.

Types of Online Ads

Any payment model can be used with any type of online advertising—and there are lots of different types of ads you can run. Take your pick from familiar banner ads to context-sensitive text ads to newfangled rich media ads. There's something here for every advertiser.

Text Ads

They're small. They're unobtrusive. And there are lots of them. We're talking about text ads, which—believe it or not—are the most prominent type of online advertisement.

Text ads are most often found on the results pages of the major search engines—Google, Yahoo!, Bing, and the like. These ads are typically listed alongside the organic search results in a section titled "Sponsored links"

(Google), "Sponsored results" (Yahoo!), or "Sponsored sites" (Bing). They're sponsored, all right, by advertisers just like you.

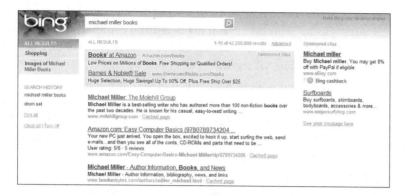

FIGURE 14.1

Text ads ("Sponsored sites") at the top and side of Bing's search results page.

Text ads can also appear on third-party websites. In most instances, these third-party sites are part of the ad network run by the major search engine. So if you advertise with Google's AdWords network, your text ads will appear on Google's search results pages, as well as on websites that belong to the AdWords network.

FIGURE 14.2

A block of text ads on a third-party website.

These text ads typically consist of three or four short lines of text but no images. The first line is a clickable headline, followed by one or two lines of body copy, and a final line consisting of the target URL. Short but sweet, these ads are; you have to write some powerful and efficient copy to encourage customer clicks.

Most text ads are pay-per-click (PPC) ads, meaning they employ the CPC payment model. You don't pay for placement; you only pay when someone clicks the ad. At that point, you pay the agreed-upon (or previously bid) cost-per-click rate.

14

In addition, most of these PPC text ads are *contextual* or *context-sensitive* in nature. This means that the ad is served only to websites with content that is directly related to the ad's content—or, more precisely, to those keywords purchased by the advertiser. As an advertiser, this works to deliver more targeted impressions for your ads; if you're advertising running shoes, for example, your ad will be served to sites related to running or to shoes, not to sites about car stereos or financial services.

As noted, PPC text ads are also served to search results pages. In fact, this is the primary means of delivery; the major PPC ad networks are owned by the major search engines. So when you purchase a keyword for a PPC text ad, your ad will appear on search results pages when someone searches Google, Yahoo!, or Bing for that particular keyword.

Take the running shoes example again. You purchase the key phrase "running shoes" for your ad, and when someone searches Google for "running shoes," your ad appears in the "Sponsored links" section of the search results page. Someone searching for "dental floss" won't see your ad; you only get visibility to those people looking for what you're offering.

Given how utterly unremarkable these text ads are, it may surprise you to discover that this is the most popular form of online advertising. They may be unobtrusive, but they're ubiquitous. Advertisers large and small employ this type of PPC text advertising as a significant part of their online marketing plans—because they work. These ads are arguably the most efficient form of advertising available, online or off, because of their unique combination of targeted placement and results-oriented payment. If you're like most advertisers, they will also be an important part of your online marketing mix.

> **note** The next move beyond contextual placement is *behavioral targeting*, where ads are targeted based on a user's past clickstream, or website visits. For example, if a user has recently visited a number of sites about musical instruments, behavioral targeting might serve him instrument-related ads. It's all done using *cookies*, those persistent little files installed on a user's PC—and tracked by PPC advertising firms and web analysis services everywhere.

Display Ads

Display ads are the visual opposite of text ads—ads that display images, animation, even videos. Display ads can be big, like the banner ads you find at the top of many web pages, or small, like graphical versions of text ads. These ads are designed to attract the visitor's attention and, in some instances, to click for further information.

In the early days of the Web, display ads—typically in the form of banner ads—were all there were. Over the next decade, PPC text ads became the advertiser's chosen format as Google took over the search advertising market. But in recent years, display ads have made a bit of a comeback, as advertisers have begun to experiment with rich media content.

Display ads can be sold on both a CPM or CPC basis. CPM used to be the more popular method and is still common in larger ad sizes. CPC is gaining ground, however, as advertisers embrace the higher accountability model; it's the de facto standard in smaller, text ad-like sizes and is even becoming popular in larger sizes.

One of the benefits of display advertising is the variety available. For example, if you're into PPC advertising but don't want to be relegated to a bland text ad, you can create a small PPC image ad instead. This type of ad is the same size as a text ad but conveys the advertising message in a graphical format; with most of these PPC image ads, the entire ad is clickable.

FIGURE 14.3
A clickable PPC image ad.

Larger display ads tend to be more popular among big advertisers. The best-known type is the so-called banner ad that stretches across the top of a web page, although "banners" can also run along the bottom of a page or down either side. (A vertical banner ad is more accurately called a *skyscraper*.) This type of ad can even sit in a box in the middle of a page; some advertisers will link two or more display ads on a page, typically a banner and a box, or a banner and skyscraper.

note Some websites display more than one banner ad per page, either from the same advertiser or from multiple advertisers. Some sites will even rotate banners every few seconds or display different ads each time a visitor reloads the page.

14

FIGURE 14.4
A horizontal banner ad.

FIGURE 14.5
A vertical skyscraper ad.

Display ads are always graphical. Most incorporate images; some incorporate Flash animations or videos. Most are clickable, although if you're going strictly for image building, that may not always be a requirement.

Interstitial Ads

An *interstitial ad* is one that appears between web pages—that is, in the transition from one page to another. Sometimes the interstitial ad appears before a visitor can view a site's landing page; other times, the interstitial appears between two pages on a site.

In any case, interstitial ads interrupt a user's web browsing session. They must be seen (or clicked away from) before a visitor can view the page he or she wants to view. As such, they're sure to be seen—and just as likely to be hated. Use them with caution, as most web surfers find them quite irritating.

FIGURE 14.6

An interstitial ad blocking entrance to the CNET website.

Of course, that very same irritation, due to forced viewing, is what some advertisers like about interstitials. Love 'em or hate 'em, you can't easily ignore them.

The other thing that advertisers like about interstitials is that they provide a large amount of real estate to work with. You essentially have the entire page for your advertising message and aren't limited to a banner or a box.

In addition, you can use all the technology you like. Most interstitials include moving images of one sort or another, and bright lights and loud noises are common. But remember, all this technological wizardry comes at a price; not only do you have the annoyance factor to deal with, but a heavily-loaded interstitial can take a long time to load over slow Internet connections. (There's nothing like forcing a potential customer to wait forever to view something they don't want to view to begin with...)

Pop-Up Ads

Speaking of annoying, we now come to the category of pop-up ads. Most reputable advertisers shy away from pop-ups, as they really are annoying; in addition, the pop-up blocking technology found in most of today's web

14

browsers means that most pop-up ads are blocked before anybody can see them. But they still exist and should possibly be considered.

A pop-up ad is one that appears in a small window that pops up over the user's main browser window. The ad is triggered by a bit of Javascript code, typically when a user first opens a page, although some advertisers prefer to trigger their pop-ups when a user exits a page. Either approach is feasible.

FIGURE 14.7

A particularly insistent pop-up ad from Netflix.

Pop-up ads can consist of almost any type of message you want. Most are like display ads in a window, with images, animations, and the like. Some are just text-based. Most include clickable links of some sort.

From an advertiser's standpoint, pop-up ads just aren't that effective. Even if your ad doesn't get blocked, it most likely will get ignored; people really don't like them. In addition, it's easy for a pop-up window to get hidden behind the main browser window, effectively obscuring your message—although you'll still be charged for the placement.

> **note** A *pop-under ad* is a pop-up ad that is sent behind the current browser window so that the user doesn't see it until he closes his web browser.

> **note** Today, pop-up ads tend to be used more by scammers than by legitimate advertisers. I see a lot of pop-ups ad masquerading as system messages, warning about viruses and spyware and the like; when a user clicks the button in the window, malware gets installed.

Online Ad Technologies

When we're talking about display ads, there are all sorts of technologies you can employ. In fact, this is one of the most interesting aspects of online advertising—the use of new technologies to help your message stand out from the clutter and pop off the web page.

For example, so-called *HTML ads* combine text and images with other HTML elements, such as pull-down lists, check boxes, forms, and the like. You can use an HTML ad to quickly obtain information from potential customers. They click the appropriate elements in the ad, and their data is sent directly to you.

Also hot are *rich media ads* that employ multimedia elements such as sound (either music or voice narration), animation, and the like. These ads can be quite creative; I've seen ads where items move across the underlying web page, which really get your attention. The problem is that these types of ads are often quite annoying, especially if you want to read the page beneath where the animated item is scurrying.

FIGURE 14.8
A rich media ad with video playback.

That said, rich media ads really attract a lot of attention; some agencies view them as the future of online display advertising. Because of this, rich media ads come at a premium over typically image-based display advertising and typically require you to employ a high-priced ad agency for the ad creation.

Notable subsets of rich media advertising include

- Audible ads, otherwise known as talking ads, where the potential customers' computer blares out a song or the advertiser's voice.
- Animated ads, where your message is conveyed via some form of animated graphic, typically using Flash-based animation.

14

■ Expanding ads, which change size when the page is first loaded. These ads typically are located at the top of a page and push the underlying page content downward.

■ Floating ads, which move across the user's screen or otherwise float above the underlying page.

■ Video ads, where a video starts playing when a page is loaded or when a visitor clicks or hovers above the ad.

■ Wallpaper ads, which change the background of the page being viewed.

Affiliate Marketing

A quick detour is now in order, to discuss *affiliate marketing*. This is when you pay another website for sales that result from their customer referrals.

Affiliate marketing is typically done through affiliate networks, such as the Google Affiliate Network (www.google.com/ads/affiliatenetwork/) and Commission Junction (www.cj.com). In addition, some online retailers, such as Amazon.com (affiliate-program.amazon.com), run their own affiliate programs.

The way it works is simple. A website signs up for the program and then displays ads for participating merchants. When a customer clicks the ad and then proceeds to purchase an item from the merchant, the host website receives a commission—typically a percentage of the final sale. No fees are paid for placement or for clicks; a purchase has to be made for the commission to be earned.

FIGURE 14.9

An affiliate marketing ad from Barnes & Noble.

As noted, the cost-per-action (CPA) payment model is most common, with the action being a consumer purchase. That said, cost-per-order (CPO) and cost-per-lead (CPL) models are also popular, depending on the merchant.

We really don't deal much with affiliate marketing in this book; it's a topic worthy of its own title. That said, if you sell items online, it may be worth checking out one of the major affiliate networks. Having a network of other websites serving as your sales agents isn't necessarily a bad thing.

Getting to Know the Big Players

Back to the topic at hand—online advertising. When you want to place an ad, chances are you'll be dealing with one of the major online advertising networks. These networks will take your ad and place it with their network of affiliated websites. Most networks also offer assistance in ad creation if you need that.

Who are the big players? Table 14.1 details the major online ad networks as of December 2009, as compiled by comScore Media Metrix.

Table 14.1   Top Ten Online Advertising Networks

Ad Network	URL	Unique Visitors
AOL Advertising	advertising.aol.com	187,023,000
Yahoo! Advertising	advertising.yahoo.com	180,909,000
Google (AdWords/Doubleclick)	adwords.google.com www.doubleclick.com	178,134,000
ValueClick Networks	www.valueclick.com	170,774,000
Microsoft Advertising	advertising.microsoft.com	165,470,000
Specific Media	www.specificmedia.com	165,230,000
FOX Audience Network	www.foxaudiencenetwork.com	156,981,000
24/7 Real Media	www.247realmedia.com	155,856,000
Collective Network	www.collective.com	153,905,000
interCLICK	www.interclick.com	148,989,000

Not surprisingly, four of the top five ad networks are associated with major search engines or web networks. Yahoo!, Google, and Microsoft, of course, place ads not only on affiliated sites but also on their own search engines. Market-leading AOL Advertising places ads across the AOL network of sites.

Which of these ad networks should you utilize? If you're interested in reach across the Internet, there's no reason you should limit yourself to a single ad network; you could (and probably should) utilize multiple networks to get your ad seen on as many sites as possible.

14

If you're more interested in placement on search results pages, then Google AdWords is the way to go. Forget the network of third-party sites; AdWords puts your PPC ads on Google's search results pages. And when it comes to search, you can't get any bigger than Google.

note Google's ad network consists of two parts. AdWords handles all the PPC ads, while DoubleClick (purchased by Google in 2007) handles all the display advertising.

Most of these ad networks work in a similar fashion. You create or submit your ad and decide on the payment model you want—typically CPM or CPC. You settle on a budget and either choose a list of keywords for your ads or desired website demographics. In some instances, you can choose the specific sites where you want your ads displayed.

You pay the ad network when the ads run or when they're clicked if you chose the CPC model. The ad network splits the ad revenue with their affiliated sites—or keeps it all for themselves if the ads are run on search results pages or on their own company-run sites.

Trends in Online Advertising

The online advertising industry has been one of almost constant change. What was standard operating procedure ten years ago are quaint practices today; even the major players are constantly in flux.

As such, it helps to know which way the winds are blowing. With that in mind, here are some of the more important trends to keep abreast of.

Mobile Advertising

Online advertising isn't all about the Web; users with iPhones, Nexus Ones, and other smartphones also use their devices to connect to the Internet. Indeed, mobile access is the fastest growing part of the Internet today. If you want to reach this increasingly important mass of mobile users, you have to include mobile advertising as a major component of your online advertising plans.

note The mobile Internet is so important that I've devoted an entire section of this book to the topic. Learn more in Part XI, "Mobile Marketing," specifically in Chapter 40, "Advertising on Mobile Devices."

Social Media Advertising

Equally important as the mobile Internet trend is the social networking trend. Facebook, Twitter, and the like are major destinations for a large number of web users; advertising to the users of these sites makes increasing sense for most advertisers.

note Learn more about social networks in Part VIII, "Social Media Marketing."

Application Advertising

Speaking of the mobile Internet, here's a relatively new form of promotion—developing your own application as an advertising mechanism. This is increasingly common on the iPhone/iPad platform, where advertisers are building their own customer-focused apps. It's a great way to entice customers into your brand.

note Learn more about application advertising in Chapter 41, "Marketing via Mobile Apps."

Paid Tweets

You heard it here first. (Or maybe you didn't; somebody probably tweeted before me.) Advertisers are going directly to popular Twitter members and paying for tweets. Yes, it's a sellout for those Twitterers, but it could turn into an important form of advertising—in addition to Twitter's formal advertising program, of course.

Going Direct

You don't have to place your ads through an ad network; many advertisers, both large and small, prefer to place their ads directly with host websites. This is most easily accomplished with larger sites, of course, but many smaller sites are also willing to accept direct ad placement. In fact, there's a subtle shift from using ad networks to placing ads directly—especially among established advertisers.

Going direct is a good way to cut out the middle man, reduce your advertising costs, and guarantee better placement. It's also popular among the big website publishers, who can book more of the ad revenue themselves. This trend seems like a win-win for everyone—except the major ad networks.

14

Independent Websites

There's a subtle shift from advertising on major websites to advertising with smaller, independent sites. It's a matter of choosing grassroots, independent publishers over major publishing networks. Good news for the little guy; it may also save you a bit of money, as it costs less to advertise on smaller sites.

Nonstandard Ads

In an effort to break out from the typical blandness of display advertising, more and more advertisers are requesting ads in nonstandard sizes. (The standard sizes, of course, being those dictated by the Internet Advertising Board, or IAB.) This trend may even find favor among website publishers, who can customize ad placement for their own content.

Bigger, More Intrusive Ads

Along the same lines, some advertisers are looking for a more dominant web page presence, which results in bigger, more intrusive ads. This trend is also being pushed by some of the ad networks, who are looking to make up for lost revenue (see "Going Direct" a few sections back) by selling bigger, more expensive ads. This isn't necessarily a good trend, as it goes against what most customers want.

The Bottom Line

Online advertising is a major component of most companies' web marketing plans. PPC text advertising, those ads placed on search results pages, is most prevalent. That said, display advertising is becoming more important, especially for larger companies looking to build their brand image; many display ads incorporate video, animation, and other rich media elements.

While most ad buys today are made through major ad networks, some large advertisers buy space directly from major websites. Placed direct or through an ad network, the trend is toward bigger, flashier ads—the better to cut through the online clutter.

14

WHAT KIND OF ADVERTISING IS BEST FOR YOU?

Plain-text ads or rich media display ads? CPM or CPC payment models? Join an ad network or deal direct with host websites?

Important questions all, as you start to put together your web advertising plan. There are lots of options, and your budget, no matter its size, is limited. Just what should you do?

Let's look at the ad type first. Both text ads and display ads have their places. Text ads—PPC text ads, to be specific—are more effective than display ads in driving direct sales. Display ads, on the other hand, are better at generating product or brand awareness. So while it's possible that both types of ads will fit into your plans, it's more likely that you'll pick an ad type based on your marketing goals for a given year or quarter.

As to payment model, that kind of goes along with the ad type you choose. CPC payment is the great pay for play bargain; you pay only for customers delivered from those text ads placed on search results pages. CPM payment is more closely tied to image-based display advertising, where you're not really tracking direct sales results.

The ad network choice is, perhaps, less obvious. If you're doing PPC text ads, of course, you'll be tied to ad networks of the big three search engines—Google, Yahoo!, and Bing. But display advertising doesn't have to be network-supported, especially if you know the websites you want to work with and have the wherewithal to negotiate directly with them. If you can cut out the middleman, why not?

In general terms, then, if you're selling directly online, go to PPC text ads through one of the big ad networks. If you're using the Web for image awareness, go with CPM display ads and bypass the ad networks if you can. That's a broad and simple generalization, of course; as always, you should pick the combination of activities that make the most sense for your business.

14

Pay-per-Click Advertising

The most popular type of web advertising today is pay-per-click (PPC) advertising. The typical PPC ad is a small text ad, placed contextually on a search results page or website with similar content. There are other types of PPC ads, of course; PPC merely explains the payment method, not the look or feel of the ad itself.

PPC ads are so prevalent because they're fairly effective and definitely cost-effective, as you only pay when they're clicked. As such, let's take an in-depth look at PPC advertising, with a focus on the largest PPC ad networks.

Understanding Pay-per-Click and Contextual Advertising

If you're in business selling baby clothing, you'd probably like your ads placed next to content about babies; potential customers will be more inclined to take an interest in your offerings if they just got done reading an article about baby care on a baby-related website. That's bound to be a more sympathetic audience than if your baby clothing ads were placed on a site about hydroponic farming methods or even a general-interest news site. You do better when the people reading your ads are predisposed to the subject matter.

You also get a good bang for your buck when your ad for baby clothing pops up for people searching baby clothing. Someone queries Google or Bing about "baby clothing" or "baby jumpers" or "toddler clothes" or something similar, and your ad appears among the organic search results. That's a good thing; you know the searcher is already interested in what you're selling, and now your ad is right in front of her to click if she likes.

15

Well, this is exactly what you get when you purchase a PPC ad. The ad is delivered contextually—that is, it's placed on search results pages and web pages that have similar content. If you're selling baby clothing, it will appear on Google, Yahoo!, or Bing when people are searching for baby clothing; it won't appear when people are searching for tractor tires or baseball gloves. It will also appear on websites that talk about babies and baby clothing; it won't appear on websites that focus on reading glasses or cocktail mixes. It's a *sympathetic placement*.

Even better, you only pay for the ad when someone clicks it. That's the pay-per-click thing; you pay for the click, not for the ad placement. It's a very efficient payment method that doesn't waste your budget.

But how do these PPC ads get placed on the right pages? And how exactly does that per-click payment thing work? Read on to learn more.

It Starts with One Little (Key) Word...

PPC ads are different from traditional ads in that they're highly relevant to the pages on which they appear. That is, PPC ad networks don't display any old ad on a web page; instead, they try to serve up the right ads for the right potential customers. To do this, PPC advertising networks utilize *keywords*, those words and phrases that users search for on Google and other search engine sites.

It all starts when a PPC advertiser purchases a particular keyword or phrase from the PPC ad network. (In most cases, the advertiser actually bids on a keyword rather than purchasing it outright; we get into this in a minute.) Ideally, the keywords purchased are somehow related to or descriptive of the product or service promoted in the ad.

The keywords purchased determine where the ad is displayed. When a user enters a query on a related search site, such as Google, the advertiser's ad is displayed on search results page in the "Sponsored links" section that appears at the top or side of the page. The ad is designed to look kind of like an organic search result—the better to entice users to click the ad.

To this end, PPC ads on search results pages are almost always text ads. That doesn't mean that you can't do PPC image ads, just that these image ads won't appear on search results pages.

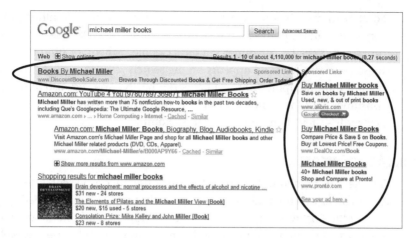

FIGURE 15.1

PPC ads at the top of and along the right side of Google's search results page.

Instead, you can place PPC image ads—along with PPC text ads—on individual websites that are part of the PPC ad network. The ad, text or image, is placed on specific pages that have content that relates to the purchased keyword. These ads can appear anywhere on the given page; the ad placement is up to the owner of the web page.

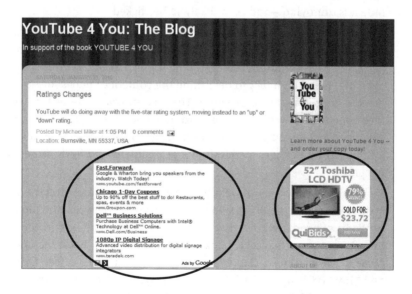

FIGURE 15.2

PPC text and image ads on an affiliated website.

15

So, for example, if you have a business that sells acoustic guitars and acces-sories, you might purchase the keywords "guitar," "pick," "strap," "amplifier," and so on. When a consumer searches Google, Yahoo!, or Bing for any of these keywords, your ad appears on the search results page. (Assuming you bought into the appropriate ad network, that is.) Your ad also appears when a consumer goes to an affiliated website that features content containing these keywords—sites about guitars, in this example.

Placing Ads in Context

The neat thing about PPC ads is that they use advanced search technology to serve content-focused ads—that is, an ad that relates to the underlying con-tent of the host web page. As any market knows, an ad that is somehow related to the content of the underlying medium—in this case, the web page—reaches a more targeted audience than a more broadly focused ad. This close relationship between ad content and page content should generate more and better traffic to the advertiser's website. It's very targeted placement.

As a side benefit, this context sensitivity also benefits the sites that host the ads. If, for example, you host a website about NASCAR racing, only ads some-how related to stock car racing will appear on your site. You won't see ads for cooking utensils or legal services or baby toys; your site's visitors will only see ads that are related to the main content of your site. This makes the ads a little less annoying—and more likely to be clicked.

How does a PPC network serve up these relevant ads? It's all about leveraging search technology. When we're talking about the Google, Yahoo!, and Bing ad networks, each company uses the same sophisticated algorithms that it uses to create its search index to determine the content of pages for sites that par-ticipate in its advertising program. The ad network analyzes the keywords that appear on a web page, the word frequency, font size, and overall link structure to figure out, as closely as possible, what a page is all about. Then it finds ads that closely match that page's content and feeds those ads to the page.

For example, my personal website (www.molehillgroup.com) is all about the books I've written. I subscribe to Google's AdSense network (the flip side of its AdWords network for advertisers), and Google serves up ads on each page that are relevant to each specific book. On the page for my book *The Complete Idiot's Guide to Playing Drums*, Google serves up ads titled "1,684 Video Drum Lessons" and "Top 10 Cheap Drum Sets." On the page for *Windows 7 Your Way*, there are ads for "Speed Up Your Computer" and "Free PC Optimizer." The right ads for the right content—which benefits both advertisers and the host sites.

Paying by the Click

Now to the PPC thing. The reason it's called pay-per-click advertising is that an advertiser pays the ad network only when customers click the link in the ad. (The link typically points to the advertiser's website or, most commonly, a special landing page on the website.) If no one clicks, the advertiser doesn't pay anyone anything. The more clicks that are received, the more the advertiser pays.

Ad rates are calculated on a cost-per-click (CPC) basis. That is, the advertiser is charged a specific fee for each click—anywhere from a few pennies to tens of dollars. The actual CPC rate is determined by the popularity of and competition for the keyword purchased, as well as the quality and quantity of traffic going to the site hosting the ad. As you can imagine, popular keywords have a higher CPC, while less popular keywords can be had for less.

> **note** As you learned in the previous chapter, PPC or CPC advertising is in contrast to the traditional cost-per-thousand impressions (CPM) model, where rates are based on the number of potential viewers of the ad—whether they click through or not.

This varying CPC rate is determined by having advertisers bid on the most popular keywords. That is, you might say you'll pay up to $5 for a given keyword. If you're the high bidder among several advertisers, your ads will appear more frequently on web pages that contain that keyword, or higher on a search results page for that keyword. If you're not the high bidder, you won't get as much visibility—if your ad appears at all.

> **note** A given PPC ad probably won't appear on every search engine results page for the keyword purchased. That's because page inventory for a given keyword is limited, while advertisers are theoretically unlimited. For this reason, ad networks typically rotate ads from multiple advertisers on its search results and affiliated websites.

Sharing Ad Revenues

Here's something else interesting about PPC advertising; revenue from PPC ads gets shared between the ad network and the hosting website. That's right, any website where the ad appears gets a cut of the ad revenues paid by the advertiser—which is why sites agree to put PPC ads on their web pages.

If you're an advertiser, this part of the arrangement is transparent; you pay the ad network, and they divvy up the funds however they do. Those sites that host PPC ads, however, get a percentage of all the funds paid by the site's advertisers. The ad network collects the revenue from the advertisers and then passes your share on to the host website.

Here's the process, in a nutshell:

1. An advertiser creates an advertisement and contracts with a PPC ad network to place that ad on the Internet.

2. The ad network serves the ad in question to a number of appropriate websites (and to search results pages on its own search site, of course).

3. An interested customer sees the ad on an affiliated website and clicks the link in the ad to receive more information.

4. The advertiser pays the ad network, based on the CPC advertising rate.

5. The ad network pays the host website a small percentage of the advertising fee paid.

And remember, nobody pays anything until someone actually clicks an ad. If no one clicks your ad, the you pay nothing—and the site hosting the ad generates no revenue. Better for all concerned, then, that the ad receives the maximum number of clicks—which is where context sensitivity and picking the right keywords come in.

Maximizing Ad Placement

As an advertiser, it's important that you pick the most effective keywords for your PPC ads. Pick keywords that no one is interested in, and your ad won't appear anywhere; pick more popular keywords, and your ad will appear more often—and, hopefully, generate more traffic back to your site and more sales.

The problem, then, is that the best keywords are also the most popular ones. That is, lots of advertisers will be interested in the same keywords. Because ad networks set their rates by having advertisers bid on keywords, the most popular keywords will cost you more than less-popular ones will.

This competition for keywords among advertisers becomes, essentially, an online auction. Those advertisers who bid the highest amounts for keywords will "win" more and better ad placements. If you don't bid high enough on a popular keyword, your ad simply won't appear as often. In fact, if you bid way too low, your ad may not appear at all.

The temptation, then, is to bid high on the most popular keywords in an attempt to get more ads displayed and drive more traffic to your website. Be careful what you wish for, however, as this approach can result in very high advertising bills.

That said, bid price isn't the only factor in determining how often an ad is displayed—at least not anymore. It used to be that the highest bidder got the most placements, but that didn't always ensure that the most relevant ads got placed. For that reason, the ad networks now utilize a "quality score" factor that attempts to determine the relevance of the ad's landing page—the page that the ad links to. If an ad's landing page consists of low-quality content, that ad gets a low quality score and won't rank high in the ad network's results. A landing page with high-quality, relevant content will rank higher and thus be displayed more frequently.

note PPC ad networks let you set a daily or monthly budget for your total advertising expenditures. Your ad will run only until your budget is maxed out; at that point, your ad is no longer in circulation.

To maximize your ad placements, then, you need to consider a number of factors:

- Keywords
- Bid price for those keywords
- Content of the linked-to landing page
- Effectiveness of your ad copy

In other words, you have to bid on keywords that are both popular and relevant; bid the going rate for those keywords; create a high-value landing page for your ad; and write an ad that encourages users to click it. Fall down on any of these factors and your ad will be less than fully successful.

Choosing the Right Keywords

PPC advertising, then, involves a combination of keywords, CPC bidding, and, let us not forget, ad copy. We look at each component in turn, starting with keywords.

As you might suspect, one of the most important factors in creating a successful PPC campaign is the set of keywords you choose. Select the right keywords, and everyone searching for a given topic will see your ad; select the wrong keywords, and your ad will never be displayed.

What Is a Keyword and Why Is It Important?

A *keyword* is a word that someone includes in a search query. Similarly, a keyword phrase (sometimes called a key phrase) is a group of words that

15

someone includes in a query. In other words, keywords and phrases are what people search for on the Internet.

Keywords are important to advertisers because Google and the other PPC ad networks use these search queries to match PPC ads to what people are searching for. This is why you must specify one or more keywords to trigger the PPC ads you create. The keywords you select are matched against the keywords that the search engine's users search for; when someone searches for one of your keywords, your ad is placed in the running to be displayed. (Whether it's actually displayed or not depends on how much you bid per click, what other advertisers are bidding on that same keyword, and other factors, as previously discussed.)

So, for example, if someone is searching for the word "pie," only advertisers who bid on the word "pie" will have their ads considered for display. If you haven't specified "pie" as one of your keywords, your ad won't be displayed on this person's search results page. So if you want to target home bakers for your advertising, you want to specify the word "pie" as one of the keywords for your campaign—and also include that keyword on the landing page linked to from your ad.

Similarly, if someone is searching for the phrase "pie crust," only advertisers that specify that phrase will register as a match. If your campaign includes the word "pie" but not the phrase "pie crust," it won't be a match for that particular query. You need to specify the entire key phrase as part of your campaign.

In short, keywords are important because they're what people are looking for. If your PPC campaign includes the keywords that people are searching for, your ads will display more often and in higher positions than ads from competing advertisers that aren't targeted by those keywords. And if you don't include the keywords people are searching for, you might as well not be advertising at all.

Conducting Keyword Research

How, then, do you determine which keywords people are searching for? It's really a matter of learning how to *think like the customer*, as I've stressed throughout this book. In other words, you need to get inside searchers' heads to determine which words they're using in their queries—and then specify those keywords for your campaign.

How do you get inside your customers' heads? In the case of figuring out which keywords they use, you can conduct *keyword research*, using inexpensive keyword research tools. These tools are software utilities or web-based services that compile and analyze keyword search statistics from Google and (sometimes) the other major search engines. You use the results from these keyword research tools to determine the most powerful keywords to include on your site.

Most keyword research tools work by matching the content of your website with keywords relevant to that content; they've already searched through hundreds of thousands of possible keywords and phrases on the most popular search engines and mapped the results to their own databases. You enter a word or phrase that describes what your site has to offer, and the research tool returns a list of words or phrases related to that description, in descending order of search popularity.

> **note** It's never a good idea to guess at what keywords searchers are using or assume that the way *you* search is the way everyone else searches. Instead, use keyword research tools or traditional market research to determine the real keywords used.

For example, if you have a website that's selling running shoes, you might describe your site with the phrase "running shoes." The keyword research tool, then, would return a list of keywords and phrases related to the topic of running shoes. Those words and phrases at the top of the list are the ones that show up most often in search results and, thus, will best improve the ranking of your site on those search engines.

None of these research tools are free; you'll pay anywhere from $40 to $70 a month to subscribe. The most popular of these tools include the following:

- **KeywordDiscovery** (www.keyworddiscovery.com)
- **Wordtracker** (www.wordtracker.com)
- **WordZe** (www.wordze.com)

In addition to these paid, somewhat universal, keyword research tools, if you're a Google AdWords subscriber, you can also use the free keyword research tools provided by Google. There are two such tools available.

Google's Keyword Tool is a free web-based utility, accessible from the Opportunities tab on the AdWords site (adwords.google.com). Enter one or more words or phrases that describe your site or just enter your site's URL; the Keyword Tool then generates a list of focused keywords, along with data about how popular each keyword is among competing advertisers, how many searches are made each month for each keyword, and search trends for each keyword.

15

If you want even more keyword ideas, try Google's other free utility, the Search-Based Keyword Tool, accessible at www.google.com/sktool/. Unlike the basic Keyword Tool, anyone can use the Search-Based Keyword Tool; you don't have to be an Adwords advertiser. This tool provides more detailed data for each keyword listed, including category information, AdWords share, and the suggested bid that may place the ad in the top three positions—always a good thing to know.

> **note** You can pick up a lot of keywords—and potential customers—inexpensively by bidding on misspellings of common keywords. For example, if you're selling golf clubs, you might want to bid on "gulf clubs" and "golf culbs" and "golf blubs" and other similar typos that fumble-fingered users might enter by mistake into a search box.

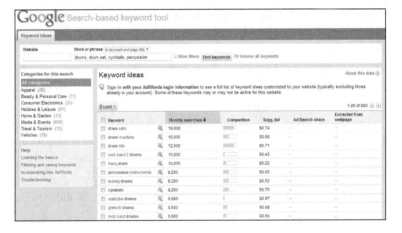

FIGURE 15.3

Keyword suggestions from Google's Search-Based Keyword Tool.

Researching Competitor's Campaigns

You can use any of these search tools to generate keywords for your PPC ad campaigns. You can also use these tools to get smarter about what your competitors may be doing with their ad campaigns.

You see, you're not limited to entering just your own website for analysis. You can also enter the URL for a competitor's site. When you do this, the tool generates the list of keywords that your competitor is likely bidding on. And, depending on the tool, you may also see the amount that your competitor is likely bidding per click.

You can use this knowledge in a number of ways. First, you may choose to go head-to-head with a successful competitor. In this instance, you'd bid on the exact same keywords, but at a higher level, stealing position away from that competitor—at least until he catches on to what you're doing.

Another approach is to use this information to develop an alternative strategy. In this instance you deliberately *avoid* the exact keywords this advertiser is using, instead generating a list of similar but different keywords and key phrases. These may be synonyms or alternative spellings, or even more precise phrases (if the advertiser is using more general keywords). In any instance, you try to outflank the competitor by not going head-to-head with the same keywords and generate page views for searches that this advertiser is currently missing.

Bidding the Right Price

Once you assemble the list of keywords you want to associate with your PPC ads, you need to determine how much you should bid on those keywords. There are a number of different bidding strategies you can employ.

The bidding strategy you choose affects the success of your PPC ad campaign. If you bid too low, you won't win enough keywords, your ads won't appear as high or as often, and you won't generate much traffic. If, on the other hand, you bid too high, then you'll end up overpaying for your ads and generating too low a return on your investment.

How the Bidding Process Works

As you've learned, the cost per click for most PPC advertising is determined by a bidding process. When you sign up as an advertiser, you pick the keywords you want and tell the ad network the maximum amount you're willing to pay for each ad placement. When it comes time to serve an ad onto a search results page or an affiliate website, the ad network runs an automated auction process to determine which ad gets placed. Obviously, the advertiser who is willing to pay the highest price has a better chance of having his ad displayed than does an advertiser with a lower bid.

This automated auction takes place whenever a user searches for a keyword that advertisers have bid on. The ad network takes various factors into account beyond just the bid price. In some instances, the advertiser's location, the date and time of day, as well as the actual content linked to by the advertiser also figure into the equation. And because most search results pages have slots for several of these "Sponsored links," there can be more than one winner for each keyword search. In this situation, the ad from the highest bidder typically shows up first in the list.

This same sort of automated auction occurs when an ad appears on an affiliate website. Whenever a page is visited on that site, the ad network conducts an auction for the ad slots available on that page. As with ads in search engine results, those ads with the highest bids—as well as highest quality content—are most likely to be displayed. When the site has placement for multiple ads, the ad from highest bidder typically shows up on the highest position on the page.

The bidding for PPC ads works much the same way as bidding in an eBay auction. You specify the maximum amount you'll pay and let the ad network's automated bidding software do the dirty work for you.

> **note** An ad on an affiliate site typically has a lower click-through rate (CTR) than does a similar ad on a search engine's results page. As such, these ads are less highly valued and typically cost less than the same ads served on search engine results pages.

That is, the ad network places a bid for you that is only a little higher than existing bids. If competition forces the bidding higher, the ad network raises your bid accordingly, up to but not exceeding the maximum amount you specified.

The result is advertisers aren't necessarily charged the full amount of their maximum bids. Because the bid raises are automated and incremental, Google and other ad networks charge the winning bidder just a penny or so more than the next-highest bid. So if you bid a maximum of $5 and the next-highest bid was $4, you won't pay the full $5; instead, you'll be charged $4.01 for your winning bid.

Manual versus Automated Bidding

The first choice you have to make is whether you want to use manual or automated bidding. If you select manual bidding, you can specify exact CPC rates for each keyword or group of keywords you create. The other option is to use automatic bidding, for which you don't have to make an exact CPC bid.

When you choose automated bidding, the only choice you have to make is the maximum amount you want to pay per click. The PPC ad network will then make the best bid below that level to maximize the number of potential clicks for your daily budget.

> **note** With most PPC ad networks, you can fine-tune your bidding more when you choose manual bidding. For example, Google AdWords' manual bidding feature lets you set bids for individual keywords, which you can't do with automated bidding.

The good thing about automated bidding is that it's less work—and guess-work—for you. You set a maximum bid, and the ad network does all the bid-ding, never exceeding your maximum amount per click. For that reason, automated bidding is the recommended approach for new or inexperienced PPC advertisers.

The bad thing about automated bidding is that it typically applies to all the keywords in an ad campaign. You can't set different CPC rates for different keywords or keyword groups, which is required for some of the more sophisti-cated bidding strategies; you give up a lot of control. For that reason, manual bidding is the recommend approach for many advanced PPC advertisers.

Bid Rates versus ROI

Of course, different keywords sell for different rates. It's logical, really. Those keywords that more advertisers want to use get higher bids and have higher CPC rates; those keywords that aren't as popular have lower CPC rates. So it's just as easy to bid high on a low-priced keyword as it is to bid low on a high-priced one.

If you bid way too low, your ad simply won't appear for a given keyword. And if you consistently bid too low on keywords, you won't generate enough traffic to make your campaign profitable—and thus reduce your campaign's return on investment (ROI). On the other hand, if you consistently bid too high on keywords, you'll spend more advertising funds than you need to—and also reduce your ROI. That's why you need to figure out how to bid the right amount—neither too high or too low—to strike the right balance between traffic and cost. This will maximize your ROI for a given campaign.

Ways to Reduce Your Maximum Bid

Whether you use manual or automatic bidding, you still enter a maximum CPC bid. This is the maximum you're willing to pay; in reality, you may end up paying less.

That's because most PPC ad networks manage your CPC bids so that you don't have to pay more than you have to. This works by the ad network's automati-cally lowering your maximum bid to a penny or so more than the next-highest competing bid. So if you bid $2.00 for a keyword but the next-highest bid is $1.50, you don't pay the full $2.00; instead, you pay $1.51.

In addition, most PPC ad networks will lower the maximum CPC bid for ads appearing on their affiliate network sites. That's because most third-party sites have less traffic—and generate lower click-through rates—than do search engine results pages. So even though you set a single maximum bid, if a click from a given site or page is less likely to result in a sale, most ad networks will reduce the bid level for that particular site. In other words, you pay less for lesser results.

Bidding Strategy 1: Bid Whatever It Takes to Be First

With those bidding basics out of the way, let's look at some of the various bidding strategies you can employ for a PPC campaign. The first strategy is one aimed at always winning the keywords you choose—no matter what the price.

The thinking behind this strategy is simple. When your ad ranks in the number one (or number two) position for a given keyword, it appears *above* the search engine's organic search results for that keyword on the search results page. That's the best position possible, as it results in more—sometimes a lot more—clicks and traffic than lower positions.

Of course, you have to pay top dollar to get that top slot, so this can be a costly strategy. That's especially so if you get into a bidding war with another advertiser following the same strategy; when two advertisers are both intent on being number one, the price for a given keyword can skyrocket.

This strategy also has its limits. Remember, your bid price is only part of what determines your final ad position; you also have to figure in your site's quality score, which factors in things like the content of the ad's landing page. So you can't guarantee top position by bidding only, as it's possible to be outbid by a competitor with a higher quality score.

That said, the key to this strategy is constant monitoring of your ad's position—at least daily. If your position starts to slip, that means someone else is outbidding you, and you'll need to increase your bid.

Bidding Strategy 2: Bid for a Specific Position

The problem with bidding for the number one or number two position is that it's costly—and apt to get more costly over time, as other advertisers also bid for those same keywords. For many advertisers, a better approach is to bid for a lower position—something in the 3–6 range, for example. These positions will cost you a lot less than the number-one position but still land you on the first page of the search engine's search results page—which typically results in a good CTR for a much lower CPC.

The key to this strategy is to fine-tune your bid once your campaign is running to find the sweet spot you want. Once the campaign is underway, check the average position for the ad in question. If your average position is below your target range, increase your CPC bid for that keyword; if your average position is above your target range, decrease your bid. Like I said, it's a fine-tuning process, but one that guarantees a decent ROI over time.

Bidding Strategy 3: Bid the Bare Minimum

The first strategy presented was to always bid high in order to capture the top display position for a keyword. The flip side to that strategy is one in which you always bid low—to contain your costs and work within a budget.

The thinking here is that you can waste a lot of money trying to get the top positions; your budget may be better spent bidding low for your traffic, especially if you have a high quality score that can pull up your position compared to lower-performing competitors. Now, you'll probably never rise to the top spot, but you may end up on the first page of search results—which isn't bad.

This cost containment strategy works if you believe users browse all the ad listings on a page, not just those at the top. That's not always the case, of course; if it were, the top position wouldn't pull as effectively as it typically does. Still, some users *do* consider more than just the first listing, at least on the first page of search results, so there's some merit to this strategy. It's certainly a strategy that's worth considering if your budget is limited.

If you decide to go this route, use manual bidding and always bid at the lower end of the suggested range. You should also consider *not* bidding on keywords that are estimated to have a high CPC; you may get better results bidding on less popular keywords.

Bidding Strategy 4: Bid High—Then Lower Your Bid

Here's a quirk in some PPC systems that can work to your benefit; this is particularly evident if you're using Google AdWords. As you know, Google uses the quality score to help determine your ad's position. And one component of the quality score is your ad's click-through rate. You get a higher CTR, and your quality score goes up; your quality score goes up, and you get a better position—which improves your CTR. And a higher CTR makes your quality score go up again...and on and on. You get the idea.

The key here is to realize that if your ad is working and your CTR is going up, thus improving your quality score, you can maintain the same ad position at a lower cost. That's right, when your CTR rises you decrease your bid level and maintain the same ad position; the improved quality score works in your favor in this regard. You end up at the same (or higher) position at a lower cost.

15

This strategy works best if you start with a higher bid level. That is, you go in strong to establish your position, and once your position has been established, you can then lower your bid. Naturally, you'll want to monitor your average position and quality score on at least a daily basis and then use your best judgment on when to change your bid.

Bidding Strategy 5: Bid What It's Worth

All the previous bidding strategies were externally focused; that is, you have goals related to ad position. But you can also bid with an internal focus—in particular, how much a given keyword is worth to you.

If you do a little research beforehand and performance tracking after your campaign starts, you can determine the *optimal* cost per click for any keyword. Here's how to do it.

Start by determining how much profit you make off a sale from your website. As an example, let's say you sell an item for $100 retail that costs you $60 to purchase or manufacture; you generate $40 profit on each sale.

Next, determine your conversion rate for a given keyword. In most instances, expect your conversion rate to be in the low single digits. For our example, let's say that your conversion rate is 1%, meaning that 1 out of every 100 people who click your ad end up buying your product.

Now it's math time. Each sale you make is worth $40 to you, and it takes 100 clicks to make one sale. Divide $40 by 100, and you discover that each visitor you attract costs you $0.40. This means you can afford to spend a maximum of $0.40 per click before you start losing money on each click. So, in this example, you'd set your maximum price per click to $0.40.

This calculation works only when you're selling products or services directly from your website, and it requires a little post-launch calculation. (That is, you won't know your conversion rate until you get some experience under your belt.) If, on the other hand, you're using PPC advertising to generate nonsales leads or build your brand image, the value of each click is much more difficult to determine—so difficult, in fact, that each company must determine this on their own.

Writing Effective Ad Copy

The final component of your PPC ad campaign is the ad itself. Given that most PPC ads are text ads, this means writing effective ad copy.

In most PPC ad programs, a text ad consists of four lines of text. The first line is the headline or title, with a relatively short character count. The next two lines contain the body of the ad, often a product description, which can hold more characters but still not a lot. And the final line is the URL of the site where you're driving traffic.

Books by Michael Miller
How-to books by popular author
Computers, music, eBay, and more!
www.molehillgroup.com

FIGURE 15.4

A four-line PPC text ad.

Writing a Compelling Headline

The most important part of any text ad is the title. This is because some ad formats on third-party pages display *only* the title and URL, skipping the two description lines. So your title has to do the heavy lifting; it has to grab potential customers at a literal glance. You can then fill in more details in the next two lines, but the title must be able to stand alone if necessary.

Even when the complete ad is displayed, as it is on most search results pages, the title is still the most important element. That's because it's the first thing that people see; a good headline will draw them to read the rest of the ad, while a bad headline will turn them off completely.

For this reason, you have to write a compelling headline for your ad. It should attract the attention of potential customers and compel them to click the ad. It's the equivalent of a carnival barker—"Click here, click here!"

Naturally, the headline must inform customers of what you're selling or trying to accomplish; in this aspect, it needs to be informative. But the headline should also trigger specific customer behavior, in most instances a click through to your chosen landing page.

A good headline includes words that grab the user's attention. I'm talking about words like "free" and "sale," "new" and "more," "discover" and "bargain." These words cause users to read the rest of the ad or click the headline to learn more. They're powerful.

Bottom line, it's worth spending a lot of time on the headline in order to get it right. In fact, the headline is so important that you may want to hire a professional copywriter to do the job. Yes, it's a short headline, but when every word (and every character!) counts, a pro can more than pay for himself.

Writing Compelling Copy

It's not just your headline that should be compelling. The two lines of descriptive or body text should also persuade potential customers to click through to your landing page.

To this end, you should use words that appeal to the customer's emotions. People want to be excited or comforted or entertained; your copy should fulfill these emotional needs.

In addition, your copy needs to solve a problem or answer a question the customer might have. What does the customer need to do that your product does? That's the solution to push in the body of your ad.

Persuasive ad copy tells consumers how to save money, how to get something done, how to learn something important, how to do something better. You do this by using certain "power words" that invoke emotion and enthusiasm in potential buyers. These words include the following:

note The most effective PPC ads include specifics—percentages, dollar amounts, product names, and the like. For example, you can show users how to "Save 10%," "Increase profits by 25%," or buy something for "$19.99."

- Free
- Cheap
- Save
- Sale
- Special [offer]
- Bargain
- Bonus
- Limited time [savings or offer]
- Discover
- Learn
- Tips
- Tricks
- Enhance

Because you only have two short lines of copy to work with, you don't have space to talk about your product's features. Instead, you must focus on the benefits—that is, how the customer will benefit from buying what you're selling. If you're selling a weight-reduction aid, don't talk about its unique chemical compound; tell people that they'll "lose weight fast." Tell readers what's in it for them.

You also need to differentiate your product from the competition's. To that end, play up your unique selling proposition—the thing that sets you apart from competing products. What makes your product better or different from everything else out there? That should be clear in your copy.

Including a Call to Action

Because most PPC ads link to the advertiser's website, you want the potential customer to do something. We're not talking generic image advertising here; PPC ads should result in a specific action—that you need to ask for.

To that end, your ad copy needs to include a strong call to action. You have to ask the customer to do something before they'll do anything at all.

What's a good call to action? Here are some common ones:

- Order now
- Buy now
- Download your free trial
- Sign up
- Get a quote
- Learn more
- Read our brochure
- Request more information
- Browse our site
- Join us today
- Start now

Notice what's *not* on this list: the phrase "click here." Asking someone to click your ad is not a good call to action for a number of reasons. First, it's implied in all PPC ads; the title is a hyperlink, after all. Second, most ad networks don't like it and may reduce your quality score and your ad placement if you include it. Third, clicking isn't really what you want users to do; you want them to get more information or buy now or something similar. Focus on that.

So remember, you want the customer to do something specific, beyond just clicking the ad—and you have to tell them what that is. Without a call to action, your ad is just a bunch of words on the page.

Including Targeted Keywords

With text-based advertising, words are important. That goes for the keywords you use to trigger the display of your PPC ads.

15

To that end, you need to include your primary keywords in both your ad's headline and body copy. That's because people look for the keywords they've queried when they're viewing search results. If someone searches for "toboggan," he's going to scan the search results page for the word "toboggan." He's more likely to click an ad that contains that word than one that doesn't because of the implication that an ad that contains "toboggan" in its headline or copy is relevant to his search.

For this reason, ads that contain the same keywords that trigger the ad tend to perform better than ones that don't. Research your keywords carefully and then include those keywords in your ads.

Writing Efficient Copy

It's important to remember the character limitations inherent with PPC text ads and to work within those limitations. You definitely don't have room for excessive verbiage; you may not even have room for proper grammar and complete sentences. Your writing has to be short and to the point. You have to get your message across in the minimum amount of space.

So don't even think about putting puff words ("lowest" or "best") or punctuation (! or *) in your text ads. There simply isn't space to waste on these unnecessary words and characters.

What is okay is to use space-saving characters, such as the ampersand (&) for the word "and." You can also use widely-understood abbreviations and acronyms where appropriate.

The whole point is to put forth a compelling message in a minimum amount of space. This takes no small amount of talent. In fact, if you're not comfortable writing this sort of super-tight ad copy, it's worth hiring a copywriter. This is the toughest kind of copywriting out there.

note You also have to present your website's URL in a certain number of characters. That effectively rules out displaying individual pages or directories; you pretty much have room to display your home page URL and nothing more. In fact, if you have an overly long domain name, there might not be enough characters to display the entire URL; you may need to establish an alternate, shorter domain instead. Of course, you can have the ad link to a more specific landing page, but it might have a longer URL. Just keep the limited space in mind.

Testing Different Copy

For your ad to be successful, then, it needs to entice users to click through to your website for more information or to place an order. This means informing them about what you have to offer, as well as presenting a strong call to action.

It also means clicking *your* ad, not somebody else's. This requires that your ad—both the information presented and the call to action—be unique. Users have to know why to click your ad instead of someone else's.

With all this in mind, you should experiment with different copy blocks—that is, presenting your message in different ways. Write several different variations of your main copy and then run them as competing ads in the same ad campaign. (This way they'll be triggered by the same keywords.) From this exercise you can determine which ad copy pulls the best and use that information to inform future ads.

Creating PPC Image Ads

Most PPC ad networks let you create both text and image ads. While text ads are most prevalent, clickable context-sensitive image ads are also popular among some advertisers.

FIGURE 15.5

A PPC image ad in skyscraper format.

A PPC image ad is like any web-based display ad; it just falls under the CPC payment method. That is, instead of buying the ad space on a web page, you

15

pay only when a user clicks the ad. In most instances, the click takes a user back to your website, where you can provide more information or try to make a sale.

Like all display ads, PPC image ads are available in a variety of sizes and formats. You can create horizontal banner ads, vertical skyscrapers, or simple squares or rectangles. Typically, the whole of the ad consists of the image you provide.

> **note** Some PPC ad networks also let you place rich media ads containing audio, video, Flash animations, and the like.

The big drawback to PPC image ads is that they typically don't display on search engine results pages. So if you want to advertise directly to Google or Yahoo! searchers, you need to use text ads. PPC image ads display primarily on third-party websites affiliated with the PPC ad network—and not on all of them. (Websites have the option of accepting either text ads or a mix of text and image ads; not all webmasters choose the image ad option.)

What makes for an effective PPC image ad? Pretty much the same thing that makes for an effective display ad, as we discuss in the next chapter. But because you want customers to click the ad, you also need to include a call for action and ask for the click, in so many words. It's a display ad that isn't a brand ad; you want the customer to click through and visit your website.

Maximizing Conversion with a Custom Landing Page

A landing page is the page that appears when a potential customer clicks your PPC ad. The landing page could be your site's home page, it could be a product page for whatever it is you're advertising, or it could be a page specially designed to accompany the specific advertisement.

Why Landing Pages Are Important

Here's the deal. Most users don't view more than the first page of the resulting web page when they click an ad. If they don't like what they find, or if the landing page doesn't contain the information they want, they leave immediately.

For this reason, you need to set up a well-structured landing page to greet those users who click your ad. The more effective your landing page, the more clicks you will convert to sales.

The best landing pages display content that is a logical extension of the advertisement. Depending on the nature and intent of the page, it should provide additional information, ask for information from the customer, or ask for the sale.

Why You Need a Separate Landing Page

As we've discussed, you could link to your site's home page, but that generally isn't a great idea. That's because most home pages are rather general in nature; they advertise your company or brand, not necessarily the specific product or service mentioned in your ad. That is, they don't follow directly from your ad—which could be confusing to potential customers.

Likewise, linking to any existing page on your site might not be the best approach. Remember, if you're looking for conversions rather than raw clicks, your landing page has to close the sale. That means that you shouldn't point to a generic brand or product page; customers need to see a page that displays the product or service you talked about in the ad. Going to any nonspecific page requires unnecessary work on the part of the customer to learn more about what's advertised and to place an order.

The best approach, then, is to link to a page on your site custom-designed for readers of your PPC advertisement. This page should display information only about the product promoted in your advertising—and include an ordering mechanism, the better to convert that click into a sale.

Why design a special landing page for each ad you create? It's simple: You want to make it as easy as possible for people to give you their money. If you just dump potential customers on your site's home page, they could get lost. Or they might have trouble finding the product they want and give up. In any instance, you don't want them randomly browsing your site; you want them to immediately respond to your specific offer.

Creating an Effective Landing Page

Though you can create a different landing page for each ad you place, you may be able to get by with a single landing page for all the ads in a campaign. In any instance, some custom page design is in order.

The connection between your ad and the landing page is of utmost importance. That means that your landing page *must* discuss or display the product or service promoted in the ad. It probably shouldn't display any other products or services; you don't want to confuse the customer. Remember, a potential customer clicks your ad to find out more about what the ad talked about.

He expects to click to a page that follows seamlessly from what was discussed in the ad.

For this reason, your landing page needs to be consistent with your advertisement, both in terms of content and presentation. That means using the same terminology employed your ad—talk about the same product in the same way. Don't change things up or get greedy about presenting other products. There will be time enough for that later if the customer decides to buy what you're advertising.

> **note** Remember that customers see your ad because they're interested in particular keywords. Make sure to include those keywords not only in your ad but also on your landing page.

And if you're designing a landing page for a PPC image ad, the page should convey the same look and feel of the ad itself. Obviously, this is less important if you're running a text ad, which really doesn't have a visual design. But a landing page for an image ad should look and feel like the ad the customer just clicked.

Naturally, the landing page can and should include more information than you had space to present in the ad. After all, you have a lot more than three lines to work with now. So the landing page should include detailed information about the featured product, as well as more detailed product photos. It should be a real sell page.

> **note** That said, you don't want to hit the customer over the head with too much information. Displaying a landing page that contains paragraph after paragraph of boring details or useless marketing drivel will kill the interest of even the most dedicated potential customers. The information you present has to be both relevant and valuable or it doesn't belong on the page.

Creating a Great-Looking Landing Page

It goes without saying that your landing page should have a professional look and feel. It shouldn't look quick and dirty, but rather have a quality design, just like your main site has. Your page needs to look trustworthy; users are never sure what's on the other side of a click and are quickly turned off by sites that don't make them feel safe.

Your landing page should also be visually clean and easy to read. Customers who can't find what they're looking for will quickly click away. Make it easy to find the information people want.

Remember, first impressions count, and your landing page is the first exposure customers have to your site after they click your ad. Wow them visually, impress them with your content, and then ask for the order. That's the way landing pages are supposed to work.

Asking for the Order

Useful information and professional design aside, the most important element on the product landing page is the click-to-order button. You want customers to buy your product, and presumably they clicked on your ad because they're thinking of buying. Don't make the customer do a lot of work; make it easy to click one button to initiate the order process.

When the customer clicks the order button, she can move to your site's normal shopping cart or checkout section. You can even present add-on items that the customer might also be interested in buying.
But don't get in the customer's way when he or she is in the purchasing mood; make sure the order button is big and obvious and easy to use.

Of course, not all advertisers are in the direct sales business. If you have a different goal for your PPC ad, your landing page should reflect that goal. For example, if you want to collect sales leads, your land-ing page should contain a form to collect customer information. Just make sure that your landing page is the natural next step after clicking your ad and that it asks the customer to take a specific action.

note Another good rea-son to create a differ-ent landing page for each of your PPC ads is because that makes it easier to track sales for each ad. You should be able to track each page separately and thus analyze your sales on a per-ad basis.

Choosing a PPC Ad Network

If you want to advertise your website or business, then you need to join a PPC ad network. The three biggest such networks are owned by the big three search providers—Google, Yahoo!, and Microsoft.

Google AdWords

The largest PPC ad network today is Google AdWords (adwords.google.com). AdWords places ads on Google's own search results pages, throughout its entire network of sites (Gmail, Google Maps, YouTube, and so forth), and on participating affiliate sites. Google claims that its AdWords program reaches more than 80% of all Internet users; most advertisers confirm that AdWords generates the overwhelming majority of PPC traffic to their sites.

note Learn more about Google AdWords in my companion book, *Using Google AdWords and AdSense* (Michael Miller, Que, 2010).

The effectiveness of the AdWords network is due primarily to the fact that with AdWords, you're advertising on the Internet's most popular search engine. Google owns more than half of the total search market; more people search Google than search Yahoo!, Bing, and all other competitors combined. If you want to reach web searchers, then, Google AdWords should be your PPC ad network of choice.

One thing that's a bit different about using AdWords, in contrast to traditional ad buys, is that you specify a *daily* budget. Most traditional advertising media work with monthly budgets; your company most likely has monthly budgets, as well. Google AdWords, however, uses daily budgeting, so you'll need to do a little math to adjust. If you have a monthly PPC ad budget of $10,000, for example, you'll tell Google that you have a $333 daily budget.

Speaking of budgets, just how much does it cost to advertise with AdWords? It's your choice. If you go with the cost-per-click method, you can choose a maximum CPC click price from $0.01 to $100. If you go with the CPM method, there is a minimum cost of $0.25 per 1,000 impressions. Your daily budget can be as low as a penny, up to whatever you're willing to pay.

At the end of each month, AdWords bills you for the number of clicks on your ads or for the number of impressions you contracted for. With CPC billing, if no one clicked your ads, you don't pay anything—but then again, you can hardly call that a success. You only get billed, of course, up to the maximum amount of your budget. If the cost of those clicks is under your budget number, you only pay for the actual clicks, not the maximum amount you budgeted.

Creating an AdWords ad is simplicity itself. Each text ad consists of a short headline, two lines of body text, and the target URL. AdWords also lets you create PPC image ads, although these will appear only on third-party sites, not on Google's search results pages.

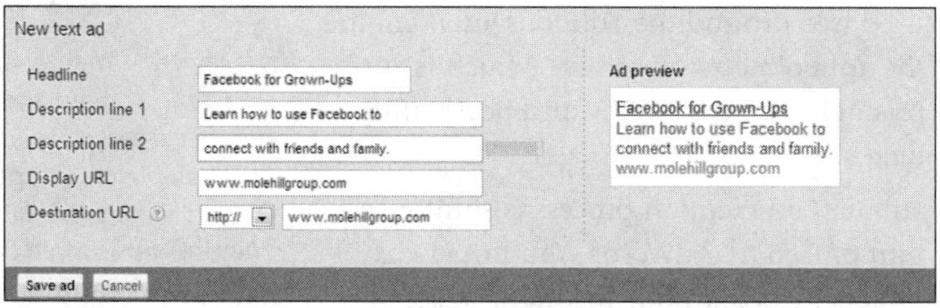

15

FIGURE 15.6

Creating a Google AdWords text ad.

You monitor your AdWords campaigns from the AdWords Dashboard. Google provides a number of different tools and reports to slice and dice your ad performance any number of ways. It's a well-tuned machine, suitable for both small and large advertisers.

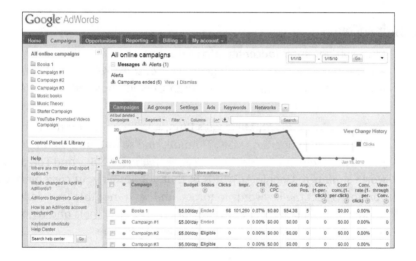

FIGURE 15.7

The Google AdWords Dashboard.

Yahoo! Sponsored Search

Google's number-two competitor in the search market is also the number-two search engine-based PPC ad network. Yahoo! Sponsored Search (advertising. yahoo.com/smallbusiness/ysm) works much like Google AdWords, except that

15

it's based around the Yahoo! search engine, the Yahoo! network of sites (which is surprisingly popular), and third-party affiliated sites.

Yahoo!'s ad creation process is similar to that of Google AdWords. You target customers by geographic location, select the keywords you want to target, set a daily spending limit, create your four-line text ads, and then let it rip. Yahoo! provides a variety of tools and reports for monitoring the success of your ad campaigns as well. You can view these reports online, download them for viewing offline, or have Yahoo! email them to you.

note Yahoo! and Microsoft have formed a formed a search alliance, which will have Microsoft power Yahoo!'s search results and merge Yahoo!'s Sponsored Search advertising platform with Microsoft's adCenter platform. For advertisers, this means that Yahoo! advertising will eventually be subsumed into Microsoft's advertising program—essentially reducing the search-based PPC ad networks from three to two.

Microsoft adCenter

Microsoft adCenter (adcenter.microsoft.com) is Microsoft's PPC advertising network, soon to become even bigger after it absorbs Yahoo!'s network. Even then it will still be considerably smaller than Google's AdWords network, but still worth considering.

adCenter places ads on Microsoft's Bing search engine, on the websites for various Microsoft properties (MSN, Hotmail, and so on), and on affiliated third-party sites—which include the *Wall Street Journal*, CNBC, and Fox Sports. It works similar to Google AdWords in that you target your customers, create your ad, select the keywords to target, and set a monthly (not daily) spending budget. Like Google, Microsoft provides a variety of tools and reports for monitoring the performance of your adCenter campaigns.

Other Sites for PPC Advertising

It's not only the search engines that are big in the PPC advertising game. Other websites have embraced targeted PPC advertising and should be considered as part of your online marketing plan.

PPC Advertising on YouTube

Let's start with two PPC advertising programs that are closely related to Google AdWords. These programs are available on YouTube (www.youtube.com), Google's popular video sharing community.

While videos themselves can be a strong marketing tool, you can make your videos more visible by advertising them on the YouTube site via YouTube's Promoted Videos feature. YouTube Promoted Videos are essentially PPC ads that appear in YouTube search results, whenever a YouTube user searches for a keyword you purchase. Your ad is a small text ad with a clickable thumbnail image; when a customer clicks the thumbnail, he or she plays the video you're promoting. You sign up for the Promoted Videos program at ads.youtube.com.

Promoted Videos

Abbey Road Drums tutorial
Abbey Roads 60s and 70s Drums:
basic parameters & the mixing desk
by **NativeInstruments**   3 weeks ago
48,941 views

2:42

FIGURE 15.8

A YouTube Promoted Videos ad on a YouTube search results page.

There are other advantages to participating in the Promoted Videos program. By default, you can't link from a YouTube video to an external website; the best you can do is include your site's URL as a graphic in your video. But when you advertise the video via the Promoted Videos program, YouTube *does* include external links in your video in the form of a clickable overlay. It's worth spending a little money on Promoted Videos just to activate this external linking feature.

note Learn more about marketing on YouTube in Chapter 36, "Video Marketing."

Promoted Videos ads work just like normal AdWords ads. You bid on one or more keywords, create an ad, and set a daily budget. The only difference is that you have to specify which YouTube video or videos you're promoting and select which thumbnail images you want to include in the ad. Tracking can be done on the YouTube site or via your Google AdWords Dashboard.

note YouTube Promoted Videos is actually part of the Google AdWords program.

You don't have to have a YouTube video to advertise on the YouTube site. YouTube uses Google AdWords to place regular text ads across the YouTube site. Again, you

note YouTube also offers a variety of display advertising options, including video ads and InVideo ads that appear as animated overlay on other videos. Learn more at www.youtube.com/t/advertising/.

purchase (or rather bid on) one or more keywords; your ad appears when someone searches for a video using that keyword or on video pages where the video content matches the keyword you've targeted. You create these ads from your Google AdWords account.

PPC Advertising on Facebook

Another site that lets you create PPC ads targeted to its userbase is Facebook, the big social networking site. Facebook advertising is targeted to specific users, matching the demographics you select with the personal information provided by each Facebook user.

> **note** Learn more about Facebook marketing in Chapter 28, "Marketing on Facebook, MySpace, and Twitter."

That's right, Facebook offers PPC advertising that appears on users' profile pages. The ads are simple text ads with a title, body copy, and optional small (110x80 pixel) image; the entire ad is clickable to your target URL. A Facebook ad can link to either a Facebook fan page or to your external website. Go to www.facebook.com/advertising/ to get started.

FIGURE 15.9

A typical PPC text ad on a Facebook user profile page.

Facebook advertising is a little different from traditional PPC advertising in that you don't use keywords. Instead, you select specific targeting options—demographic criteria that ultimately determine which users are shown your ad. You can target potential customers by the following criteria:

- **Location**—You can target by country, state/province, or city.
- **Age**—Specify an age range to target.
- **Birthday**—Lets you display ads to people on their birthdays.
- **Sex**—Target either males or females.
- **Education level**—Target college graduates, college students, or high school students. You can also target students of particular schools or universities.

- **Workplace**—Lets you target employees of specific companies.
- **Relationship status**—You can target singles, married people, engaged people, or those "in a relationship."
- **Relationship interest**—Lets you target people who are interested in either men or women (or both).
- **Language**—Target speakers of a given language.
- **Connections**—Lets you target people who are members or users of a specific Facebook group, event, fan page, or application.
- **Likes and interests**—This is the closest Facebook has to keyword targeting; you can target specific types of music or movies, hobbies, and the like.

So, for example, you can target gay males (males interested in other males) who are single, college graduates, and work at the United States Postal Service. Or over-40 females who are interested in death metal and read books by Dr. Seuss. As you make your selections, Facebook displays how many users match your criteria; this provides interactive feedback on your targeting.

note Facebook offers both CPC and CPM payment models, although most advertisers go the CPC route.

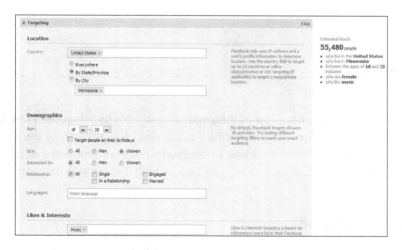

FIGURE 15.10

Creating a Facebook PPC ad.

Once you've selected the targeting criteria, you select the maximum CPC you're willing to pay and your daily budget. Set a schedule for the ad campaign, and Facebook does the rest, displaying your ad to people who fit your targeted demographics.

PPC Advertising on Twitter

As this book is being written, Twitter has announced that it, too, will join the ranks of ad-supported services and start offering PPC ads on its search results pages. Twitter's "Promoted Tweets" are initially open to a select group of large advertisers (Virgin America, Best Buy, Starbucks, and the like) but are expected to be available to other—and smaller—advertisers at some point.

These Promoted Tweets are just that—regular tweets (not ads, per se) that are promoted by their creators. They appear at the top of the search results page, with a "Promoted by *Advertiser*" tag under the tweet.

If you want to advertise in this fashion, you have to do it within Twitter's 140-character constraint. As you'll learn in Chapter 28, there's a lot you can say within 140 characters, but this is an even shorter message than you have with typical Google or Yahoo! text ads.

FIGURE 15.11

A Promoted Tweet on Twitter.

There's not a whole lot of information available as yet on the Promoted Tweets program; it's unclear how much each ad costs or how the ads are synched to Twitter searches. Undoubtedly more information will be forthcoming as the program progresses; check in with Twitter to learn more.

The Bottom Line

Pay-per-click advertising is the dominant form of advertising on the Web today—particularly among smaller advertisers and online retailers. PPC ads are typically small three- or four-line text ads, although some ad networks offer PPC image ads.

PPC ads are most often context-sensitive ads, in that the ad content is matched with the content of the host web page. PPC ads also appear on search results pages from Google and the other major search engines when someone searches for a keyword associated with the ad.

A PPC advertiser bids on one or more keywords, which determine where the ad is displayed. No payment is made when the ad is displayed; payment is due only when a person clicks the ad. PPC ads are typically sold by PPC ad networks, such as Google AdWords. PPC ads can also be purchased on YouTube, Facebook, and similar sites.

DEALING WITH CLICK FRAUD

When it comes to placing PPC advertising, there's one important issue you need to be aware of: *click fraud*. This type of fraud is a deliberate effort to defraud advertisers who pay for their ads by the click; it occurs when a link within an online ad is clicked for the sole purpose of generating a charge per click, with no actual interest in the ad itself or the site linked to within the ad. It drives up your ad costs without generating additional revenue.

Most instances of click fraud directly benefit the entity doing the clicking. Typically the ad that is clicked resides on the perpetrator's own website. Because host websites receive a portion of all PPC revenues via a PPC ad hosting program, such as Google AdSense, every click on a site's ads results in money flowing into the pockets of the site's owner. By perpetrating click fraud, the site owner artificially inflates the revenue his site earns from the hosted ads.

Here's the way it often works. An individual obtains a web domain and creates a website, often nothing more than a "link farm"—a site without any real content of its own, just links to other sites and text designed to attract hits from popular keywords at the major search sites. The site owner signs up with AdSense or another ad program and places a variety of PPC ads on the site. To generate revenue, then, the site owner—through manual or automated means—clicks multiple times on the ads on his own site. Each click generates PPC revenue, thus lining his own pockets.

15

Other instances of click fraud are designed more to harm the advertiser than to benefit the host website. For example, a competitor of an advertiser might use click fraud to generate a bevy of irrelevant clicks, thus draining the competitor's advertising budget with nothing to show for it.

Fortunately, all the major PPC ad networks have mechanisms in place to identify and block click fraud inside their ad networks. But they can't block all attempts; Click Forensics estimates that in the third quarter of 2009, 14.1% of all ad clicks were fraudulent. (For what it's worth, Google disputes this figure, claiming that click fraud on its network is less than 2%).

Whatever the rate, click fraud does exist and can impact your online advertising campaign. For this reason, as an advertiser you need to constantly monitor your click-through rates and your conversion rates (measured by information requests, leads, merchandise sales, or whatever). If you see a spike in PPC traffic that is not offset by a corresponding increase in conversion rates, you can suspect click fraud. You can also use click fraud detection tools, software programs that monitor your website traffic for irregular patterns, and then flag potentially fraudulent clicks.

If you suspect that you're a victim of click fraud, you need to report your suspicions to your PPC ad network and ask for a refund. Most ad networks will work with you on this; it's in their own best interest to weed out click fraud and keep their advertisers happy.

Display Advertising

When it comes to online ad spending, about a third of all web ad budgets are devoted to display advertising. For our purposes, we define display advertising as any type of web advertising that isn't a text ad; that includes banner ads, image ads, video ads, even those ads that creep down or across the page of their own volition.

The very first online advertising, back in the 1980s, was display advertising; for the record, these ads were on the pre-Internet Prodigy network, promoting products from co-owner Sears. On the Internet proper, the first clickable ad was a 1993 banner ad on the old GNN (Global Network Navigator) site, promoting a Silicon Valley law firm. (The term "banner ad" was coined by HotWired CEO Rick Boyce in 1994. HotWired was one of earliest proponents of clickable, trackable ads.)

The point is that display advertising has always been a big part of the online marketing mix and remains so today. Just how you employ display advertising depends on your own particular goals and, to some degree, your creativity.

Are Display Ads Effective?

Display advertising is big business and getting bigger. From those first web banner ads in 1994, display advertising grew to become the economic foundation of the online advertising industry throughout the rest of the decade.

Display advertising's dominance receded at the turn of the century, replaced by text-based PPC search advertising of the type discussed in the previous chapter. But a decade later, display advertising is again on the rise, led by many of the same players who dominate the PPC advertising industry— Google, Yahoo!, and Microsoft.

Sizing the Display Advertising Market

How big is the display advertising market? The Internet Advertising Bureau (IAB) estimates that display advertising represents about a third of the $20 billion or so online advertising market in the U.S., or close to $8 billion in revenue. That's second only to search advertising, which accounts for about half of all online advertising revenue. (For what it's worth, the U.S. advertising market is about half of the global market, so figure global display advertising revenue at $16 billion or so.)

Display advertising's share of the market is rising slightly, especially with the easing of the so-called Great Recession. During the economic downturn of 2008–2009, many advertisers switched from relatively expensive display advertising to lower-cost PPC text ads. With the economy returning, advertisers are shifting some of their dollars back to display ads.

Judging the Effectiveness of Display Advertising

Know, however, that even as display advertising appears to be increasing in popularity, it also appears to be decreasing in effectiveness—at least as measured by click-through rates.

One chief example of this is a March, 2010, study by research firm comScore, which found that the percentage of U.S. Internet users who clicked display ads at least once a month fell from 32% to 16% over a 20-month period ending in March, 2009. That's not necessarily a good thing.

However, counting clicks is just one way to measure the effectiveness of display advertising. Unlike PPC text ads, display ads also have a brand-enhancing function. So as comScore Director of Industry Analysis Andrew Lipsman said, measuring the success of a display ad solely by its clicks "grossly understates the importance of an advertising campaign."

That is, some potential customers remember an ad without clicking it; it has impact from being viewed without necessarily being clicked. Studies have found that merely looking at a display ad increases the likelihood that a viewer will later search for the brand or make a purchase. To that end, many display ads are aimed solely at building brand awareness; for these image-building ads, clicks are relatively unimportant.

Quantifying this, a Yahoo! study found that 78% of the sales effect from display advertising comes from those who view but do not click display ads. Only 22% of the sales come from those who do click the ads.

When to Employ Display Advertising

Knowing that display advertising has impact even (if not especially) when people don't immediately click the ad, how should you incorporate display advertising in your company's online marketing mix?

While display advertising can be used to drive direct sales of a product or service, it's better used to raise awareness of a product or brand. That is, display advertising is primarily a brand-building vehicle.

As such, you should use display advertising to push a higher-level brand or product message. Use display ads to build or reinforce your brand or to introduce new products or product lines. Don't expect a large sales increase to immediately result.

If you do employ display advertising to drive direct sales, be prepared for extremely low click-through rates. Most display ads have CTRs less than 1%, which isn't going to drive a lot of traffic.

Choosing a Payment Model

The low CTR explains why most display ads are sold on a CPM basis instead of the CPC model used for most text advertising. Paying for impressions—the CPM model—has been the most common model for display advertising. That doesn't mean it will remain the most common, however.

CPM ads are the de facto standard because display ads are all about capturing eyeballs rather than capturing clicks. That is, because you're not necessarily encouraging clicks with an image-building ad, there's no reason to pay for clicks. Instead, the goal is to get the ad in front of as many eyeballs as possible, which means you want to pay for impressions. That's the CPM model.

note CPM rates today tend to range from $20 to $100 per thousand impressions, with $50 being about average. Know, however, that where the ad is placed significantly affects both response and CPM rates. Placing your ad high on the home page of a major website will not only deliver more viewers, but you'll have to pay more for them, too.

That said, there is a subtle but definite shift from the CPM to the CPC model. As you should be familiar by now, with the CPC model you pay only when an ad is clicked; you don't pay for placement or impressions.

This shift to the CPC model may reflect advertisers' movement toward higher accountability; they want to be sure that people are actually viewing their ads, so it's natural to push for a click to register some sort of action. That action doesn't have to lead to a sale; you can simply ask viewers to click to learn more, to download a brochure, or whatever. The key is to ask for action and then register (and pay for) the click.

Setting a Display Ad Budget

Display advertising isn't really for small advertisers. To get sufficient reach, you have to pay for a large number of impressions. That typically means buying space on high-traffic websites that charge a high CPM.

So how much does a display ad cost? That depends on a lot of factors, of course. You'll pay more for larger ads, for better (top of fold) position, for higher-traffic websites. And of course you pay more for running your ad more often.

That said, a top-of-page banner ad on a high-volume website like AOL.com can cost you upward of a half million dollars. On the other hand, the same ad on my personal website can be had for a ham sandwich and a handful of beads. Ultimately, however, you get what you pay for; if you want a lot of impressions, you have to pony up the appropriately large budget.

Examining Rich Media Ads

When it comes to display advertising, there's no one single type. Today's display ads can be image ads (that is, they consist of a static graphic image) or rich media ads. And when it comes to rich media, the sky's the limit.

What is rich media? It's anything that moves or plays or that delivers dynamic content to the targeted audience. In short, you can look at ads that offer any or all of the following:

- Voice narration or music
- Video playback
- Animated elements
- "Frame-breaking" construction, where elements of the ad break out of the traditional ad frame and move across the underlying page
- Expandability, where the ad itself shrinks or grows dependent on some action

- Dynamic content, such as live Twitter or blog feeds inserted into the ad
- User interaction

FIGURE 16.1
A rich media video ad for VeriSign—playback is automatic.

FIGURE 16.2
Hovering over this ad for JW Marriott causes it to expand down the top of the New York Daily News *home page.*

FIGURE 16.3
This rich media ad from Insurance.com encourages viewers to play a game of "catch the coins."

Image ads are also typically interactive ads. That is, there's something that happens when the viewer clicks the ad. Maybe a video starts to play, or the animation changes, or there are additional options, such as more photos or things to download or such. In any case, you use the rich media to engage the customer—to make him do something that brings him closer to you.

An image ad, in contrast, is just a picture. A *still* picture. That isn't necessarily a bad thing, especially from a technological standpoint. There are several issues with rich media ads, concerning both download time (audio and video files can be rather large and slow to download over a slow Internet connection) and compatibility (not all users have the state-of-the-art technology installed to play back all rich media ads). If you want to guarantee a no-hassle experience with all users, ditch the rich media and stick with a simple image ad.

On the other hand, rich media ads can really pull viewers into your message. Watching a character walk across the web page while talking directly to the viewer can be a compelling experience. And some people will always stop to watch a video on any web page.

Rich media content also enables an unparalleled degree of creativity. Volvo, for example, used rich media to embed a Twitter feed from the New York Auto Show into ads for its new XC60 vehicle. (The ad also used copious amounts of Flash animation and used Flash to offer additional videos, photos, a 360-degree product tour, and online games.) And an ad for Harley Davidson encouraged viewer participation via both embedded video and the capability for viewers to add their own comments and "send a tribute to our troops." Pretty creative in both instances.

FIGURE 16.4
Volvo's rich media ad, complete with Twitter feed.

FIGURE 16.5
Harley Davidson's rich media ad with embedded video and viewer comments.

The real benefit of rich media ads, of course, is their effectiveness—which is measurable. By most accounts, rich media ads typically have a CTR two to four times that of simple image ads, which means moving from a 1% (or less) CTR to something in the 3% range. That's significant.

So if you want to stretch your imagination, stand out from the pack of static image

note Neither the Volvo or Harley Davidson ads were easy or cheap to produce. Both required the skills of pricey web advertising agencies to implement; these are probably not the kinds of ads you can create in-house on a small budget.

16

ads, and increase your CTR, by all means incorporate rich media into your display advertising. You won't be alone; by most accounts, more than 40% of all display ads incorporate some form of rich media content.

Choosing a Display Ad Format

Whether you go with a plain image ad or a fancy rich media one, you also have to decide on the size of the ad you want. For many years, display ads were synonymous with banner ads, those horizontal ads that stretch across the top of the page. But there are places on a page other than the top where you can place an ad, and that placement will to some degree determine the size and shape of the ad.

Display ads can, of course, be horizontal banner ads. They can also be vertical skyscrapers or smaller square or rectangular ads. In fact, the IAB has compiled a list of 18 common web ad formats of various shapes and sizes, as detailed in Table 16.1. Pick the format that works best for your particular message.

Table 16.1   IAB Recommended Ad Units

Ad Unit	Size (width x height, in pixels)	Recommended File Size
Leaderboard	728 x 90	40kb
Pop-Under	720 x 300	40kb
Full Banner	468 x 60	40kb
Large Rectangle	336 x 280	40kb
Half Page Ad	300 x 600	40kb
Medium Rectangle	300 x 250	40kb
3:1 Rectangle	300 x 100	40kb
Square Pop-Up	250 x 250	40kb
Vertical Rectangle	240 x 400	40kb

(continued)

Table 16.1 IAB Recommended Ad Units (continued)		
Ad Unit	Size (width x height, in pixels)	Recommended File Size
Half Banner	234 x 60	30kb
Rectangle	180 x 150	40kb
Wide Skyscraper	160 x 600	40kb
Square Button	125 x 125	30kb
Skyscraper	120 x 600	40kb
Vertical Banner	120 x 240	30kb
Button 1	120 x 90	20kb
Button 2	120 x 60	20kb
Micro Bar	88 x 31	10kb

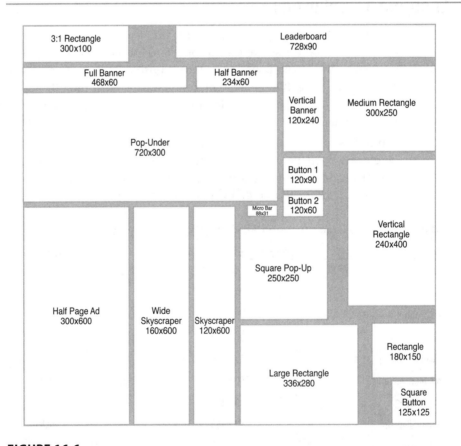

FIGURE 16.6

Standard web display ad sizes, as recommended by the Interactive Advertising Bureau (IAB).

Of course, you're not limited to a single ad format. You can employ different formats on different sites or even place multiple ads in multiple formats on the same page. This particular approach can be effective; if you don't get their attention with a top-of-page banner, the smaller rectangle ad further down the page might just do the trick. Or, even better, the two ads work together to reinforce your message. It's an increasingly popular approach.

FIGURE 16.7
Dual ads for Breaking Bad on the Salon website; a banner at the top, reinforced by a rectangular ad a little lower on the page.

Best Practices: Creating Effective Display Ads

Want to create an effective display ad? To do so, you need to consider not only ad media and size, but also position, content, and all sorts of other stuff. Read on for some tips on best practices for display advertising.

Choose the Best Ad Format

When it comes to deciding on what ad format to employ, the first thing you need to do is to adhere to IAB standards. Many websites simply won't accept non-IAB standard ads.

With that in mind, know that when it comes to advertising effectiveness, bigger is better. It should come as no surprise that wider ad formats tend to outperform narrower formats—even if the narrower ad is also taller. It's all about readability. Visitors can read more at a glance with a wider ad than they can with a taller one.

To that end, advertisers have found the following formats to be among the most effective:

- 728×90 leaderboard
- 468×60 banner
- 336×280 large rectangle
- 300×250 medium rectangle
- 160×600 wide skyscraper

That's two horizontal banners, a vertical skyscraper, and two largish rectangles. As you can see, these are all fairly large ad units and thus are dominant on the underlying page.

Obviously, you should experiment with different ad sizes, as well as ad positions, to find the ones that work best for your ads. But there's nothing like size for getting you noticed.

Keep It Small

While we're talking about ad sizes, you also need to consider the file size of the ad—the size of the image or video or Flash file that loads when the ad is displayed. In general, you want to keep file sizes as small as possible—for most formats, under 40kb. Anything larger and you will affect the viewership of the ad.

There's a good reason for keeping things small. While many Internet users connect over fast broadband connections, many don't. And if the connection speed is constrained, it takes a long time to download big files. Given that your display ad is likely on the top half of the page, that means it gets loaded before the underlying content. You don't want to tick off potential customers as they wait for your ad to load before they can view the page content they came there for.

Choose the Best Position

You don't always get a vote in where your display ad appears on a page. But if you can choose your ad position, where should you place it? That is, what position delivers the best results? It isn't always (and in fact seldom is) the very top of the page.

There are some variables to consider, but in general the best position for a display ad is nearest the page's core content that can be seen without scrolling. That typically means near the top-middle of the page, either above, to the left, or below the main content.

note In general, ads perform better on the left side of a page than on the right. That's because we all read from left to right and see the left-side content before that on the right.

To help you determine the best ad position, Google put together a "heat map" of possible ad positions and ranked the different positions in terms of click-through potential. Place your ads in one of the slots marked 1 or 2 to get the best results; avoid those slots with higher numbers.

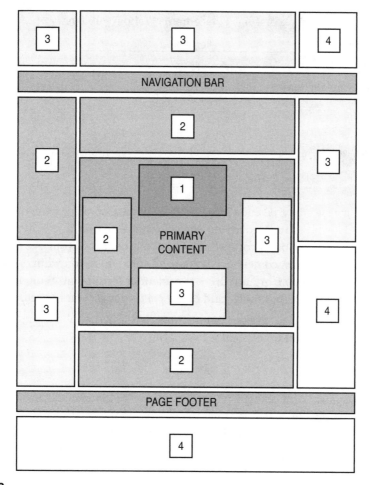

FIGURE 16.8

Position ads in the lower-numbered positions to achieve the best results. (Heat map courtesy Google.)

As you can see from this map, it's important to place your ads near important content; you want visitors to see the ads when they view must-read content. That points out another good position for ads—directly after the end of an article, blog post, or other editorial content. You also get a good bang for your buck by positioning ads *between* other elements, such as between articles or blog posts. Also good is placement near navigational elements, such as menus and back/up buttons.

This advice is reinforced by a 2007 pool of websites by the Yahoo! Publisher Network, shown in Table 16.2. These publishers found the best results came from ads embedded near important content on the page, followed by ads placed "above the fold" (on the top half of a web page) and between the top navigation and the page's main content.

Table 16.2   Most Successful Ad Placements (Yahoo! Publishers)

Ad Placement	Response
Embedded in content	44.66%
Leaderboard (top of page banner)	27.32%
Right rail	9.28%
Left rail	7.88%
Rotating positions	4.73%
Below the fold	1.93%

Of course, "best position" for an ad depends to some degree on the content and layout of the underlying page. To that end, take a look at the page from the viewpoint of one of the site's visitors. Where does your eye go? What's the most important content on the page? That's where you want to place your ads—somewhere around this key content or focal point. Yeah, it might be a little intrusive, but that's kind of the point—it gets you noticed.

Bottom line: Top is better than bottom, left is better than right, and butting up against important content is best of all.

Blend In

This next bit of advice isn't quite as strong as the previous tips but still should be considered. When it comes to considering the color scheme of your ad, are you better to blend in with the underlying page or stand out from it?

Now, you might think that contrast with the page would draw eyeballs to your ad. That's probably true, but it also easily identifies your ad as an ad, something apart from the underlying page—and to many readers, something undesirable. You get more *clicks* by blending into the page's color scheme. To some readers, it must look as if your ad is part of the native content and thus more valid than a blatant advertisement.

> **note** To further help your ad blend in with the underlying content, don't put a border around your ad.

Of course, you don't always know what the color scheme will be of the pages where your ads will appear, which is why this tip may be of lesser value to you. But if you have the choice, especially if the underlying page has a light background, manipulate your ad's color scheme to blend in with this background.

That said, many advertisers have found that bright colors in their ads result in higher CTRs. To that end, blue, yellow, and green are better colors to use than simple black or white. And you should use red only sparingly; it attracts attention, but not in a good way.

Include a Call to Action

It should go without saying that if you want the reader to click your ad, you need to make that clear. Include some sort of call to action, such as a "submit" or "click for more information" button. Without such a call to action, most readers assume a banner ad is like a billboard, not meant for interaction.

Keep It Short

If you have an animated display ad, keep the animation relatively short. Surveys show that viewers spend less than 10 seconds looking at the top of a web page. You have to display all your content within this time frame, including—and especially—your call to action. Dispense with long animations and get your message out there as quickly as possible.

Link to a Landing Page

We've discussed this before, but it bears repeating. You should never have your display ad link to your site's home page or to some other generic page on your site. Create a landing page specific to each ad that continues the ad's look and feel and message. You want the potential customer to have a seamless experience when he clicks your ad; it should be a continuation of the path started when the customer first viewed the ad.

Test It

Don't assume that you'll get everything right on the first try. You should always include a period of testing for different display ad approaches. You can test different sizes, placements, content, and the like. Evaluate responses on a regular basis and go with the ads that perform the best. You might be surprised how something small, like changing the font or background color, can improve an ad's performance.

Where to Purchase Web Display Ads

We've done a lot of talking about web display ads. Assuming you can find your own source for creating these ads (either in-house or via an ad agency), where do you go to purchase the display ad space?

Directly from the Site

For some advertisers, the first stop for purchasing space is at the sites where you want to advertise. Now, not every website accepts ad buys directly, but many do. It's not just the big sites, either; many smaller sites like to bypass the middlemen (and their commissions) and accept advertising directly.

If you have the staff and the experience and you know precisely where you want your ads to appear, there's no harm in asking those sites for direct ad placement. If you can go direct, it'll probably cost you less—and put more money into the pockets of the host websites.

Display Ad Networks and Exchanges

For most advertisers, however, display ad space is purchased via some sort of ad network or exchange. The big three PPC ad networks all have space advertising arms; there are also a number of other large display ad networks that would be glad to help you get your ads placed.

Let's start with the big three PPC ad networks, who aren't necessarily the big three display ad networks—although they're all near the top of the list. The advantage of going through these networks is that you're likely to have a prior relationship with them, and it's easy to extend from your PPC ads to include display ads to the mix.

Here are the networks to start with:

- DoubleClick by Google (www.doubleclick.com)
- Yahoo! Advertising Display Solutions (advertising.yahoo.com)
- Microsoft Advertising (advertising.microsoft.com)

Other display ad networks were listed back in Chapter 14, "Understanding Online Advertising." Many, such as AOL Advertising (advertising.aol.com), are associated with a specific network of sites; others sell ads across a variety of sites. And, as with all online advertising, there's nothing wrong with using more than one network to further extend your reach.

Purchasing Remnant Inventory

Most ad networks sell premium space—the exact space you want on the sites you specify. But most sites don't sell out all the premium space; they still have space available on their sites that goes unsold.

This *remnant inventory* is the same exact space as a site's premium space; it's simply space that is left over after the primary space has been claimed. As such, it sells at discount and could be a good buy for your advertising program.

There are ad networks that specialize in selling remnant inventory. These networks buy up the unused space from a variety of websites and then package it to their advertisers for pennies on the dollar. Now, you don't always get the choice of websites for your ad to appear, but you don't pay as much as you do with premium space, either.

For the host websites, selling remnant inventory is a lot better than leaving the available space empty; they get a little bit of income, and they don't have to leave white space on their pages. For advertisers, the benefit is purely monetary; you get your ads out there for less than you would if you purchased premium space.

To that end, including remnant inventory in your advertising plan might make sense. Even if you still purchase premium space on the sites you really want to use, you can supplement these placements with additional remnant purchases. It's certainly cost effective.

The Bottom Line

Display advertising is the best way to establish your brand or product online. Most display ads are sold on a CPM basis, which is fine if you're most interested in generating impressions. There is, however, a movement toward PPC display ads, if in fact you have actual conversion in mind.

Display ads can be image-only ads, or they can include all manner of rich media. State-of-the-art display ads often incorporate Flash animations, video and audio playback, and even interactive elements for the consumer to click.

As such, display ads come in all sizes and shapes and can be placed virtually anywhere on the underlying web page; the dominance of the top-of-page banner ad is long over.

HOW ANNOYING IS YOUR ADVERTISING?

Advertising has always been a bit of push and pull between what advertisers want and what consumers want. In general, advertisers want more people to notice their ads. And in general, consumers want to read what they want to see without having ads pushed in their faces. Somewhat of a conflict, isn't it?

This is particularly true on the Web. If you want your display ads to be noticed, you have to try more and more intrusive stunts—big images, autoplay music and video, annoying animations, even ads that capture the page until the customer performs some action. All this fancy stuff gets your ad noticed—and hated by a majority of web users.

I have to side with consumers on this one. I hate, absolutely despise, ads that interrupt my web browsing. I don't want to see an animated mascot cavort across my screen, obscuring what I'm trying to read. I don't want the article I'm reading to be pushed down to the bottom of the screen by an expanding ad. I don't want my valuable Internet bandwidth taken up by an unwanted video playing in the background. And I certainly don't want loud music or an annoying voice blaring out from my computer speakers just because I happened to load a page that hosted a particular ad. These are all unwanted and unnecessary intrusions and earn more ill will than good for those advertisers.

(And it's worth remembering that the most popular and arguably most effective form of web advertising remains the nondescript PPC text ad. That says something, doesn't it?)

On the other hand, I understand the need for advertisers to stand out from all the background noise. The simple fact is that most users ignore banner ads unless something is going on to draw their attention. You have to do *something*, don't you?

Maybe you do; maybe you don't. Making noise and creating animations just to be *doing something* probably isn't in your customers' best interests. Loud noises and fancy animations in and of themselves don't lend a lot of value; they're bells and whistles for the sake of having bells and whistles.

If, however, you can employ these technologies for the benefit of potential customers, you may have something. Maybe you incorporate a live Twitter feed into a display ad or use HTML technology to let customers take part in a poll or provide feedback on a new product or feature. You could employ Flash animation to let customers take a 360-degree product tour—but only if they click to do so. You get the picture. Implement useful features that interested consumers can use and that don't automatically engage and annoy.

So when it comes to display advertising, which practices are acceptable and which should you avoid? To me, the guiding rule comes down to this: Don't interrupt the underlying content of the page. You can try to draw attention away from what the customer is reading but never ever obscure it.

First off, then, you should avoid rich media animations that prance about outside the main ad frame. Nothing obscures the underlying content more than an animated figure dancing on top of it. It's more than just annoying—it's rude.

Along the same lines, resist the temptation to employ automatically expanding ads, the kind that either expand on top of underlying content or push that content further down the page. I don't want an article to keep moving up and down while I'm trying to read it; it makes me want to leave the page completely, which isn't good for either the advertiser or the owner of the underlying page. (You can, of course, have an ad that expands when the viewer clicks it; just avoid those that expand without warning.)

To that end, you should avoid ads that play music without prompting. Loud, unexpected music is certainly intrusive. It's okay to allow music playback when a button is clicked, but don't force the 99% of page viewers who aren't interested to listen to your musical choices.

I'd also recommend against video playback that starts as soon as a page is loaded. This one is more about unnecessary bandwidth usage than it is interfering with the page viewing experience, but should still be avoided; not everybody reading a page has a fast broadband connection.

16

16

These are my suggestions, in any case. Just remember, it's a fine line between being interesting and being annoying, as anyone dealing with a drunk at a cocktail party can tell you. Your job is to be engaging, not bothersome—and certainly not so drunk on the technology that you force your message on those who just aren't interested.

Tracking Ad Performance

Once your ad campaign is underway, it's time to start tracking its performance. That means looking at different types of raw data and then analyzing that data in various ways. You can learn from both your successes and your failures and use this information to create better-performing campaigns in the future.

Using Tracking Tools

How do you track ad performance? Most ad networks offer their own set of reports and tracking tools, and for most advertisers these are sufficient. Just display the report that contains the data you want and then view the results—piece of cake.

Tracking with Google AdWords

The reports and tools vary from ad network to ad network, but we can use Google AdWords as a representative example.

AdWords provides much of its reporting data on the main page, or Dashboard, located at adwords.google.com. Select the Campaigns tab and then select different subtabs to view specific types of data:

- **Campaigns**—Tracks performance of whole campaigns, including your daily budget, campaign status, total number of clicks received, total number of impressions for your ads, the click-through rate, average cost per click, total cost of the campaign, average position for your ads, and various conversion data.

- **Ad Groups**—With AdWords, a group of ads revolving around a group of keywords is called an *ad group*. This subtab lets you track performance by ad group—clicks, impressions, CTR, and the like.

- **Settings**—This subtab lets you view and edit various account settings.

- **Ads**—Tracks performance of the individual ads you've created.

- **Keywords**—Tracks performance for each keyword you've bid on, including clicks, CPC, CTR, cost, and so on.

- **Networks**—Tracks performance by AdWords channel—Google's search site, search partners, and content network.

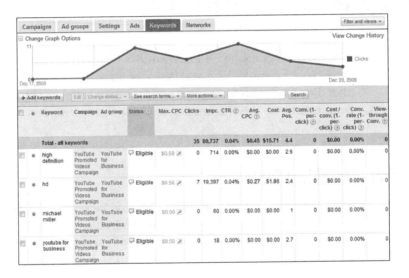

FIGURE 17.1

Tracking keyword performance with Google AdWords.

AdWords also lets you create custom reports based on this raw data. Use the AdWords Report Center to select which data you want displayed in your report, along with time frame you want analyzed. You can display your reports onscreen, download them in Excel or .html format, or have them emailed to you on a set schedule.

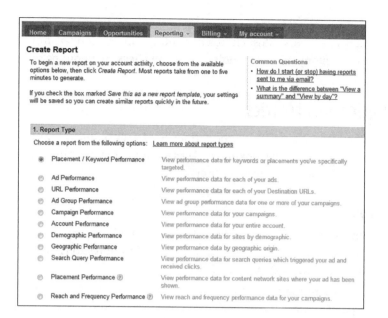

FIGURE 17.2

Creating a custom Google AdWords report.

Using Third-Party Tracking Tools

You may be satisfied with the tracking tools provided by the ad networks you use. Or you may not. In either case, you may want to check out some third-party online ad tracking tools.

Most of these tools offer reports and analysis that go beyond what you get from your ad network. One thing you get from a third-party tracking tool is the ability to track ads across multiple ad networks and compare the performance of each network.

Some of the more popular third-party ad tracking tools include the following:

- AdWatcher (www.adwatcher.com)
- Clickable Pro (www.clickable.com)
- Conversion Ruler (www.conversionruler.com)
- CrucialStats (www.crucialstats.com)
- HitsLink (www.hitslink.com)
- OneStat (www.onestat.com)

note In addition, many of the web analytics tools discussed in Chapter 9, "Tracking Website Analytics," including Google Analytics, track various ad-related metrics.

Of course, you pay to use these tools; they're not free, like the ones are from your ad network. Most charge a monthly subscription fee, from $10/month on up, but many offer free trials so you can check them out before you invest.

Evaluating Key Metrics

When you're tracking the performance of your online ad campaign, what data should you be looking at? Let's examine the most important metrics for both PPC and display advertisers.

Impressions

How many times was your ad displayed? That's the *impressions* metric, which is key for CPM display advertising; the more impressions, the more people who were exposed to your ad.

Impressions are also important for PPC advertising. You need your ad to be displayed before it can be clicked; the more impressions you get for your ads, the more clicks you'll theoretically generate.

Obviously, when it comes to impressions, more is better. If your ad or campaign is generating a low number of impressions, you won't get your message across—or generate a lot of clicks.

There are a number of ways to increase the number of impressions an ad receives. This may be as simple as increasing your ad budget or raising your bids on selected keywords; higher bidders get more and better ad placements. You can also increase your impressions by selecting higher-traffic or more appropriate websites for your ads.

In addition, improving the performance of the keywords you select will increase your impressions. That might mean changing from inexact to exact matching or even selecting a different set of keywords for a particular ad. You can also work to improve the effectiveness of your ad's landing page—a low quality score for this page can result in your ad not being displayed as often.

Clicks

How many times was your ad clicked? That's the *clicks* metric, key to PPC advertising; the more clicks, the more traffic you have to your landing page.

As with impressions, the more clicks you get, the better. Of course, you can't get a lot of clicks if you don't start with a lot of impressions, so that's always job one. But a large number of impressions doesn't always result in a large number of clicks; if your ad isn't interesting or compelling, people won't be inspired to click it.

You can improve the number of clicks by improving the effectiveness of your ads. For text ads, you should include more powerful words in your copy, make sure you talk about your unique selling proposition, and include a compelling call to action. For display ads, consider changing your image, including animation, and adding other rich media content. Just remember, the more effective your ad, the more clicks you'll get.

Click-Through Rate (CTR)

Raw clicks are important but not necessarily the best measurement of an ad's effectiveness. You can't generate a lot of clicks, after all, if you have minimal impressions.

A better measurement of ad effectiveness, then, is the click-through rate (CTR). This metric measures the number of clicks as a percentage of the number of impressions. A high CTR indicates that your ad is doing its job; a low CTR indicates that you need to retool your ad copy.

> **note** You can estimate the number of clicks you might generate if you increase the number of impressions by multiplying your current CTR by the higher impressions number.

Remember, CTR is totally independent of the number of impressions your ad receives. This enables advertisers on a budget to compare the effectiveness of their ads against big-budget competitors. If your ad has a high CTR, increasing your budget is sure to result in more absolute clicks—and more customer conversions.

Percent of Clicks Served

When looking at the performance of individual ads within an online ad campaign, take a gander at the *percent of clicks served* metric. This data point tells you which ads in an ad group are getting the most displays. It divides the number of impressions for a given ad by the total number of impressions for all the ads in the ad group.

An ad with a higher percent of clicks served number is outperforming the other ads in the campaign; an ad with a lower number is underperforming the other ads. Of course, this isn't so much a measurement of the ad as it is the keywords chosen to display that ad, so consider this in your analysis.

Average Position

In what position was your ad displayed on a search engine's results pages? That's the *average position* for an ad, and higher is always better.

The higher an ad's position, the more clicks the ad will get and the more traffic that ad will drive to your landing page. Advertisers are always striving for higher positions—to a point. You don't want to outspend your campaign by bidding to achieve one of the top two positions. You may be better off aiming for a slightly lower position at a corresponding lower cost.

> **note** Higher positions also cost more per click, so keep that in mind.

Cost

How much have you paid in total for a given keyword, ad, or campaign? That's the *cost* metric—as in, this item cost you this much money over a specific time frame.

Note that your cost for an ad campaign will never exceed your specified budget. In fact, it most often will come in *under* your budget, as you won't always be the high bidder on all the keywords you choose. Consider your daily budget as a max spend amount; your actual spending is reflected in the cost metric.

Conversions

Next, we come to the topic of *conversions*. A conversion occurs when someone clicks your ad and then proceeds to purchase what you're selling, or otherwise do what you want them to do.

Most ad networks let you track a number of conversion-related metrics:

- **Conversions**—The total number of actions taken by people who clicked your ad. Conversions can never exceed clicks.
- **Cost per conversion**—How much each conversion cost you.
- **Conversion rate**—The number of conversions divided by the number of clicks.
- **View-through conversions**—Tracks the number of conversions that happen within 30 days of a customer clicking your ad. (Regular conversions measure actions that occur immediately after a click.) The assumption here is that just viewing your ad can lead to a sale some time later; the sale doesn't have to happen immediately after the ad is served.

Obviously, if you're trying to generate sales revenue from your advertising, tracking conversions is important. While clicks matter, revenue matters more—and conversions are directly related to revenue generated.

Customer Engagement

Now we focus on a new type of metric, and a rather nebulous one at that. *Customer engagement* revolves around the concept that the more you can engage the customer with your product or brand, through your advertising or other online activities, the more you enhance your brand identity and ultimately the more products you sell.

Customer engagement is particularly important when you're doing rich media advertising—especially ads with an interactive component. That is, you want consumers to listen to your audio pitch, watch your video, click your buttons or other interactive components, and so on. The more that people interact with your advertising, the closer you are to converting them into customers.

Unfortunately, there aren't any cut-and-dried metrics to measure customer conversion. You can, however, analyze a collection of existing metrics to get a feel for customer engagement.

These are the metrics that factor into customer engagement:

- **Duration of visit**—Presumably, the more time a visitor spends on the host page, the more likely it is he's viewing or interacting with your rich media ad.
- **Frequency of visit**—If a visitor returns to the host page, it may be to interact further with your ad.
- **Percent of repeat visits**—Again, a returning visitor is likely to be returning because of your ad.
- **Click-through rate**—You do want the consumer to click through to your website, after all.

The key is developing some algorithm that effectively translates this data into some accurate measurement of customer engagement. As noted, there is no industry standard to do this; customer engagement is still a relatively new and mostly untested concept. Still, it's something you need to take into account—and try to measure as best you can.

Revenue

All of this brings us to our final advertising-related metric: revenue. If you're in the business of selling products or services online, what really matters is how many sales result from your advertising campaign. Impressions and clicks and even customer engagement are fine, but dollars pay the bills.

Now, your ad network probably doesn't directly track the sales resulting from your ads. That's okay. You can do that yourself because you know what you sell and who you sell it to. Your job is to tie each sale to the ad that generated it. You want to know which ads generated the most sale revenue. That's how you tell which ads are truly successful.

Even if you're not in the click-to-sell business, even if all you do is image-oriented display advertising, you still want to track revenue over the course of a campaign. Ultimately, you're advertising to build your brand and increase your sales. Your display advertising is part of that effort and should be measured accordingly.

After all, you're not advertising for the fun of it, or you shouldn't be in any case. You also shouldn't be advertising because your competitors are doing it or because your boss expects you to or because the technology is, frankly, enticing. You're advertising to grow your business. So you need to track that growth and tie it back to specific advertising—whether that advertising is online or off. Track your revenue and decide where they came from. That's how you determine a successful online advertising campaign.

Testing and Tracking Ad Strategies

It's good to know how well your ads are performing. It's even better to use this information to fine-tune your campaigns and become a more effective—and efficient—online advertiser.

To this end, you want to use these data tracking tools to test various ad strategies. Don't just look at the numbers when a campaign is over and say, that was pretty good (or not, as the case may be). Instead, look at the data over the course of a campaign to help test different ad variations.

This typically means running two or more variations on a given ad, which may include different ad copy, different images, and the like. You can also test regular content versus rich content ads to see which pulls better.

But that's not all you can test. You can test different ad sizes and placements. You can also test *where* your ad is placed—on what sites. You want to find out what combination of factors gives you the best bang for your buck.

With PPC advertising, you should test the effectiveness of individual keywords. You should also test your bid levels on these keywords—what prices produce the best or most effective positions.

You can use your ad network's reporting tools to generate the data for these tests or use one of the third-party tools previously discussed. The key is to isolate one variable among test ads and determine which variation is most effective.

As all marketers should know, tracking and testing your strategies is an essential part of marketing. Concentrate your efforts on those strategies that produce the best results and you'll be a smarter and more successful online marketer.

The Bottom Line

Most web advertisers use the tools supplied by their ad networks to measure the effectiveness of ad campaigns. You can also use third-party tools, which are especially effective in tracking a campaign across multiple ad networks.

For online advertising, the most important metrics to track include impressions, clicks, click-through rate, percent of clicks served, average position (for PPC search ads), cost, conversions, and revenue. If you're serving rich media ads, you should also try to track customer engagement, although there are no discrete metrics for doing so.

17

THE DARK SIDE OF ONLINE ADVERTISING

Online advertising isn't a completely clean business. Yes, you operate your campaigns on the up and up, but there are other advertisers who engage in activities that some may view as intrusive, if not illegal.

Let's start with the subject of *malware*—malicious software. When most of us think of malware we think of destructive computer viruses, but that's not the only malicious software out there. Even more common than viruses is *spyware*, which is used to spy on users or otherwise affect their web browsing experience.

Unfortunately, spyware is sometimes used by the advertising community in the form of *adware*. Unscrupulous or uncaring advertisers install adware on users' computers when they click an ad or go to their websites. Adware is then used to display pop-up windows, change the browser's home page, or insert unwanted advertisements into web pages viewed—in short, to alter the user's web browsing experience to benefit the advertiser.

However adware is used, it's unwanted and malicious, operating in the background without the user's express approval. Most of us would concede that adware of this sort goes well beyond the norm in promoting an advertiser's message.

But that isn't the only malicious behavior engaged in by some advertisers. You see, there are many advertisers today who deliberately or otherwise infringe on users' privacy. In fact, this is becoming more the norm, as cookies are used to track user behavior online. Cookies can be used to follow users from one website to another and then serve up appropriate ads based sites visited. This is a form of behaviorial advertising, and privacy experts are not big fans of it.

Now, you might think nothing of using cookies to track visitor behavior; it's how most web analytics tools work, after all. But just how far should you follow users around the Web—and how should you use the information you glean? Is it really your business what other websites your customers visit?

Okay, so you say you don't do any of these things. Except you probably do, at least where cookies are concerned. And it's a short step from placing a cookie on visitors' computers to dropping adware on their machines to control the ads they see. The question remains, then: How well do you respect your customers' privacy? There are some tough issues ahead.

18

Understanding Email Marketing

The next type of online marketing we discuss has been around even longer than web advertising. (Email predates the Web, as those of you steeped in Internet history well know.) It's a form of direct marketing over the Internet, and it's bigger than traditional postal mail marketing and has been since 1995.

Email marketing is simple in concept; it involves sending promotional messages via Internet-based email. But it's not so simple in practice, as you have to differentiate between opt-in and unsolicited email messages. The former qualifies as legitimate email marketing; the latter is spam, pure and simple, and nothing you want to be involved with.

Email Marketing Is Big Business

How important is email marketing? Well, it's not as ubiquitous as search engine marketing or web advertising, but it's still widely used.

Most companies who have an online presence utilize email marketing to some extent and see it as an important part of their mix. A recent survey[1] revealed that 39.4% of marketing professionals said that email marketing was their strongest performing channel in 2009; that's the highest response, better even than search marketing (23.6%).

---

1. Datran Media, Fourth Annual Marketing & Media Survey, 2010.

Putting some dollars to those figures, JupiterResearch[2] estimates that spending on email marketing will reach $1.1 billion in 2010 and top $2 billion by 2012. Just over half (53%) of email marketing spending is targeted at customer retention (cajoling additional sales from existing customers); the balance is spent on new customer acquisition.

These numbers reflect the fact that email marketing is not the next big thing, nor is it the most recent big thing. Email marketing has been around for almost two decades, so if you're just now considering it, you're a little late to the game.

Email Marketing Is Effective

How effective is email marketing? Do people actually read these things, or do they just hit the Delete key?

Email marketing effectiveness depends on a number of factors. First is whether or not promotional emails actually get delivered or if they get stuck in a server queue or spam filter somewhere. To this end, you'll be pleased to find that 98.8% of all email messages do get delivered, or so finds Bronto[3], a provider of email marketing software. (Other research firms report similar numbers in the mid- to high-90s.) So unless you're sending out genuine spam, you should be able to get your messages into the desired email inboxes.

Once your message has been delivered, Bronto reports that 23% or so of the people who receive your message will actually open it. That's not bad; almost a quarter of your audience will read (or at least glance at) your message.

Finally, somewhere between 5% and 6% of the people who receive your message will end up clicking the included links back to your website. That's a darned good response rate for direct marketing of any type.

Email Marketing Is Direct Marketing

Notice my comparison between email marketing and traditional direct marketing. That's because email marketing *is* direct marketing. It's not mass marketing, as web advertising is, displayed blindly to hundreds of thousands of unwitting recipients. Email marketing is targeted marketing, aimed directly at specific consumers. It's just like those promotional pieces you send via postal mail, except better; the recipients of your email promotions have to agree to

---

2. JupiterResearch, U.S. E-mail Marketing Forecast, 2007 to 2012, January 2008.
3. Bronto delivery statistics, April 25, 2010.

receive your mailings, which means they have a built-in receptivity to your marketing messages.

It's that one-to-one communication that makes email marketing so effective. Most traditional direct marketing done via postal mail is still rather broad; yes, you send mailings to customers on your mailing list, but you also buy mailing lists that contain names of people who have no connection to you. You may get a decent response rate from an internal mailing list, but response rates for those purchased names are, more often than not, abysmally low.

In contrast, email marketing is true one-to-one direct marketing. Unless you're engaging in spam activities, you send your email messages only to existing customers or to consumers who've opted in to your mailings. They're willing recipients, less likely to view your emails as unwanted junk. As such, you get a higher response rate, especially if you tailor your message to individual recipients—which you can and should do.

The best email marketers send mailings that present offers specific to each customer. Maybe it's an offer of plane tickets from the recipient's home airport to desirable destinations; maybe it's a promotion for accessories to an item previously purchased by that person. In any case, when you match the offer directly to the consumer, you get pretty good response rates—and are less likely to annoy those individuals who aren't interested in buying just now. Targeted promotions are relevant and valuable, even for those who don't immediately take advantage of them.

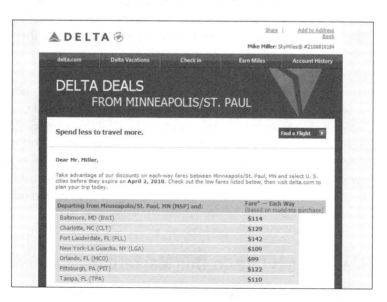

FIGURE 18.1

A targeted frequent-flyer email from Delta.

As you can probably surmise, then, email marketing is best suited to marketers who have a product or service to sell directly to the consumer. (Or, in the case of B2B marketing, directly to a business.) Email marketing is less suited for more generic brand or image marketing; if that's what you want to do, stick with web display advertising. But when you have something to sell on a one-to-one basis to your customers, email marketing is hard to beat.

Email Marketing Is Customer Retention Marketing

As noted previously, the majority of email marketing is customer retention marketing—messages sent to existing customers. These are people who have previously purchased something from you and agreed to receive future emails. They're proven customers and willing customers, ripe for further engagement.

As most smart marketers know, it costs much less money to sell an additional item to an existing customer than it does to create the first sale from a new customer. And on the Web, the primary means of contacting your customer base is via email.

The key, of course, is to capture your customers' email addresses. You can do this when they order from you online by including a box for email address, as well as an option they can check to receive email messages from you in the future. You'd be surprised how many people willingly sign up for this option.

What kinds of emails can you send? Customers like to know about upcoming sales and promotions. They also like to know about new products. They're also big fans of things that work with or accompany things they've already purchased—add-on sales, in other words.

Of course, you can also use email marketing to gain new customers. This is a more difficult undertaking—and a potentially dicey one. You have to purchase or borrow lists from other retailers or list brokers, and even if these are people who opted to receive mailings from "partners" of that company, they don't have a direct relationship with you; they certainly won't be expecting to receive your emails. Because of this, your mailing is more likely to end up in spam folders or manually deleted by the recipients. You almost certainly will get a lower response rate than you would with an opt-in mailing to your own customer list.

Email Marketing Is One-to-One Marketing

Of course, the more targeted you can make each email, the better. Successful email marketers don't send out generic emails containing dozens of products or offers; they limit the number of items offered, selecting only those that appeal directly to specific customers. This requires a bit of database management, of course; you need to know who bought what and when and then match that information with the various offers you have in the hopper. When done right, you end up with highly personalized offers that will not only retain existing customers, but will elicit additional purchases from them.

If you *don't* personalize your emails, you'll not only get a lower response rate, but you'll also find people removing their names from your mailing list. Let's face it, your customers are busy people, just like you and me. They have a finite amount of time and attention, and if you don't send them something that's relevant and interesting to them, they'll get turned off very quickly. You have to keep their attention, or they won't allow you to send them emails for long.

It's all about the relationship between your business and the individual customer. It's not a mass message; it's an individual message designed to foster the individual relationship. And it's a long-term relationship; each email is like a brick in the wall you're building to cement that relationship. You have to keep up the mailings to keep building the relationship.

Email Marketing Is Database Marketing

Key to email marketing is the ability to manage large databases of information—in this case, databases of names and email addresses, along with accompanying customer information.

Remember, email marketing is targeted marketing, not mass marketing—even more so than traditional direct marketing. With postal mail direct marketing, such as what you find in the catalog business, you have databases of names and addresses, but that's about it. You get a big enough list of names, dump a lot of pieces in the mail, and figure you'll get a set percentage of people who respond. The more names you buy, the more pieces you send, and the more money you'll make. It's all a numbers game.

With email marketing, however, you're managing more than just name and (email) addresses. You're also managing information about each individual customer. The databases you assemble include data about what each person has purchased in the past, what they've looked at on your website, the communication they've made with you, and so on. It's this data that holds the value; without it, you're just carpet bombing a bunch of anonymous email addresses.

With this customer data, however, you can tailor your mailings to each individual. That means tailoring not just the content of each message, but also the timing and frequency. Manage the database correctly, and you can put relevant messages in front of interested customers when they're most likely to buy. That makes each message you send more valuable to the recipients and should increase the response rates.

For this to work, you have to do a bit of database management. You have to create the right type of database, populate it with the right data, and then extract that data in an appropriate fashion. This isn't a simple mail merge like what you can do in Microsoft Outlook; it's sophisticated database management, often involving multiple databases.

To that end, frequent email marketing may not be something you can do in-house. Many companies, large and small, engage the use of professional email marketing firms. These firms can help you develop an email schedule, create your promotional emails, build and manage your customer databases, and create and send your email messages—or any subset of the above. Database management expertise is imperative; if you don't have it, hire it out.

Email Marketing Is Permission Marketing

Let's be clear about one thing. Legitimate email marketing is opt-in marketing; that is, you've received the customer's permission in advance to send out your email messages. If you send out emails without this prior permission, you're a spammer (and spamming is not part of any legitimate marketing mix).

The theory is that emails that users consent to receive will be better received than those unsolicited messages that arrive blind in their inboxes. If you're providing true value in your emails, you'll find that your recipients look forward to receiving your emails once a week, once a month, or on whatever schedule you have them set to be sent out.

Permission marketing typically involves some sort of regular communication with your customers. This may be a weekly or monthly email newsletter, a list of weekly deals, a list of weekly new releases, or something similar. It can also include unscheduled mailings triggered by specific events, such as new product releases, special sales, or announcements or promotions tied to current events.

How do you build your database of people who willingly agree to receive your mailings? There are a number of ways. Many companies request permission to send mailings when a customer purchases something online, as part of the checkout process. Others encourage signing up elsewhere on their websites or blogs, sometimes offering incentives (free merchandise, typically) for customers who do.

FIGURE 18.2

A mailing for a one-time-only special promotion from AV123.

It's especially important to tie the database of names with other databases that hold additional customer information. That way you can trigger emails based on customer characteristics, such as items they've purchased or expressed an interest in.

You can also program your databases to send out mailings on a regular schedule; this is useful for weekly announcements, for example. Do your programming work well and you can have your entire message put together automatically, dropping in the right notices and products for each customer in your database.

Email Marketing Is Frequent Marketing

When you're marketing via email, it's important to keep in front of your customers on a fairly regular basis. If you only send one email a year, customers are likely to forget that they gave permission to receive mailings from you and thus regard them as spam—which is not a good thing. (Heck, it's even possible they'll forget who you are completely!)

Setting up a regular schedule of mailings, then, makes sense. Unlike postal direct mail, it doesn't cost you much if anything more to send 50 emails a year than it does to send one; that's one of the benefits of email marketing, after all. So you might as well send as many emails as the customer can stand.

Scheduling regular emails is called *email drip marketing.* That is, you "drip" frequent emails to your customer base, one mailing at a time.

For example, once you purchase a DVD from Amazon.com and agree to receive their mailings, you get a "new release" email from them every week. The hope is that you'll eventually buy something else advertised in these emails—little drips add up.

FIGURE 18.3

A weekly new releases email from Amazon.com.

The point is for your emails to become a constant and welcome presence in the lives of your customers—without becoming an unwelcome annoyance. This may be a fine line, and the frequency certainly differs from company to company, but once you achieve it, you'll maximize your response rate, week in and week out.

Email Marketing Is Inexpensive Marketing

In the old world of postal direct marketing, you were on a budget; you could only do so many mailings each year because you had to pay for paper and envelopes and (of course) postage. But with email marketing, you don't have any of those costs—which means you can, in theory in least, send out as many emails as you like.

What's the cost of an email mailing? You have to manage your database of names, of course, but that's an ongoing cost. You may also pay for an outside firm to develop your mailings or just to develop a template that you use going forward. But you don't have to pay for names (assuming people proactively sign up), you don't have to pay for the individual emails themselves (no paper or ink involved), and you don't have to pay to have the emails delivered.

To this end, it doesn't matter whether you send out one email or a hundred thousand or if you send them once a month or once a day. Whatever the quantity or frequency, your costs are essentially the same.

Basically, email marketing does not incur media or delivery costs. Yes, you still have creative costs, and you have the cost of managing the database. But beyond that, the incremental costs are minimal.

This makes email marketing ideal for companies who want frequent contact with their customers. It's also ideal for companies with a complex message that would otherwise require multiple printed pages to get across; a short email message costs the same as a long one.

Like much online marketing, email marketing is also a great leveler, providing a somewhat level playing field for companies large and small. This introduces a kind of "marketing democracy" to the game in that a small company can be just as professional and persuasive as a larger one.

While you don't need a huge budget to be competitive with email marketing, you do need a certain level of intelligence and creativity. To that end, a smaller company can actually be more competitive than a larger one. A smaller company that is more receptive to new ideas and faster on its feet can run rings around a larger company with too many entrenched political systems in place.

18

Email Marketing Is Trackable Marketing

Another nice thing about email marketing is that it's quite trackable. That is, it's easy to track your results—the sales you make and where they came from.

It's a simple matter of tracking site visits (and resulting sales) from the specific links you include in your promotional emails. You record that X number of visits, Y number of sales, and Z amount of revenue were generated by visitors who came from the specific link included in a given email. You know how many messages you sent out, so it's easy enough to calculate all the percentages you want. You don't have to speculate where a given sale came from—you know.

Assuming, then, that you've kept an accurate log of all costs involved, you can then calculate a fairly accurate return on investment for each and every email you send out. And don't be surprised if you find that email marketing provides an ROI second only to search engine marketing in your mix.

The Bottom Line

Email marketing, or the sending of promotional messages via email, is an important part in the marketing mix for most companies. Legitimate email marketing requires the permission of the recipient; email sent without permission is spam.

As such, email marketing is a fairly efficient and effective form of direct marketing. It's best suited for soliciting direct sales; it's easy to track results from the links included in the promotional emails.

The majority of email marketing is directed at existing customers. A certain frequency is necessary for maximum effectiveness; you have to keep your name in front of your customer base. You also need to present a targeted message in your emails; use sophisticated database marketing techniques to match the message with the needs of specific customers.

EMAIL MARKETING IS NOT SPAM

Opt-in emails are sent with the explicit permission of the recipients. Emails sent without this permission are unwanted commercial emails (UCEs), or spam for short.

Nobody likes spam. Really, nobody. Not the recipients who find this junk email overrunning their inboxes, nor Internet service providers who find their bandwidth eaten up by the huge number of unwanted messages, nor other advertisers who find their legitimate emails marginalized by all the spam messages for Canadian drugs, "performance enhancing" products, and the like.

So why does spam exist? Because it's cheap (remember, it costs almost the same to send out a million spam messages as it does to send a thousand legitimate ones) and because, to some degree, it's profitable. That's right, some small percent of people actually click spam messages and order. Even a miniscule response rate can be profitable when you send out millions of unsolicited messages at no or low cost.

Legitimate marketers, of course, don't engage in spam and reject any connection to the junk email industry. They go to great lengths to stress the opt-in nature of their mailings and feature large and noticeable "unsubscribe" links in their mailings so that anyone who no longer wants to receive emails can be removed from future mailings. Legitimate email marketing is all about giving consumers emails that they want to and expect to receive.

That said, you need to make sure that your email marketing efforts do not violate those anti-spam laws that are on the books. In the U.S., that means reading up on and adhering to the terms of what is known as the CAN-SPAM Act of 2003. (That stands for—take a deep breath here—Controlling the Assault of Non-Solicited Pornography and Marketing.) You can read the entire thing online at http://uscode.house.gov/download/pls/15C103.txt; like most official government documents, it's scintillating reading.

Even better, work with an established email marketing firm and let them sweat the details. But the best advice is to not do anything that would annoy you as a consumer. You don't want to receive emails in your inbox that you don't want; tailor your email marketing campaigns appropriately.

18

Building Email Mailing Lists

Key to a successful email marketing program are the lists of names to which you send your mailings. This is not unlike traditional direct mail, of course, but we're talking email addresses instead of postal addresses—and it costs virtually nothing to send an email versus the increasing expenses of printing and mailing physical pieces.

Where, then, do you get the names and email addresses for your email marketing programs? As you'll soon see, the best names are those found close at hand.

Creating an Email List

The best email mailing lists contain names of people who you know are interested in what you have to offer. The worst lists contain names picked seemingly at random and have nothing to do with anything you do. Obviously, you want to collect as many names as possible that are pretty much prequalified and avoid the junk names that will never respond to your mailings.

Where to Find Names

So where can you find names and email addresses of people who are predisposed to purchasing what you have to sell? The best names are those of people who've already bought something from you; the second-best names are those of people who have shopped for what you're selling. What you want to assemble, then, is a list of existing customers and visitors to your website.

How do you get customers and website visitors to give you their email addresses and agree to receive your mailings? Well, you have to ask for it.

You can ask for customers' email addresses in lots of different places—and the more often you ask, the more names you'll collect. Here's just a short list of places where you can include requests for customers to opt into your mailings:

- On the home page of your website
- On a special email preference center page of your website (discussed later in this chapter)
- On any product page on your website ("click here to receive more product information via email")
- On your site's checkout page ("click here to receive future product announcements")
- On your site's technical support and customer support pages
- On any other page of your website
- On your company blog
- At the bottom of all email messages you send—especially those sent to purchased lists of names
- Via telephone, when a customer calls for customer service or technical support

> **note** In most instances, you can only use purchased names for a limited number of mailings. To add these customers to your email list permanently, you have to ask their permission—which you can do via a link at the bottom of the email.

- If you have retail locations, at a sign-up sheet at the cash register
- If you do traditional direct mail, on the printed order form in your catalogs and brochures
- If you exhibit at trade shows, at your booth

In addition, you and other employees should actively solicit customer names wherever you travel. Ask for business cards and add those people to your email lists.

How to Ask for Names

Asking a customer for permission to send him what might be perceived as annoying email messages takes a bit of skill. And, in most instances, you have to do it in a line or two of text.

How do you convince someone to fork over his or her name and email address? Well, you have to provide some benefit for doing so; you can't just say, "Give us your address," without offering something in return.

What benefits, then, can you offer in exchange for permission to email your offers to a person? Here's a short list:

- More information.

- Updated information—new product announcements, product updates, and so forth.

- Technical support. If you charge for support, you might offer a few months of free support (or a few free tech support calls).

- Deals and specials. This may take the form of weekly sale prices or something similar.

- Free access to otherwise-paid information, such as archival content.

- A discount on their next order.

- A free gift of some sort.

In other words, you may have to bribe people to give you their email addresses. Such is the way of the world.

You can also, of course, try to convince them that the emails themselves are of value. The best way to do this is to show them or tell them about what they'll be getting. Talk about the benefits of subscribing to your email mailings, tell them what they'll receive and how often. You can even link to a sample mailing or to past mailings so they'll see for themselves what you send out.

In any case, you have to explicitly ask for customers' permission to send them emails, and they have to respond in the affirmative. This is typically done via a simple checkbox; if the customer checks "yes," you can add his or her name to your list—if not, you can't.

> **note** For those of you familiar with the book club or record club business, you cannot use a negative option process to procure email names. In this approach, you assume you have their permission unless they check a box saying *not* to send the mailings. It's kind of permission by negligence, more implicit than explicit—which is why it's not recommended.

It's also a good idea to include a link to your company's privacy policy near the email signup block. For those customers who are aware of and concerned with privacy issues, you need to assure them that you'll hold their data close and not share it recklessly with other firms.

> To take advantage of your Joann.com account, please complete the information below.
> * indicates a required field
>
> e-mail: [＿＿＿＿＿＿＿] *
>
> confirm e-mail: [＿＿＿＿＿＿＿] *
>
> password: [＿＿＿＿＿＿＿] *
>
> confirm password: [＿＿＿＿＿＿＿] *
>
> Your password must be at least 4-35 characters in length
>
> ☑ I would like to recieve e-mail messages from Joann.com

FIGURE 19.1

A typical opt-in email signup request from Jo-Ann Fabric and Craft Stores; the option box must be checked for the customer to start receiving emails.

Serving Multiple Lists via an Email Preference Center

If you offer more than one email newsletter, you can give your customers the choice of which newsletter(s) to receive. This is typically done via a separate page on your site that functions as an email preference center.

Key to this type of page is a positive presentation of all the different mailings you have available. This is ad copy and should have the most positive, bene-fit-laden marketing spin you can create. You have to make each newsletter uniquely appealing—without being too terribly misleading, and you need to convince customers to sign up for as many newsletters as you can.

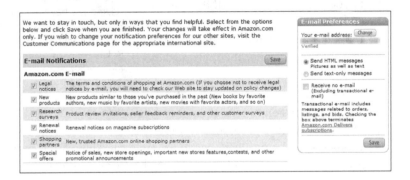

FIGURE 19.2

The email preference center page from Amazon.com, presenting multiple email options.

To that end, an effective email preference center page needs to include the following components:

- A description of each newsletter or mailing available
- A link to a sample copy of each newsletter or mailing
- A check box to sign up to receive each newsletter or mailing
- A check box to unsubscribe to each newsletter or mailing
- A single check box to unsubscribe to *all* newsletters and mailings
- Delivery preferences—plain text or HTML
- A box to enter or correct the recipient's email address
- A link to your privacy policy
- A "contact us" link to your customer support department, which either sends an email to you or opens a separate web form page where the customer can enter comments, complaints, and the like

In addition, you may use this opportunity to ask for more information about the customer. This may take the form of a few check boxes related to specific activities or intentions; just don't overwhelm people so that they back off before they actually subscribe to your mailings.

> **note** Instead of calling them newsletters or emails, you may want to refer to your mailings as "special offers."

Another popular option is a way for customers to recommend your mailings to other people. This typically takes the form of a "let your friends know about this" section with a text box for them to enter their friends' email addresses. If you go this route, however, you can't just automatically add these addresses to your lists; you'll need to send them an introductory mailing to convince them to sign up on their own.

The key thing to remember is that an email preference center is the hub where customers can manage their email preferences. That includes not only subscriptions to specific mailings, but also their names, email addresses, and so forth.

> **note** Giving customers the option to manage their email subscriptions is likely to result in higher retention rates than offering a single "unsubscribe" option.

19

Finding Email Addresses for Existing Customers

If your business includes a physical component, or if you're transitioning from traditional direct mail, you probably already have a huge list of customers' names and implicit permission to send out regular mailings. The problem is you might not have email addresses for some or all of these names.

In this situation, you need to contract with a direct mail or email specialist to run an *email append* on your list. The vendor will take the names on your list and, as accurately as possible, find email addresses for them. The vendor then sends emails to these people on your behalf, asking for permission to send more emails. Those people who respond in the affirmative (and whose names accurately matched their email addresses) get added to your email mailing list.

Purchasing or Renting Names

Back in Chapter 18, "Understanding Email Marketing," I mentioned that a little over half of all legitimate marketing emails were in support of existing customers. That leaves the rest of the mailings, 45% or so, that are sent to solicit business from new customers.

But wait, I hear you saying, isn't email marketing supposed to be permission marketing—all opt-in, all the time? Well, yes and no.

Yes, in that the best results come from mailing to people who've explicitly said they'd like to receive mailings from you. Yes, also in that mailings to people who have not opted in are considered spam. But no, in that there's a muddy middle ground.

That middle ground consists of people who agreed to receive mailings from another company and also agreed for that company to share their names. This sometimes takes the form of a "would you like to receive special offers from our partners" sort of option, which a surprising number of people check. Names gathered in this fashion can be sold or rented to other companies— which is where you get all those new names to solicit.

This use of names and addresses from people who opted in at another site is called *co-registration*. It can be effective if you choose your partners carefully. That is, if you share names from a site that has a similar demographic to yours, you'll stand a better chance of success than if you use a random list. In this respect, list sharing is one area where quality is much more important than quantity.

note It's always a good idea to test some names before you do a full-scale purchase of another list. Send out a hundred or so test mailings and see if you get an adequate response rate.

You can send two types of mailings to these shared names:

- Special offers, where you try to sell directly to recipients

- Sign up offers, where you instead use the mailing to solicit recipients' approval for you to send them further mailings

Obviously, the first approach is likely to generate faster revenue than the second. The second approach, however, is probably the best for building a long-term mailing list. You'll get a higher response rate, though, when people don't have to buy anything.

note Most co-registration comes in the form of either list swaps (you share yours and they share theirs) or list rentals. It rarely takes the form of list purchases. In fact, most lists offered for sale are spam lists, constructed without the owners' permission or knowledge. You should avoid purchasing spam lists; not only will you get a very poor response, you'll risk the ire of those people who receive your unsolicited mailing (along with hundreds of others).

Managing Your Lists

Email lists are just like traditional mailing lists. It's all about creating a big database of names and other information.

Collecting the Data

What, exactly, should the database contain? Well, with email marketing, you will probably know a lot more about the people you deal with than with traditional marketing—because you have their online behavior to track.

Here's a short list of data that is relatively easy to collect and quite useful in targeting specific mailings:

- Customer name (of course)
- Email address (also of course)
- Item(s) purchased—including price, when purchased, and so forth
- Web pages browsed
- Referring websites—the sites that led them to yours
- Keywords used—if they came to your site via search, what keywords they used to find your site

19

Now, not all this information has to be kept in a single database. It's possible that you have your names in one database and your sales information in another. But it's easy enough, at least for the tech guys, to link names in one database with information in another.

So, for example, if you want to send an email to people who have (a) opted in to your mailings and (b) purchased an item in the last 90 days, you can do it. Just merge your opt-in names against your sales transactions, and you get a subset of people who've recently purchased. Easy enough.

But why do you want or need all this data? It's all a matter of how sophisticated you want your marketing to be. If you're just blasting a monthly special to all the names on your list, you don't need anything that fancy. But if you want to segment different offers to different customers, then all the data you have is valuable.

Let me provide an example. I purchase a lot of items from Amazon.com, and they do a very good job of tracking and using customer data. That's why I recently received an offer with a special price on Microsoft Office products. I had been browsing Amazon for Office and other software, and Amazon captured my browsing data (each product has its own page that can be tracked). They then sent me an email offering Microsoft Office because they knew that was what I was interested in. Simple logic, nice use of technology, and a very targeted email message.

FIGURE 19.3

A targeted email offer from Amazon.com, enabled by sophisticated data tracking and database management.

Keeping Your List Clean

It's not enough to create an email mailing list and corresponding database(s). You also have to keep that list clean.

Proper list hygiene, as it's called, helps keep your response rates high. You have to periodically cull bad or unresponsive names from your list; otherwise you keep sending emails to people who either don't exist or who clearly don't want what you're selling. It may cost a little time and money to purge bad names from your list, but you'll save that money—and more—in the long run.

What do you need to do to clean your list? Here's a short list of things to look for and then purge:

- Addresses that bounce. A *hard bounce* is a known bad address; it simply doesn't exist, and the email bounces back to you. A *soft bounce* is due to some sort of temporary problem, such as a server being down or the recipient's inbox being full. You can try resending a message after a soft bounce, and if it goes, good for you. If messages to a given recipient continue to bounce, however, you may want to consider removing the address from your list.

- Addresses with typos, including missing @ signs.

- Customers who have never responded to your mailings. This could be a sign of your emails going directly to a person's spam folder without them ever being seen or of a person who just isn't interested in buying from you.

> **note** You can improve the accuracy of your addresses at the sign-up stage by requiring customers to enter their email addresses *twice*—and then flagging them if the two attempts don't match.

- Customers who haven't responded in a given period of time. The longer a customer goes without responding, the less likely he is to respond in the future. Just make sure, however, that you're giving the customer enough time; don't purge a name just because the person didn't respond to your last two or three mailings.

Turning Inactive Names into Active Ones

Once you've identified those people on your list who have never responded to your emails or who haven't responded in a long time, you could just purge those names from your list. Or, even better, you could give these folks one last nudge in the form of a good reason to respond.

This attempt at *reactivation* typically takes the form of a "last chance" mailing. This mailing may simply state that unless the recipient responds to this message (in the form of actively resubscribing), they'll be forever deleted from your mailing list. Or it may make a great offer to get them buying again—a bribe, as it were, to retain them as customers. (I prefer the latter approach, as it's more positive and results in some degree of immediate sales.)

Avoiding Spamming—by Asking Permission

However you build your email list, you have to do so by requiring customers to opt into your mailings. It's called *permission marketing*, and it's how you avoid being lumped in with all the spammers out there.

We've already talked about including a permission box that customers have to check to receive your mailings. That's a good first step, but there are other safeguards you probably need to consider to ensure your nonspam status.

The first thing concerns the permission box. It needs to be an opt-in box, not an opt-out box. As we've discussed, email marketing is not the place for a negative option approach. Don't ask customers to check the box *not* to receive your mailings; ask them to check the box to opt in.

In addition, this little box should always be displayed in its empty state. Never prefill the box with a "yes" checkmark; don't assume that all customers will opt in. Permission marketing requires a distinct action from the customer, which you remove if you precheck the box. Besides, if the box is prechecked, just clicking the OK button automatically provides a positive response, which may not be what the customer wanted. Bottom line, you have to make them check the box.

If you want to go the extra step, you can use a double opt-in approach. The standard "check the box, click OK" approach is a single opt-in; the customer does it all on a single page. In contrast, a double opt-in adds a further verification step to the process. That is, they check the box and click OK, and then they're sent a confirmation email to the address they provided. They have to click a link in that email to verify their subscription.

There are a few benefits to the double opt-in approach. First, you'll get more accurate email addresses; any bad or false addresses get immediately bounced back to you, so they never get added to your mailing list. Second, the extra effort provides you with some really dedicated subscribers; it's a cleaner, better performing list. On the downside, however, you'll get fewer subscribers because the extra effort won't be worth it for everyone.

What you don't want to do is assume that because a customer purchased something from you in the past they also want to receive emails from you in the future. A purchase is not a permission to email. Route your purchasing customers through the email opt-in process as part of the checkout; most will opt to receive your mailings, but some won't, and that's okay. At least you asked.

By the way, it's always a good idea to include some sort of opt-out option in all your emails, as well as on your email preference center page. You want to serve your customers, even those who don't want to hear from you on regular basis. Give people an option to unsubscribe from your mailings, and you'll be a better marketer for it.

> **note** Just because someone unsubscribes from your emails doesn't mean you actually delete their names from your database. You should retain all the names, just turn "off" the option for regular mailings under their names. You can always re-email inactive customers with special offers, including those to resubscribe to your mailings.

You are subscribed as: ████████@MOLEHILLGROUP.COM. Edit Subscription or Unsubscribe.

FIGURE 19.4

An unsubscribe option at the bottom of an email message.

Who Does the Work?

Now we get down to the nuts and bolts of things. When it comes to creating and managing a list of email names and addresses, who does all the work?

Well, if you're a relatively small shop with some degree of internal technical expertise, there's no reason why you can't do it yourself. It's not as simple as doing a mail merge between Microsoft Outlook and Microsoft Word (in fact, several companies offer email marketing software just for this purpose), but it's still doable.

Larger firms and those with more sophisticated marketing needs are more likely to farm out their list management—of both a traditional and digital nature. There are

> **note** Some of the more popular email marketing software programs include Bronto (www.bronto.com), Constant Contact (www.constantcontact.com), iContact (www.icontact.com), and Yesmail (www.yesmail.com).

lots of vendors who can handle all or part of the email marketing process, from managing your list to creating and sending your mailings. You'll pay for this service, of course, typically on a per-name or per-piece basis, but a quality vendor can often achieve better results than you can on your own.

note Most ethical email service providers are members of the Email Sender & Provider Coalition (www.espcoalition.org). Visit their website to learn more.

Who are these email vendors? Here's a list of some of the larger ones, all of which handle accounts of various sizes:

- Benchmark Email (www.benchmarkemail.com)
- Campaigner (www.campaigner.com)
- Datran Media (www.datranmedia.com)
- ExactTarget (www.exacttarget.com)
- VerticalResponse (www.verticalresponse.com)

The Bottom Line

Email marketing is permission marketing, which means you need to get permission from the people you want to email to. That means building your lists from a series of opt-in forms, typically presented to customers when they check out or visitors who browse your website. You can then merge these opt-in names with other important data, such as what they browsed or purchased, and create targeted email messages.

You can also solicit names from shared or rented lists, typically people who opted to receive emails on other websites. You can't automatically add these names to your list, however; you have to ask their permission first. (It's all about permissions, isn't it?)

Once you assemble your list, you need to manage it. That means purging bad names and addresses and sometimes trying to reactivate people who haven't responded in awhile. You can do this work yourself or hire an email marketing vendor who specializes in this type of email list management and creating effective email promotions, which we discuss in the next chapter.

PRIVACY MATTERS

Assembling a database of names for your email marketing means collecting a lot of information that some would consider private, starting with a person's email address and moving on to data about a person's purchases, website visits, and the like. Most people, quite rightly, take their privacy seriously—and so should you.

Let's start with the data you collect, which needs to be kept private. This means using it solely for your own internal purposes and not sharing it or selling it with other companies—unless such sharing is expressly agreed to by your customers. And some information, such as purchase information, probably shouldn't be shared at all.

So if you're going to be doing any sharing, it probably should be limited to names and email addresses—and only of those customers who have opted in for such sharing. You should never share or sell names and email addresses of customers who have not given this explicit permission; to do so would not only be a violation of customer privacy, but also would be contributing to the overall spam problem.

Finally, you need to tell your customers how you're handling their private information, in the form of a posted privacy policy. This policy should be a separate page on your website, linked to from your home page, your email sign-up page, and every single email you send out. This policy should state, in very clear terms, how you collect customer information as well as what you do with that information. You should be explicit about things like cookies and data sharing; you should also include an email link or postal address where customers can write with their questions or comments.

The key here is transparency. No privacy policy will please 100% of all consumers, but at least you'll be up front about what you're doing—and that's what's important.

19

20

Developing an Email Marketing Campaign

When you have your list of names and email addresses assembled, it's time to put that list to good use. That means developing your email marketing campaign(s)—figuring out what to email to your customers and how.

Deciding What—and When—to Promote

How you use your email mailing list is entirely up to you; different companies, even in the same professions, do different things. And it isn't just a matter of choosing which products or services to promote. There are different strategies you can employ about which types of mailings to send to specific types of customers—and how often. Let's look at a few of the most popular.

Promotional Blast

One of the most common types of promotional email is the simple promotional blast. This is a sales mailing, pure and simple; it promotes one or more items at a special price.

There are several different ways to use promotional blasts. What's common is that these are occasional mailings, not regular ones. You can use promotional blasts to promote a once-a-year sale or clearance, a special purchase that you're promoting, or a sale targeted to a big holiday. It's *not* a mailing that drops into inboxes once or twice a month; it's truly something special.

You can promote one item or many. In fact, you don't even have to promote individual items; a promotional blast can announce store-wide savings, such as "20% off all items in stock."

FIGURE 20.1

A promotional blast offering various items for sale from Gardener's Supply Company.

In most cases, promotional blasts talk about individual sales prices or dollar or percentage discounts. You can also use a promotional blast for a coupon promotion; that is, the email itself serves as an electronic coupon that can be redeemed during the checkout process. This is actually a great way to track performance from individual mailings.

Promotional blasts can be true blasts, sent to your entire email list. Or they can be targeted mailings, aimed at specific customers or customer types in your list. This latter approach lets you tailor your offer to specific types of customers. For example, you might send out a promotional blast with an offer customized for frequent customers or one promoting a specific product for customers who've purchased similar products in the past. As you learned in Chapter 19, "Building Email Mailing Lists," and as we discuss in more depth later in this chapter, the more personalized the offer, the higher the likely response rate.

The key to a successful promotional blast, then, is to offer a relevant and enticing offer to the people on your list. You don't want to promote something that people aren't interested in, nor do you want to extend a wimpy offer. Promote products that customers want at a price they can't resist, and you'll have a winning campaign.

Regular Mailing

Promotional blasts should be something special; if they show in someone's inbox too frequently, they lose their impact.

There are mailings you can send, however, on a more regular schedule. These are mailings you send out once a quarter, once a month, or even once a week. If you do it right, customers will look forward to receiving these mailings—and the information or offers they contain.

One type of regular mailing is the monthly special. Maybe it's an end-of-month clearance, maybe it's just an item or group of items that you discount over the course of a month. The point is that these are sale items good for the current month only (or, in some cases, until they're gone). It's a use-it-or-lose-it kind of mailing, and customers learn to anticipate the next month's sales.

Another type of regular mailing is the weekly or monthly announcement. For example, Ticketmaster sends out a weekly TicketAlert email that announces upcoming local concerts, as well as new tickets on sale for a given week. Each email is targeted locally, so I find out about concerts in the Twin Cities, where I live, while people who live in other cities receive emails with content for their locations. It's a useful mailing, in that I'm notified of concerts I might want to attend; it's also a definite promotional mailing, as each email contains links to purchase tickets for the concerts listed.

FIGURE 20.2

The regular weekly TicketAlert mailing from Ticketmaster, targeted to a specific location.

20

There are any number of regular mailings you can send, including the following:

- Weekly or monthly new product announcements (great for companies or places that offer a lot of new items on a regular basis, such as CD, DVD, and book retailers)
- Weekly or monthly specials
- Monthly activity statements (these can offer not only a summary of a customer's activity for the previous month, but also additional promotions)

FIGURE 20.3

A monthly activity statement from Priority Club Rewards; note the special offers beneath the statement itself.

Email Newsletter

There's one special kind of regular mailing that bears individual examination—the email newsletter, which can be a great promotional tool even if it doesn't promote any specific items.

An email newsletter is the electronic equivalent of the traditional printed newsletter. Newsletters are typically delivered on a somewhat regular schedule—one a month, typically, although quarterly, weekly, and even daily newsletters also work in some instances.

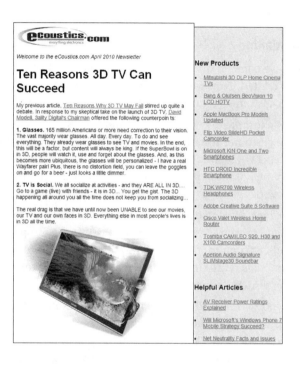

FIGURE 20.4

An email newsletter from eCoustics.com.

If you're a business, you can use a newsletter to let your customers know what's new with your business. That might be new products or services, new routes or destinations (if you're in the travel business), new locations, new hours, new employees, new you name it. Naturally, you also use your newsletter to announce sales and other promotions, but you don't have to. A newsletter can be strictly news, or it can be a mix.

Newsletters require a bit more work in the writing department than do other forms of promotional emails, which explains why

> **note** News media can also send out newsletters. For example, the *Indianapolis Business Journal* sends out a daily email summarizing the lead articles in its print edition—which functions as a promotion to entice new paid subscribers.

20

you don't see a lot of daily newsletters. You have to include real news and write real articles; it's not just a bunch of advertising blather. In fact, that's what makes newsletters so effective—readers actually get something out of them. We're talking real news and information, stuff your customers will find interesting and useful.

Related Items Mailing

Finally, we come to an interesting and quite effective type of mailing that I'll call the related items mailing. This is a promotional email that offers something to customers related to something else they've purchased or looked at.

The best example of a related items mailing is one offering accessories for an item the customer recently purchased. For example, if a customer purchased a flat screen TV, you might send out an email promoting cables, DVD players, wall mounts, and the like. This type of mailing is all about add-on sales, and it often works.

Another type of related items mailing promotes items that a customer was looking at on your website. If someone was browsing pages for lawn mowers, you send out a promotional mailing offering special prices on selected lawn mower models. This kind of email strikes while the iron is hot; you know someone's interested in that product, so push the heck out of it.

The category of related items mailings includes notification emails. These are mailings that notify the customer about something they should be doing. For example, a car dealer might send out emails to customers notifying them when their cars are due for oil changes or other maintenance. Naturally, a notification email can also include promotions on the given product or service; typically, this takes the form of a coupon the customer can use online or print out and use in the store.

Constructing the Promotional Message

Whatever type of promotional email you go with (and you're not limited to just one, of course), you have to construct the message in such a way as to maximize the response rate. That means focusing on each and every part of the message, from the very top to the very bottom.

Subject Line

The subject line of an email is the first thing a recipient sees, typically in his or her email inbox. But it's also the part of the email that often receives the least attention from marketers. That's too bad, as it's the subject line alone that often determines whether or not the email gets read.

Let's start at one extreme. The worst subject line is one that's entirely blank. Don't laugh; I've seen them. I don't know why you'd put the time and money into a big email campaign and then leave the subject line blank, but some companies do. Trust me, a blank subject line will result in close to a zero response rate.

> **note** The worst case scenario is that a recipient reads your email's subject line in her inbox and from that determines that your email is spam—marking it so all further mailings from you go directly into a spam folder.

The next-worst subject lines are those that really don't have anything to do with the contents of your mailing. The subject simply states the company name or says something generic like "Important Message." These subject lines do nothing to entice the recipient to open the message and can doom even the best-constructed email promotion.

The best subject lines offer a unique benefit to the recipient. They don't just describe the contents of the email but tell the recipients how they'll benefit from reading the email. It's just like standard ad copy; you get better results by talking about benefits than by listing features.

That said, you do have to mention the content of the mail, to some degree. The subject line, then, has to be both informational and promotional—and do it in a relatively small number of characters. The most effective subject lines are no more than 50 characters long; anything longer gets truncated in most inboxes. So short and punchy is the way to go.

> **note** The 50-character rule changes somewhat when emails are read on mobile devices—many of which can only display the first 20 characters or so of email messages.

The content of the email typically takes the form of some sort of offer or promotion. This needs to be included in the subject line. That might mean using the words "discount" or "save" or "coupon" or "X% off" or something similar. It's always good to get these action words into the subject line—the same way you would want to work them into the headline of an online ad.

> **note** It might sound like a good action word, but you probably want to avoid using the word "free" in your subject line. Many spam filters are constructed to look for this word in the subject and automatically label the corresponding email as spam.

20

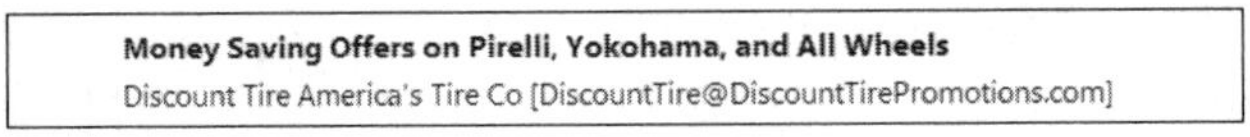

> **Money Saving Offers on Pirelli, Yokohama, and All Wheels**
> Discount Tire America's Tire Co [DiscountTire@DiscountTirePromotions.com]

FIGURE 20.5

A compelling subject line from a Discount Tire America mailing.

Within the subject line's 50-character limit, you also need to mention who you are or what you're selling. That means shoehorning in the brand or company name or a short variation thereof. Otherwise, some recipients won't know what the email is about and will automatically delete it.

And if you can, try to personalize the subject line. A subject that says, "Special offer for Mr. Miller" will get my attention more than one that just says, "Special offer on Product X." People like to see their names, especially in emails; a personalized email is also less likely to be viewed as spam.

Here's the bottom line: Effective subject lines result in a high response rate. Knowing that, you need to spend the appropriate amount of time concocting a subject line that grabs the recipient's attention and entices him to read the entire message.

Sender

This one seems simple. The sender, or From line, is you. But how do you best represent yourself? You have several different choices.

The email can come from:

- The company itself (From: The XYZ Company)
- A brand or product name (From: Product X)
- A department within the company (From: XYZ Customer Service Department)
- A person within the company (From: Bob Roberts, CEO)

The question is which type of sender is more likely to be trusted by the recipient? That depends on which is most recognizable.

If you have a strong brand or company name, that might be the way to go. People are sure to recognize Diet Coke, for example, or IBM. This is especially true in the consumer marketplace, where brand names matter.

note If you're sending an email newsletter, the sender line can be the name of the newsletter (From: XYZ Newsletter).

In the B2B marketplace, however, your company's president or CEO might be well known enough to warrant using his name instead of the company or product name. It depends, to some extent, on the size of the industry; people are more likely to recognize other players in smaller industries.

However, if your name is Bob Roberts, your company is Bob's Big Bundles, and your product is the Bundlematic, well, neither one is likely to be easily recognized. In this instance, you might be better off having the email come from a specific person, even if that person isn't well-known. That's because an email sent by a specific person can sometimes be viewed as more "real" than a "form message" coming from a company.

> **note** While you have some leeway over whose name you put in the From: line, it does have to accurately reflect where it's coming from. Unless you want to fall victim to the CAN-SPAM act, you can't lie about who's sending the email.

Bottom line, pick the From: line that is most likely to be recognized by your recipients. That means thinking like the customer, of course, and figuring out what (and who) they know—and what (and who) they don't.

Recipient

Okay, this one is pretty easy. The To: line should contain the recipient's name and/or email address—but *only* the recipient's name/address. If you fill the To: line with the email addresses of everyone on your mailing list, you're doing a few things wrong.

First, you're telling the recipients (all of them) that they're getting the same email sent out to dozens or hundreds of other people. It's not personalized, which makes it less relevant—and less likely to be read or clicked.

Second, you're exposing your customers' email addresses to other customers. That's a big privacy no-no.

So manipulate your email sending software to list only a single recipient's name and email address in the To: line. That's really the only way to do it.

Message Format

Ah, now we come to the message itself, in particular its formatting. Here, you have a lot of leeway.

The content of your email can be either text, image, or a combination of both. An all-text email is more likely to make it past the spam filters, as well as be visible to users who have turned off images in their email programs or are using older programs that have trouble displaying HTML email. It also takes longer to download image-heavy emails and may not be visible if the user is reading the email offline.

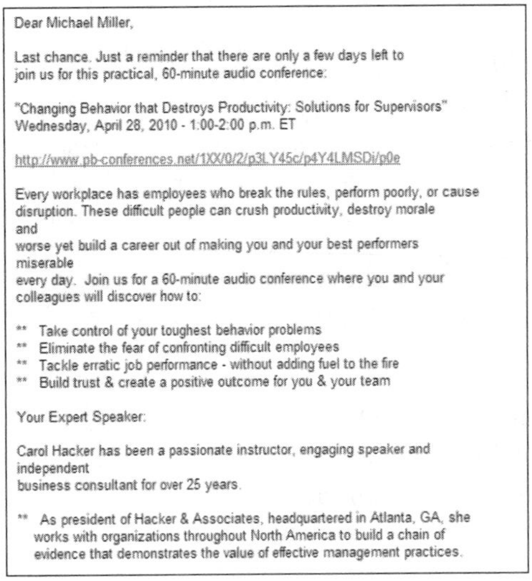

Dear Michael Miller,

Last chance. Just a reminder that there are only a few days left to join us for this practical, 60-minute audio conference:

"Changing Behavior that Destroys Productivity: Solutions for Supervisors"
Wednesday, April 28, 2010 - 1:00-2:00 p.m. ET

http://www.pb-conferences.net/1XX/0/2/p3LY45c/p4Y4LMSDi/p0e

Every workplace has employees who break the rules, perform poorly, or cause disruption. These difficult people can crush productivity, destroy morale and
worse yet build a career out of making you and your best performers miserable
every day. Join us for a 60-minute audio conference where you and your colleagues will discover how to:

**   Take control of your toughest behavior problems
**   Eliminate the fear of confronting difficult employees
**   Tackle erratic job performance - without adding fuel to the fire
**   Build trust & create a positive outcome for you & your team

Your Expert Speaker:

Carol Hacker has been a passionate instructor, engaging speaker and independent
business consultant for over 25 years.

**   As president of Hacker & Associates, headquartered in Atlanta, GA, she
     works with organizations throughout North America to build a chain of
     evidence that demonstrates the value of effective management practices.

FIGURE 20.6

An all-text email from Progressive Business Audio Conferences—visually boring but loads quickly.

FIGURE 20.7

An all-image email from FTD—pretty, but there's nothing there if the image doesn't display.

FIGURE 20.8

A nice mix of text and images from Blue Nile.

On the other hand, an all-image email lets you display just about anything you want to display. It can be pretty, too. So there's that.

But you can run into problems when you use images to present your email message. Someone reading your message on a mobile phone, for example, won't be able to see what you're talking about; most mobile devices display text-only email messages by default. And some PC users disable image display in their email programs, too. The result is the same—recipients see only your text, not your images. For this reason, you probably shouldn't rely on images to convey your entire message; it certainly doesn't hurt to supplement your images with appropriate descriptive text.

Most emails, however, mix text and images; it's hard to resist using at least a few images, especially that image file that contains your company's logo. Just keep the images small to minimize download problems, include enough text to satisfy nonimage viewers, and you should be okay.

note It's always a good idea to offer subscribers the option of receiving either HTML or plain-text emails. Putting this decision in the hands of your customers saves you from sending the wrong type of email to people who can't receive it.

20

Message Content

Beyond the format of the email is the email's content. Key here is to keep your emails short and to the point. It's tempting, given that it costs the same to send a long email as a short one, to throw everything but the kitchen sink into your messages. Resist the temptation—long emails work against you.

First, remember that people don't like to read much these days. Emails, in particular, are more likely to be grazed than deeply read. To that end, if you can present your entire message at a glance, you're more likely to keep your customers' attention than if you make them scroll through an extra-long message.

Second, a shorter email focuses attention on the most important point you're making. A longer email is more likely to contain multiple messages, in which case how is the customer supposed to know which is most important? If you have multiple points to make, send out multiple emails. Keep each email focused on a single message, and each message is more likely to be remembered.

Beyond the length of the email, make sure that it presents a clear and compelling marketing message. That includes presenting benefits ahead of features, using lots of action words, and including a strong call to action. Make it clear what you want the recipient to do, and make it easy for the recipient to do it. That might include putting a link to your website in the email, presenting a printable coupon, or who knows what. Just be very clear about what the next steps are—and how to take them.

All of this is direct mail copywriting 101, of course. If you can create a great direct mail piece, you can probably create a great email piece as well. Just remember that your email copy has to be a lot shorter than what you'd put in a direct mail piece—shorter, even, than a single-page letter. In an email promotion, you have space for the key message and not a lot more.

As you no doubt know, selling the deal with words—lots of them—is what typically works in direct mail. It's a copywriter's medium. Email, however, doesn't work quite the same way, and it's because of customers' expectations. People expect to receive long letters that they read in their postal mailboxes. That's not what people expect in their email inboxes, however—and you have to adjust for that.

So if you think your message needs a lot of supporting detail, think again. You don't have to and shouldn't present all that detail in the email itself. What you need to do is take advantage of the Internet's linking nature. Emails can contain links, after all. Just link the customer back to your website for more content if it's necessary.

Fine Print

One last thing. As noted in the previous chapter, you need to include some standard fine print in all your email messages. This includes some sort of unsubscribe link, as well as a link to your company's privacy policy. You don't have to draw attention to these details (which means very small print is fine), but you do need to include them.

> **note** A working unsubscribe link isn't just a nicety; it's a legal requirement under the CAN-SPAM act.

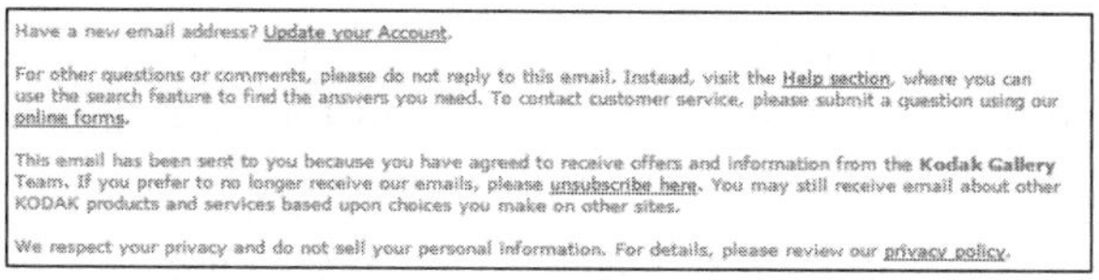

Have a new email address? Update your Account.

For other questions or comments, please do not reply to this email. Instead, visit the Help section, where you can use the search feature to find the answers you need. To contact customer service, please submit a question using our online forms.

This email has been sent to you because you have agreed to receive offers and information from the **Kodak Gallery** Team. If you prefer to no longer receive our emails, please unsubscribe here. You may still receive email about other KODAK products and services based upon choices you make on other sites.

We respect your privacy and do not sell your personal information. For details, please review our privacy policy.

FIGURE 20.9

The fine print at the bottom of a Kodak Gallery email.

Personalizing Your Mailings

One surefire way to increase the response rate of your email campaigns is to personalize the mailings you send out. When someone reads an email that sounds as if it were written just for him, he's much more likely to take it seriously and act upon it.

How can you personalize the emails you send? There are lots of ways, including the following:

- Make sure the email is addressed to the person by name. That means including the recipient's name, not just his or her email address, in the To: line.

- Include the recipient's name in the email's subject line.

- Tailor the content of the email to the specific customer. That means using the information in your various databases to send relevant messages based on prior purchases, web pages browsed, and the like. You can also use demographic information to better target the message content.

- Include the recipient's name in the content of the message. This can be in the form of a simple "Dear Mr. Jones" salutation at the top of the message or inserting his or her name in appropriate places within the message text, including (and especially) in the message's call to action.

20

The point is to make each customer think that he's receiving an email tailored just for him or her. We all respond better to personalized messages than we do to mass-produced ones.

What *Not* to Do

We've talked a lot about what to do when you're creating an email promotion. There are also a few things *not* to do.

Avoid Spam Techniques

First, you need to make sure that your emails don't fall into the recipient's spam filter. That means avoiding those techniques commonly used by spammers.

What are these techniques? Well, they tend to change over time, but here are a few to look out for:

- Including dozens of recipient addresses in the To: field
- Writing subject lines in ALL CAPS
- Excessive use of exclamation points and other inappropriate characters (!, #, *, and the like) in the subject line
- Using the word "free" in the subject line

As you can no doubt tell, it's the subject line that gets examined most by spam filters. You need to do the same and make sure your subject line doesn't sound like a typical spam message.

Don't Promise One Thing and Deliver Another

Beyond spam, you have to make sure you give the customer what he thought he signed up for. Email marketing is permission marketing, after all, and a customer opts in expecting to receive a specific type of thing. If you deliver something different, you'll have a very annoyed customer—and potentially be viewed as sending unwanted spam.

So make sure the content of your email promotions match the content you described on your email signup page. If you send emails that differ in content from what people signed up for, they'll either delete your message or unsubscribe from all future mailings.

20

Don't Be Annoying

Finally, remember that you're being invited into your customers' homes, via their email inboxes. Don't abuse the invitation. That means you should avoid sending out too many emails—don't want to overstay your welcome. Remember the old show business adage about leaving them wanting more applies just as well in email marketing.

The Bottom Line

You can send out various types of promotional emails—promotional blasts, regular mailings, email newsletters, and related items mailings. Whatever type of email you send, you need a short and compelling subject line; a sender name or address that the recipient knows; a relatively short and direct promotional message; and the necessary fine print, including an unsubscribe option.

Your emails will draw better response if they're somehow personalized to your recipients. That includes everything from including the recipient's name in the salutation to customizing the email's content to the recipient's past behavior or demographics. And, whatever else you do, avoid using techniques that might identify your emails as spam; you don't want your messages to end up in the recipient's spam folder.

HOW OFTEN IS TOO OFTEN?

What's the right frequency for email mailings? Should you email customers once a day, once a week, once a month, or once a year?

There's no single answer to this question, other than often enough to be remembered but not so often as to be annoying. The exact number, of course, depends on what you're offering and what the customer expects to receive.

Some types of email are actually looked forward to by many recipients. Speaking for myself, I like seeing the weekly announcements of upcoming concerts from Ticketmaster, Jam Mail, and other promoters; I also find value from weekly fare specials from Delta and other airlines, as well as new release announcements from Amazon.com and other music and movie retailers.

20

In these instances, once a week is the right frequency. But for other marketers, that might be too much. For example, I really don't need to see the weekly specials from my local computer reseller; I'm not in the market to buy a new PC once a week.

So here's the thing. You need to keep your name out there in front of your customers, which argues for a minimum frequency of once a month. But unless you really truly have something new and valuable to announce each week, going to a once-a-week mailing is probably too frequent.

Of course, you can always tailor your frequency to what your customers want. Ask your customers how often they want to receive emails. When the customer opts into your mailings, give the option of once a week, once a month, and so on. Then send out your mailings on the desired schedule. You'll be giving your customers exactly what they asked for.

20

Tracking Email Marketing Performance

Tracking the performance of an email marketing campaign is similar to tracking a direct mail campaign, except more so. That is, when you're dealing with email, there are more metrics that you can directly track—which is a good thing.

Determining Key Metrics

With traditional email, about the only metric you can track is sales—that is, the percentage of respondents who bought directly because of the mailing you sent out. Well, you can track sales (we call them *conversions*) with email campaigns, too, along with a lot of other important data points.

Delivery Rate

Let's start with the *delivery rate* metric. This is important, as it tells you precisely how many people received your emails.

Wait, you may be saying. I sent out 1,000 emails, so there must have been 1,000 emails delivered. Au contraire, mon frère; not every email you send out ends up in a valid inbox. Some emails are sent to an incorrect address, some get bounced from full inboxes, and some end up in spam filters. None of these missed messages are actually received, and none can be read or acted upon.

> **note** Not all direct mail pieces are received, either. Some percentage of every mailing gets sent to wrong postal addresses or are simply lost in transit.

The problem is that delivery rate is the one metric that is not easily tracked. You can track the number of emails that get bounced back to you (if you're not sure how, ask your IT guys), and hence the *bounce rate*, but you have no idea how many emails get caught in spam filters. So getting an exact delivery rate number isn't in the cards.

That said, most email experts believe that 20% or so of legitimate (nonspam) emails mistakenly get blocked as spam. So calculate your bounce rate from a given mailing, add 20% to the number, and subtract the total from 100%. This gives you your approximate delivery rate for that mailing.

Open Rate

Next, you want to see how many recipients actually open your emails versus how many ignore them or delete them without reading. The percent of messages opened is your *open rate*.

How do you determine when someone opens your email? It's all done with HTML. To be precise, you insert a snippet of HTML code into your email message that tracks when an image in your email shows up in someone's inbox. The image doesn't get downloaded (from your website) and displayed (in the email message) until the recipient actually opens the email message. When the message is opened, the image is displayed, and your server tracks that action.

Note that you can calculate two different open rates. The first divides the number of messages opened by the total number of messages sent out and may not be the most useful calculation. The second approach divides the number of messages opened by the number of messages actually delivered; this rate is a better measurement of the effectiveness of your campaign.

note Because open rate tracks the display of an image, it doesn't track any text-only emails you send; it only works with HTML messages. It also doesn't track emails that are opened in email programs configured not to display HTML images.

If you're looking to compare your results to industry averages, JupiterMedia estimates an average permission email open rate of around 30%. If you're getting less than this, you need to examine your campaign's subject lines; it's the subject that entices recipients to open and read the accompanying message.

That said, don't assume that just because a message was opened that it was actually read. A message appearing in the preview pane of an email program counts as read (the tracked image was displayed), even though the recipient may not have really read it. (How many emails that appear in your email program's preview pane do you yourself read?) Still, the open rate, as well as the total number of opens, is a good thing to track.

Click-Through Rate

You send out your email. It gets delivered. It gets opened. The next step in the process, then, is the recipient acting on the email by clicking one of the links included therein.

Clicks are the easiest part of the process to track. Your IT guys can easily track site visits coming from specific links; just make sure they know to track the links you include in specific email campaigns.

You can track either total clicks or unique clicks. Unique clicks tell you how many recipients clicked on a link in the email; total clicks help you determine if recipients click on multiple links or respond more than once. As such, unique clicks are probably more useful to measure.

Once you know the number of clicks you receive, you can calculate the click-through rate (CTR). You can calculate CTR as clicks versus emails sent, clicks versus emails successfully delivered, or clicks versus emails opened. You can also calculate CTR using either unique or total clicks. Most marketers calculate unique clicks versus emails delivered, so if you're looking at benchmarks, use this approach.

What's a good CTR? For what it's worth, JupiterResearch estimates the average CTR for permission email at about 12%, although this number varies wildly depending on whether you're doing B2B or B2C mailings and the types of names you mail to.

Conversion Rate

Clicks are great; sales are better. For this reason, you want to calculate the *conversion rate*, based on the percentage of recipients who actually do something when they get to your website. This could be (and often is) purchasing the item promoted, but it could also be asking for more info or other action you specify.

You calculate conversion rate by dividing total conversions by the number of emails successfully delivered. If you're looking for benchmarks, JupiterResearch estimates an average 4% conversion rate for permission emails. That's pretty good—better than you typically get with most other forms of direct marketing.

21

ROI

Once you count the total sales you generate from an email campaign, you can calculate your return on investment (ROI) for that campaign. You know how to calculate ROI—divide the profits generated by the money spent.

When you calculate ROI for a given campaign, you're probably going to discover that you're very pleased with the results. That's because email marketing typically has a higher ROI than all other types of marketing, online or off. And that's a very good thing.

What level of ROI should you be looking at? The Direct Marketing Association estimates a $43.62 average ROI for email marketing campaigns,[1] which is 70% higher than the ROI for any other direct response vehicle. Assuming that your ROI is in this range, you gotta love it.

Unsubscribe Rate

There's one final email metric you probably want to track, and that's your total unsubscribe rate—the percentage of people who are removing their names from your list. If you have too high an unsubscribe rate or a rate that's increasing, you have a problem somewhere that you need to address. Maybe you're sending out too many mailings, or maybe the mailings aren't targeted enough. Whatever the cause, let the unsubscribe rate alert you to potential problems.

Tracking Email Data

When should you track the performance of an email campaign—and how often? Email is unique in that you're likely to get almost-immediate responses to your mailings, unlike traditional advertising where responses can trickle in for days or weeks, or even traditional direct mail, where you have to wait a few days for your pieces to be delivered. Email gets delivered in a matter of seconds and read almost as soon as it shows up in people's inboxes.

For that reason, most email campaigns get the majority of responses within the first 72 hours after sending. This argues for an almost-immediate measurement.

21

---

1. Direct Marketing Association, Power of Direct, 2009

In reality, you probably want to check the response a few times during the campaign. I recommend tracking responses after 24 hours, 48 hours, and 72 hours after sending. This will provide the majority of tracking data, but you should also track again after a week and then after a month; some responses will continue to trickle in over time.

You can analyze your tracking data at any point in this continuum, although there's no reason not to do so immediately after collecting the data. Just know that the first tracking point (24 hours) is likely to provide an incomplete view of the campaign's performance; it's probably better to wait until you have two or three days' worth of data before you make any final judgments.

The Bottom Line

When evaluating the performance of an email marketing campaign, the key metrics are delivery rate, open rate, click-through rate, and conversion rate. You should also measure the ROI of each campaign, as well as your email list's ongoing unsubscribe rate. Check the results one, two, and three days after sending the emails and analyze the data after the third day.

SEGMENT YOUR ANALYSIS

When analyzing your email marketing performance, it's good to look at the overall numbers. But it's even better to look at performance by segment so you know which parts of your list are performing better than others.

To that end, you need to segment your email lists in whatever fashion makes sense for your business. Maybe you segment demographically (gender, age, and so forth), maybe you segment by when customers last made a purchase, or maybe you segment by what customers last purchased. What's important is that you break out your list in a way that works for you.

Once segmented, you can see which groups were more likely to open and act on your mailings. Find the group that's most responsive and market more aggressively to them. Find the group that's least responsive and figure out why; maybe you need to change your promotion message or mailing frequency—or maybe you just need to give up on them.

21

This is the nice thing about email marketing—you have a lot of information available. And the more you know, the smarter decisions you can make going forward. Online or off, smarter marketers are more successful marketers.

21

Understanding Blog Marketing

Next up on our tour of online marketing vehicles is blog marketing. This one is kind of a nebulous concept—does it mean marketing to or through third-party bloggers or marketing via your own corporate blog?

In reality, blog marketing encompasses both of these activities. To take full advantage of the blogosphere, you need to put on a PR push to get mentioned in other people's blogs as well as create and maintain your own company or product blog.

Getting to Know the Blogosphere

Okay, just what is this blogosphere, and where can you find it?

What Is a Blog?

First off, a *blog*—short for "web log"—is a journal of sorts that is hosted on the Web. Most blogs are updated frequently with commentary, links to other sites, and anything else the author might be interested in. Most blogs also let visitors post comments in response to the owner's postings, which often results in a community that is very similar to that of a message board. It's a twenty-first century version of self-publishing, enabled by the Internet.

note As for the terminology, the word *blog* is a noun describing a web-based journal. The word *blog* can also be used as a verb, meaning to add content to a blog. The activity of updating a blog is called *blogging*; someone who runs a blog is a *blogger*; and the entire universe of blogs is the *blogosphere*.

Blogs are composed of individual *posts*, typically a paragraph or two or three long. Blog posts are displayed in reverse chronological order so that the newest posts always appear at the top of the page. Older posts are typically accessed via some sort of archive link.

FIGURE 22.1
A typical blog, with posts down the main part of the page and additional content in the side-bar on the right.

Blog posts can contain text, photos, videos, music, and links to other blogs and web pages. Blog content ranges from personal opinion and rants to quasi-news reporting and marketing-type announcements.

The most popular blogs tend to be updated on a fairly regular basis—weekly, daily, or even hourly, depending on the blog. The process of updating a blog is facilitated by blog publishing software and requires little or no technical expertise on the part of the blogger. This means, of course, that virtually anyone can blog—which makes for an interesting mix of blogs in the blogosphere.

Who Are the Bloggers?

Blogs can be hosted by individuals, groups of individuals, or by businesses. Obviously, an individual's personal blog is likely to be a little different from a blog run by a big business, even if they might superficially look similar.

Some individuals create blogs that are a kind of personal-yet-public scrap-book—an online diary to record their thoughts for posterity. Even if no one else ever looks at it, it's still valuable to the author as a repository of thoughts and information they can turn to at any later date.

Other blogs are less personal and more focused. There are blogs devoted to hob-bies, to sports teams, to local events, to particular industries, and so on. Bloggers write about music or video games or travel or cooking or whatever they're interested in, and their blogs include their thoughts on the topic at hand, as well as links to interesting news articles and websites.

> **note** The most serious individual bloggers are like columnists in the traditional media. They write with a passion, a point of view, and a personal sensibility that make their blogs extremely interesting to read. Even bloggers who don't inject personal comments still offer a viewpoint based on what they choose to include and link to in their blogs. It's an interesting world out there in the blogosphere, and it's revolutionizing journalism (and journals) for the new online reality.

Then there are those blogs that exist in the service of companies, brands, and prod-ucts. Let's label these *company blogs,* as they are run by companies (or organiza-tions), not independent individuals. You can include a company blog as part of your company's website or as a freestand-ing site; the key is that you or others in your company write the blog posts and moderate and manage the resulting cus-tomer comments. You can use a company blog to post the latest company news, announce new products and promotions, or just talk about topics of interest to your customer base.

What Are Company Blogs Good For?

You should consider a company blog a marketing tool, a way to talk directly to your customer base on a regular basis. It's a mix of public relations and promotion, a source of constant information about your company and your products.

Just how can you utilize a company blog? There are lots of different approaches.

Disseminating News and Information

One of the primary uses of a company blog is to get the word out about what-ever it is you want your customers to know about. Maybe you talk about the new stores you're opening or a new product line you're developing or maybe a

22

series of upcoming trade shows or product demonstrations. You can even talk about your current advertising campaign, changes in company policy, or what's new in your industry.

For example, the Nuts About Southwest blog (www.blogsouthwest.com) features posts from employees throughout the company. The individual bloggers talk about upcoming schedule changes, feature photos and tours of their newest planes, go behind the scenes of advertising photo shoots, and discuss the company's community service programs. Southwest even hosts some guest customer bloggers who blog about their customer experiences with the airline. It's a very newsworthy blog that puts a real human face on the company.

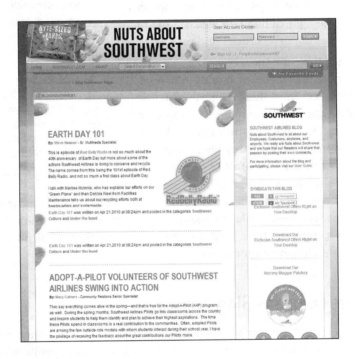

FIGURE 22.2
The Nuts About Southwest company blog.

Promoting Products and Services

You can also use a company blog as a pure promotional tool. You can use it to announce new products, upcoming promotions, big sales—you name it. All you have to do is post your promotional announcement as a blog post; that means couching ad copy as a news article, but that isn't so different from writing a standard press release.

22

Of course, you can also promote your products and services in a more subtle fashion. Instead of saying, "Here's our new product!" you write an article about how a particular customer is using that product or how a given company adopted your product line, or how easy it is to use your product in a particular situation. You get the gist of it; create a news event that features the product or service in question and talk about it on a blog post.

Interacting with Your Customers

A blog doesn't have to be one-way communication. You can foster a closer relationship with your customers and create a burgeoning online community by encouraging reader comments to your blog posts.

These customer comments serve several purposes. First, it makes your customers feel as if they have a direct relationship with your company; this customer-company connection makes for a more loyal customer base. Second, and equally important, it lets you know what your customers are thinking. This type of customer feedback is terrific market research; if you pay attention to these comments, you can better *think like the customer* and thus better serve your customers' needs.

And you don't have to passively wait for comments to use your blog for market research. You can proactively ask questions of the blog's readers, either in blog posts or via polls posted on the blog site. You can ask questions to find out more about the demographics of your customer base (where do you live, how old are you), how they use your products, what improvements they might like to see, even what new products they might be interested in.

Providing More Exposure—and More Search Opportunities

Here's another benefit you get from running a company blog—it's one more thing for people to stumble over online. Now, I don't necessarily mean that in a negative or even a passive way; having one more home on the Web is a good thing and part of a smart marketing strategy.

If you have both a website and a blog at different URLs, that's two different ways that customers can find you online. It's also two different ways that search engines can find you—which can double your visibility in search engine results.

Think about it. If you have both a website and a blog that focus on a particular topic and are optimized for the same keywords, anyone searching for that topic using those keywords is now likely to see both your website and your blog in her search results. Whether your two sites rank number one and number two or end up somewhere further down the page, you still have two

22

chances of getting clicked instead of just one. That's a terrific way to increase your site traffic coming from the search engines.

It gets even better than that. Because your blog is probably going to be updated more frequently than your website, it may actually rank *higher* with the search engines than your more static website. Search engines love fresh content, which a blog can supply on a very regular basis; the search engines use your blog's RSS feed to update their search indexes on a daily basis. Fresh content equals high rankings—which result in more traffic to you.

Running Your Own Blog

By now I hope you're convinced that there are benefits to running your own company blog. But just how do you incorporate blogging as part of your online marketing mix?

First, you need to decide whether you want to include the blog as part of your existing website or set up a separate blog site. I'm generally in favor of the latter approach, a separate URL. Even if it's a subdomain, it gives you two shots at the search engines. Having your blog in a subdirectory of your main site isn't going to help you much in that regard.

Next, you have to develop a blogging strategy—that is, what you want to blog about and how often. Blog content can range from simple product announcements to in-depth articles about how your company works. Your blog posts define the character of your blog and should reflect the brand or product image you want to convey; this includes not only the content but also the writing style. Should your blog be light-hearted or deadly serious? Should the articles be short and sweet or long and detailed? These are key strategic decisions you need to make.

note One popular approach is to use a subdomain for your blog. For example, if your main domain is mybusiness.com, your blog might be located at blog.mybusiness.com.

When it comes to posting strategy, you can decide to post monthly, weekly, daily, or even more often if that makes sense. In general, you keep customers coming back with more frequent posts; certainly, anything less frequent than weekly isn't going to do the trick. If you have enough unique content to post several times a week, or daily, that's even better.

You also have to determine *who* should be doing the blogging. Should your posts come exclusively from a copywriter in the marketing department, or should you solicit input from throughout the organization? Do you want to go with consistent style and subject matter, which argues in favor of a single poster, or go for more variety in content, which you get if you use multiple posters? And what about soliciting posts from people outside the company, including customers? Again, important decisions must be made.

You also have blog design issues to consider. The blog page itself is merely a container for your blog posts, but it's an important container. You should surround the posts with elements of use to both you and your customers. This includes links or buttons to share your blog's content with various social media sites, such as Facebook and Twitter; links to email blog content to other users; links to subscribe to the blog's RSS or Atom feeds; and links back to your website, either to the home page or to individual product pages.

The goal, after all, is to convert blog readers into paying customers—if not immediately, then eventually. You can do this subtly by inviting the customer back to view more content or more overtly by promoting weekly specials or including other calls to action. Think of your blog as an extension of your existing web presence, and you'll be headed in the right direction.

Marketing to Other Blogs

Posting to your own blog isn't the only way to include the blogosphere in your marketing plans. You can also utilize third-party blogs to promote your company and products—by getting those bloggers to talk about you and what you offer.

This approach incorporates the blogosphere as a key component of your online public relations efforts. In the old days, you sent press releases to various press outlets, such as newspapers and magazines. Today, however, that traditional press is supplemented by both professional and semi-professional bloggers. In fact, you should consider some bloggers as part of the press; they function similarly in terms of informing the public, even if they don't share the same journalistic code.

And here's the thing. Many companies are finding that blogs send more traffic back to their sites than do traditional media. Within any given industry or topic area, there are some blogs that are quite influential; they have a large readership that trusts the blogger's opinions. If such a blogger writes about your company or product, lots of traffic—and, hopefully, sales—can result.

You need to expend effort, then, to get in front of (and in the good graces of) these influential bloggers. That means identifying these bloggers, of course,

22

but also getting to know them, the same way your PR folks might get to know the most important newspaper columnists or magazine reviewers. This sort of thing is done on a personal basis, not just by sending out press releases or their electronic equivalent—although you still need to do that, of course, to hit the second- and third-tier bloggers. With the big guys, there's a lot of talking and cajoling involved; it's a relationship kind of thing.

If you can get in front of these bloggers, however, and get them to write about your products, you can then benefit from that implied endorsement. You can't always tell how many readers of a blog will act on the blogger's advice, but it's "free" placement that carries with it a legitimacy similar to true word-of-mouth marketing. Directing your PR efforts to these influential bloggers is every bit as important as cultivating traditional media contacts—and perhaps more so. It's the kind of exposure you just can't get from paid media.

The Bottom Line

Blogs are an important part of the Web, places that people visit to get both news and opinion. As such, you need to incorporate blogs into your web marketing plan in two different ways.

First, you need to establish your own company or product blog. This should probably be separate from your main website in order to maximize your search results exposure. Use this blog to broadcast company and product news and announcements, as well as cultivate a closer relationship with your online customers and learn more about them.

Second, you need to direct your PR efforts to the most influential bloggers in your industry or topic area. When your company or products get mentioned by these bloggers, you get great word-of-mouth exposure that carries a greater legitimacy than paid advertising. Treat these top bloggers as you would your contacts in the traditional media; establish personal relationships in addition to sending out press releases and the like.

SHOULD EMPLOYEES BLOG?

When we talk about a company blog, you have to decide which employees can or should contribute to that blog. But your blog isn't the only place on the Web where your employees might be blogging; don't be surprised if you discover a number of your employees hosting their own blogs—where they may, on occasion, talk about your company.

Therein lies the issue. Do you really want your employees talking about you? After all, if they're blogging on their own time, they can say anything they want about the company or your products—positive or negative.

Imagine a disgruntled employee (and we all have them), venting about his boss, workplace conditions, or even product quality in a blog post. Even worse, envision an employee divulging company secrets on his blog. It can—and does—happen.

And even positive comments can be problematic. The happiest, most satisfied employee can talk about your company or your products in a way that doesn't hew the company line. You have a particular image you want to maintain; an exuberant employee might paint a much different picture. Like I said, even positive comments can have a negative result.

The question, then, is how much control should your company have over its employees' personal blogging activities. The answer is quite a bit—if you address it upfront. What you can't do is crack down on someone, or even fire them, without laying down the rules first. You do this by establishing a company blogging policy, where you spell out precisely what employees can and can't do when it comes to blogging on their own when the company's name is involved. And, yes, you can specify just what types of information they can divulge and how. You can even, if you wish, state that employees can't blog about their work at all, which that's not an unusual policy.

How strict a policy you concoct depends on how much control you want over your company's public image. Just make sure your employees are aware of the policy, even to the extent of making them sign the darned thing. If an employee then decides to blog outside of the defined parameters, you can take whatever action is necessary with confidence.

Creating a Company or Product Blog

As noted in the previous chapter, there are two aspects to blog marketing—running your own company blog and promoting your company and your products to other bloggers. This chapter focuses on that first of these—creating a blog to promote your company, your brand, or your products.

Why Create a Company Blog?

Before we delve into all the details, let's re-examine the fundamental question of just how a company blog fits into a company's marketing mix. Do you really need to blog—and if so, why?

There are many distinct advantages to creating a quality blog for your company, brand, or product. In general, however, a blog provides an efficient way for you to communicate to customers and potential customers and to engage in an ongoing conversation with these people. It creates a closer relationship between you and your most loyal customers.

A blog is also a great tool for gaining insight about your customer base. It's not just a one-way communication; comments left about your blog posts let you know what's your customers' minds, especially those loyal trendsetters who follow your blog on a regular basis. That's invaluable research.

That said, running a blog isn't right for every company. As with every aspect of online marketing, you have to figure out where your community of customers is and then determine which tools and channels will best reach and resonate with them. A blog might be more trouble than it's worth—or you might just not have that much to say on a regular basis.

Establishing a Public Face for Your Company

One big advantage of a company blog is that the blog lets you establish a public face for your company, brand, or product. Instead of remaining a faceless, soulless corporation or empty brand, your blog lets you connect to customers on a person-to-person basis. In essence, you put a human voice to your company or product.

Consider two companies, one with a blog and one without. The company without a blog looks like every other company online, offering the same benefits and promises as all its competitors. "We have the lowest prices, we have the best customer service, we're open 24 hours a day, blah blah blah." You've heard it all before, and who really cares? There's virtually no differentiation between this site and the competition.

The company that has a blog, however, can make the same claims but augment them with real-world comments and experiences—especially if employees from throughout the company are contributing to the blog. "Hi, I'm Paul, and I'm really excited about the new snow tires we're offering this season. They give great performance in the mush, and the tread lasts 50% longer than other brands."

See what you get from the blog? Instead of boring facts and numbers, you get a personal experience. Paul clearly is passionate about what he's doing and describes the new product in a way that standard copy just can't do. Customers get the facts but with a very human spin.

Putting this personal face on your company or products will inspire more customers to purchase what you're selling. Customers like the personal approach, so they'll probably like Paul and his blog posts—and, by extension, they'll like the products that Paul blogs about. It's a great form of promotion, not really advertising, that doesn't cost much but generates impressive results.

note A company can also use a blog to address potential issues before they become big problems. Again, it's the human face thing. If you get a real human being in front of an issue, you can most likely defuse things before they get bad.

Establishing Your Authority

A blog can also help you establish your company (or a person within your company) as an authority in your industry or just the place to come for the latest news. This requires you to post a lot of fresh content on a very regular basis, of course, but it can make your blog a go-to site for those interested in specific industry buzz.

Let's start with the facts first—posting the facts, that is. The concept here is using your blog to disseminate news relevant to your company or product. Not just your own press releases (in fact, never your own press releases—how transparently self-serving!), but rather honest-to-goodness headline news from your particular industry.

What you end up offering, then, is a blog chock full of news headlines, articles, and links that provide unique value to a specific customer base. Interested customers visit your blog on a daily basis for the latest news or subscribe to the blog's newsfeed to have the news delivered to them automatically. In either case, you get in front of your customers on a regular basis and establish your company as an authoritative source for news and other important information.

note Where you generate or gather these headlines is another issue, of course. Most companies end up scraping news from other websites, and that's okay; in this instance, you're a news consolidator, which has its own particular value.

You can also establish your company as an authority by *making* news. Here I'm talking about the new and unique content you provide via your blog. This may be detailed information about new products or industry developments, it may be hands-on advice or instruction on how to use a give product or perform a specific task, or it may be pure opinion about issues of interest to your customer base. In any instance, your blog becomes an important source of information for customers who are interested in whatever it is you're blogging about.

Providing Fresh Content for Your Website

Here's another advantage to creating a company blog and posting to it on a regular basis: All that blog content provides fresh material for what might otherwise be a dreadfully static website. (And let's face it, most corporate websites are dreadfully static; they're about as dead as dead can be.)

The goal, you see, is keeping your home page new and lively. Constant blog

note For a blog to contribute to the freshness of your website, you have to host your blog content on your website, not on a separate blog site. Your blog could be on a separate web page or domain, although it works best if you at least feed the latest post headlines to your site's home page.

updates do that; there's always something new on your home page when you're making daily blog posts. The rest of the page's content—contact information, mission statement, pretty pictures of your corporate headquarters—can remain constant; new blog posts will still make your site appear fresh and relevant.

Blogging as Part of Your Search Engine Marketing Strategy

There's another advantage to feeding fresh blog content to your website: All that fresh blog content gets eaten up by Google and the other search engines. They just *love* blog posts, and that will improve your standing in those search results.

This love of blog posts is something relatively new in the search world. In years past, the search engines only indexed traditional web pages, but lately Google and its peers have started accepting RSS feeds and indexing those feeds. This lets them index much fresher content than is typically available from relatively static web pages, and fresher content is a good thing when you're searching.

What happens, then, is Google and Yahoo! and Bing and the rest now display relevant blog posts when someone conducts a search. If your blog contains information relevant to a given search, chances are that post will show up in the search results.

And I mean in the *main* search results. That's not how it's always been. Google, for example, used to not display blog results on its main search results page, instead opting for a separate Google Blog Search page and results. (Which still exists, by the way, for those determined to conduct blog-only searches.) Now, however, Google displays blog posts within the same search results as they do web pages. It's what Google calls *universal search*, although it's really universal (or unified) results, but who's to argue?

The point is, when you maintain a fresh and relevant blog, you increase your chances of popping up in those search results. Let's say you sell baby food, and your website is all about baby food, and your blog contains posts about baby food. When a curious mother searches Google for "baby food," it's possible that both your main web page and your blog page will show up in the search results. That's two slots on the results page, which more or less doubles your chances of generating a click through.

In other words, a blog provides the opportunity to occupy multiple search results for the same query. Sweet.

Where Should the Blog Reside?

One of the first decisions you have to make about your blog is where it should reside on the Web. You have three choices:

- At its own domain or on the domain of one of the major blog hosting services. So you might end up with a blog with its own URL (www.ourcompanyblog.com) or a Blogspot or Wordpress URL (ourcompanyblog.blogspot.com).

- As a separate page or subdomain on your website. In this scenario, your blog has a URL such as www.ourcompany.com/blog/ or blog. ourcompany.com.

- On the home page of your main website. In this instance, your blog doesn't have its own URL at all; it exists as content on your site's home page.

There are advantages to each approach.

Hosting the blog at its own domain is easy enough to do, and provides the blog with both its own unique address and unique identity. It also positions the blog as separate from your main website, which may not be a good thing; you want to integrate your marketing efforts as much as possible. That said, this approach probably provides the best shot for maximizing your search engine exposure because you have two separate sites to place.

Hosting the blog at a blog hosting service, however, and using the blog host's domain doesn't have a lot of advantages. In fact, it's just plain lazy. All the hosting services (Blogger, WordPress, and so on) let you place the blogs they host at any URL you specify. Why would you subsume your corporate brand to a blogspot.com URL when it could exist at your own brand's domain? To me, this option is a nonstarter.

Then there's the option of hosting the blog on your site, but on its own page or subdomain. This is nice option, as you gain the benefits of a distinct page for your blog while retaining the advantages of existing under your main corporate domain. Kind of the best of both worlds, if you ask me.

The final option, posting your blog to your site's home page, certainly gives your blog prominence, as well as provides a constant stream of fresh content to your home page. It doesn't, however, provide a unique URL for your blog, which kind of diminishes its own identity. You also lose the benefits of having a second strong URL for your content.

23

There is, however, a compromise option of which I'm particularly fond. In this scenario, you put your blog on its own page or subdomain but then feed the most recent blog posts (or, more typical, the post headlines) to a module on your home page. What's nice about this approach is you get a separate URL and identity for the blog while still feeding fresh content to your home page. You also don't overwhelm the home page with the blog content—we're talking about a smallish module, either above or below the fold, that is constantly updated with fresh blog posts.

FIGURE 23.1

Blog posts incorporated on the home page of clothing retailer Patagonia.

Building the Blog

If you work for a large company, blog creation is probably just one more task you assign to the internal team or outside firm who handles your website design and maintenance. They can easily build you a blog to go along with your website and provide the tools necessary to make your regular posts.

They may also simply utilize the tools available at one of the major blog hosting services. It's easy enough to plug a Blogger or WordPress blog into your own website, and savvy site designers might do just that.

Blog Hosting Services

If you work for a smaller firm or just have a very tight budget, the blog hosting route is probably the way to go. These services let you quickly and easily create a blog, assign it to a given URL, customize its look and feel, and then start making posts. It's a turnkey solution.

Most of these blog-hosting services are free, so you don't have to pay a single penny to get your blog up and running. The downside is that you may not be able to completely customize the blog as you would if you were designing it from scratch, although it's really a matter of degree. Most of these services let you provide your own HTML templates for the blog design.

What's nice about these services is how easy they make it. Setting up a simple blog is as easy as making a few choices in a form; posting is as easy as writing what you want and clicking a button. They take the process and make it extremely user-friendly.

The chief downside, at least for inexperienced users, is that your blog's URL is tied to the hosting service's domain. For example, a blog hosted by Blogger exists in the blogspot.com domain, like this: yourblog.blogspot.com. That's less than ideal for any company wanting to establish its own online identity. Fortunately, most of these services let you publish your blog to any domain you specify, even if it requires a bit more effort to set up in that fashion. So you can have a blog hosted by Blogger or WordPad, while the blog itself resides at the URL of your choosing—either a distinct URL or a page or subdomain of your existing website.

Which are the top blog-hosting services? Here's the list I go by:

- Blogger (www.blogger.com)
- TypePad (www.typepad.com)
- WordPress (www.wordpress.com)

For that matter, your web hosting service might offer blog hosting, too; many do. It's worth checking into.

> **note** Of these blog hosting services, Blogger is by far the most popular. Learn more about Blogger in my book, *Using Blogger* (Michael Miller, Que, 2010).

Blogging Tools

If you decide to skip the blog hosting services and build your blog yourself, there are several blogging tools you can use just for that purpose. No sense in reinventing any wheels, you know. These tools let you create a master blog page design, insert a blog onto its own web page on your site, start posting, and then manage all your posts and comments.

Some of the more popular of these blogging tools include the following:

- b2evolution (www.b2evolution.net)
- Blog:CMS (www.blogcms.com)
- Movable Type (www.movabletype.com)

Designing Your Blog

What should your blog look like? Well, it should look like the rest of your website, of course; you should carry over your site's look and feel and color scheme as much as possible. You want all your online efforts to be consistent and holistic. Everything has to fit together like pieces of a puzzle, your blog included.

That said, a blog has unique elements that you need to take into consideration. Most blogs have a sidebar that feature a variety of blog-specific content modules. Think of this sidebar as a kind of frame for static content around (or beside) the constantly changing content of your blog posts.

FIGURE 23.2

A Thousand Words, the official Kodak blog—looks pretty much like the Kodak website.

Some of the more important content modules include the following:

- **Archive**—This is a list of links to older posts, typically organized by year, month, or week.

- **Tags**—This is a list of keywords included in your blog posts; it's a way for readers to find posts about specific topics. They click a tag and are shown a list of posts that contain that keyword.

- **Categories**—Sometimes used in lieu of tags, sometimes alongside, this helps you organize your blog posts by topic category.

- **Search**—If you really serious about helping readers find older content, add a search box to your blog. This way readers can search for what they're interested in.

- **Blog roll**—This is a list of other (typically related) blogs that you recommend.

- **Subscribe**—This is a button that lets readers subscribe to an RSS or Atom feed of your blog content.

Categories
Announcements
Community
Japanese
Learning Resources
New Feature
Prototyping
Uncategorized

Archives
May 2010
April 2010
March 2010
February 2010
October 2009
September 2009
August 2009
July 2009
May 2009
March 2009
February 2009
January 2009
December 2008
November 2008
October 2008
September 2008
August 2008
July 2008
June 2008

Recent Posts
Fireworks CS5 post-launch news
Fireworks CS5 is now shipping!
Fireworks CS4 10.0.4 Updater for Mac OS X
now available
Fireworks CS5 demos and details
Announcing Adobe Fireworks CS5

FIGURE 23.3

Content modules in a blog's sidebar.

I also recommend providing means for your readers to easily share the blog content they like. This means incorporating a series of buttons for the most popular social media/bookmarking sites (Twitter, Facebook, MySpace, Digg, and so on) as well as an email button. These buttons should appear below each and every post on your blog. Make it easy for readers to share content, and you'll spread your content among a wider audience of potential customers.

FIGURE 23.4

A group of sharing buttons accompanying a blog post.

Even with these elements factored in, don't assume that all blogs have to look alike. Suspend everything you think you know about blogs and remember that a blog can be designed to look like any other web page. There's no reason why your blog can't have a bar running down the side of the page advertising your weekly specials, or links to other pages on your site, or a call to action to talk to a representative or download a whitepaper or whatever. Anything you include on a normal web page can also be included on your blog page.

Allowing Comments—or Not

One other decision you have to make about your blog is whether or not you want to allow reader comments. This isn't necessarily an easy decision.

Most blogs allow comments. Know, however, that if you let readers comment on your posts, not all those comments will be positive. Some will be slightly disagreeable, some will be way off topic, and some will be just plain hateful. It happens.

With that in mind, how accepting is your corporate culture of criticism? If you want to present an everything is peaches and cream image, then you're not going to take kindly to troublemakers in your midst. Rather than risk the occasional reader disagreeing with you, you might just want to disable comments completely.

If you do enable comments, you probably need to monitor them. At its most basic, monitoring comments means assigning someone to read them all and respond as necessary. This is a PR job if there ever was one; your online responses to negative comments have to be diplomatic while presenting the company line. It's not for the faint of heart, especially when dealing with controversial topics.

note You also need to be on the lookout for comment spam, where spammers post their junk messages in blog comments. While you can use comment moderation to monitor comment spam, most blogging platforms offer plug-ins to block these junk comments automatically.

You also have the option of *moderating* comments. When you enable comment moderation, you have to approve each and every comment made before they go live. This reeks a bit of censorship, but then again, it is your blog. Moderation is a good way to keep comments on topic, weed out the obvious complainers and naysayers, and avoid flame wars and spamming. It's a nice middle ground.

That said, I always opt for openness—and open conversation. Some of the best corporate blogs let pretty much everything stay up, including negative comments. The thinking here is it's better to address issues openly and to establish a reputation for openness and honesty. I can't say I disagree with that.

note Some companies moderate comments not so much for opinions but rather for appropriateness. That is, they want comments to stay on topic and not become a forum for general complaints—which are better handled via personal email, in any case.

Determining Who Contributes to the Blog

Which person in your organization, then, should write your blog?

Some companies assign blogging to the marketing department, which kind of makes sense. In this instance, it may be thought of as an advertising function or maybe part of public relations.

Other companies leave blogging to the big shots. That is, it's the company president or CEO who handles the blogging chores. This certainly lends a bit of authority to the blog, but may not always be realistic. How much free time does your CEO have to spend on the blog?

Other companies leave blogging to their product people to the sales department, or sometimes even to HR. There are certainly arguments to be made for each of these decisions.

But here's the thing. Blogging doesn't have to be assigned to a single person. Many companies are quite successful in incorporating contributions from multiple individuals throughout the organization—including, in some instances, key customers.

Personally, I like the multiple-blogger approach. When you go this route, you allow lots of people within your organization to talk about your business—about what they do, how they help customers, and the like. You end up providing multiple perspectives on your business, which really works to humanize the organization. That's a good thing.

It's also a good thing to draw on the expertise of individuals who do—and are expert in—different things. Let's say, for example, that you work for a car dealership. You can assign one person to blog about new cars, one to blog about used cars, one to blog about service-related issues, and so forth. Or maybe one person blogs about mini-vans and family cars, another economy cars, and a third sports cars. You get the idea; tap into the expertise of everyone in your organization. The more bloggers you have, the merrier.

note Some companies even extend blog posting to some of their favored customers. There's nothing like adding a real-world customer perspective to flesh out your blog's content and cement your relationship with those customers.

Deciding What to Write About

Of course, deciding who writes what depends to a large degree on what you want to write about. This is the big question: What is your blog about?

The first thing you need to decide is if you're writing for your existing customer base or to a larger base of potential customers. If it's the former, you're safe writing about things your company is doing—new products, etc. But if you want to expand your base, you need to attract people who don't know that much about you, people who aren't "insiders" to your world. In this instance, your blog has to include posts that are interesting to casual readers.

This means writing about more than just your company and products; you need to write about the world outside your company. This probably means writing about industry-related news and topics. You thus aim for your blog to become a valued industry resource.

For example, if your company sells sporting goods, you don't limit your writing to the kinds of balls and sticks and sportswear you sell. Instead, you write about individual and team sports in general. Maybe you focus on local teams and athletes (professional or amateur), maybe you focus on a particular sport; the point is, by talking about sports, not just about the sporting goods you offer, you attract a wider audience to your blog.

That's not to say that you can't write about your company and products; you can and should. But you need to do so in a way that engages both current and potential customers and creates a community for readers. Remember, your blog is your company's public face; it's the home base of conversations and content for and about your company and your customers.

Writing Blog Posts

Now we come to the nuts and bolts of writing blog posts. There are some guidelines.

Creating the Title

Let's start at the top, with the title you assign to each post. The title is very important, as it factors heavily into the post's searchability and, in many RSS and Atom feeds, might be the only part of the post that readers are first exposed to. Besides, the title of a blog post is like the title of a newspaper or magazine article or even a print advertisement; it's what attracts the reader's attention and persuades them to read the text that follows.

To that end, you have to write powerful, compelling titles for all your posts. The title has to draw the reader into the post. It has to be interesting and informative in its own right, as well as descriptive of the post itself.

There are many ways to do this. You can and probably should communicate a customer benefit in the title. ("Meet Our New A-9 Widget: Better Performance That Improves Your Bottom Line.") You can also pique the reader's interest by asking a question ("What's the Secret Behind the New A-9 Widget?"), or making a provocative statement ("Our New A-9 Widget Will Change the Face of Business in America.").

23

It goes without saying that power words should be part of your title-writing arsenal. You can't go wrong by including words like "free," "bargain," "new," "discover," "easy," and the like in your titles.

You also need to include your most important keywords in your title. I'm talking keywords that describe the post content, of course, but also keywords that apply to the blog itself or to your company or product. Now, you can't pack too many keywords into a title, so you have to choose judiciously. But titles are what count most when the search engines are indexing blog posts, so fitting in the primary keywords is essential.

The challenge in accomplishing all these goals is that the title of a blog post has to be relatively short. While there are no practical limitations on the length of a blog post title, you need to know that search engine results pages will only show the first 65 characters or so of a post title. Anything past that 65-character mark simply gets truncated. So you can go long if you want to, but a lot of people won't see the words at the end.

Writing the Post Itself

Effective blog writing is conversational yet direct. It has to reflect the personality of the contributor, while still getting across the company message. To that end, the author's voice is important; the writing needs to be personal, not corporate.

Getting that personal feel is important. A blog post shouldn't sound like a regurgitated press release nor like a piece of catalog copy. It should sound like a letter from a trusted friend—a little chatty, perhaps, but full of useful and interesting information.

Blog posts also need to be relatively short. Not as short as a tweet or Facebook status update, of course, but not near as long as a magazine article, for example. We're talking posts that are measured in paragraphs, not pages. Write too much and no one will read the complete post; write too little and the post won't be informative. You have to strike a middle ground fit for the short attention spans of today's Web users—somewhere between 250 and 1000 words.

note You probably want to "break" longer blog posts so that the entire post doesn't appear on the main blog page, thus making it harder for the reader to scroll through all the posts. Break a long post after the first two or three paragraphs and let the reader click to view the rest of the post "after the break."

As to how fancy the writing should be, the key descriptor is "conversational." You also need to know your customer base and gear the writing to that level. There's nothing wrong with aiming at a fifth-grade reading level, which seems to be the American average these days (and woe is that), but you can notch it up a tad if you have a more educated or technical audience.

By the way, remember that a blog post doesn't have to be text only. You can include pictures and videos in your post, both of which can help to humanize the experience. There's nothing like a picture of someone making or using a product to grab the reader's attention and pull him into the process.

Determining the Right Frequency

How often should you post to your company blog? That's a good, strategic question. If you post too often, you could overwhelm readers with unwanted information. If you don't post often enough, your blog will appear stagnant and irrelevant. You need to strike a happy medium.

For most companies, the optimal posting frequency is somewhere between once a day and once a week. It kind of depends on what actual news and information you have to convey, as well as the strength of the relationship you have with your customers. Obviously, the more you have to say, the more often you can legitimately post. And the more your customers are like fans, hanging on your every word and action, the more often they'll want to hear whatever it is that you have to say.

If you publish more than once a day, at least on a regular basis, you're probably going to start boring your readers. At some point, they're going to look at all the posts you write and say, "Who cares?" I'm not sure exactly where useful information turns into useless blather, but you want to be someone on the useful side of that point.

On the other hand, if you post less than once a week, customers will forget you're there. You need to stay in front of them, and that means putting something out there on a somewhat regular basis. If your last post was a month ago, you just won't appear serious about this whole blogging thing. Your loyal customers will feel abandoned, and that's definitely not what you're going for. If you can't post more often than that, you're better off not having a blog at all.

So aim for posting daily or every few days. That leaves something new out there just about every day for customers to read; it keeps their interest without overwhelming them—and demanding too much of their time.

Optimizing Your Blog for Search

We talked earlier about a blog being an important component of your search engine marketing efforts. That's only the case if you optimize your blog for search. That's right, we're talking SEO for blogs, which is a little different than normal website SEO.

I discussed SEO for blogs in more detail back in Chapter 12, "Advanced SEO Techniques," but it's worth repeating some of the important advice here:

- **Optimize the blog template**—You have to think of your blog template (that area that contains the individual blog posts) and the posts themselves as two separate entities and optimize each individually. Optimizing the template means including important keywords in the blog's descriptive text, <TITLE> and <META> HTML tags, and alternative image text.

- **Optimize individual blog posts**—The major search engines index all posts individually, so instruct your bloggers to include important keywords in all their posts. They should include keywords in both the post's title and main text—especially the first paragraph of each post. Contributors should also assign relevant tags to each post—and these tags should include those same keywords we've been focusing on throughout.

- **Submit your site feed**—It's your blog's site feed that updates the search engine indexes, so make sure you activate the feed and submit to each of the major search engines.

You should also make sure that your blogging engine supplies unique URLs to each of your blog posts. That is, each post appears on its own separate page when you click the post title. Creating this kind of individual post URL helps the search engines index individual posts.

note Learn more about SEO for blogs in Chapter 12.

Common Corporate Blogging Mistakes

With all these things you should do to create a successful company blog, let's take a quick moment to look at a few of the things you *shouldn't* do—those common mistakes that can drag down a blog's readership.

First, you don't want the blog to be too "inside." Remember, you're writing for your customers, not for your own internal benefit. You have to think about who is reading your blog and why. Figure out what they want to read and then give it to them. It's not about what you want to talk about; it's about what your customers want to read.

You should probably also avoid the "senior executive" blog. It's nice to think that your CEO can be the public face of your company, but that's seldom a good idea. In reality, senior executives seldom blog themselves; they have a staffer (probably someone in PR) do the ghost writing for them. Everybody knows this, so don't try to fool your readers. Besides, what does your CEO know about the day-to-day workings of your company and your products? It's much, much better to get an in-the-trenches perspective by letting real workers write—and having multiple people write, as well.

The other big mistake is not devoting enough time or resources to the blog. You want to post something at least once a week, probably once a day, and that takes time. You need to devote the time it takes to do this, as do the people you assign to do the writing. If someone can't commit the time, get someone else to do it. The worst thing in the world is a blog that is left unattended for long periods of time. What's the point?

Finally, you can blow the whole blogging thing by being too obviously promotional. Your blog has to be transparent, not a blatant attempt to sell product or put forth an approved corporate image. Your blog has to reflect your company's culture—what you are, not the image you'd prefer to project. Be real, be honest, and be transparent. That's how you create a winning blog that people want to read.

Promoting Your Blog

Finally, we come to the topic of promoting your blog. What do you need to do to make people aware of what you're doing?

First, if your blog doesn't appear on your site's home page, you at least need to link to it from there. Include a prominent link to your blog, not just a hidden menu item, to drive traffic from there.

You also need to link to your blog from all your other online efforts. That means linking from your Facebook and Twitter pages, as well as other social media pages. You should also include blog links in all your email newsletters and promotions. (And don't forget mentions in your offline promotional efforts, as well.)

Next, work with other blogs to do some cross-promotion. If you're a local business, link to other local blogs in your blog roll and get them to link back to you. If you're in a particular industry, develop cross-links with other industry players. (But not competitors, of course.)

You should also consider specific PR and promotion for your blog. When you're first launching your blog, for example, put your PR people to work. Same thing when there's a notable event worth talking about. Drive interested visitors to your blog, and they may end up as customers in the future.

The Bottom Line

A company or product blog is an ideal way to promote your company and products. It's really an adjunct of your normal website—and, in fact, can feed fresh content to your website, which the search engines will certainly like.

Corporate blogging is also a bit like social networking, in that you have to constantly feed the beast. One or more people need to be assigned to write new posts, ideally daily but no less frequently than weekly. The more people you have writing, the more different points of view you can project—and the more content you'll create, faster.

What you want to avoid, however, is executive pontificating. No one (except for the CEO and his immediate family, perhaps) wants to read the CEO's thoughts on life, the universe, and everything, or on how great the company is under his management. Stick to topics of interest to your customers, written by employees who are knowledgeable and close to the action.

Of course, you need to make sure your blog is easily found and easily subscribed to. You also need to optimize your blog and all your blog posts for search; that's a surefire way to get another placement in Google's search results.

BLOGGING VERSUS SOCIAL NETWORKING

Here's an interesting question: Just how relevant are blogs today? After all, blogs were a really big deal a few years ago, but then social networking came along and stole some of the buzz. Should you still bother with doing your own blog, or should you turn your attention more toward social networking?

That's a good question, at least on the surface—or if you believe that social networks have made blogs obsolete. But that doesn't appear to be the case, as the blogosphere is flourishing like never before.

At least the business and professional areas of the blogosphere are flourishing. I'm not so sure about personal blogs; these do appear to have been affected by the rise of social networking. It's a lot easier to make one's personal opinions or activities known via a Facebook status update than via a post to a freestanding blog, after all. It takes zero skills and effort to get set up on Facebook, whereas there is some work involved in creating a personal blog, even with the easy-to-use tools of Blogger and WordPress.

So I definitely see a movement from personal blogs to social networking. But that movement doesn't apply to business and what I'd call professional blogs, which really can't be replicated via Facebook and other social networking sites. Naturally, you can (and should) establish a Facebook presence, but that presence is nothing like what you get with a well-run blog. For businesses, then, social network marketing supplements and complements blog marketing. You need to do both.

23

24

Marketing to the Blogosphere

In the previous chapter we discussed the value of creating a company or product blog. But that's not the only value the blogosphere offers to online marketers. There are lots of third-party blogs out there that can help you promote your company or product. That's right, marketing to the blogosphere is just as important as blogging on your own.

This form of blog marketing is really a kind of public relations. That is, you apply somewhat traditional PR techniques to get bloggers to talk about or mention or link to your company or product. The more and more influential bloggers you have on your side, the more exposure you get—and exposure is the name of the game, here.

Why Blogs—and Bloggers—Are Important

Here's the deal: Big name bloggers have huge followings, and blogs can drive more traffic to your site than can traditional media. Because of this, the blogosphere should be an important component of any company's online public relations efforts.

If you're not involved in the whole blogging thing (and if not, shame on you), it may come as a surprise to learn that bloggers are becoming household names—at least within those households interested in a given topic. Blogs are notoriously topic-specific, of course, which means people are apt to follow blogs that concentrate on those topics in which they're interested. It's not that there's one major blog that everyone in the country reads; it's more a network of small, focused blogs that are important to narrow groups of consumers.

When someone is a regular reader of a blog, they come to know and trust the opinions of the person (or people) writing that blog. It's really a personal thing; the best bloggers become something like trusted friends.

Certainly, bloggers are major influencers. One kind word about a product or service functions as an endorsement and has a lot more impact than any advertisement you might target to that customer base. It's the ultimate in word-of-mouth promotion.

Because of all this, blogs play a big part in the decision process when consumers are looking to make a major purchase. When people are gathering information about what to buy and where to buy it, they often turn to blogs for that information and advice. In some product categories, blogs contribute more than half the information on which customer choice is finally based. That's a big influence.

What this means to marketers is that you need to tap into this resource. You need to develop and nurture a network of key contacts in the blogosphere and feed those contacts information that you want your customers and potential customers to hear. One good word from a major blogger can have a huge impact on your bottom line; you need to do whatever it takes to get the most influential bloggers on your side.

How to Get Bloggers to Notice and Mention You

In some aspects, targeting a blogger is just like targeting any other member of the media—reporters, critics, and the like. You send information their way and, if you're persistent and a little bit lucky, they mention you or your products in their writing. Public Relations 101, as it were.

Except it isn't quite the same. You don't reach bloggers the same way you reach newspaper or magazine writers. And they're not looking for the same things, either. There are some subtle differences of which you need to be aware.

As with most PR efforts, reaching bloggers starts with you treating them as people, not just contacts on a list. Sending out blind emails or making cold calls isn't going to work; you have to establish a personal relationship with these folks. You have to learn a little about them, starting with their names. (The worst thing in the world is contacting a blog without having the name of the actual blogger.) Find out what they like and don't like, which is easy enough to do by reading their blog posts. (Yes, you have to read their blogs; that's how you get informed about what they're doing.) Get a judge of their temperament, what gets them excited, what they really hate, and so forth and so on. Get inside their minds.

Once you're comfortable with how a blogger thinks, it's time to introduce yourself. Not via a press release or unsolicited email, mind you, but by leaving comments on the blogger's posts. That's right, you make yourself known by posting a comment or two or three. This establishes you as a participant in that blog's community, not as an outsider wanting PR favors.

So you should get to know the blogger through his posts and let him get to know you through your comments. Then you can attempt a direct contact, typically via email. Introduce yourself, reference some of the aforementioned posts and comments, and let the blogger know you'd be glad to provide him with any information he might find useful. Plant the seeds, as it were.

Then, when it comes time that there's some news you want to publicize, call in your favors. Email the blogger and let him know what's cooking. Plug your product or service or whatever it is you're plugging and suggest that the blogger might want to mention it in an upcoming post. Point out how the blog's readers might be interested in or benefit from this information. Make it sound like readers deserve to hear about this news. And offer to provide more information or resources if the blogger needs them.

Knowing how bloggers tend to work will help you in this task. Unlike traditional journalists who have a traditional 9-to-5 workday, bloggers don't necessarily keep the same hours. Some bloggers have day jobs and blog in their free time, so it may be better to contact these bloggers in the evenings or on weekends.

> **note** For really influential bloggers, offer some sort of exclusive interview with a product person, member of the management team, or whatever—anything that the blogger can view as an "exclusive" to his blog.

Obviously, because you're both working online, you want to communicate online, as well. That means email instead of postal mail and instant messaging instead of phone calls. Find out what the blogger prefers and go that route.

As to what you send the blogger, a traditional printed press release or press kit is out. Instead, put together an electronic press kit, something you can send to bloggers via email. The email message itself should probably serve as the press release; use attachments to send product photos and other key items.

That email press release, by the way, should include a link back to whatever it is you're promoting. That could be your company's home page but more likely should be a dedicated landing page for this PR event. You want to send the blogger's followers to a web page that relates directly to whatever it is the blogger wrote; don't rely on generic links.

You should also include your own contact information in the email so the blogger can contact you directly for more information. Most bloggers want to personalize the information they present, which means you shouldn't expect exact regurgitation of your press releases. Instead, help bloggers turn your message into something unique to their blogs.

note One of the transformative features of online PR is that you can directly measure the effectiveness of your efforts by tracking where links to your site originate—in this instance, which blogs drive the most links. Learn more about online PR in Part IX, "Online PR."

By the way, bloggers tend not to react too well to traditional press releases. Instead, make the accompanying email conversational and personal. Use bullet points to highlight main topics but always bring the content around to how it will benefit this blogger and the blog's readers. That means customizing your press releases for each individual blogger, but it's an effort well spent.

As to who you should target, do your research and find out which blogs are read by your current customers or desired customers. Identify those blogs that are big in your industry, those that have the most followers and the most impact. These blogs are the ones that matter.

note Don't focus exclusively on the biggest A-list bloggers. Smaller blogs, in aggregate, can generate a lot of traffic back to your site.

Once identified, you should treat these bloggers as you would members of the mainstream press. Treat them as friends, yes, but as very important friends.

These are also friends with their own unique worldviews and their own very definite opinions. Don't expect to tell a blogger what to write; you can suggest all you want, but in the end they'll do what they want to do and nothing more than that. Bloggers, in other words, are beyond your control. (In fact, most bloggers can't be controlled at all.) They're not corporate drones, and they don't work for you. They're important people with their own opinions and should be treated as such.

Giving Bloggers Everything They Need

Once you convince a blogger to mention your company or product, you need to provide him with everything he needs to create an effective blog post. Some of this stuff can be included in or attached to your initial email; other items can be linked to and downloaded from your website.

This means, of course, creating a section of your website devoted to the press and the media. This part of your site should include product photos at various resolutions; bloggers love to include pictures with their posts. Offer a variety of photos so that a blogger can choose the one best suited to his blog and readers.

In short, you have to give bloggers all the information and details they need to put up an interesting post. The easier you make it for them, the more likely they are to write about you.

> **note** Learn more about providing press materials online in Chapter 32, "Creating an Online Press Room."

Buying Blog Placements

There's a new wrinkle in blog PR that bears examination. Instead of begging for placements, you buy them. That's right, product placement for blogs is now a reality.

There are several companies out there that offer blog product placement. That is, they take your products or services, as well as your money, and offer them up to their networks of bloggers. These bloggers decide to mention said products and in return get paid for it.

Blog product placement can also be handled directly. You or your PR firm identifies and contacts key blogs and then make direct offers for some sort of product placement. Maybe it's a cash deal, maybe you just send them a free copy (or multiple units) of whatever it is you're selling. In return, the blogger gives you a plug.

Using a Product Placement Service

Probably the easiest way to pursue this is to sign up with a product placement network. They sign up a large number of independent bloggers and then try to match advertisers with the appropriate blogs. Any blogger who writes about a given advertiser (or its products) gets paid a small amount, typically in the $5–$10 range.

With these networks, bloggers are under no obligation to mention any given product; they only get paid for what they do blog about. They're also under no obligation to write positively about a given product, but you can imagine that they probably will—otherwise, they won't last long in the network.

The upside of these networks is you can get a lot of blogs written about your company or products. The downside is that a lot of these blogs are nothing more than advertising mills; they don't have a lot of regular followers and exist primarily to write shill posts.

Heck, even those legit sites in a network might have nothing to do with your industry or have any cachet among your customers. Do you receive any benefit from some random site mentioning your product? Maybe a little, but not as much as you would from a well-known and relevant site doing the same.

For these reasons, you may not want to invest too heavily in these "blogvertising" networks, at least until you check them out a little. They do make things relatively easy for you, however.

Who are these pay-for-play networks? Here's a short list:

- Blogitive (www.blogitive.com)
- Blogsvertise (www.blogsvertise.com)
- LinkFromBlog (www.linkfromblog.com)
- LoudLaunch (www.loudlaunch.com)
- PayPerPost (www.payperpost.com)
- PlaceVine (www.placevine.com)
- ReviewMe (www.reviewme.com)
- Smorty (www.smorty.com)

How much to these services cost? It varies somewhat from service to service, but expect to pay at least $10 per placement. How many placements you pay for is negotiable.

Arranging Placement Directly

Paying cash for mention in a blog is pretty blatant promotion and doesn't always generate the results you want. You can go a little lower key if you contact bloggers yourself.

Here's an example. A few years ago my sister, who is a writer, wrote a fiction book about a "super mom" and set up a "super mom" blog to support the book. Shortly after, she was contacted by representatives of Procter & Gamble, who offered her a large quantity of Swiffer products if she would mention said products in her blog. I don't know if she took them up on their offer, but the P&G folks obviously thought that a mention in her blog was worth a box of Swiffers.

How do you identify the best blogs to proposition? You have to get your hands dirty. Survey your customers to see what blogs they're reading. Do a search for the keywords you typically use and see which (if any) blogs also appear in the search results. Check your website analytics and see which blogs are sending you traffic already. In other words, do your homework.

Now, not all bloggers will respond positively to this sort of pay-for-play offer. It's kind of an ethical dilemma for some idealistic bloggers, the online equivalent of the church v. state issue eternally facing newspapers and magazines. And that's okay; you don't want to force a blogger to sell out his principles. But for those willing to do so, why not take part in the fun?

> **note** Product placement isn't just an ethical issue for bloggers; it's a legal one. New FTC regulations stipulate that bloggers must disclose any payment or special treatment they receive for product mentions. This can be within the body of a post or in a small tag at the end, but your involvement can no longer be hidden.

The Bottom Line

Bloggers are great influencers; readers are likely to support any product or service that their favorite bloggers endorse. To that end, bloggers should be a primary target of your online PR efforts.

That means not just adding bloggers to your press release list, but also personally cultivating their favor. You also need to provide bloggers with everything they need to easily write about your products—links to your product pages, web-sized image files, and the like. If you do your job right, you'll get favorable mentions in influential blogs—and corresponding traffic back to your website from the blogs' readers.

BLOGS VERSUS TRADITIONAL MEDIA

I mentioned earlier that you need to treat bloggers as you would members of the traditional press. That's because in many ways, blogs are supplanting traditional media and becoming the new trade press.

It used to be that there was this notion of "the press" and "blogs," and there was just about zero intersection. Blogs weren't taken as seriously as was the traditional press, and that was that.

But over the past few years blogs and bloggers have grown in importance. To some degree, it's because members of the traditional media have become bloggers, but it's also because bloggers have stepped up to the task. Blogs have broken a lot of news stories that traditional media have ignored; in fact, blogs are threatening the dominance of the old school press. They're not bound by the same restrictions, they're not owned by the same corporate masters, and thus they can raise more than a little muck if they want to.

It's not surprising, then, that some bloggers have really big audiences and can drive as much if not more traffic to your site as can traditional media. As such, you really need to regard bloggers—at least the most serious ones—with the same respect you do your contacts in the traditional media. It's a changing world out there, and bloggers are at the forefront of this change.

24

Tracking Blog Marketing Performance

Blog marketing is an important component of your online marketing plan. But how do you measure its effectiveness? After all, you have to measure both the performance of your company blog *and* the performance of your PR efforts toward other bloggers. That's a lot to track.

What you have to do is split your blog marketing into these two key areas, blogging and what is essentially online public relations. You can then measure the first component (your blog) using standard website analytics and the second component (your influence on other bloggers) using analytics common to your other PC efforts.

Tracking the Performance of Your Company Blog

Let's start by looking at how you track the performance of your company or product blog. As I said, it's pretty much the same as tracking the performance of your website—with a few key differences.

Applying Web Analytics

When it comes to tracking blog performance, it's important to know that a blog is really nothing more than a fancy web page. As such, you can use the same web analytics tools and metrics to track your blog's performance as you use to track the rest of your website.

So if you're using Google Analytics, for example, on your main website, you can add Google Analytics code to your blog, as well and then use the Google Analytics dashboard to track your blog's traffic, pageviews, visitors, and so on.

Most web analytics tools can easily be used for blog tracking; it's just a matter of inserting the proper code into the body of your main blog page. Then you track whatever metrics you want to track.

note Some blog hosting services offer their own analytic tools. For example, Blogger offers Blogger Analytics, which measures your blog's performance in real time.

And what metrics *should* you track? In essence, you want to find out how many people are reading your blog posts, who they are, how much time they spend reading your posts, and where they come from—basic web analytics stuff.

This means you want to track the following metrics:

- **Pageviews**—Track this one over time to see if your traffic is increasing or decreasing.
- **Unique visitors**—Same as with pageviews, helps you track traffic over time.
- **Session duration**—This tells you whether visitors are fully reading an article or getting turned off before they get to the end.
- **Traffic sources**—Use this metric to determine where your blog traffic is coming from—search engines (and if so, for which keywords), links from other blogs, and so forth.

What's slightly different about blog analytics as compared to general web analytics is that you want to track these metrics for *each individual post* on your blog, as well as for the blog itself. You then want to develop a matrix to compare these metrics

note Learn more about each of these metrics in Chapter 9, "Tracking Website Analytics."

between all the posts so you can determine which posts are drawing the most traffic, keeping readers engaged, and the like.

The goal here is to determine which types of posts are getting the most reads—and then to write more of them. Identify which posts aren't getting read and post fewer of them. Figure out what's working and why and use that to fine-tune your blog content going forward.

Beyond Basic Analytics

Beyond basic web analytics, you also want to measure how engaged the readers of your blog are. This means finding out how many readers subscribe to your blog's feed, how many click through to links on your main website, and how many bother to leave comments on your articles. You're also interested in the comments, themselves, of course, which is a bit more subjective analysis.

All of this means you need to be looking at the following new metrics:

■ **Feed subscriptions**—This is a simple and important number to track. Readers who subscribe to your blog's feed obviously find it important enough to them to do so. The more subscribers you have, the more you're doing something right—something that's essential to those subscribers. You can track subscriptions using FeedBurner and other feed services; it's not a metric tracked by traditional web analytics tools.

> **note** Because subscribers read your posts in their newsreader programs rather than visiting your blog itself, an increase in feed subscriptions will actually result in a decrease in page views and visitors to your blog. For this reason, you need to track pageviews and subscriptions in tandem.

■ **Inbound links**—You know you're doing something right when other blogs start linking to your posts. A post with a large number of inbound links has a perceived level of authority that a less lined-to post does not. For this reason, you want to track inbound links—and do so for each of your posts individually.

> **note** A *trackback* is an automatic notification that enables you to automatically track links from other blogs back to your blog posts. Most blog hosting services and blogging tools support automated trackbacks.

■ **Comments**—When you want to increase the interaction with your customer base, the best way to measure this is via the comments left on your blog posts. A post that has a large number of comments has obviously touched a nerve (positively or negatively) with your customers. They read the article and were involved enough to spend the time to leave their comments. That's a good thing. So you should definitely measure the number of comments for each blog post—but don't stop there. These comments are an invaluable source of feedback from your most-interested comments, which means you need to read them and digest what your customers are saying. Ignore comments at your peril; they can help you not only fine-tune your blog posting, but also improve your business.

■ **Click-throughs**—It's important to remember that your blog is a means to an end, and that end involves driving customers to your main website to make a purchase, request more information, or whatever.

To that end, you need to track the number of click-throughs from the blog itself and from each blog post back to a page on your website. Track the sheer number of click throughs, as well as which pages are clicked to. Which blog posts are driving the most business to your site, and which, while perhaps interesting, aren't helping your business that much? These are the questions you want to answer.

The point with these blog-specific metrics is to determine which posts are best engaging your readers and thus driving the most traffic back to your main web pages. That means comparing these metrics for each post on your blog to determine which posts are working the best.

For example, if you work for a car dealership and find that posts about auto repair perform better than posts about used cars, you should write more auto repair posts and fewer about used cars. Now, this may cause some consternation in management ranks, especially if the management really, really wants to push used car sales. But if your readers (that is, your potential customers) don't respond well to that kind of content, you have to listen to and respect their wishes, management wishes be damned.

That's one of the unique aspects of blog marketing and all social media marketing, for that matter: The ongoing conversation with your customers determines what you write about and promote. It should also tell you what your customers are interested in and thus can help shape the direction of your business. If you find that customers are interested in something other than what you're focusing on...well, that argues for a shift in overall business strategy, doesn't it?

Tracking the Effectiveness of Your Blog PR Efforts

Then there's the matter of tracking how effective you are in getting other blogs to write about your company and your products. This is online PR tracking, and it will tell you not only how effective you are in gaining publicity, but also how effective other blogs and websites are in driving traffic back to your website.

There are really two aspects to this type of performance tracking. First, you can track how many mentions you receive from a given press release or publicity drive. Second, you can track how many clicks you get back to your website based on these mentions.

You see, the number of placements alone doesn't mean squat if nobody reads those blogs or if no one is so moved to click back to your site for more information or to make a purchase. This is where online PR differs from traditional PR. With traditional PR, you can only track placements; with online PR you can track actual effectiveness.

This is because of hyperlinks, of course. When a blogger mentions your company or product, he also includes a link back to a page on your website. (Ideally, some sort of specific landing page.) Because links can be tracked, you now know how much traffic is driven by a given PR effort. That's not a bad thing.

So what we want to track here are these metrics:

- **Placements**—We're talking mentions by other bloggers, online articles, and the like. As with placements in traditional media, you'll probably have to do this manually.

- **Click-throughs**—This is easy enough to do via web analytics. Just look for traffic generated from specific websites, blogs, or URLs. It gets even easier if you provide each blog with its own unique landing page; just track pageviews for each URL to see how much traffic is being generated from each source.

- **Conversions**—If your ultimate goal is to sell a product or get a customer name or whatever, then track how many of these PR-generated visits results in the desired outcome. That's right, you can assign an actual dollar value to each PR activity. Wild!

Just getting mentioned in a lot of random blogs may be nice for your corporate ego but really doesn't matter much if those blogs don't reach and inspire potential customers. Ultimately, those PR efforts that deliver the most traffic and conversions are those that are working the best for you.

> **note** Learn more about measuring online PR in Chapter 33, "Tracking Online PR Performance."

The Bottom Line

To determine whether your company blog is performing to expectations, you use standard web analytics to track pageviews, visitors, session duration, and the like. You should track these metrics on each blog post in addition to the blog in general; you should also track subscriptions to your blog's feed.

To determine the effectiveness of your PR efforts to thirty-party bloggers, you should track placements or mentions of your product, clicks back to your website, and conversions. It's not enough just to get mentioned; you need to convert those placements into sales or other quantifiable actions.

OTHER INDICATORS OF BLOG PERFORMANCE

We've looked at the most obvious and reliable ways to measure the performance of your blog marketing efforts. But there are a few other factors you can look at if you're so inclined.

For example, if you want to see how popular your blog is compared to other similar blogs, check out Technorati (www.technorati.com), a free blog ranking service. Technorati provides several interesting metrics, including overall ranking and an "authority" number, which is based to a large degree on the number of inbound links a blog receives. Compare your numbers with those of your competitors.

You can also track mention of your blog in traditional media. It happens, especially among the most influential or notorious blogs. (Think The Huffington Post for politics or Engadget for technology.) If your blog is getting mentioned in the print or broadcast media, you're doing something right—or at least something interesting.

I also like to track how a blog is being tagged by various social bookmarking services, such as Digg and Delicious. These services help you measure popularity; the more tags you get, the more people are liking what you're doing.

Finally, you can measure how often or how high your blog and blog posts appear in search engine results. One reason you're blogging, after all, is to increase your chances of appearing in these search results. So search Google, Bing, and so on for those keywords that matter and see if and where your blog posts rank.

26

Understanding Social Media

Now we come to the section on social media. Tell all your friends and have them tell their friends—because that's what social media is all about, passing information back and forth between friends, family, and business associates. For marketers, that makes social media a twenty-first century form of word-of-mouth promotion.

There are lots of different social media—a lot of different channels of communication—and they all are important to modern Internet marketing. So get ready to learn all about friends and fans, tweets and diggs, Facebook and MySpace. Social marketing is the hottest form of online marketing today!

Inside the World of Social Media

What is—or, rather, what *are*—social media? Get a few of your friends together, and I'll tell you.

That's because social media are all about friends—real ones and virtual ones. Social media lets you create a list of friends and then share things within them. Things like what you're doing and thinking, pictures and movies you've taken, events you're attending, even web pages and online articles you find interesting. In return, your friends share the same with you. The end result is a giant online community, facilitated by the many social media sites and services available on the Web.

In a nutshell, social media are those websites, services, and platforms that people use to share experiences and opinions with each other. They cover everything from *social networks* (users share the details of their own lives) to *social bookmarking services* (users share the sites and articles they like), and include blogs, microblogs, and other forms of online communities.

Social media is differentiated from traditional media because of its two-way, conversational nature. Traditional media (newspapers, magazines, radio, television, and the like) are one-way; these media broadcast their static messages to the widest possible audiences. Social media, on the other hand, are interactive, encouraging two-way (or more-way) conversations between multiple parties.

Look at it another way. Participating in traditional media is a consumer activity; you consume what the broadcasters send you. To participate in social media, however, requires both consumption and creation. That is, you not only consume messages sent by others, you create your own messages that others consume. It's a participatory activity, not just a spectator sport.

It's this participation that makes social media of interest to marketers. There are plenty of media available, both online and off, that let you broadcast your message to consumers. But how many media enable you to engage your customers in an active conversation? That's where social media shine.

The History of Social Media

Just where did today's social media come from? Well, it's not a new concept; aspects of social media have been around since the late 1970s, if you can believe that. In fact, today's social media can be seen as combining a mashup of features that other online media have offered for years—message forums, instant messaging, email, media sharing, and the like. So it's not what they do that's new; it's the way they bring it all together into a single site or interface.

If you consider a social network as a kind of virtual community, you can see the history. In fact, the concept of online virtual communities dates to the earliest dial-up computer networks, bulletin board systems (BBSs), and online discussion forums, including The Source, The WELL (short for Whole Earth 'Lectronic Link), CompuServe, Prodigy, America Online, and Usenet. These proto-communities, many of which predate the public Internet, offered topic-based discussion forums and chat rooms, as well as rudimentary forms of private electronic communication.

note Bulletin board systems (BBSs) were private online discussion forums, typically hosted on a single computer and accessed by other computers via a dial-up telephone connection. BBSs were how people communicated online before the advent of the Internet.

Some of these early online communities were quite popular in their day. CompuServe, for example, was a large commercial dial-up computer network, in operation from 1979 through 2009; it offered a variety of topic-based discussion forums and at one point had more than three million members. Prodigy was another commercial dial-up network, in operation from 1984 to 2001, with more than a million subscribers. And America Online, founded in 1985 (as "Quantum Link"), is still around today as a web portal—even if its user base is far less than the 30 million subscribers it had at its peak as a commercial online service.

Other components of what is currently considered social networking developed in the 1990s and 2000s. The concept of topic-based website communities, as typified by iVillage, Epicurious, and Classmates.com, arose in the mid-1990s. Personal blogs, which let users post short articles of information and opinion, emerged around the year 2000. And photo-sharing sites, such as Flickr and Photobucket, became a part of the Internet landscape in the early 2000s.

Social media as we know it today was born in 2003, when Friendster combined many of these online community features into the first large-scale social networking site— and introduced the concepts of "friends" and "friending" to the social Web. Friendster enjoyed immediate popularity (more than three million users within the first few months of operation) but was soon surpassed by MySpace, which launched later the same year. MySpace became the most popular social networking site in June 2006 and remained the top social network for almost two years.

note Friendster is an interesting example of a company being done in by its own success; its remarkable early growth brought about a series of technical problems that drove users to competing sites, such as MySpace. Friendster was purchased by News Corporation in 2005, and while it's no longer a major player in the United States, it remains one of the largest social networking sites in Asia.

26

Another social networking site, LinkedIn, also launched in 2003. Unlike Friendster and MySpace, LinkedIn targeted business professionals and became known as a site for career networking. Today, it has more than 60 million users.

The year 2004 saw the launch of Facebook (initially called "Thefacebook"), which was introduced as a site primarily for college students. Sensing opportunity beyond the college market, however, Facebook opened its site to high school students in 2005 and to users of all ages (actually, users above the age of 13) in 2006. This broadening in Facebook's user base led to a huge increase in both users and pageviews, which led to Facebook surpassing MySpace in April 2008. Today, Facebook reigns supreme in the social media space, with more than 500 million users—a truly staggering number.

Examining Different Types of Social Media

As noted earlier, there are many different forms of social media, all of which can be important to your online marketing efforts. Everybody divides them up a bit differently, but I tend to see them in this fashion:

- Social networks, such as Facebook, MySpace, and LinkedIn
- Blogs
- Microblogging services, such as Twitter
- Social bookmarking and news services, such as Digg, Delicious, and StumbleUpon
- Media sharing sites, such as Flickr and YouTube
- Virtual communities, such as Second Life

In addition, you can probably throw in social review sites, such as Yelp, web-based message forums, and any number of topic-specific websites that create their own online communities. In other words, any place online where social interaction occurs has the makings of being a social medium.

Social Networking with Facebook, MySpace, and LinkedIn

Social networking is, perhaps, the most popular social medium today because it's a true online community; it's where friends and family can hang out online and share their experiences.

In practice, a social network is a large website that hosts a community of users and facilitates public and private communication between those users. Social networks enable users to share experiences and opinions with each other via short posts or status updates.

Some social networks, such as school or alumni networks, are devoted to a specific topic or community. Other social networks, such as Facebook, are more broad-based, which allows for communities devoted to specific topics to develop within the overall network.

How popular are social networks? *Really* popular. According to the research firm Alexa, Facebook is currently the number two most popular site on the Web (after Google), with MySpace (which is admittedly on the decline) also appearing in the top 20.

And just why are these sites so popular? It's because they enable easy and immediate interaction between friends, family members, fellow students, and co-workers. Users can interact via public posts, private communication, event calendars, and even community-based games and applications. It's a way to be social with large numbers of people without having to interact personally with each and every individual—which is a big time saver. It's a way of being social without necessarily being personal, perfect for the new millennium.

In short, social networks help people keep up-to-date on what others are doing and keep others updated on what they are doing. They also help establish a sense of community based on shared experiences at school, in the workplace, or at play.

> **note** In today's busy world, many people simply don't have time to meet face-to-face with all of their friends, family members, and colleagues. It's easier to catch up with one another on a social network, where a single status update is broadcast to an entire community of online friends. The social network becomes a way to maintain existing relationships and make new ones, even if on a somewhat superficial basis.

As to who uses social networks, while it's true that college and high school students used to comprise the bulk of the active audience, the demographics are rapidly changing. In fact, the fastest-growing demographic for social networks today is the 45-and-older age group—which means that users of social networks have some money to spend.

In practice, then, social networks are home to all sorts of users, including:

- Business colleagues who use the site for professional networking
- Friends who want to talk online
- Singles who want to meet and match up with other singles
- Classmates who need study partners and homework advice
- Hobbyists looking for others who share their interests
- People looking for long-lost friends
- Musicians, actors, and celebrities connecting with their fans

And, of course, college and high school students.

When you're targeting social networks as part of your Internet marketing mix, far and away the largest player is Facebook (www.facebook.com). This site not only delivers the largest audience but also the

> **note** When we talk about social networks, it's easy to focus on the big dog (Facebook) and neglect everybody else—which would be a mistake. Niche social networks represent unique opportunities to reach distinct communities of consumers. LinkedIn, for example, is heavily used by business professionals; Eons targets baby boomers; and BlackPlanet is a community for African American users.

26

most general audience, which makes it perfect for all types of businesses. Other big players, in the U.S. at least, are MySpace (www.myspace.com), with younger-skewing demographics (and a big appeal to musicians and other entertainers), and LinkedIn (www.linkedin.com), which targets an older, more affluent, professional audience.

Blogging as a Social Medium

It may surprise you to think of blogs in the same breath as Facebook and Twitter, but it's true; blogging is a form of social connection. A blogger makes a personal connection with his readers, and a community is formed when those readers comment on the blog posts. (And on other comments, of course.)

As such, blogging is one of the key social media. In terms of sheer number of blogs, and those who read them, blogging is right up there with tweeting and social bookmarking and all that. And that should get your attention.

> **note** Learn more about blogs in Part VII of this book, "Blog Marketing."

Now, we've already covered blog marketing, so I won't repeat that information here. Know, however, that as blogging is a type of social media, you probably should consider blog marketing when you develop your overall social media marketing strategy.

Microblogging with Twitter

Then we have microblogs. As the name implies, a microblog is a little bitty blog—more accurately, a service that broadcasts very short blog posts to a group of subscribers.

In reality, microblogging has more in common with social networking than it does with traditional long-form blogging. A microblog is what results when you separate the short text messages or status updates from a social network into a separate feed. Microblogs, typified by Twitter and Tumblr, exist solely to distribute short text posts from individual users to groups of followers. These posts are similar to traditional blog posts but are much shorter, typically in the 140-character range.

That said, a microblog is considerably different from both a social network and a traditional blog. Microblogs do not offer any of the community features found on larger social network sites; there are no topic-based groups, one-to-one private messaging, photo sharing, and the like. The only service a microblog offers is public message distribution. It's all about the tweets.

Here's how it works. A user signs up for the microblogging service and posts short messages. Other users sign up to follow the posts of individual members; they are then notified when someone they follow makes a new post. Microblog posts are used to convey personal information and opinions; businesses also use them to make commercial announcements—which is where microblog marketing comes in.

The most popular microblogging service today is Twitter (www.twitter.com), at least in the U.S. Twitter has more than 100 million users, most of them followers of friends, celebrities, and businesses. The next-largest service is Tumblr (www.tumblr.com), with just 3 million users.

Social Bookmarking with Digg, Delicious, and StumbleUpon

Social bookmarking services—sometimes called *social news* sites—represent a subset of features found on a social network. A social bookmarking service lets users save and share their favorite web pages with friends and colleagues online. It's all about finding something you like and then letting others know about it.

In operation, it's fairly simple. A user visits a website, web page, news article, or blog post that he or she likes and then clicks a button or link to bookmark that site. This bookmark then appears in that user's master list of bookmarks on the social bookmarking service site; the user can share all or some of these bookmarks with anyone he or she designates.

Most social bookmarking services use *tags* to help users find bookmarked sites. When a user bookmarks a site, he adds a few tags or keywords to describe the site. Other users can then search by keywords to find the most popular matching bookmarked sites—just as they search Google and the other traditional search engines.

Users can also vote on the bookmarks submitted, typically on an up or down basis; this helps quality and relevant bookmarks rise to the top of the list. Users can also add their comments to bookmarks, thus helping to create a thriving community.

Social bookmarking services are great ways to spread timely and interesting content. The most notable bookmarks on these sites quickly turn viral, as one user after another shares his or her links with other users. Because of this, you want to make it easy for users to bookmark content on your website and blog.

The most popular social bookmarking services include Digg (www.digg.com), Delicious (www.delicious.com), Reddit (www.reddit.com), and StumbleUpon (www.stumbleupon.com). Digg is the big dog of this bunch, with 23 million or so users; bookmarking a site with Digg is referred to as "digging" the site.

Social Sharing with Flickr and YouTube

One interesting aspect of the social Web is social sharing, the passing around of pictures, movies, music, and such between friends and family. Social networking sites, such as Facebook and MySpace, offer media sharing features; in fact, Facebook is probably the number-one photo sharing site on the Web. But there are lots of sites dedicated solely to sharing specific types of media online.

All of these sites work in a similar fashion. Users upload their media—photos, movies, whatever—to the site. The uploaded media are made available either publicly to everyone on the site or privately to selected lists of friends and family. Other users, invited or otherwise, then view the uploaded media as they wish.

Most media sharing sites also offer some degree of community interaction, typically by letting users share the media they find and like with others. YouTube, for example, makes it easy for users to email links to their videos, as well as embed videos in blogs and other websites. Flickr goes a step further by encouraging user-created groups devoted to particular subjects or types of photography. Most sites also offer private email-like communication between users.

In terms of photo-sharing sites, Flickr (www.flickr.com) is the big dog. In the video-sharing arena, it's YouTube (www.youtube.com) standing head and shoulders above the completion.

> **note** Learn more about YouTube and video sharing in Chapter 36, "Video Marketing."

Social Location Sharing with Foursquare, Gowalla, and MyTown

Talking about sharing, if you take social networking mobile and local, you end up with something called social location sharing. This particular social medium helps consumers connect with one another—and with local businesses and location—while they're on the go. These services track your location via your iPhone or other smartphone and either broadcast your location to other users or let you know if other users are in the neighborhood. They attempt to create real-world connections via the virtual medium.

As you might suspect, social location sharing holds lots of promise for marketers, especially local businesses. In fact, social location marketing, as it's called, is a great way to identify and put your name in front of nearby customers.

Social location sharing is a relatively new social medium, so it's still in a bit of flux. Currently, the largest players include Foursquare (www.foursquare.com), Gowalla (www.gowalla.com), and Loopt (www.loopt.com).

> **note** Learn more about social location sharing for marketers in the book *Social Location Marketing* (Simon Salt, Que, 2010).

Virtual Social Networking with Virtual Communities

Then there's the unique form of social media known as virtual communities. A virtual community is kind of like a social network as filtered through an animated cartoon. That is, users interact with other users in much the same fashion as they do on Facebook, except they're represented onscreen by cartoon-like avatars, little animated people who walk around the virtual world as you would a real-world amusement park.

Some virtual worlds closely resemble the real world. Others present fantasy worlds, where an avatar might be a wizard or a knight or a superhero. These later virtual worlds are more obviously descendants of traditional role-playing games, although all virtual worlds incorporate role playing to some extent.

A typical virtual world is part chat room, part multiplayer online game, all accessed via the user's onscreen alter ego. Most of these sites let users do virtually everything they can do in the physical world. People can talk to other users, play games with them, shop for virtual merchandise, even participate in virtual political campaigns. It's a computerized version of the real world that is played on a computer over the Internet.

Virtual communities look so much like computer games that it's easy to lose sight of their social nature. But even game-oriented online environments have many social networking features, specifically the ability for users to interact via chat rooms, discussion forums, instant messaging, and the like. More sophisticated virtual worlds feature even more opportunities for social interaction by enabling entire communities

> **note** Virtual worlds evolved as a form of online role playing. The first networked multi-user game was Maze War, which was played on Arpanet (the forerunner of today's Internet) as early as 1974. This type of Dungeons and Dragons-like game soon evolved into a type of multi-player game called a *MUD* (multiuser domain or multiuser dungeon). MUDs moved onto the Internet in the 1990s with larger and more complex environments and eventually morphed into *MMPORGs* (massively multiplayer online role-playing games) and today's virtual 3D communities.

26

to develop within their worlds. Users can interact with other users just as they would in the world, by "talking" directly to each other, forming groups and clubs, and even conducting e-commerce transactions with one another.

I like to think of a virtual community as a social network with avatars. That is, users engage in all the activities typical of a social network, but through their chosen onscreen graphical identities.

When it comes to choosing a virtual community for your online marketing efforts, Second Life (www.secondlife.com) is the easy choice. Second Life has the most social features of all of today's virtual communities as well as the largest user base. Many marketers literally set up virtual shop in the virtual world, selling virtual merchandise and gaining new real-world customers in the balance.

Why Social Media Matters to Marketers

Why is all this important to marketers? As with most things, it's all in the numbers—but also the connections.

Numbers first. More than a half-million users today are connecting with one another via social media. That's a huge potential customer base to tap into, and I'm not just talking about bleeding-edge technophiles; you'll find just about anyone online, from preteens to senior citizens, students to retirees, blue collar workers to high-level executives. It's truly a universal media.

As an example of the universality of social media, consider the demographics of Facebook, the leading social network site. Now, you might think that all Facebook users are teenagers giggling with their pals, but you'd be way off base. While youngsters do represent a strong component of Facebook's user base, a full 41% of users are age 35 or more; 64% are 26 or older. These are real adults with real spending power, well worth your attention.

Indeed, social media is becoming so mainstream that it's likely you'll find many of your existing customers already there, ready to hook up with you when you make the plunge. In fact, they may already be talking about you online. Social media is all about conversations between people, and people talk about a lot of different things. Even if you aren't listening, your customers may be talking about you on Facebook or Twitter or Digg. These conversations go on with or without your active participation; can you afford not to join in?

note Facebook's maturing demographic is so important that I wrote a book about it: *Facebook for Grown-Ups* (Michael Miller, Que, 2010). Consider this an old-school cross-promotion for that book.

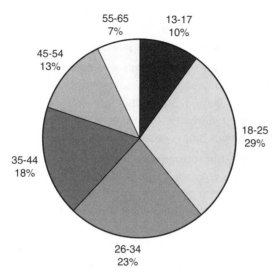

FIGURE 26.1

Facebook demographics—it's not just for kids anymore.

Speaking of what you can or can't afford to do, there's the matter of cost. Do it right, and social media can deliver a large number of highly targeted customers at a relatively low cost. It's one of the more efficient marketing vehicles available to you.

As you know, traditional advertising is expensive; building word of mouth through social media, less so. To that end, if you can build a large friends or fans list on Facebook, get bookmarked on Digg, or become the subject of a popular tweet on Twitter, you can see a significant spike in website traffic—as well as a lasting long-term increase in your customer base. Social networks have a lot of users, and getting in front of them can make or break a company's traffic goals.

I like the notion that social media is a great equalizer. Given that it doesn't cost big bucks to participate, little guys can play right alongside big marketers. In reality, little guys can actually outsmart the big guys in social media, just by being more attentive and active. It's all a matter of how you play the game.

Then there's the benefit you get from getting mentioned on Facebook, Twitter, or one of the social bookmarking sites. Each link or bookmark you receive creates a new link back to your website. Links are good in and of themselves, of course, but these inbound links also increase your site's ranking in the search results of Google and other major search engines. That's because, if you recall, search ranking is at least partly dependent on the number of inbound links a site receives. The more you're "dugg" or tweeted about, the higher your site will rank with Google and its competitors.

Another upside to participating in social media is that links coming from these sites are organic. Individual users make the decision to create these links; they're not being paid or otherwise induced to do so. To the business' benefit, search engines view these organic links as high-quality links and reward the site with higher search rankings.

Quantity is nice, but so is quality. It's important to remember that social media marketing is a form of word-of-mouth marketing. Online or off, a strong word-of-mouth campaign trumps any form of paid advertising or promotion. It's quality attention, which results in quality traffic to your company's website.

Finally, we come to connections—those social connections you establish between your company and your customers. Social media provide a unique opportunity to conduct ongoing conversations with your most loyal customers, which not only helps to cement customer ties, but also provides valuable feedback about your company and products. When you get your customers involved with social media, they become more invested in your company; they feel like they're part of your team, participating in the day-to-day workings of your company and products. There's nothing better than that.

The fact that all these benefits can accrue with minimal financial investment is the final plus for social media marketing. You don't have to buy expensive advertisements, you don't have to spend a lot of big bucks; all you have to invest is your time. Spend the time participating in social media and you'll find you have a new and interactive Internet presence, one that can potentially reward you with large numbers of new and highly devoted customers.

Developing a Social Media Marketing Strategy

How, then, can your business participate in social media? I won't kid you; there's a lot of work involved.

The most obvious way for a business to participate in social media is to literally participate—to become part of the community. That means establishing pages for your business or products on all the major social network sites, creating a Twitter feed, and the like. You can use this type of presence to notify interested customers of upcoming products and promotions, as well as to connect one-on-one with your online customer base.

This participation should be two-way, of course. Not only should someone from your company monitor posts to your social pages, that person should also post to other pages on the social network—for both other businesses and individuals. It's a matter of being an active participant in the community, not just hosting a passive web page.

In addition, you need to make it easy for various social media to link to your web-

note In addition to letting you participate in social conversations, many social network sites also offer third-party advertising. This advertising is typically contextual, meaning that you can target certain demographic qualifiers, such as age range or gender, and have your ads displayed only to users who match those demographics. While advertising on a social network costs more than "free" social media marketing, its targeted nature can make it more effective than other types of online advertising.

site, blog posts, and the like. You start by making your website linkworthy so that there's something of interest for people to link to. Then you need to include buttons or links that visitors can click to automatically bookmark the page with the most important social bookmarking services and to share it with the largest social networks. Having dedicated Digg and Facebook buttons will make it pretty much a no-brainer for users of social media to link to the given page.

Your goals, then, can be both objective (numerical) and subjective. Numerical goals might include signing up a set number of fans or friends to your Facebook page, getting a set number of subscribers to your Twitter feed, generating a set number of Diggs or other social bookmarks, and the like. Subjective goals should concern the quality of conversations you develop with your customers via these social media; the ideas generated, topics addressed, and so forth.

When it comes to these subjective goals, perhaps the most important goal is to simply get the conversation started. With social media, you really don't know what's going to develop until it develops; the key thing is to simply establish the mechanism for engaging online customers and make sure that those engagements are fostered. What happens next is sure to be interesting.

26

The Bottom Line

Social media marketing is the hottest thing happening in web marketing today, and for good reason. Social media are being embraced by web users of all ages and demographics, primarily as a means to connect and communicate with friends, family, and business associates. Facebook, Twitter, and the like are some of the largest and fastest-growing sites on the Internet, and look to get only bigger.

To take advantage of these social media, you need to develop an effective social media marketing strategy. That means exploiting all forms of social media—social networks, blogs, microblogs, social bookmarking services, social sharing sites, social location sharing services, and virtual communities. Do so effectively, and you can establish unique two-way communications with your most loyal customers—and benefit from the ongoing conversation.

ARE SOCIAL NETWORKS REPLACING OTHER FORMS OF ONLINE ACTIVITY?

Many people consolidate some or all of their online activities through a social network. The social network, then, becomes the user's primary means of communication and is used for posting public messages, sending private messages, sharing photos and other media, and engaging in group discussions.

For these users, separate forms of communication are superseded by those features on a social networking site. Instead of blogging, emailing, instant messaging, and sharing photos via separate sites and applications, users perform all these activities on a single social networking site. This efficiency of usage helps explain the popularity of Facebook and other social networks; it's easier to do all of these things on a single website than on several different sites and services.

This doesn't mean that blogs and email and instant messaging is going away; each has its place in the pantheon of online media. But for many users, especially younger ones, they're using these older online media less and less, preferring to consolidate their activities on Facebook or similar sites. Which, of course, makes social networking even that much more important for marketers.

26

27

Participating in Social Networking

When it comes to social media, social networks are the big dogs. Hundreds of millions of users participate in social networking sites, connecting with friends and family and establishing new online communities.

As such, to fully realize the marketing potential of social networks, you need to participate in them. I'm not talking about advertising; I'm talking about active participation in conversations with your customers on these sites. Only by participating in these social activities can you establish that invaluable one-to-one connection with your online customer base.

What Goes On in a Social Network

Before you participate in a social network, you need to know exactly what you'll be participating in. What exactly goes on in these sites?

Social networking is a great way to connect and communicate with friends and family. It's all about hanging out—virtually, that is. Users tend to spend much of their time online cruising through the personal profiles on a site, looking for people they know or who share similar interests. They view photos, play music, and watch videos posted by their friends. They see who's online, and they communicate via public posts, private emails, and instant messages.

Now, while the specifics differ a bit from site to site, these general activities remain constant. For the purposes of our examination, however, let's focus our attention on Facebook, far and away the largest social network today. In fact, Facebook is such a major player that some companies focus on it exclusively, in terms of their social media marketing.

Looking at Facebook as a decent example of all social networking sites, know that everything that goes on tends to revolve around users' personal profiles and their ongoing status updates. Think of a profile page as the user's home on the site and status updates as the way people tell others what they're up to.

Profile Pages

As you might suspect, a profile is a collection of personal information posted by an individual user. There is enough personal information in each profile to enable other users with similar interests to connect as "friends;" one's growing collection of friends helps to build a succession of personal communities.

All this profile information is displayed on a user's profile page. This page includes the user's personal photo, personal information, and a list of her most recent status updates and activities. It's kind of a home page for each user and also hosts any photos, videos, and events shared by that user.

FIGURE 27.1
A typical user profile page on Facebook.

Status Updates

Users keep their friends informed of current activities via short text posts called status updates. A status update is a bit like a long tweet or a short blog post; it's a line or two or three of text, sometimes accompanied by a photograph, video, or link to another web page.

People use status updates to tell their friends what they're doing, what they're thinking, and how they're feeling. Some people post updates weekly, some daily, and some pretty much every hour on the hour. (These more-frequent posters may be overdoing it just a bit, however—whose lives are so interesting that they need to post hourly updates?)

These status updates are broadcast to everyone on that person's friends list. These updates appear on their friends' home pages via a news feed; a user's news feed contains updates from all their friends. Reading the news feed, then, lets you know what all your friends are up to.

FIGURE 27.2

Status updates in a Facebook news feed.

Friends

The people you associate with on Facebook are called *friends*. To communicate with another user, you have to add that person to your friends list. All the people on your friends list see your status updates in their news feeds; you see all your friends' status updates in your news feed.

In addition, Facebook friends can view and share photos and videos, events, web links, and other items. Facebook also facilitates private communication between friends via an email-like private message system and real-time instant messaging (what Facebook calls *chat*).

Fans and Pages

Everything we've mentioned up to this point is available to individuals using Facebook. As a business, however, things are a little bit different.

27

First, businesses don't create simple profile pages. Instead you create what I like to call fan pages, or what Facebook just calls *pages*. That is, you create a page for your business that contains many of the same elements as a personal profile page—a conversation wall, photo albums, information about the business, and the like. This business page can also include a discussion tab, where your customers can engage in ongoing conversations with and about you.

Instead of your customers adding you and your page to their friends list, they instead opt to "like" or become a fan of your page. Your page includes a Like button; customers click this button, and they're now official fans. That means that any status updates you make are posted to their news

note Learn more about creating Facebook pages in Chapter 28, "Marketing on Facebook, MySpace, and Twitter."

feeds so they can be automatically notified of any news or other information you care to post. It's a great way to keep your name in front of your most loyal customers and keep them informed of sales, new products, and other important developments.

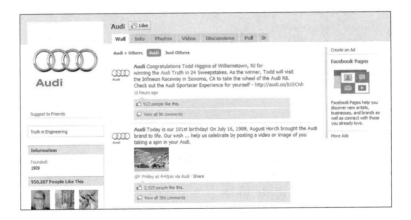

FIGURE 27.3
A typical Facebook business page—from Audi.

Becoming Part of the Community

That's pretty much how Facebook and other social networks work. Your challenge is to infiltrate and become part of these communities. You can't just sit back and wait for customers to come to you; you also won't succeed if you insist on broadcasting static messages.

Social marketing requires active participation. That's because social media is a two-way street. You can't just ask for attention; you have to provide something in return.

In most instances, that something is your own input—comments on blog posts or status updates, joining in on message board threads, and the like. You have to become an active member of the community to be taken seriously.

That means connecting and contributing on a fairly regular basis. You want to connect often and personally. That means either you or someone specifically assigned to your social media marketing efforts. You don't want to be anonymous in these conversations; it's better for users to connect with "Phil from Jascorp" than with "Jascorp Marketing."

Connecting on a social network involves both your corporate presence and your presence on other pages on the site. Yes, you need to establish a corporate page on Facebook and a company Twitter feed, but you also need to read and contribute to other Facebook pages and comment on other tweets. You have to get out there and participate—you can't wait for your customers to come to you.

What you have to do, then, is get off of your page and out into the community. On Facebook, that means reading and participating in pages that are relevant to your business; on Twitter, it means finding and commenting on feeds that are similarly relevant. These could be pages and feeds from other business, topic-oriented groups, or even individuals that are visible players in the community. Find out who the players are and then join in on their conversations.

For example, if you work for a home and garden retailer, become a fan of your suppliers' Facebook pages and Twitter feeds. Seek out groups that have to do with gardening and landscaping topics. Identify the major contributors to these groups and add them to your personal friends list. Build a network of people interested in what you do and establish ongoing contact with them.

And when you're participating in these other conversations, you can't be blatantly promoting your business. It's no good to leave a comment along the likes of "Great post! Look for our new widget in stores near you." That's self-serving and doesn't do anybody any good. Instead, you need to contribute relevant and useful comments; you have to advance the conversation, not hijack it.

To this end, one of the best things you can do is to offer helpful advice. If you can personally be helpful in a social conversation, benefits will accrue to you and the company you represent. Become known as a helpful person, and you'll build a loyal following of your own.

Monitoring Social Media

Naturally, you need to be proactive about taking part in social media conversations. But there may still be lots of conversations about you that you're not taking part in because you're not aware of them.

You see, conversations don't always take place in expected places. A disgruntled customer can tweet or post a Facebook status update that will be read by hundreds of his friends—and hundreds more of their friends, if they forward it along. Perhaps customers are talking about you in forums you're not even aware of. You might want to respond, but you can't if you don't know what's being said and where.

To that end, it pays to monitor the social media for conversations involving your company and products. This way you can be notified if your name is taken in vain (or justly praised), you have the opportunity to respond, and you're made aware of other groups and forums in which you should be participating on a more regular basis.

Short of monitoring every possible social media site and service and participating in every group and forum you can think of, how do you monitor conversations about you on the social Web? Fortunately, there are tools available that let you search it. Some even let you save and subscribe to the searches you make.

Free Monitoring Tools

Some of these monitoring tools are free; others require a paid subscription. As you might suspect, the free tools require a bit more work on your part, typically in the form of entering manual searches on a regular basis; there's less automation available. (Although several of these tools let you save your searches or subscribe to RSS feeds of search results.) But hey, they're free!

The most popular of these free monitoring tools include the following:

- **BackType (www.backtype.com)**—A relatively new (still in beta as I write this) service that monitors how users are engaged with specific websites. Enter a URL to list the total number of comments found, display individual comments, and display the top "influencers" (commenters) about the site.

- **BoardReader (www.boardreader.com)**—A nice little search engine for web forums and message boards.

- **BoardTracker (www.boardtracker.com)**—Another search engine for web forums and message boards.

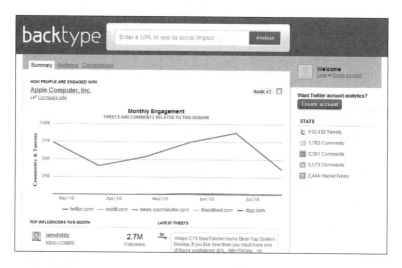

FIGURE 27.4

Monitoring comments and influencers with BackType.

- **IceRocket (www.icerocket.com)**—A search engine primarily for blogs and blog posts but can also be used to search Twitter and MySpace.

- **Hootsuite (www.hootsuite.com)**—A full-featured tool that, among other things, lets you track mentions of your company or brands across multiple social media.

- **SocialMention (www.socialmention.com)**—A search engine for blogs and most of the major social media sites, including Facebook, Twitter, Digg, Reddit, and StumbleUpon.

- **Technorati Search (www.technorati.com/search/)**—One of the oldest and best-respected blog search engines.

Of course, you can also directly search any given social media website. Facebook, Twitter, Digg, and all the rest offer their own site-specific search boxes; just enter your company or product name to call up a list of relevant pages or posts or bookmarks.

And what should you search for? Your company name, of course, and also the names of your major products or product lines. You may also want to search for the

> **note** You can also use Google to search for news items, blog posts, Facebook pages and status updates, and Twitter tweets. Start by conducting a normal search and then when the search results page appears, click News (for news items), Blog (for blog posts), or Updates (for tweets and Facebook posts) in the sidebar.

27

industry you're in, important industry topics, and competing companies and products. In addition, it's probably a good idea to search for the names of your company's key management—just in case someone is taking your boss' name in vain.

Paid Monitoring Tools

These free monitoring tools are fine, but if you want more sophisticated and more automatic monitoring, you need to upgrade to a paid tool. These tools, typically available via paid subscription, are better when you're trying to monitor across a large number of sites or if you expect to find a lot of mentions online.

The most popular of these paid monitoring tools include the following:

- **Alterian SM2 (socialmedia.alterian.com)**—An enterprise-level monitoring service that collects and analyzes mentions of your brand or product in the social media space. Pricing starts at $600/month.

- **Radian6 (www.radian6.com)**—Another enterprise-level monitoring system for all social media. Radian6 lets you monitor most major social media and filter results by media type or keyword. Pricing starts at $600/month.

- **Scout Labs (www.scoutlabs.com)**—A social media monitoring package for larger firms. Tracks mentions across more than 100 million sources—blogs, social media, websites, and so forth. Charges are based on the number of terms you track, starting at $249/month.

- **Trackur (www.trackur.com)**—A less-expensive, easier-to-use social monitoring tool. Lets you track trends and measure "sentiment"— positive, negative, or neutral. Pricing starts at $18/month.

Responding to Online Comments

What do you do if you identify a conversation out there on the social Web that mentions your company—and not in a positive way? It's your choice how you should respond, if at all.

Sometimes the better part of valor is to walk away from a potential flame war. Rather than engaging hostile commenters, it might be better to let the comments stand without response. That's not to say you should pretend the comments don't exist; even highly negative comments can prove useful for designing new products or formulating marketing campaigns. After all, if you know what people *don't* like, that can help guide you producing something they do.

If you do decide to respond to a social conversation, keep a few things in mind. First, speed is of the essence. There's no point responding to comments made a month or two ago; you need to jump in while the conversation is fresh. This shows that you take the conversation seriously enough to respond quickly.

You also need to respond positively, even to the most negative comments. Don't be defensive, and certainly don't be offensive; don't resort to name-calling or other insults. You need to be the adult in what might otherwise be a childish situation. Be professional, be calm, be cool, be collected. Don't let yourself get angry.

But don't be so calm cool and collected that you come off as being a PR flack. Yes, you probably should toe the company line, but you also have to genuinely respond to comments on a personal basis. Admit to mistakes, if there are any. Offer help or advice if any is to be given. Be sympathetic. Apologize. (You'd be surprised how far a genuine "I'm sorry for your problems" will go.)

> **note** If you're dealing with a rash of negative comments, you may have a bigger crisis on your hands. Work with senior management and your PR team to draft the appropriate public response and stick to it in your response to social media.

If you're responding to more positive or general comments, your job is a little easier. Again, respond in a personal manner, friendly without losing sight of your corporate responsibilities. Most people will appreciate your getting involved, sometimes to the point of overwhelming you with additional comments or questions. Try to take it all in stride and be gracious with your input and comments.

There's a certain amount of acceptance involved in all this. You simply can't control what people say about you, no matter how much you (or upper management) might like to. You're always going to have some people saying bad things about your company, your products, and even your people. (Especially your people, trust me on this one.) You can't take it personally. You have to accept that negative comments exist and learn to live with it. A thick skin is a must, but it also helps to develop an understanding of how people use the Internet to amplify their petty (and more-than-petty) complaints. Remember, as a company you are a lot bigger than any single complaint or complainer.

27

Finally, you should log all the comments you find and all the responses you make for immediate action and future reference. For example, if you're getting a lot of comments about a particular product feature not working, you may have an actual problem on your hands that you need to address. If a lot of people are confused about a particular process, then you may need to rethink that process—or at least your instructions for it. The social conversations you discover provide valuable feedback and information that you should put to use in your day-to-day operations.

The Bottom Line

To get the most out of social networks, you have to fully participate in the ongoing conversations. That means establishing your own company or product page, encouraging customer input and discussion, and then responding to customer comments. You also need to regularly post new news and information, in the form of tweets or status updates.

It's all about becoming part of the community, which requires no small amount of work. You need to monitor conversations not only on your company pages but also across all social networks, and respond in a proper fashion. That last bit is an acquired skill; you're going to be doing a lot of talking directly with customers, and you need to be polite and politic when doing so. Not all comments will be positive, after all; you need to be able to defuse and turn around potentially harmful situations, while at the same time presenting your company and products in a positive light. It's not easy, but it's what needs to be done when engaging your customers via social networking.

EVERYBODY CONTRIBUTES

When it comes to participating in social media, it's not just you personally or your marketing department that's responsible. Anyone in your company can take part in social conversations—which means you need to make sure everybody is on the same page.

You see, when anyone in your company can get on Twitter or Facebook and start responding to other conversations—or create new posts of their own—the potential for disaster is there. Not every employee will know the company line; more important, not every employee will have the necessary tact and skill to respond to baiting by angry customers.

There have been too many instances of lower-level employees taking the bait and putting the company in the uncomfortable position of either defending the employee or backtracking from his remarks.

To that end, you need to develop a company-wide social media policy. You need to spell out under what circumstances an employee can talk about the company online and how. While you can't ban employees from Facebooking on their own time, you can try to control how employees represent your company.

Not that you want employees to completely disassociate with the company on social networking sites. You can pick up a lot of free PR by encouraging your co-workers to blog or tweet or Facebook about your company and products. Word of mouth is great advertising, remember. In fact, you want your employees to develop large personal followings on Facebook and Twitter and the like, especially if they enjoy where they work and what they do and the products and services they're involved with. (Everybody is a happy camper, right?) The more they and their social friends talk about the company and products, the more exposure you get online.

It's even better that it's personal exposure, helping to put a human face on what you are and what you do. Just make sure that employees know what they can and can't talk about, and you have a sweet situation.

27

Marketing on Facebook, MySpace, and Twitter

Now we come to the important stuff—how to market your company and your products on Facebook, Twitter, and the like. There's a lot you can do, from hosting Facebook pages and Twitter feeds to placing "share" buttons on your website and blog to targeting full-blown PPC advertising campaigns to the users of the major social networks.

At this point I'll assume you're sold on the importance of social media marketing. So let's get right to work and learn what you need to do!

Marketing via a Facebook Fan Page

We'll start with the largest social media site—Facebook. As you know, this popular social network is a community with more than 500 million users. Ignore Facebook at your peril.

There are many ways to market your company and products on Facebook. We'll examine the most popular methods here—hosting a Facebook "fan" page, creating a Facebook application, and cross-marketing Facebook via your own website or blog. First up is your Facebook page.

Understanding Facebook Pages

Individuals on Facebook are represented by their profile pages; other users become "friends" with a person to receive his or her status updates. Businesses, however, aren't individuals and as such don't have individual profile pages or friends.

Instead, your business creates what Facebook simply calls a *page* (or what I call a *fan page*), and you get people to "like" your page to become fans. Your fans can read all about you on your fan page, contribute to hosted discussions, and receive all the status updates you make.

> **note** Who can create Facebook fan pages? Businesses, brands, organizations, performers, celebrities, and other public figures all have fan pages on the Facebook site.

FIGURE 28.1

A typical business Facebook page for the Dakota Jazz Club in Minneapolis.

A Facebook page is a great way to keep in touch with your most loyal customers and fans. You can use your fan page to announce new products and promotions, hold contests, and solicit customer opinions. Obviously, you can also link to your main website from your fan page so customers can find out more information at the source.

Any official representative of your business can create your company's Facebook page. (This prevents customers or competitors from hijacking your name and presence on the site.) There's no charge to do so; the only thing you have to spend is your time.

Creating Your Facebook Page

Creating a Facebook page is relatively easy. You start by going to www.facebook.com/pages/ and then clicking the Create Page button. When the Create a Page screen appears, select the category for your page: Local Business; Brand, Product, or Organization; or Artist, Band, or Public Figure.

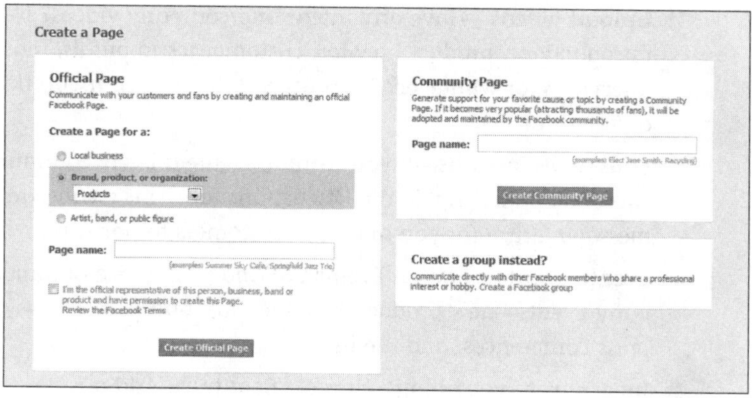

FIGURE 28.2

Creating a Facebook page.

If you select Local Business, you can then select the type of business you're in: Automotive, Automotive Dealer/Vehicle Service, Banking and Financial Service, Bar, Café, and the like. If you select Brand, Product, or Organization, select from Communications, Consumer Product, Fashion, Financial Service, and so on.

You then need to enter the name of your page, typically the name of your company or brand or product you're promoting. Confirm that you're an official representative of your company and then click the Create Official Page button. That's it. Your company now has a brand new Facebook page.

Customizing Your Page

You're not done yet, however. You can now customize the look and feel of your page, as well as which elements appear. This is how you brand your presence on the Facebook site.

What can you customize? Here's a short list of available features, all of which are accessible from the page itself:

- **Upload your logo**—You can add your logo to your Facebook page simply by uploading it as the page's default picture.

- **Upload pictures**—Create photo albums for your major product lines, key employees, management team, corporate offices, or whatever you think your customers will be interested in. Then populate those albums with the appropriate photos.

28

- **Upload videos**—Have any interesting company videos? New product introductions, product how-tos, customer testimonials, management interviews, or whatever? Then upload those to your Facebook page on a Videos tab.

- **Enable discussions**—If you want to create a lively community on your Facebook page, enable the Discussions tab. This creates an organized message forum for you and your customers to participate in.

- **Create events**—Add an Events tab and post notice of important company events—new product introductions, online meetings or webinars, press conferences, and the like.

- **Incorporate your blog**—Here's a neat trick. Add a Notes tab to your page and then use it to pull in your blog's RSS feed.

- **Add applications**—There are tons of Facebook applications available, some of which might be applicable to your business. For example, if you run a restaurant, you might want to add the OpenTable app to a tab on your page. Look around and see what's available and then add the ones that make sense.

I also recommend that you create a custom URL for your fan page. You have to have 100 fans before Facebook offers this option, but it's worth striving for.

Promoting Your Page

Of course, just having a Facebook page doesn't guarantee that you'll get scores of fans. You need to make people aware of your page by promoting it in various ways.

The first thing you should do is invite people to visit and like your page. You want to find friends on the Facebook site and then suggest your new page to your friends. There's a Suggest to Friends link in the sidebar of your page; use this to send invitations to these folks.

There are lots of other ways to promote your fan page, of course. You can include your fan page's URL in company emails, newsletters, press releases, advertisements, and other company marketing materials and correspondence. You can also mention your Facebook page in other social media, such as your Twitter feed. And don't forget your main website and blog; you should include links to your Facebook page there, as well.

note Another option is to promote your fan page on the Facebook site by purchasing Facebook advertising, discussed later in the chapter.

Posting Status Updates

When you sign in with your company account (the same one you used to create your fan page), you can then post status updates to Facebook. These updates get displayed on your fan page as well as in the news feeds of all your official fans—people who click the Like button on your page. What should you update your fans about? There's some strategy involved here.

You can use status updates as promotional notices, kind of like press releases to your Facebook fans. That means updating your fans of new products and services, company events, and the like.

You can also use status updates to relay favorable notices and reviews, announce upcoming events, and even run contests and sweepstakes. For that matter, you can use status updates to share useful or interesting content, such as YouTube videos or customer photos.

If you're a restaurant, for example, you can post your daily specials as status updates on your Facebook page. If you run an auto repair shop, post about common service procedures. If you're a landscaping business, post about seasonal landscaping and gardening issues. If you run a design firm, post about some of your more interesting projects. You get the idea.

The key is to use your status updates to engage your community. Point out interesting trends, repost comments from fans and reviewers, take the opportunity to ask your fans what they're interested in. Try to encourage comments and posts from your fans. Make it interesting.

As to how often you should post, some companies post daily, some weekly, and some only sporadically. I'm a fan of more regular updates, a few times a week or more. Obviously, it helps if you have something genuine to post about, but you still need to keep your name in front of your fans and customers. There's no point in establishing a Facebook presence if you're never there.

Marketing via a Facebook Application

This next bit isn't for everyone, but it may be worth considering. I'm talking about developing a brand- or product-specific Facebook application, something that Facebook users can run or use while they're using Facebook.

There are thousands of Facebook applications available, most from third-party developers. Some are quite useful, such as those that help you manage your book and music libraries or find relatives on the site. Others are more

28

fun than useful; I'm talking about the plethora of social games, of which Mafia Wars and FarmVille head the bunch.

That said, there may be an application you can develop (or have developed for you) that helps to expand your presence on the site. For example, a gardening firm might offer an app that helps users categorize their garden flowers or schedule lawn and garden maintenance. An auto repair shop might offer an app where users can track their scheduled oil changes and other maintenance. A music store might have an app that helps local musicians connect with each other for gigs. And just about any business can do some sort of quiz-type app.

FIGURE 28.3

An interesting company-sponsored Facebook application: Home Depot's What's Your DIY-Q? quiz.

The point is, a custom Facebook application, if truly useful, can help you better serve your customer base and attract new customers. If you can think of such an app, it's a great marketing opportunity.

How do you create a Facebook application? That's a bit beyond the scope of this book and my own personal abilities. We're marketers, after all, not software developers. That said, Facebook offers a variety of developer tools and services, all centralized at developers.facebook.com. You'll probably want to partner with a local development firm to let them turn your ideas into reality.

Cross-Marketing with a Facebook Like Button

You can also establish and promote your Facebook presence from your existing website or blog. Facebook offers the opportunity to connect your site with Facebook and your presence on the Facebook site. You can log customers onto your site using their Facebook logon info and then share customer information between your site and Facebook.

You have to understand that Facebook's goal (other than making money, of course—and lots of it) is to connect practically everyone with practically everyone else. As such, why limit said connections to the Facebook site proper? There are a lot more connections to be made if Facebook can turn other websites into extensions of its social network.

This approach is easy to understand when you see the linkage between Facebook and other social media sites. For example, you can sign into YouTube with your Facebook ID and then have the videos you post or the favorites you make cross-posted as status updates to your Facebook feed. The two sites share information about you, the user, and use it to connect the two communities. It makes the entire Web more social.

There are a number of ways you can take advantage of this interconnection. All involve forging closer ties between your site and Facebook, so if that bothers you (especially in terms of sharing user information), feel free to back away now. But if you're interested, there are some opportunities to be had.

This kind of social cross-pollination is possible thanks to Facebook's Open Graph technology. Probably the most common implementation of Open Graph is the Facebook Like or Recommended button that many websites and blogs display. It's easy to add such a button to your site; just insert a small bit of code in your page's underlying HTML. When one of your site's visitors clicks the button, that shows up as a status post in that person's Facebook feed. For example, someone clicking the Like button on Big Belly Burger's website would generate a post along the lines of "Joe Jones likes Big Belly Burgers." It's a nice little promotion.

FIGURE 28.4

A Facebook Like button.

There's more. When someone clicks the Like button your website, he becomes a "fan" of your site. This means that all the status updates you post are listed in that person's news feed. It's a great way to convert your existing customers into Facebook fans.

note Open Graph was previously known by the more descriptive title of Facebook Connect. (Great marketing work, Facebook, in changing that name!)

Clicking the Like button also adds your website to that user's Facebook profile. Your site is listed in that person's Interests section as a clickable link. Friends of that user who view his profile can click the link to go directly to your website.

By the way, you don't have to settle for just a single Like button on your site's home page. You can add Like buttons for different sections or topics on your site; this lets you segment your customer base according to product line or service or whatever. For example, if you run a travel agency, you can have a "master" Like button on your home page for the agency itself but then have other Like buttons on pages for specific destinations. You can then push status updates about location-specific tours or offers to those users who "liked" that destination.

That's not all. Facebook also lets you add a Like Box to your website. This is actually a widget that displays a live stream of all the people who have "liked" your site. I'm not sure the real value of this, but it's an interesting little feature.

FIGURE 28.5

A Like Box.

Learn more about adding a Like button at developers.facebook.com/docs/ reference/plugins/like/. Learn more about the Like Box at developers.facebook. com/docs/reference/plugins/like-box/.

Utilizing More Facebook Social Plugins

The Like button and box are two of what Facebook calls *social plugins* or what others might call *widgets*. A Facebook social plugin lets users see what their friends have liked, commented on, or shared on sites across the Web. Install these plugins on your site to better connect your existing customers to Facebook—and Facebook users to your website.

There are several of these social plugins available for online marketers. We've already discussed the Like button and Like box; the other plugins include the following:

- **Recommendations**—This plugin provides personalized recommendations (from Facebook) to your site's users. The plugin works by considering all the social interactions that Facebook users have with URLs on your site; it tends to recommend pages that a person's Facebook friends have visited.

- **Comments**—This plugin lets users comment on your site's content. Comments are listed on your web page, and users have the option of sharing those comments via a status update to their Facebook friends. This is a great way to get more visibility on the Facebook site by encouraging user comments.

- **Activity Feed**—This plugin displays what Facebook calls "the most interesting activity taking place" on your website. In reality, it displays when users "like" or share the content on your site. If a user is currently logged into Facebook, it highlights content from his friends.

- **Live Stream**—This plugin lets your site's visitors share their activity and comments in real time. It's best suited for sites offering real-time events.

- **Friendpile**—This plugin displays the profile pictures of a user's friends who are already signed up for your website. As the name implies, it really does display a "pile of friends;" it's a way of confirming that a person likes the same sites as his friends do.

FIGURE 28.6

The Facebook Recommendations plugin.

FIGURE 28.7

The Facebook Comments plugin.

FIGURE 28.8

The Facebook Activity Feed plugin.

Facebook also has an Authentication feature that many websites are starting to use. With Authentication installed, visitors to your site or web-based application have the option of signing in with their Facebook IDs. The nice thing about this is that you then get access to all the general information in that person's Facebook profile—name, picture, gender, and friends

note Not all of these plugins are suitable for all sites. You also have to get comfortable with the fact that when you install one of these plugins, you're linking yourself inextricably with Facebook; you may be okay with this, or you may not.

list. That gives you a real head start in personalizing your site's services for that particular user—and forging a deeper connection with that user.

Learn more about Facebook social plugins—including how to install the necessary code—at developers.facebook.com/plugins/. Learn more about Facebook Authentication at developers.facebook.com/docs/authentication.

Marketing on MySpace

Facebook is the big dog of social networking, and thus of social media marketing. But for certain types of businesses, MySpace is also worth considering as part of your online marketing plans.

It's a fact that MySpace isn't nearly as popular as Facebook among the general populace, at least not anymore. It still has some appeal among younger teenagers, but even they are moving to Facebook. No, where MySpace shines is in the entertainment community, among musicians, comedians, actors, and other performers. If you're in the entertainment business, MySpace is the place to show your wares.

That said, many non-entertainment businesses also use MySpace to connect with their "fans" and promote their goods and services. Just as with Facebook, businesses of all types, from travel agents to restaurants, create their own MySpace profiles to connect with their customers online.

As to how you market on MySpace, it's pretty similar to how you do so on Facebook. You create a MySpace profile for your company or brand, try to get a large number of "friends" for your page, and then post regular status updates to these friends. It's all free, save for your time, and very similar to managing a Facebook page.

I won't go into all the details of creating a MySpace page; it's pretty much a fill-in-the-blank process, starting with the Sign Up link at www.myspace.com. Suffice to say, you can customize your MySpace page with your company logo, specific color scheme, and all manner of specific content modules.

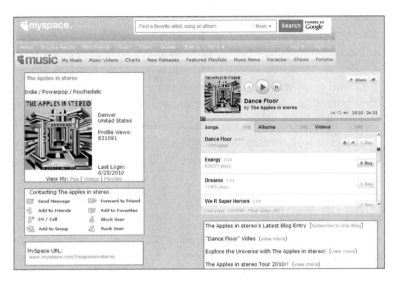

FIGURE 28.9

A typical MySpace page.

After you've created and customized your MySpace page, you start feeding the beast in the form of status updates. These are just like Facebook status updates, and you enter them from the What Do You Want to Share? box on your page. The updates you post appear on your profile and home pages, as well as in the Stream module on your friends' home pages.

> **note** If you're in the music business, MySpace offers even more options, including streaming audio playback and the ability to sell music downloads directly from your profile page.

Your status updates appear in multiple places on the MySpace site. Your most recent status updates appears near the top of both your Profile and Home pages. Your status updates also appear on your friends' Home pages in their Stream module. This way your friends are kept updated as to what you're doing and thinking.

To succeed on MySpace you have to actively participate in the community. You can't expect your fans to follow you on MySpace (or on any social network) unless you post with some regularity. If you go too long without posting something new, people will quit following you. In reality, that means going online and writing *something* at least once a week. You can talk about upcoming product releases, industry happenings, or even your boss' birthday—whatever you think will interest your customers. Just put yourself out there to connect with your customers on a regular basis.

FIGURE 28.10

MySpace status updates on a user's home page.

Marketing with Twitter

Then there's Twitter. Twitter isn't a social network, so there's no built-in sense of community. There are, however, lots of conversations.

If Twitter isn't a social network, what is it? Well, Twitter is what we call a microblogging service. Users post short text messages,

> **note** Unlike Facebook or MySpace, Twitter is not a full-featured social network. It only offers message posting and following; it does not offer any other community features, such as photo sharing, instant messaging, or groups.

28

called *tweets*, which are the equivalent of Facebook status updates, except a lot shorter, limited to 140 characters, max.

Marketing with Twitter is all about the tweets. You set up a Twitter account for your company or brand and then start tweeting. As with Facebook or MySpace marketing, you need to post something new on a fairly regular basis—once or twice a week, or even more often if you have something of value to impart. You gather a group of *followers* (Twitter's equivalent of Facebook's friends), and they receive every tweet you make. It's how you broadcast your promotional messages.

FIGURE 28.11
Tweets on Twitter.

Your Twitter followers can respond to your individual tweets or tweet you back privately. Other users can search for your company name to find all the tweets made by or about you. And, of course, you can choose to follow other Twitterers—which means you'll see everything they post to the site.

Tweeting

You sign up for a Twitter account and do all your tweeting at www.twitter.com. Once you sign up, you can create and customize your Twitter profile; this provides some small degree of promotional value, as it's what your followers will see if they are interested in who you are.

28

FIGURE 28.12

A typical Twitter profile page.

Tweeting is as simple as going to the Twitter home page, typing your message into the What's Happening? box, and then clicking the Tweet button. Remember, a tweet can be no more than 140 characters in length.

FIGURE 28.13

Tweeting from the Twitter home page.

Because of that 140-character limitation, tweets do not have to conform to proper grammar, spelling, and sentence structure—and, in fact, seldom do. It is common to abbreviate longer words, use familiar acronyms, substitute single letters and numbers for whole words, and refrain from all punctuation.

> **note** You can also tweet from your mobile phone by sending a text message to the number provided by Twitter.

For example, you might shorten the sentence "See our new Friday specials" to read "C R new Fri spcls." It might not make sense to you now, but it will eventually.

28

The 140-character limitation presents a challenge when you want to include links to your website (or other websites) in your tweets. Entering a link is as simple as typing the URL, but long URLs might not fit. To that end, consider using a link-shortening service, such as bit.ly (www.bit.ly), to create shorter URLs to better fit within Twitter's limitations.

Links aren't the only things you can insert in your tweets. You can mention other Twitter users in your tweets and make their names clickable. All you have to do is type an "at sign" (@) before the user's name, like this: @username. Clicking a referenced name displays that user's Twitter profile page.

You can also enter the equivalent of keywords, called *hashtags*, in your tweets. A hashtag is simply a word that is preceded by the hash or pound character, like this: #hashtag. When you add a hash character before a specific word in a tweet, that word gets referenced by Twitter as a kind of keyword, and that word becomes clickable by anyone viewing the tweet; it also helps other users find relevant tweets when they search for that particular topic. Clicking a hashtag in a tweet displays a list of the most recent tweets that include the same hashtag.

One thing you can't add to a tweet is a picture; by default, Twitter is a text-only service. However, certain third-party applications, such as TwitPic (www.twitpic.com), enable you to include links to photos within your tweets. Upload a photo to TwitPic, and it creates a tweet with a link to that picture hosted on their site. It's actually pretty easy and pretty common.

Tips for Successful Tweeting

A few words of advice. First, determine who does the tweeting for your company. As with a blog, it can be one or more people; in fact, the more people you have tweeting, the more tweets you can post.

Second, consider the frequency. Twitter users expect a regular stream of tweets from the people and companies they follow. Tweeting once a week probably isn't going to be enough. Heck, once a *day* might not be enough. Successful twitterers tweet several times a day. It's all about maintaining a constant presence, and given the barrage of tweets out there, more is definitely better.

Remember, tweets don't have to be long. Actually, they *can't* be long—there's that 140-character limitation you have to work with. But shorter is better and might even make it easier for you to tweet more often. Think in terms of single-sentence communications—a single thought sent out into the Twitterverse. Instead of saving up all your thoughts for one long blog post, post them throughout the day in short, individual tweets.

28

What should you tweet about? Whatever your customers want to read, of course. If you're a restaurant, tweet your daily lunch and dinner specials. If you're a retail store, tweet your latest sales or promotions. If you're a movie theater, tweet the latest show times. If you're a bookstore, tweet the latest releases. If you're a clothing manufacturer, tweet about the latest styles and fashions.

Here's what you *don't* want to tweet about: The fact that you just got yourself a cup of coffee. How you feel this morning. The weather. (Unless it's really interesting or extreme.) When you're ready to take a nap. How much you hate your boss. Or just about anything else that is self-involved, self-referential, or just too personal or insipid to interest anyone else but you.

In other words, you need to find some snippit of real news or information and make that your tweet. In most companies, that shouldn't be too much of a problem; there's always something new and interesting to tweet about. And if you can't find anything interesting to tweet about, then maybe you shouldn't be tweeting.

As to the form and style of your tweets, what I recommended for Facebook updates applies here, as well. Make your tweets informal and personal. Use the opportunity to show the human face behind your organization or brand. That means being conversational as well as helpful.

Which brings us to a final point. Many customers will use Twitter as a means to contact you with questions and customer support issues. That's cool—it's nice to have another support channel. This means, however, that you have to answer these questions and in a timely fashion. If you can't answer the questions directly, forward them to your customer support department. However you do it, make sure the customer is satisfied.

note While the temptation is to answer questions and complaints via private responses, there is value in posting your responses in public tweets. Public replies show how responsive your company is, which is a good thing. In addition, posting a public response will answer other similar questions that other may have but haven't tweeted yet.

Responding and Retweeting

Any Twitter user can respond to any tweet they read. It's as easy as clicking the Reply button next to the sender's username in the original tweet. The reply will be sent as a tweet back to the original sender.

In addition, Twitterers like to pass on or "retweet" those tweets they find most useful or interesting. In fact, there's a Retweet link next to each tweet. It's an efficient way to obtain wide distribution for popular tweets and something you as a marketer should encourage.

> **note** Once a tweet has been retweeted, it's out of your control. There's no way to delete an errant tweet once it's been retweeted.

Following and Followers

Obviously, you want to encourage your customers to follow you on Twitter. To that end, listing your Twitter name in all your marketing materials is a good start; you should also mention your Twitter feed on your website and blog.

Of course, it also helps to have a useful and interesting Twitter feed. If your tweets are nothing more than short promotional announcements, you won't attract too many new followers and are likely to lose existing ones as well. Create more valuable tweets and you'll have your existing followers retweeting and telling others about them, which will gain you even more followers over time.

Then there's the issue of whether you should follow the people who follow you. It doesn't have to be a two-way street; you can pretty much assume that Ashton Kutcher doesn't follow each of the million or so people who follow him.

That said, when you do follow your followers, you're sending the message that your customers are important to you. That's a good thing and will help cement customer loyalty.

Fortunately, following someone creates no responsibility on your end to respond to their tweets or even read them. It does, however, clog up your Twitter home page; if you have a thousand followers and choose to follow them all, that's a lot of potential tweets. It's your choice.

Getting the Most Out of Twitter with Third-Party Tools

Even though some followers will respond to your tweets and some will tweet you directly with their questions or complaints, Twitter is mainly a one-way social medium. That said, there are a few tools available to help you manage your tweets and followers and help you determine what to tweet about.

The most useful of these tools include the following:

- **CoTweet (www.cotweet.com)**—This service is designed for use by large companies and organizations. You can manage multiple Twitter accounts and users, manage Twitter workflow among multiple users, monitor keywords and trends, and view click-through statistics of the URLs you include in your tweets.

▪ **Hummingbird (www.hummingbird2.com)**—Use this tool to determine which of your followers you should follow. It generates a "quality score" for each follower to help you identify users who are relevant to what you're offering.

▪ **Tweepdiff (www.tweepdiff.com)**—Use this tool to compare the followers of different Twitterers. It's a good way to see if there's any overlap between followers of different accounts.

▪ **Trendistic (www.trendistic.com)**—Use this tool to compare the popularity of different topics among Twitterers. Displays trend charts that track frequency of mentions over time; also displays individual tweets about the topic.

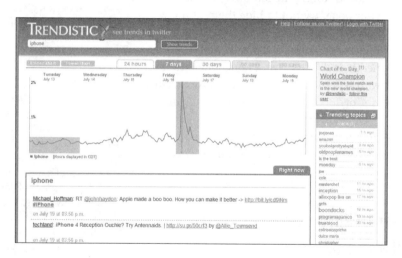

FIGURE 28.14
Tracking Twitter trends with Trendistic.

Sharing and Bookmarking via Social Media

Now we come to a bit of a no-brainer that not all sites do, surprisingly. I'm talking about making it easy for your website or blog to be shared and bookmarked with the major social networks and social bookmarking services.

28

If you want your website or blog to be bookmarked and shared, you need to include buttons or links (I like buttons better; they're more visual) that make bookmarking a one-click process. That means picking the social media you want to target and adding buttons to each page on your site or blog that users can click to automatically bookmark those pages.

FIGURE 28.15

"Quick add" buttons for a variety of social bookmarking services.

Add these buttons in a prominent position on each page on your website, typically in a sidebar along the left or right side of your page; try not to hide them at the very bottom. On your blog, include these buttons in the page's sidebar as well as underneath each blog post. Preface the buttons with text along the lines of "Share this article" or "Bookmark this page." You can even get fancy and use Javascript to display a pop-up menu of social bookmark links when a user clicks a "Share This" link.

> **note** As you've probably guessed, the Facebook Like button discussed previously is one instance of this type of social sharing/bookmarking.

> **note** You may want to include a list of relevant tags or keywords alongside the "quick add" buttons so that bookmarkers will know how to tag their bookmarks. These should be a subset of your site's existing keyword list. You may also want to include suggested text that people can use when they create links to your site.

Constructing an Effective Social Media Campaign

Knowing how to use Facebook, MySpace, Twitter, and the like, how do you use these media to conduct an effective promotional campaign?

While there are lots of ways to approach this, it's important to note that when you're talking to your social media audience, you're talking to your most loyal customers—true believers, as it were. Communicating directly to these folks via tweets and status updates creates a bit of an echo chamber, but in a good way; you end up amplifying your message and building excitement and anticipation among those customers who matter most.

Let me give you an example, In August, 2010, musician Brian Wilson released a new CD, titled *Brian Wilson Reimagines Gershwin*. Now, Brian has a huge number of very loyal follows, many of whom date back to his Beach Boys days. His new releases are few and far between, so the news of a new release gets the fan base really excited.

Brian's marketing team decided to use social media to stoke the fires for this new release. They started with a single, rather cryptic message across all services (Twitter, Facebook, et al) in March, five months before the album release:

> **Brian is busy mixing his upcoming "George Gershwin" album.**

That attracted a lot of attention. On Facebook alone this message got more than 350 "likes" and almost a hundred comments.

Then, about a month later, came this follow-up message:

> **Fans are speculating and rumors abound, but Disney has NOT yet set a release date for Brian's Gershwin album. You'll be the first to know as soon as we get word from Disney.**

In June, Brian and his camp posted photos and artwork from the upcoming album, which now had a title. Later in June, they announced a release date for the album, and a few days later posted a link to Amazon where the album could be preordered. That's right, they started encouraging sales a full two months before the album was released.

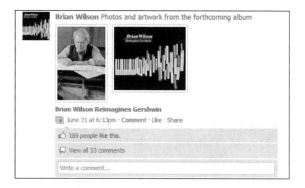

FIGURE 28.16

A teaser post for Brian Wilson Reimagines Gershwin *on Facebook.*

Toward the end of June came a further enticement, in the form of a link to a prerelease track from the album, downloadable in MP3 format. As you can imagine, the fans went nuts; there's no better way to drum up support for a musical release than to let fans listen to the music, even if it's just a taste.

More teasers followed. There were links to newspaper articles about the upcoming album, the official press release and final track list, video clips showing the artist at work, links to favorable blog posts and prerelease reviews, posts from prerelease listening parties, you name it. By the time the album actually hit, the fans were stoked and sales were high.

This was a masterful use of social media to promote a new product to a loyal fan base. Social media is great for leaking information in dribs and drabs, teasing customers about what's to come, keeping the interest level high. Use it as a textbook example of what you could be doing in this area.

Advertising on Social Media

So far we've discussed ways to organically use Facebook and other social media as part of your online marketing activities. But there's an inorganic side to the social media business, too. I'm talking good old-fashioned advertising, which you can now do on most of the major social networks.

> **note** Learn more about online advertising in Part V of this book, "Online Advertising."

PPC Advertising on Facebook

Let's start with Facebook. Yes indeed, Facebook now offers pay-per-click (PPC) advertising. It's actually kind of neat in that you can target your PPC ads based on user interests and demographics; you don't buy keywords, per se, but rather specify what topics and interests you want to target.

Facebook ads are displayed in the sidebar of a user's home and profile pages in the Sponsored section. Ads include a short title, brief descriptive copy, and an optional image. The title is clickable.

What you advertise is your company's Facebook fan page. Your ads point to this page, and when your ad clicked, users are taken to your fan page.

As I mentioned, these are primarily PPC ads; you pay only when the ad is clicked. Facebook also sells ads on a CPM basis, but that's really not the way to go. The option is there, however, if that's what you want.

FIGURE 28.17

A couple of typical Facebook ads.

Creating an ad is relatively simple. Go to your fan page and click the Get More Connections button. This displays the Advertise on Facebook page; click the Facebook Content arrow and select the page you wish to promote.

Now you get to create the ad. Enter the destination URL for your ad (can be your Facebook page or your own website), the ad's title (up to 25 characters), and the Body Text box (135 characters max). You can also choose to include a photograph or other image in your ad, up to 110 pixels wide x 80 pixels tall.

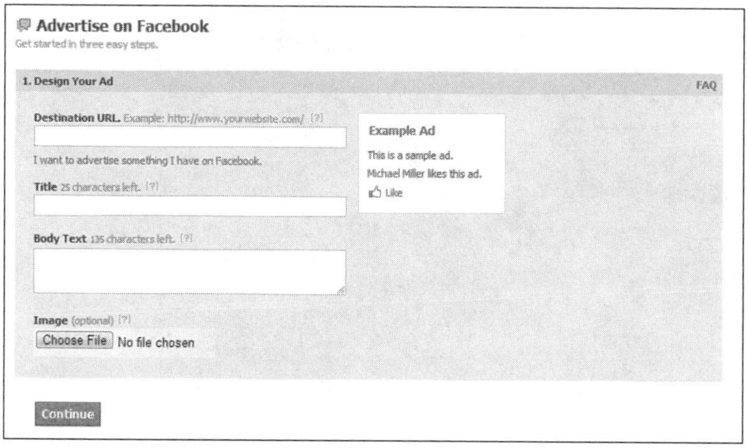

Advertise on Facebook
Get started in three easy steps.

1. Design Your Ad   FAQ

Destination URL. Example: http://www.yourwebsite.com/ [?]

I want to advertise something I have on Facebook.

Title 25 characters left. [?]

Body Text 135 characters left. [?]

Example Ad

This is a sample ad.
Michael Miller likes this ad.
Like

Image (optional) [?]
Choose File No file chosen

Continue

FIGURE 28.18

Creating a Facebook ad.

28

When you're ready, click the Continue button. You now get to select who sees your ad via the options in the page's Targeting section. Facebook uses the personal information entered by its members to identify those members to which your ad will be served. Select from these targeting options:

- Location
- Age
- Birthday (target people on their birthdays)
- Sex
- Interested In (Men or Women)
- Relationship
- Languages
- Likes and Interests
- Education
- Workplaces
- Connections
- Friends of Connections

Make your selections; the more options you select, the smaller the target audience.

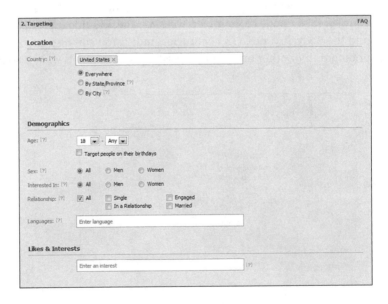

FIGURE 28.19

Selecting targeting options.

When you click the Continue button, the page expands again to display the Campaigns and Pricing section. You can assign a name for this particular campaign, as well as determine a daily budget. As with Google AdWords and other PPC advertising networks, Facebook runs ads up to but not exceeding your specified budget level. You can then determine whether you want your ad to run immediately or only during specified dates.

Next, you select whether you want to pay via CPM or CPC. Assuming you pick the latter, you then enter the maximum bid per click you're willing to pay. Review your ad and then start things running.

note Learn more about Facebook advertising at www.facebook.com/advertising/.

You monitor the performance of your ads via the Campaigns dashboard. You can view the following data:

- Status of your campaigns
- Amount you've bid for each ad
- Number of clicks received
- Number of impressions
- Click-through rate (CTR)
- Average cost per click (or average CPM, if you went that route)
- Amount spent

You can also generate three different campaign reports: Advertising Performance, Responder Demographics, and Responder Profiles. The latter two reports help you fine-tune your demographic targeting.

Should you advertise on Facebook? I can't make that decision for you. I do know that many marketers find that Facebook ads perform much weaker than do similar search advertising, such as with Google AdWords. You might find that organic marketing on Facebook provides the results you want and that additional advertising isn't necessary. Or you might experiment a bit with Facebook's ads just to see whether or not they're worth it. What I wouldn't recommend is jumping into a big ad campaign without doing some testing first; you may be disappointed in the results.

PPC Advertising on MySpace

Not surprisingly, you can also do advertising on MySpace, via the MyAds platform. MyAds lets you place ads on MySpace pages, on either a CPC or CPM basis.

MyAds offers three ad sizes: A top-of-page horizontal banner, a vertical sky-scraper, and a simple square. These can be graphic ads by uploading your own images. Or you can use a predesigned ad template to create what is effectively an enhanced text ad. You don't have to get all fancy if you don't want to.

FIGURE 28.20

A typical MySpace banner ad.

A typical ad has the expected components—title body copy and click-to URL. As with Facebook advertising, you target your ads demographically, specifying the following criteria:

- Gender
- Age
- Education
- Relationship
- Parental Status
- Location
- Interests and Occupations

When you create your ad, you specify your daily budget and maximum CPC you're willing to pay. There's also a dashboard to help you monitor your ads' performance.

How does MySpace advertising compare to Facebook advertising? The big difference you'll probably see is the age of your potential customers. Whereas Facebook has a fairly broad demographic, MySpace delivers a much younger audience. So don't be surprised when you see the average age of your MySpace ad traffic skewing well under 21. That's just the nature of the beast.

Learn more about MySpace ads at www.myads.com/myspace/.

Advertising via Promoted Tweets

Then there's Twitter. For the longest time, Twitter didn't accept any advertising. Not surprisingly, they also didn't report much in the way of revenues.

All things change, however, and Twitter has since announced their own in-house advertising platform. These Promoted Tweets, as they're called, look more or less like regular tweets, not like ads. They appear only on search results pages, when someone searches for a topic linked to keyword purchased by the advertiser. These tweets appear at the top of the search results page, with a distinctive "Promoted by *Advertiser*" tag.

FIGURE 28.21

A Promoted Tweet on Twitter.

As with traditional tweets, Promoted Tweets are subject to Twitter's 140-character limitation. The only graphic included is the advertiser's profile picture. (Which argues for using your logo as your Twitter profile picture, of course.) Surprisingly, Promoted Tweets are sold on a CPM basis, not via CPC.

And that's all I know about Promoted Tweets right now. As I write this text (August 2010), Twitter has yet to roll this out to the general advertiser base, still testing it with a select group of major advertisers. Keep checking the Twitter site to learn more over time.

Integrating Your Efforts Across Multiple Social Media

If you follow the advice given in this chapter, you have a lot of work cut out for you. Status updates on Facebook and MySpace, tweets on Twitter, and don't forget the regular blog posts we talked about previously. That's a lot of different messaging vehicles to manage.

Constructing Compatible Messages

But here's the thing. You don't have to create different messages for each vehicle. There's no rule that says what you post on Facebook has to be different

28

from what your tweet about on Twitter. For that matter, you can post the same message in your company blog.

What you don't want to do is write completely different messages for each media. That would be a lot of unnecessary work—and not very smart. The reality is if there's something important enough to announce on Twitter, you want to tell your Facebook and MySpace and blog followers about it, too. There are very few messages that you want to limit to the followers of a particular social medium. Instead, you want to tell everybody everything—and, in most instances, the same thing.

There are space limitations to deal with, of course. Blog posts can be longer than Facebook updates, and everything is longer than tweets. But if you plan your messages carefully, you post substantially similar messages across multiple media; you don't have to reinvent a lot of wheels.

Consider the messages you create. Start with the shortest medium first—Twitter. Begin by constructing a message that fits within Twitter's 140-character constraint. Then see if that same message works with Facebook and MySpace. If so, you're good to go. If not, you may need to flesh it out a bit—or at the very least unabbreviate the tweet's abbreviations and shorthand.

You can then move on to your blog. You may need to expand the message even more for this media—or not. You may find that a Facebook update works just fine as a short blog post. It probably will.

Using Integration Tools

If you choose, you can construct a message and then manually post it on all the relevant social media—Facebook, MySpace, Twitter, your blog, you name it. But that's still a lot of work. There has to be a way to write once and post in multiple places, doesn't there?

In fact, there does, and there is. Or "are," as several tools are available that enable you to make a single post to multiple media. The most popular of these tools include the following:

- **Amplify (www.amplify.com)**—A Twitter-like service that cross-posts your messages to Facebook, Twitter, and other social media.
- **Hootsuite (www.hootsuite.com)**—A self-described "social media dashboard" that enables team collaboration and task assignment, tracks mentions of your company or brand, and cross-posts messages to Facebook, Twitter, LinkedIn, and other social media.

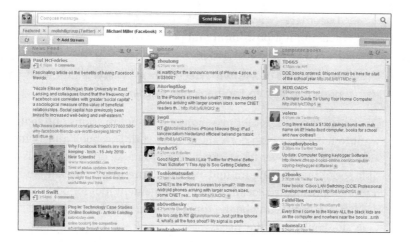

FIGURE 28.22

Managing multiple social media with Hootsuite.

■ **Ping.fm (www.ping.fm)**—A one-stop posting service that posts your messages to Facebook, Twitter, MySpace, LinkedIn, and other social media—including WordPress and Blogger blogs.

FIGURE 28.23

Posting to multiple social media with Ping.fm.

■ **Tweetdeck (www.tweetdeck.com)**—A consolidation service that lets you monitor posts from and post to Facebook, MySpace, Twitter, LinkedIn, other social media.

■ **Twitterfeed (www.twitterfeed.com)**—A service that feeds your blog posts (via RSS) to Facebook and Twitter.

Obviously, these tools all have slightly different missions and features. If you want to have your blog posts show up in your Facebook and Twitter feeds, Twitterfeed is the way to go. If you want to make one post that is sent to multiple social media, Ping.fm and Tweetdeck are worth checking out. If you want a more sophisticated social media management tool for both viewing and posting, Hootsuite may be the thing for you. Check 'em out and see which tools suit your particular needs.

The Bottom Line

Facebook, MySpace, and Twitter are the big three social media sites. As such, they need to be the focus of your company's social media marketing strategy.

For Facebook, that means establishing a "fan" page for your company, brand, or product, and then using that page to engage interested customers. You need to post frequent status updates, to keep your fans interested. And you may want to consider creating a Facebook application, to get even more face time on the Facebook site.

You should also cross-market by adding a Facebook Like button to your website. You can also consider other Facebook social plugins, such as Recommendations or Comments widgets.

Marketing on MySpace is similar. You need to create a MySpace page for your company or brand, and post frequent status updates to that page.

Twitter is a little different, in that there isn't much community involved. Instead, you need to make (very) frequent tweets, pretty much as often as you can, to feed the beast. The goal is to attract a large number of followers, and then promote to them as effectively as possible.

You should also pursue social bookmarking services, by making it easy to bookmark content on your website and blog. You may also want to consider advertising on the social sites; Facebook, MySpace, and Twitter all accept some form of PPC ads.

THE DOWNSIDE OF CONSOLIDATION

When you're trying to market to multiple social media, some form of posting consolidation tool makes sense. It's certainly more convenient to post once than to post multiple times to multiple sites.

That said, however, there is some potential downside to consolidating all your social media posts. For example, if you default to the lowest common denominator in terms of length (Twitter's very short posts), you're missing out on the opportunity to elaborate more fully on Facebook and even more so in your blog.

Then there's the frequency thing; not all media are suitable for the same posting frequency. For example, Twitter is conducive to more frequent posts (several a day), whereas you probably don't want to post quite that often on Facebook or on your blog. If you try to post once for all media, you'll either post too frequently for some or not frequently enough for others.

More important, you don't want to ignore any conversations that might develop on individual sites by focusing purely on the posting. Social media is all about the conversation, which requires you to actually visit each site to see what others are saying. If all you do is use Ping.fm or Tweetdeck to make your posts and then never visit Facebook or MySpace or the other sites, you'll miss out on your customers' comments. You still need to visit these sites or at least use a consolidation tool like Hootsuite that shows all the conversations on every site you subscribe to. There's more to social media than just posting, after all.

28

Tracking Social Media Marketing Performance

As you've seen, social media marketing is growing in importance. It's also somewhat multifaceted, which makes measuring performance somewhat tricky. How do you know when your Facebook and Twitter efforts are paying off?

Fortunately, there are some objective performance measurements we can employ, along with some more subjective ones, as well. Success in social media is a combination of hard numbers and soft indicators.

Tracking Hard Performance Metrics

Social media is all about conversation, but how do you measure conversation? Obviously, there are subjective evaluations that can be made, which are discussed later in this chapter. But there are also some tried-and-true hard metrics that can at least measure how many conversations you're engaging in online—and, to some degree, the quality of those conversations.

Measuring Eyeballs

Let's start with the easiest thing to measure—the number of people with whom you're engaging via social media. That's right, we're talking about measuring eyeballs, which is something you should all be accustomed to by now.

What are the best ways to measure how many people you're reaching with your social marketing efforts? Here are the key metrics to consider:

- **Pageviews and unique visitors coming from specific social media sites**—Okay, this is a bit of a combined metric. Most web analytics tools track pageviews and unique visitors, as well as traffic sources. What you need to do is correlate the data so that you know how much traffic to your website is being driven by each of the major social media—Facebook, Twitter, Digg, and so on.

- **Subscribers and fans**—These are metrics that come directly from the individual social media sites. You can track how many subscribers you have to your Twitter feed, how many fans you have of your Facebook page, how many friends you have on MySpace, and so forth.

- **Shares and bookmarks**—Now we move onto the social bookmarking and sharing services, such as Digg and StumbleUpon. What you want to track is how many Diggs you receive, how many times your site is bookmarked, how often your content is shared.

As you can see, many of these metrics are site-specific. That is, you measure how many fans or likes you get on Facebook, how many times you're bookmarked on Delicious, and so forth. You can then compare and contrast the eyeballs you're receiving from each of these social media and determine which are performing best for you.

Measuring Engagement

Measuring how many people you engage with via social media is one thing. Measuring the quality of that engagement is something else, indeed.

Not all followers of your Twitter feed are going to read every tweet. Not all people who "like" your Facebook page are going to actively engage in conversations. Not all conversations are going to result in new customers or leads.

How, then, can you determine if your social media efforts are effectively engaging your target audience?

The first measure of engagement is also our first eyeball metric—the number of unique visitors and pageviews coming from specific social media. This tells you whether people who read your tweets or your Facebook page are inspired to follow through by visiting your website.

Next, look at time onsite and pageviews per visit. The longer a visitor spends on your site, the more engaged he is—and the deeper the relationship you're building.

Bounce rates are also important, for just the opposite reason. People who leave your site quickly are most definitely *not* engaged—which means there's something about your site that doesn't build on what people first experienced on your Facebook page or Twitter feed. There's something wrong somewhere.

That said, know that some forms of social media—in particular, social bookmarks and shares—don't necessarily result in strong engagement with visitors. When someone bookmarks or shares your site with others, people checking out that bookmark (by clicking to your site) don't necessarily know what to expect. You're going to get a lot of "lookers," more than you would normally get, which results in lower time onsite numbers and a higher bounce rate. Yes, your traffic will go up, but these aren't necessarily qualified visitors. Some of them will turn into customers or leads, but certainly not all.

Back on the individual social media sites— another good indicator of engagement is how many comments you receive on your posts. Measure the number of comments you receive on each Facebook status update and Twitter tweet; the more comments you receive, the more you're engaging your audience. Those posts that don't inspire a lot of comments aren't that engaging; posts that result in tons of comments are a better draw.

> **note** Not all posts with lots of comments are good for you. Some controversial posts will generate a lot of responses, but if the negative comments outweigh the positive ones, you've done yourself more harm than good.

Evaluating Social Media Performance Subjectively

Social media, by definition, is somewhat subjective. How can you measure the effectiveness of one conversation versus another? How can you value a tweet versus a Digg?

When examining the performance of your social media marketing, a lot of it is open to discussion. While the big bosses might not like this immeasurable facet of your marketing program, it's something you have to get used to. There really is no hard and fast way to measure the quality of a conversation, after all. It's a form of word of mouth marketing, and that is inherently immeasurable.

As previously discussed, you can certainly measure the *quantity* of conversations that take place in the social media universe. The more comments your posts receive, the more discussions you host on your Facebook page, and the more that people are engaging with you online. But what exactly are these comments and discussions about?

The best conversations draw customers closer to your company and your products. You get the feeling that these people have a vested interest in what you're doing and that they want to share in your success. These are in-depth conversations about your products, their features and functions, how they work, what people use them for, and what people would like to see in the future.

Less useful are conversations that amount to online bitch sessions, customers just complaining about this or that thing or another. That's not the same as customers asking for help or advice; those conversations can actually prove useful, especially when you provide helpful solutions. No, I'm talking about people who use your online forums to vent about how much they hate your company and your products. That's not a quality conversation.

Also of lesser quality are those conversations that are nothing but gossip. What's the CEO up to this week? Who's sleeping with whom? Do you think the stock price will go or down next quarter? Gossip isn't a positive conversation; it's wasted time.

Another type of negative conversation is the one that goes unanswered. A customer asks a question, publicly, and you don't reply. That's not a conversation, that's a wasted opportunity. Don't let that happen too often.

Instead, use each and every comment as an opportunity to more fully engage both the customer who started the conversation and others who might be reading—or waiting to add their two cents' worth. Someone skilled in social marketing can turn any comment into a quality engagement with the customer base. It just takes a little imagination—and the willingness to engage.

Take, for example, a typical comment along the lines of "Your new product rocks!" Okay, not a very meaningful comment but still something you can work with. Instead of not replying at all or posting something like "Thanks," turn this into a learning experience. Reply with a question, like "Cool, thanks. What is it you like best about the product?" or "How does it help you get your job done?" Don't let the customer get away too fast; pull him into what could become a far-reaching conversation.

The key here is to use social conversations to more fully engage your existing and potential customers. To this end, expanding your reach to new audiences is paramount. Now, this probably won't happen on a Facebook page or in a Twitter feed but can happen when your fans and followers share their comments with their friends. It's this sharing nature of social media that exposes your company and brand to new faces. When one of your fans shares your post or tweet with a hundred or so of his friends, that's a hundred new impressions you're making. (And these impressions are from someone these people trust; your existing customers become influencers to new customers.)

To that end, you want to make sure that at least some of your posts are of a general enough nature that your fans and followers will want to share them. Posting about the detailed construction of your latest widget probably won't do it, even though hard-core fans might get all drooly about it. Instead, you need some posts that reach out in a more general fashion that civilians might find interesting.

And when you make these general posts, make sure you include some sort of call to action, even if it's just a link back to a product page on your website. Saying "Isn't this new product really neat?" doesn't go far enough; you have to say "Isn't this new product really neat? Go to our website to learn more." That's a call to action that drives new visitors to your site—which you can then track and convert to your heart's content.

Different Metrics for Different Social Media

As you might suspect, not all social media is created equal. Different sites require different metrics to determine their effectiveness in your social marketing campaigns.

With that in mind, let's look at the metrics that make the most sense for different types of social media.

Social Networking Metrics

When it comes to full-featured social networking sites, such as Facebook and MySpace, there are a lot of things you can measure. The most important metrics include the following:

- Number of fans or friends acquired
- Number of comments made on your status updates
- Number of discussions started on your discussions tab—and the number of replies to each discussion
- Number of photos and videos uploaded by your fans
- Number of photos or videos in which your company or product is tagged

- Number of participants to any polls or questions posed
- Direct traffic from each social networking site to your website or blog
- The amount of time visitors from the social networking site stay on your site and the number of pages visited
- If you have a social networking application, the number of downloads or users of said application

Microblogging Metrics

The metrics you measure with Twitter and other microblogging sites are essentially a subset of your social networking metrics. These include:

- Number of followers acquired
- Number of followers who respond to your tweets
- Number of total replies
- Number of retweets your tweets receive
- Number of tweets that occur around the hashtags you create

It's the replies and hashtag tweets that create conversation in the Twitterverse; these are your most engaged customers. The retweets indicate potential reach to new customers and measure to some degree how influential you are.

note There are a lot of spammers on Twitter. When you're measuring followers, try to weed out the spammers from the real people.

Social Bookmarking Metrics

Social bookmarking sites are unique among other social media in that they can drive traffic directly to your website. As such, several key metrics are traffic related:

- Number of bookmarks that reference your site or blog
- Number of votes (positive and negative) on these bookmarks
- Number of comments on these bookmarks
- Traffic driven to your website from the social bookmarking site
- The amount of time visitors from the social bookmark site stay on your site and the number of pages visited

Social Sharing Metrics

We haven't talked a lot about social sharing sites in this section, although we will later in this book. Of course, I'm talking media sharing sites, such as Flickr and YouTube. What metrics measure your success with these sites? Here's the short list:

- Number of times a photo or video is viewed
- Number of times a photo or video is commented on
- Number of times a photo or video is added to a "favorites" list
- Number of "up" or "down" (positive or negative) sentiments
- User ratings for each photo or video
- Number of links or embeds of a photo or video
- Number of times a photo or video is added to a group
- Number of friends or subscribers to your media on the site
- Number of mentions or shares of a photo or video in other social media
- Traffic driven to your website from the social sharing site
- The amount of time visitors from the social sharing site stay on your site and the number of pages visited

The Bottom Line

When measuring the effectiveness of your social media marketing efforts, you can track hard metrics and softer ones.

In terms of hard metrics, you can track pageviews and unique visitors coming from each social site, as well as subscribers and fans you have on each individual site. You should also track shares and bookmarks on the major social bookmarking services.

Softer metrics measure customer engagement. Obviously, you want to track visit duration, bounce rate, and such. You also want to evaluate the comments and conversations generated on the social networks—not just the quantity but also the tone and tenor of what customers are saying. How substantial are these discussions—is it all gossip, or are customers truly interested in your products and services?

29

Evaluating social media performance isn't easy; there's a lot of subjectivity involved beyond the raw data. The key is to determine how well you're connecting with your customers—and whether those connections are leading to future sales.

WHAT REALLY MATTERS

Social media is tough for numbers-oriented marketers and management to get their heads around. Because of the way social media works, you might determine that a site that registers fewer fans is actually more important to you, and that may be difficult to explain.

What matters with social media is the quality of your interaction with customers. That's not something you can measure with numbers. It's engagement over eyeballs, pure and simple.

That said, you need to come up with some way to track this customer engagement, even if it's purely subjective. This is your opportunity to get a little creative; you have to find some way to describe and measure a positive interaction as opposed to a negative one. It can be done, as long as you're comfortable with the wiggly nature of soft metrics.

But that's the way it is with social media marketing. We all know it's important, we know we need to do it, but we're unsure of exactly what we're getting for our efforts. That makes it unlike other online marketing activities, which typically are more measurable than their old world counterparts.

Still and all, social media does matter, from the number of fans and followers you amass to the insights that accrue from the conversations that ensue. Expend the effort, and you'll see what I mean.

Understanding Online PR

Public relations has always been an interesting component of the marketing mix. It's not like advertising because you don't pay for placement. And it's not like direct mail because you can't directly track results. What you have is a marketing method that can't guarantee placement and doesn't produce measureable results. Marvelous!

That all changes on the Internet, however. Not the bit about guaranteeing placement; you still have to influence other media to take up your story. But public relations activities on the Web *can* be tracked, and you can measure direct results—the number of sales that come from a given PR effort.

In addition, there's a lot more you can do online with your public relations efforts. There are new people to talk to (bloggers and social influencers) and different methods to employ (email, instant messaging, social media). Like I said, it all changes on the Internet.

What Is Online PR—and How Does It Differ from Traditional PR?

Like traditional PR, online PR is all about influencing people. It's not about buying placement; it's about generating word-of-mouth attention.

But who do you influence online—and how? That's where online PR differs from the traditional model.

Who You Influence

When we're talking online PR, we're talking about influencing a different group of people than you do with traditional PR. Old-school PR is about influence of traditional media—newspapers, magazines, radio, and television. Now, you can still use online methods to influence the people in these traditional channels (which is discussed shortly), but there are a whole other group of people online to target.

Online PR deals with another group of influencers. These are people who've become trend setters to their online followers; a mention or endorsement from one of these folks is as good as gold.

Who are these online influencers? It's a diverse group, including the following:

- Professional writers, columnists, and reviewers for various websites
- Bloggers, both personal and professional
- Twitterers with large and loyal followings
- Facebookers with similarly large and loyal followings
- Amateur contributors to various review and sharing websites

Of these influencers, only the first group—writers, columnists, and reviewers—are similar to your traditional media targets. After all, a paid reviewer for an online publication isn't that much different from a reviewer for a print magazine or newspaper.

But the other influencers on this list are much, much different from the people you're used to dealing with. First of all, most of them aren't paid professionals. That is, they're not paid (although a few might generate some PPC ad revenue from their blogs), and they're surely not trained professionals. In fact, most of the influencers online are civilians, people who do what they do merely because they like to, not because it's a job. That makes for a bit of a different push, as you might imagine.

In addition, your online PR efforts often get seen directly by consumers. That is, your press releases go out into the ether and end up getting reproduced on this website or that message forum exactly as you wrote them. Now, this sometimes happens in the print world, but those kinds of placements are traditionally in low-value publications. Online, a reprinted (or reposted) press release can get a huge number of views and lead traffic directly back to your website. Which means, of course, that you need to take the consumer in mind when you're writing your online press releases; you can't rely on the target media to do any filtering for you.

Your press releases are also likely to end up in the search results of people searching for the topic mentioned. So someone querying Google for "widgets" will see your press release for your new widget line in their search results. That's added exposure, which is a very good thing.

So when you're putting together your online PR plans, your goal is to get placement in a number of important online channels:

- News websites
- Industry websites
- Topic-related websites
- Review websites
- Media-sharing websites (YouTube, Flickr, and so on)
- Industry message forums
- Topic-related message forums
- Topic-related blogs
- Topic-related Twitter feeds
- Topic-related Facebook pages
- Social media bookmarking sites (Digg, Delicious, and so on)

What kind of placement are you looking for? It could be anything, including straight-up press release reproductions, brief mentions, official endorsements, news stories, interviews, reviews, you name it. The important thing is to get the word out and then hope the word goes viral.

How You Influence Them

Online PR differs from traditional PR not only in who you try to influence, but also in how you do that. It mainly concerns the methods of contact available.

Obviously, you can still contact people in new media using old media, but why would you want to? I'm not sure a blogger would appreciate getting an old-fashioned press kit in the (postal) mail. It's kind of incongruous.

Instead, you want to use the new media at your disposal to connect and interact with your new media contacts. It only makes sense that bloggers and Twitterers and the like will respond more positively to an outreach via the Internet than they would via a phone call or letter.

To that end, how do you reach your online contacts? It's a list you should be familiar with by now:

- **Email**—A bit passé among the younger crowd, email is still the best way to reach most online professionals.

- **Instant messaging**—Maybe not the best approach for an initial contact, instead a great way to work a continuing conversation with a busy online writer.

- **Blog comments**—If you're trying to reach an influential blogger, what better place than his blog? You can leave a public comment on an existing blog post, of course, but it may be better to get the blogger's email address and contact him that way.

- **Twitter**—Twitter allows private tweets, so why not use them? If you want to reach a prominent Twitterer, tweet your initial contact.

- **Facebook**—You can send private messages to fellow Facebook members, or you can just go to a person's profile page and write on his wall.

- **LinkedIn**—Many online professionals are members of the LinkedIn social network; sometimes this is the only contact information you can find for people. Use this to your advantage to make professional contact via LinkedIn's private messages.

As to what you send these folks, it all depends. An initial outreach may consist of nothing more than a short email or IM or perhaps even a private message on Facebook or Twitter. More extensive information can include an online press release or digital press kit or a link to a "media room" on your website where you provide digital photos, backgrounders, and the like.

Using the New Technology

The Internet makes available a great deal of new technology that can benefit PR professionals. While some tools are relatively recent, some have been around quite a long time.

Online PR Databases

The earliest digital tools for PR professionals were and are online PR databases, such as Dow Jones Factiva (www.factiva.com), Cision (www.cision.com), and, to a lesser degree, LexisNexis (corporate.lexisnexis.com). These databases are the digital equivalents of old-school clipping services,

note Cision is the new name for Bacon's, which previously acquired the competing MediaMap database and publications.

where you can find both articles and contact information. It's what you use to find out who to contact and how, as well as to discover whether your previous efforts have borne fruit.

What do you find in the Factiva or Cision databases? Here's a short list:

- Contact information for both old and new media publications and journalists
- Print articles in which your company or product is mentioned
- Where your product or company is mentioned online—websites, blogs, even social media
- Tools for monitoring and analyzing the impact of your PR activities
- Early warning of new trends and issues

You can use these services to plan your PR campaigns, identify target publications and people, and, in some instances, place your online press releases. Equally important, you can track the placements you receive, both online and in traditional media. (For that matter, you can track the placements your competitors receive.)

These online databases, however, can be expensive—especially when you realize that much of the data they house can be had for free elsewhere online. While these databases remain popular with large PR companies, and they are admittedly tailored for PR use, you can find similar information by searching Google, Bing, or any other free general search engine. Now, you may have to search harder, and the results may not be as easy to use as what you get from the paid services, but what you get from Google is free.

Social Media Search

These online PR databases do a great job of tracking mentions in traditional media an on major news-related websites. They do less well in tracking mentions in social media, such as Twitter, Facebook, blogs, and social bookmarking sites. For this, you may want to invest in software or services that search the social media for mentions of your company or products or any other terms you specify.

We discussed some of these tools in the previous chapters on social media marketing. I won't repeat all that information here but will remind you of some of the top tools for tracking mentions in social media:

- Alterian SM2 (socialmedia.alterian.com)
- CoTweet (www.cotweet.com)

- Hootsuite (www.hootsuite.com)
- IceRocket (www.icerocket.com)
- Radian6 (www.radian6.com)
- Scout Labs (www.scoutlabs.com)
- SocialMention (www.socialmention.com)
- Trackur (www.trackur.com)

Press Release Distribution

How do you distribute your digital press releases? Naturally, you should send press releases directly to the online media you've targeted. But you can also get general distribution for your press releases by using an online press release distribution service.

We'll look into these services more in Chapter 31, "Developing New Sources and Techniques." Suffice to say, it's a whole new way of distributing your press releases!

The Benefits of Online PR

Your goals with online PR should be similar to what you've always tried to achieve with traditional PR. In fact, many of the activities are the same—you write press releases, establish relationships with key contacts, and follow through to see if your efforts bore fruit.

That said, one of the key differences between online and traditional PR is the interactive conversations that develop online. Whereas traditional PR is pretty much a one-way effort (you put the press release out there and that's that), online PR is a two-way street. That's because a significant portion of your online PR efforts are targeted at customers, encouraging them to contact your company directly.

It's this two-way conversation that provides some of the primary benefits of online PR. A successful online PR effort results in more than just a placement in a prominent publication; it drives measurable traffic and sales to your website.

Note the word "measurable" in the previous paragraph. That's something new with online PR. Traditionally, you couldn't really measure the effects of your PR efforts; all you could track were articles that mentioned your company or product.

Online, you can go beyond tracking placement to measuring how effective each placement is. It's a simple matter to track clicks back to your site and where those clicks came from. You can measure, with relative ease, which of your PR efforts produced the most concrete results.

This trackability has several benefits of its own. Obviously, you can now determine which PR efforts are working and which aren't and fine-tune your activities accordingly. But you can also hold your PR people accountable—for sales, no less! This may be the first time in their careers that PR people have fiscal responsibility, and it may be a bit of a shocker for them.

There's another big difference with online PR: There are a lot more places where you can get mentioned. Online media don't necessarily displace traditional media; (most) newspapers and magazines and television outlets continue to exist, even with new online competition. But there are a lot of new media outlets, from websites to blogs to Twitter feeds, and they're all ripe for news about your company and products.

Reaching all these sources means a lot more work for the PR department. It's fair to say that because of the increased number of influencers online, PR has never been more important than it is today. You have to put forth the effort to reach all these folks—and that's what public relations is all about.

The Bottom Line

Online PR is a lot like traditional public relations, except that it takes place online. That means using all the tools available online, but also exploiting new media (such as blogs and web reviewers) for online exposure.

Fortunately, there are a lot of new online tools available for your use, including online PR databases and press release distribution services. This makes it easier to both distribute and track your online press releases—which need to be sent to all possible online influencers.

USING NEW MEDIA TO PITCH OLD MEDIA

When it comes to public relations, old media and new media are not exclusive. That's especially true when it comes to how you contact your media contacts.

In the old days, you had two ways to contact people. If you had a really good relationship with someone, you could pick up the phone (which, back in the day, had a curly cord between the handset and the base) and give them a call. For everybody else, you mailed them (via the United States Postal Service, of course) a printed press release or press kit.

Today, however, I'm not sure how effective phone calls and mailed press materials really are. I mean, how many people can you get on the phone these days? And how many press mailings get thrown out with the daily junk mail?

It may be more effective, depending on your contacts, to contact them via new media. Most old media journalists and editors tend to prefer contact via email these days, assuming your emails get through their spam filters. And some writers and publications accept solicitations via Facebook, MySpace, and Twitter.

In fact, many writers prefer electronic contact. Some even like to use instant messaging or Skype to conduct interviews, which can be a nice touch.

The point is, get to know your most important contacts in all media and learn how they like to be contacted. If you have an important contact with Luddite tendencies, stick to printing and mailing. But if you know an editor or writer who's hip to latest media, then use it to your utmost benefit. Just don't assume that old media writers are averse to contact via new media.

Developing New Sources and Techniques

Successful online PR requires adding a few new clubs to your bag. You have to develop new sources in the new media and learn some new techniques for contacting those sources and getting the word out.

Granted, public relations is public relations, no matter which media are involved. But working online means more direct contact with the end consumer, which requires a slightly different approach to the press releases you write—and the materials you make available to your media contacts.

Developing New Online Sources

Let's start with the new sources you need to develop for your online PR efforts. The Internet has created a large number of new outlets for the dissemination of news and information, and you need to learn how to take advantage of them.

Targeting Websites and Online Publications

The online outlets most like traditional media outlets are websites and online publications. In some instances, websites are actually offshoots of traditional media; in other instances, they're unique entities. But in most cases, news-oriented websites and online publications operate a lot like their old media counterparts.

What this is means is that you have to deal with a mix of editors, staff reporters and reviewers, and freelance writers. If anything, there are probably more freelance writers online than there are with traditional media, but that's purely a subjective assessment; you still have to deal with the mix.

You'll find a familiar chain of command at the larger websites and publications. When the site's big enough and the staff's large enough, you're likely to find separate editors and writers and reviewers to pitch your stories to. Just go to the website and look for an About or Contact Us link to see who's responsible for what. Email is probably the best way to contact these folks.

Smaller websites and publications, however, are likely to have much smaller staffs. In fact, some sites have one-person staffs—it's all run by a single guy or gal, with most if not all of the writing outsourced. If nothing else, this makes it easier to figure out who to contact; there's no big bureaucracy to slow things down.

Targeting Online Writers and Reviewers

You can also pitch your wares to individual writers and reviewers—those who provide content to the websites and online publications and blogs. Most of these folks write for multiple sites, so you can often get a good bang for your efforts by pitching across multiple segments.

How do you find these writers? By email, of course, but finding a good email address might take a bit of work. Start by seeking out articles across the Web that fit into your target profile and then find out who's writing them. If you're lucky, the articles you like will be bylined and have the writer's email address attached. You can always Google a given writer if no email address is handy. And there's nothing stopping you from contacting the hosting site or publication and asking to contact the writer of an article you like. Work hard enough and you'll get to the person in question.

I've found freelance writers to be particularly receptive to PR efforts. They're often struggling to find the next article to sell, and you can provide a nice angle for a given site or publication, which gives the writer a nice leg up. That's sure to be appreciated.

Targeting Bloggers

Blogs are a great place to plug your wares. There are lots of bloggers out there, and they have lots of posts to write. Convince the bloggers that speak directly to your target audience to talk about your company or product, and you'll gain a certain legitimacy among the followers of those blogs.

Once you identify a particular blog as reaching the audience you want to reach, you now have to establish a relationship with the person or persons who write that blog. This is old-school PR updated for the Internet age.

You can make your presence known by posting some comments to posts on that blog and then follow up from there by emailing the blogger directly. The key is to treat the blogger like a real human being (which he probably is, to some degree) and get to know him on a personal level. Find out what he likes and what he doesn't, what he thinks is important, what makes him laugh. Get him to like you and to trust you. Then, and only then, can you pitch him for a story or product placement.

It's the same way you used to (and still might) get to know important contacts in traditional media. The big difference is that for many bloggers, it's not a 9-to-5 job. In fact, many bloggers have another day job and do the blog thing after work and on weekends. Don't assume that you can IM or call a blogger in the middle of the afternoon and get an immediate response.

Another big difference is that (most) bloggers are not trained journalists and as such don't follow the same rules and practices as do folks in the traditional media. If you play things by the book, this shouldn't make much of a difference. But do know that some bloggers can be easily influenced or even purchased outright. Not that you'd ever think of doing so, but I'm just saying.

When it comes to pitching a blogger, keep these points in mind:

- Personalize the pitch. Don't send out blind emails to bloggers. Get to know the bloggers first and then contact them with personal messages.

- Be relevant. A generic pitch won't cut it. Make sure you tailor your pitch to the particular blog to the point of suggesting specific blog posts the blogger might make.

- Make it easy. Provide everything the blogger needs to create a post. That probably means posting your press release or landing page online and providing bloggers with the URLs to link to this info. Also provide links to photos (sized appropriately for blog use, of course), as well as your email address and IM they can use if they have questions or need more information.

You also need to be persistent. As with traditional media contacts, not every blogger will respond to the first pitch you make. If at first you don't succeed, keep trying—and keep fine-tuning your pitch as time goes by. And when a blogger does mention your product or company, make sure you follow up with a thank-you email—and another pitch if you have one.

note Learn more about promoting to bloggers in Chapter 24, "Marketing to the Blogosphere."

Targeting Online Message Forums

Online message forums are ripe for PR attention. But who do you contact?

The answer is no one—and everyone. PR on a message forum is more about interacting socially than it is about sending out press releases and pitching contacts. It's a matter of monitoring the appropriate forums for threads that best suit your interest and then participating in those threads.

That's right, I said *participating*. Message board PR is a form of social media marketing, which means you have to monitor and participate in the community conversations. If that's not your cup of tea, tough; it has to be done. Either learn how to be social or hire someone to do it for you.

> **note** Participating in online forums and social networks should be natural, not blatantly promotional. Don't fall into the practice that some call "astroturfing," where you leave favorable messages about your products without disclosing your official affiliation—or honestly engaging the rest of the community.

Targeting Social Media

It's the same thing with other social media—Facebook, MySpace, Twitter, and the like. You really can't post a press release on Facebook and expect a positive response; nor can you condense a press release to a 140-character tweet and broadcast it to your legion of followers.

You can, however, translate the key information in a press release to a format that should work on Facebook and Twitter. You can even include a link in tweet or status update to the complete press release posted elsewhere online. But you can't just tweet "New press release posted;" you have to convey the message in the press release as information of interest to your Twitter followers and Facebook fans.

So, for example, if you issue a press release announcing your new fall product line, you don't want to post "New fall product line announced." That's boring and offers no real benefit to readers. Instead, you might want to tweet something along the lines of "Muted colors are in for the fall. See photos here." or "Update your look with our new fall fashions" or "Discover the fall fashions that everybody's talking about" or "Are these the winning fashions for fall?" It's like writing an ad headline; you have to entice readers to click for more information.

> **note** Learn more about marketing to social media in Part VIII of this book, "Social Media Marketing."

Not sure how this fits into your PR efforts? Maybe it doesn't. Maybe you create a dedicated social marketing department and let them handle this sort of thing. But for many companies, social media is going to fall under the purview of the PR department, so you better get used to it.

Skills and Techniques for Online PR

When moving into the world of online PR, what tools and techniques will help you get the job done? Well, it's a blend of old ones and new ones; you need to take what you already know how to do and augment that with online-specific methods.

Using Traditional Skills and Approaches

Let's start with what you already know. To some degree, PR is PR, no matter who you're pitching. Traditional PR skills still matter.

What skills am I talking about? Here's a short list:

- Writing press releases
- Writing letters to the editor and op-eds
- Writing articles (re: thinly-disguised product placement)
- Writing white papers and reports
- Writing newsletters
- Giving and arranging interviews
- Pitching story ideas and product placements

Learning New Skills and Techniques

Then there are all the new things you can do and need to do that take advantage of different aspects of the Internet. These are new skills to an old PR hound, although they may be somewhat second nature to younger Turks.

Here are the new PR skills you'll need to master:

- Creating online media kits
- Optimizing press releases for search
- Creating podcasts
- Search engine optimization for press releases

- Social media monitoring and communication—including social networks and message forums
- Commenting on blogs (and soliciting bloggers)

In addition, you need to learn the rudiments of online media tracking, especially web analytics. Because your online PR efforts can be tracked to specific website visits, you need to know how all this tracking works—and then apply your newfound knowledge to measure the results of your PR efforts.

Learning the Art of Online Press Releases

Online PR isn't completely dissimilar from traditional PR. At the heart of both old- and new-school PR is the press release, that little piece of text that announces something new and exciting from your company.

Writing an Online Press Release

An online press differs significantly from a press release meant for old media consumption in that the target audience is different. A traditional press release is targeted at editors and journalists, in the hope of interesting them in writing an article based on the content of the press release. In contrast, an online press release is targeted directly at the end consumer, not at the middle man. Websites, blogs, and online publications will link to your press release, which will then be read as-is by prospective customers.

You might think this isn't a big change. Journalists and customers both read English, and in either case you're talking about your latest product or promotional initiative or whatever. But the message you impart is subtly different. When the target is the end consumer, you have to tell that person precisely what benefit this new product or initiative will have for him. It's less talking about the product's features and more about its benefits.

In this aspect, writing an online press release is more like writing ad copy. It's all about features versus benefits and speaking directly to the customer.

With consumers in mind, you also need to include a strong call to action in your online press releases. You want readers to click through to your website, so give them a reason to do so. That may be a simple

note Because of this consumer orientation, you can't just put your old press releases online and expect them to be effective; you need to rewrite them with the target consumer in mind.

admonition to click for more information, or it may be a unique incentive of some sort—a special discount, a free guide, or whatever.

That means you need to include your URL in your online press releases. While you want to mention your main URL, the link in question should probably be to a unique landing page that follows directly from the content of the press release. You want the movement from press release to website to be seamless—and trackable.

Applying SEO to Your Online Press Releases

So the audience for your online press releases is both the press and your customer base. But these aren't the only audiences; you also have to target your press releases at Google and the other major search engines.

For the search engines to display your press releases in their search results, which is something you want, they have to be able to *find* your press releases. Yes, that means implementing basic search engine optimization (SEO) techniques for each and every press release you write.

SEO for press releases involves carefully choosing the keywords you want to use and then incorporating those keywords into the writing of your press releases. The most important keywords should go into the press release's title; all the keywords should be written into the main text.

You want to make sure that whatever terms your customers are searching for are found within the body of your press release.

> **note** No matter what one might personally think, Google and the other search engines treat online press releases no differently than they treat legitimate news articles—which is why SEO is so important when you're writing a press release.

If you sell small kitchen appliances and potential customers are searching for things like "toasters" and "blenders" and "mixers," those are the words you should include in your press release. It doesn't matter that your company has just introduced a "premiere line of kitchen electrics," as your product people might refer to them; you still want to say "ApplianceCo Announces Innovative New Toasters, Blenders, and Mixers." Write the words that people are searching for.

That argues, of course, for keyword research—the same kind you use when optimizing your website for search. Find out what keywords are most searched for and incorporate them in your press releases.

That's not to say, however, that you should sacrifice style and substance for keyword placement. The primary audience of your press release is your customer, not Google, so make sure that it speaks to your customers. Get the message right, and then you can optimize the release for search.

Distributing Press Releases Online

Distributing your online press releases requires a two-pronged effort. First, you should distribute your releases directly to those contacts you've targeted or with whom you've established a prior relationship. But you should supplement this effort with the use of an online press release distribution service to get even wider distribution of your message.

These distribution services post press releases from a variety of sources across a large number of industries. By posting releases on their sites, they make the press releases searchable by Google and other search engines. That's a good thing.

Most distribution services also distribute your press releases directly to appropriate online and offline media outlets. They'll also send your releases to other outlets you specify.

In addition, some of these services will work with you to make your press releases more effective, particularly in the area of SEO. Some will even host photos and other accompanying media if you need that.

The major online press release distribution services include

- Business Wire (www.businesswire.com)
- CisionWire (www.cision.com)
- Free Press Release (www.free-press-release.com)
- i-Newswire (www.i-newswire.com)
- Marketwire (www.marketwire.com)
- Online PR News (www.onlineprnews.com)
- PR Leap (www.prleap.com)
- PR Log (www.prlog.org)
- PR Newswire (www.prnewswire.com)
- PR.com (www.pr.com)
- PRWeb (www.prweb.com)
- SEO Press Releases (www.seopressreleases.com)
- Wired PR News (www.wiredprnews.com)

The big dogs here are Business Wire and PR Newswire, along with Business Web, CisionWire, Marketwire, and PRWeb. While many of the other services are free, these are not—but then again, they have a broader reach.

As to pricing, they're all over the place. As one example, PRWeb charges anywhere from $80 to $360 per press release, depending on how widely you want it distributed, whether you want to work it over for your for search engine optimization and such, and whether it includes multimedia attachments. Do your homework before you sign up.

The Bottom Line

There are a lot of new outlets on the web for your PR activities. In addition to using email and other online channels to contact traditional sources, you should be cultivating relationships with online publications, topic-specific websites, freelance writers, online reviewers, and bloggers. You can also focus your efforts on online message forums and other social media, although these media are more participative than you might be used to.

In terms of conducting online PR, you need to supplement your existing skills with some new ones, such as creating online media kits, optimizing press releases for search, and commenting on blogs and such. Of these, applying SEO to press releases might be the most foreign to you, but it's important if you want your press releases to be featured in the results pages of the major search engines.

GETTING CREATIVE

Throughout this chapter we've talked about the various tools and techniques you use in your online PR efforts. Yes, you have to develop personal relationships with online movers and shakers; yes, you have to write effective online press releases. But beyond these nuts and bolts approaches to getting the word out, what kind of things generate the most publicity online?

Let's face it, announcing a new product line or letting people know that you just sold your one millionth item isn't that interesting to anyone outside of company management. Now, this sort of by-the-book content accounts for a major of both traditional and online press releases, but that's why you'll probably get lost in the noise.

31

I suppose there's no such thing as bad press, but there is such a thing as unmemorable press. Somehow you need to move past the barrage of standard-issue announcements and give people something really interesting to talk about, something truly worthy of a press release and subsequent media coverage.

This requires no small amount of creativity. Unfortunately, I can't tell you how to be creative; it's not something you can really teach. I can tell you, however, that creativity will get you noticed. Do something fun, do something entertaining, do something memorable, and then tell people about it. It's that kind of creativity that can take a press release and turn it into a viral online event that everyone is talking about.

Yes, you still need to do those press releases about the new fall product line and the opening of your latest store and the latest management promotion. Can't get around it. But you also need to step it up and do something creative that will get you noticed on the Web. It's this unique aspect of online PR that will set you apart from the pack—and drive your success online.

32

Creating an Online Press Room

Digital press releases aren't the be all, end all of online PR. There's another aspect of online PR you need to manage, and that concerns the images and other media files that both the traditional and online press need to complete their stories.

This is where the Internet really shines. Instead of waiting for a journalist to request a particular photo and then snail mailing or emailing that particular item, you can place all your available media for the press in a dedicated section of your website—an online press room, as it were. This makes it easier for print and online journalists to find key company information and all the picture and media files they need.

Why Do You Need a Press Room on Your Website?

An online press room is a section of your website for the press. It contains all your press releases (archived by date, typically), product photos, brochures and catalogs, and how-to videos that you make available to members of the press. In fact, it can be used by both traditional print media and today's online media; it's a virtual storehouse of digital media of all sorts.

As such, an online press room is a very important part of your website and critical to your traditional and online PR efforts. The pages within your online press room, if you don't hide them behind some sort of password-protected firewall, also help your

> **note** An online press room is sometimes called a *media room* or *press page*.

site show up in the search results for Google and competing search sites; someone searching for product information, for example, is likely to find links to that product's spec sheet, press release, and digital photograph in the search results.

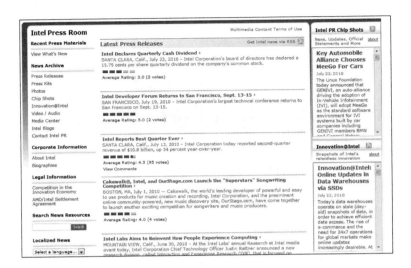

FIGURE 32.1

Intel's online press room—digital media and information for everybody.

A well-done online press room can be one of the most highly-trafficked areas of your website. It can turn journalists who were just browsing into interested writers about your company and products. It can also, of course, make life a whole lot easier for journalists on a deadline; they can download what they need when they need it, without the traditional approval and shipping delays.

Who uses an online press room? Members of the press, of course, but more than that. Potential visitors include any or all of the following:

- Print publications looking for photographs and artwork to accompany articles in progress
- Websites and blogs looking for photographs and artwork to accompany articles and posts
- Journalists (traditional and online) and bloggers looking for story ideas or details for a story in progress
- Investors or potential investors looking for company information

- Dealers and distributors who need images and information for the ads they run
- The general public, looking for product information about potential purchases

Keep this in mind when you design and stock your online press room. It's for the press, of course, but also for investors and customers.

Stocking Your Online Press Room

What sort of things should you include in your online press room? Just about anything the press might need to write or produce a story, of course. That includes photos, press releases, detailed spec sheets, even management bios and headshots. Let's take a look at the major items you'll want to include.

Press Releases

One important function of an online press room is to serve as the organized depository of all your company's press releases. The press releases have to be in electronic format, of course, and should be viewable online or downloadable for offline use.

As to format, you have a choice. You can go with simple HTML format so that the press releases appear as web pages in a browser. You can also go with Word-format press releases, although I'm not a big fan of this; it's too easy for anyone to edit or even "doctor" a Word doc, which can lead to embarrassing instances of official-looking but quite obviously altered press releases hitting the Web.

Personally, I like supplying press releases in Adobe PDF format. This way you can control the look and feel of the press release without providing something that can be easily altered. Journalists can still cut and paste text from PDF files, so life is still easy for them.

Most companies place press releases in their press rooms in reverse chronological order—that is, the latest releases appear in the top of the list. That's fine and helps visitors identify the most recent news. You should also, of course, organize your press releases into monthly or yearly archives so older releases can be easily found if anyone's looking.

32

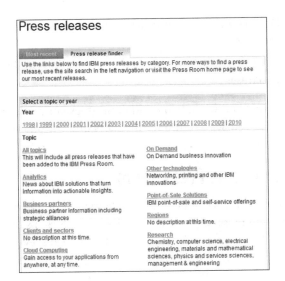

FIGURE 32.2

The "Press Release Finder" in IBM's press room; organizing press releases by topic.

I also recommend a subsidiary organization by category or topic. This way journalists interested in all the news about a particular topic can click that link and see all the related press releases. It's a bit more work but could have a big payoff.

Product Photos

Another key component of an online press room is a section of product photos. The photos are intended to accompany stories and blog posts about your products, so they should be easily downloaded.

A few words about what types of product photos to include. First, know that these photos will be used by both traditional and online publications, so you'll have to size and format the photos appropriately. For online publications, that means a smaller, lower resolution photo in JPG format. For print publications, you need a much larger, much higher resolution photo suitable for printing. TIFF is a good file format for print, as is EPS, although high-res JPG files also work. In any case, you need to provide both low-resolution and high-resolution files and make the choice simple.

Catering fully to the needs of the media, you may want to supply several different photos for each of your products. I'm talking about shooting the product from different angles, as well as supplying photos of various product details. For example, if you sell consumer electronics products, include photos of the product's front panel, back panel, and remote control. Think of any particular need the press might have and provide photos that fill those needs.

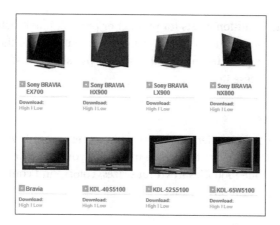

FIGURE 32.3

Low-resolution and high-resolution photos available for download from Sony's online press room.

Product Videos

With both the Web and traditional broadcast media in mind, you should also consider adding any product videos you might have to your online press room. These might be introductory product videos, how-to videos, even videos talking about your company or its management team. If there's a possibility that some online outlet might use the video and provide you with additional exposure, it's worth including.

As to format, it's similar to working with photos. Include both high-resolution and low-resolution versions of any video file you offer. Traditional broadcast media can use the high-res video; websites can link to or embed the low-res version.

Product Spec Sheets

It's not just images that the press need. They also need information.

To that end, include detailed product spec sheets in your online press room. These might duplicate items already present on individual product pages on your site, but that's okay; the press is more likely to find these documents from the press room gateway than by browsing or searching your main website. PDF is always a good format for these.

Brochures

A similar situation exists for product or product line brochures. You may offer them on the consumer site of your website but provide them to the press in your online press room as well. As with spec sheets, PDF is the format of choice for these items.

Logos

Given that one audience for your online press room is your dealer or distributor base, don't forget to include images of your company, brand, and product logos. Include logo files in various sizes, colors, and configurations for a variety of print and online uses.

Company Background

Members of the press and potential investors often come to your online press room to find out more about the company. To that end, include a detailed company backgrounder as part of your offerings. Include anything you might think the press and investors might be interested in, including a company timeline. PDF is a good format for this information.

Management Bios

As part of the company background information you provide, you should also include brief bios of key company management. That includes your President, CEO, and other top-level people. The bio doesn't have to be long, but it should include the basics.

Management Photos

Naturally, you should include downloadable photographs of each person highlighted in your management bios. This should be your typical headshot; if you don't have any yet, just get some. As with product photos, offer both a low-and high-resolution version of each headshot.

Other Company Photos

What else might the press be interested in using to accompany an article about your company, brands, or products? How about pictures of your corporate offices, factories, or warehouse? What about a picture of how your product is made? What about pictures of your product in use? What about pictures of customers using your products? Get a little creative here and think about what sort of eye candy might be interesting to accompany various types of articles. As with all images, make them available in both low- and high-resolution formats.

> **note** If your company uses official endorsers, devote a section of your online press room to these endorsers and include photos of your endorsers using said products.

Press Kits

Your job (or one of your jobs) is to make life easier for the press. The easier you make it for them, the more likely it is they'll cover you.

That probably means gathering various items we've previously discussed into online press kits. You might create kits around specific product lines, product releases, promotions, or whatever. Include all relevant information and media—press releases, spec sheets, product photos, logos, and the like.

Remember, the goal is to make things easier for journalists who may be writing about you. That means throwing some company background info into the press kit, just in case. Include management bios, a company timeline, whatever you think might be useful. And don't forget your own contact information!

Upcoming Events

Let the media know that your company is a busy one. Include a list of and links to all upcoming conferences, trade shows, and other events that your company is attending or participating in. This enhances your corporate credibility and your image as an industry leader.

Media Coverage

Here's a good one. Be sure to include copies of or links to favorable media coverage your company and products have received. Include mentions and reviews in traditional media, as well as reviews and mentions in blogs and online news sites. Filter the list, of course, so that you don't draw attention to negative reviews and mentions. Show journalists and potential customers all the good things that people are saying about you.

32

FIGURE 32.4
The News Coverage section of The Gap's online press room.

Contact Information

Finally, include a link that visitors can use to contact you for more information. Make this a personal contact—a link to a specific person in your PR department. Definitely include an email address; unless you're averse to direct communication (and if so, why are you in the marketing business to begin with?), you should probably include a direct-dial phone number, too. Heck, include your IM info if you're online doing instant messaging most days. Make it easy for reporters and reviewers to get in touch with you—and make sure you return said emails and phone calls in a timely fashion!

Locating Your Online Press Room

Where should your online press room be located? That's a very good question, even if there doesn't appear to be a single good answer.

Some companies hide their online press rooms, thinking that it's for the press only, not for the general public to stumble onto. As such, they don't publicize the URL nor make it linkable from their main website.

I think that's shortsighted. You can actually generate consumer sales from a well-organized online press room; customers browsing the images and press releases will get more interested in the products you offer. Hiding this valuable resource from the general public dismisses these potential sales.

In addition, if you hide your press room from the general public, you also make it difficult for legitimate media to find it. So you keep the URL a secret and only hand it out to qualified journalists, but then how do those journalists get in touch with you to access the press room? It's a nice little Catch-22 and one that's sure to frustrate writers on a deadline who just don't have time to jump through all your little hoops. They're more likely to not include a product photo in their stories or just not write about you in the first place. You can be sure that you have at least one competitor who makes things easier for the pros.

That's why I like making the press room a link from the company's home page. It doesn't have to be a link from the main menu at the top of your page; it can be a little link at the bottom of the page. But at least it's there for anyone interested to explore.

You should also consider giving the press room its own easily remembered URL or subdomain. For example, IBM's press room is located at www.ibm.com/press/; Ford's is located at media.ford.com. Both are pretty easy to find and remember.

Organizing Your Online Press Room

As you're designing your online press room site, easy navigation should be paramount. You want visitors to easily find what you have available.

FIGURE 32.5

The main navigation menu of Ford's online press room—note the links to News (press releases), Products (spec sheets and other info), Bios, Facilities, Photos, Videos, Audio, and PR Contacts.

To that end, I recommend navigational links to all the major sections of your press room: press releases, product info, product photos, videos and other media, management bios, company information, and contact info. Make it a one-click affair to find whatever it is a journalist is looking for.

When you're organizing your product information and photos, think like a journalist or customer looking for information. This affects how you organize and label things. Eschew the model number organization many companies default to; nobody knows your products by model number except the folks inside your company. Instead, group and label things in plain English terms, the way an uninitiated stranger might think of them.

That also extends to the file names you assign your product photos. Instead of labeling a file 42xbr730f.jpg, call it something like 42-inch-lcd-monitor-front-view.jpg. Obscure file naming not only makes it difficult to find items on your site, it makes it nearly impossible for journalists to find the files they download on their own computers. Plain English, please!

Finally, you should supplement your normal navigation with a search box specifically for your press materials. Let journalists search for what they need; that's often the faster way to find specific photos and information.

Informing Journalists of New News

Here's another interesting concept for your online press room. What about offering a way for journalists to keep informed of the latest company and product news? This may be important for journalists and bloggers covering a specific industry.

There are a couple of ways to do this. The first is via a somewhat traditional email mailing list. Get the journalists' email addresses and then pump out news alerts via email. Let them choose the types of alerts they want to receive and then let them know when something new and interesting happens.

You can also push your latest news alerts via RSS feeds. Let journalists and bloggers subscribe to your feed and then publish all your news releases into the feed. They'll be automatically notified whenever you publish something new. To implement this notification strategy, have your IT guys include an RSS sign-up button on your main press room pag, and let them do the heavy lifting in terms of creating the feed and making sure it gets updated when you post new content.

note If you're a larger company, you may want to establish multiple feeds for different brands, product lines, or businesses. You may also need separate feeds for investors, events, and the like.

The Bottom Line

An online press room is a repository on your website for everything the media might find useful—product photos, press releases, videos, management bios, and the like. It's a great way to get these items in the hands of the press, much quicker than sending them through the postal mail.

Once you make journalists aware of your online press room, you should also keep them updated when you add new materials. You can do this by encouraging them to sign up to an email mailing list, or just create an RSS news feed to publish your latest news alerts.

OPEN OR CLOSED ACCESS?

Many, if not most, companies make their online press centers freely available to all comers—traditional journalists, nontraditional bloggers and their ilk, and the general public. Other companies, however, consider their press materials somehow proprietary and not suitable for use by the general public. How a product photo or specification, which ultimately is used in public media read by the general public, isn't fit for public consumption escapes me. But this is the way some companies think (especially those ruled by a heavy-handed legal department worried about copyrights) and why they make their press rooms private.

There are multiple drawbacks to having a closed online press room, not the least of which is the issue of controlling access. Who decides who gets in and who doesn't? How does an interested journalist gain access? (Typically by emailing the contact and getting a password in return—but how do you know who to contact in the first place?) How fast can a journalist get access to the site? Issues abound.

In addition, if your press room is closed to the public, then potential customers can't see what's there. Not that a press room is optimized for consumer use, but it can be another gateway for people to find out more about what you sell. Keep it private, and you lose that advantage.

My advice is to keep your online press room open and don't hide anything from anybody. Hey, if an interested consumer wants to view a spec sheet or download a product photo, what's the harm? And who's to say who's a consumer and who's a journalist, anyway? The line between "fan" and journalist is really blurred online, especially in the blogosphere; if a so-called personal blogger wants to talk about your product and include a photo, all the better!

In my eyes, there's nothing to be gained by controlling access to your press materials, either by password protection or requiring users to register before being granted access. You want your products to gain the widest possible exposure, don't you? Then let anyone who wants to access and download your photos, press releases, and the like. The more placements you get, the better.

Tracking Online PR Performance

One of the new aspects of online PR, as compared to the traditional type, is that you actually measure the success of your efforts. I'm not talking about seeing how many blogs you pop up on, although that's still an important measurement. Online, you can track how many people thought enough of your placement to click through to your website and get more information or buy something.

If you're an old school publicist, that sort of accountability might be a little scary; you can actually have sales targets you need to achieve. But I tend to think of this as a positive advancement, where everyone in the marketing department can be held accountable for the success (or failure) of his or her efforts.

Tracking Placements

Before we get into web analytics and other ways to track traffic, let's examine the traditional metrics of the PR specialist. I'm talking placements—how many outlets picked up your press release and mentioned your company or product.

In traditional media, you typically track this by using a clipping service. A month or two after you issue a press release, you count up how many publications wrote about you; the more mentions you get, the more successful you are.

How do you know how many placements you've received online? While some clipping services purport to measure online placements, I don't really trust their results. You're better off searching Google, Yahoo!, and Bing for mentions of your company or product, perhaps keying off a keyword or phrase in a particular press release. If you want to get fancy, set up a Google alert for a particular search phrase, so you'll be notified when a new placement appears online.

And what exactly are you looking for—and where? Your press release can be picked up just about anywhere on the Internet. You need to look at mentions on websites (news sites, industry sites, enthusiast sites, you name it), blogs, review sites, message forums, and social media—including Facebook, Twitter, Digg, Delicious, StumbleUpon, and the like.

note You can also use blog search engines to search blogs for mentions of your company or product and social media search engines to search Facebook, Twitter, and others for mentions that might result from your online press releases.

Obviously, you should directly track those blogs and websites that you specifically targeted in your campaign. If you lobbied a blogger for a mention, follow that blog to see if he followed through. You should aim for a fairly high pickup rate among those blogs and websites you personally targeted.

You can also use web analytics to discover some online placements. Watch the referrals metric to see where traffic to your site is coming from. If you discover a new referring site, follow the link backward; you may find out that traffic is being generated from a mention that flowed from one of your online press releases.

Of course, there's the whole question of "how many placements equal success?" That issue remains online, if all you're doing is measuring placements. As you'll soon see, however, there is a way to more directly measure the effectiveness of your efforts online—by tracking actual click-throughs from your press releases.

Tracking Traffic and Conversions

Tracking placements measures how effective you were in getting your press release noticed—the effectiveness of your placement efforts, in other words. It does not, however, measure the effectiveness of the press release itself.

For that, we turn to web analytics. The Internet is different from traditional media in that you can track all traffic that comes to your website. If a particular visit is the result of someone reading your online press release or other mention, you can track where that visitor came from, how long he stayed on your site, and whether he did what you wanted him to do—get more information, leave his contact info, or buy something.

This ability to measure performance in concrete terms is a huge change from tracking traditional PR efforts. In many ways, PR professionals had it easy in the pre-Internet world; they really couldn't be held accountable for anything more than the clippings they produced. I'm reminded of a story told to me of a publicist who, in the old days, put a stack of press clipping on his boss' desk, only to be told something to the effect that these were just little pieces of paper. If he could deposit them in the bank, then he'd know what they were worth. Until the publicist could show a relationship between those little pieces of paper and sales, he shouldn't waste his boss' time.

Well, on the Internet you can show a relationship between the online equivalent of those little pieces of paper and resulting sales. Just about everything that happens on the Internet can be tracked, after all. It's not enough, not anymore, to claim that your PR efforts are "increasing brand awareness;" you can now point to specific metrics that show just how much traffic and even sales you're producing.

If you're not measuring clippings, then, what do you measure? It's a list of metrics that, if you've read this far in the book, you should be quite familiar with:

- **Rankings with the major search engines** (Google, Yahoo!, and Bing)—That's right, your press releases, if well written and well optimized, should pop up in the search results when someone queries the relevant topic. The higher you appear in the results, the more visible—and more effective—the press release.

- **Pageviews and unique visitors**—In other words, traffic from referring websites and blogs. That should include traffic coming from your archived press release, hosted either on your site or with a service like PRWeb, back to your main site. An effective press release will generate more traffic. It's as simple as that.

> **note** Smart marketers put tracking links in their press releases that link to unique landing pages. That way there's no confusion over someone stumbling over that page by accident; visitors to that page are a result of your PR efforts only.

- **Time on site**—Generating more traffic is great, but not so if people quickly lose interest and vamoose. An effective placement directs visitors to a targeted landing page and keeps them there long enough to register an impression—or generate an action.

- **Conversions**—Speaking of actions, just what is it you want these visitors to do—get more information, leave their contact info, buy something, or what? Whatever it is, you need to track it. Find out how many conversions are coming from the referring sites where you've placed your press release or received a sympathetic mention. Assign a dollar value to each conversion and use that to calculate your contribution and ROI. That's the true measure of your PR campaign's effectiveness.

When you start tracking the true effectiveness of your PR campaigns, you might be surprised at the results. Some surprises are pleasant, such as the company that tracked $2.5 million in sales from just four press releases. Other surprises are less pleasant; it's possible to find that you're generating next to zero in the way of sales from your efforts. But the important thing is to find out what's really happening and learn from your results.

In this way, then, you can now start to think of PR as part of your company's sales efforts. It's not just warm and fuzzy glad handing; PR now results in actual trackable sales results.

The Bottom Line

Probably the biggest change for publicists regarding online PR is that the web makes all PR efforts trackable. Management certainly will like this; not all PR staff will. (Fuzzy measurement has been a welcome refuge for some.)

Obviously, you can track placements or mentions as a result of your online PR efforts. But you can also track links directly from your online press releases back to your website, and from there you can track other web metrics—including conversions. It's not out of the question to assign specific sales targets to the PR department, which might kick some staff into high gear.

GETTING PR OUT OF THE SILO

Now that we can track PR effectiveness the same way we track the effectiveness of our other marketing efforts, it's time to more fully integrate PR into the balance of our marketing mix.

For most of the modern era of marketing, every part of the mix was a separate thing—in its own silo, as it were. Advertising had its own lingo and metrics, direct marketing had its own lingo and metrics, and PR certainly had its own lingo—even if it didn't have much in the way of metrics. This typically manifested itself in separate and distinct groups within the marketing department. You had an advertising group, a direct mail group, a trade show group, a PR group, and so forth. Seldom did paths cross.

With web marketing, however, everybody is working toward the same goals, using pretty much the same metrics to measure their success. When it comes to driving traffic to your website and converting that traffic to sales, it makes little difference whether that traffic was driven by PPC advertising, email marketing, social media marketing, or online PR. Traffic is traffic, and sales are sales, and we're all trying to maximize them both.

This argues for greater coordination and cooperation between the different silos of the marketing department. If the email guys discover a useful technique, that discovery shouldn't get hoarded by the email department; it should be shared with the advertising and social media and PR guys, as well. We should all be able to learn from each other's successes and failures online.

It's time, then, to break down the silos and get all the marketing people interacting with each other. Do so and you'll discover there's quite a lot they can learn from each other.

34

Understanding Multimedia Marketing

There's a lot of different stuff on the Web. Not just websites and email; there are also blogs and social networks and all manner of social media, as well as music and videos—you name it.

We've already covered websites and email and blogs and social media; now it's time to look at the other media online, chiefly audio and video, what some call multimedia. As you might suspect, there are lots of ways to incorporate multimedia into your web marketing mix—in the form of podcasts and web videos.

What Is Multimedia Marketing?

Multimedia is kind of an old school technology term for content presented via text, graphics, audio, and animations or video. (Technically, the term refers to any content that uses a combination of two or more media forms.) The first multimedia content was delivered to computers via CD-ROM in the mid-1990s, which makes the whole concept appear a bit dated.

In Internet terms, however, multimedia simply refers to web content that goes beyond simple text and graphics—again, typically in the form of audio and video. Audio can be anything from MP3 music files to sounds that play automatically when a web page is open; video is typically just that, moving pictures of people or things.

When we're talking about web marketing, however, we can narrow our definitions a bit. In the context of web marketing, then, audio is pretty much exclusively in the form of *podcasts*, talk radio-like presentations that are made available for anytime download. Video in the web marketing world is...well, video—any type of professional or self-produced video file available on the Web for either streaming or downloading.

Multimedia marketing on the Web, then, is any promotional effort involving either podcasts or web videos. Which, when you think of it, opens a whole new world of marketing activities. You could create your own podcasts talking about your company or products or simply sponsor other podcasts. Likewise, you can produce your own videos to promote or support your products and services and make those videos available on your own website or on third-party video sharing sites, such as YouTube.

Read on to learn more.

Understanding Podcasts

When it comes to using online audio to market your business, your primary tool is the *podcast*. Podcasts let you reach listeners at their computers or on the go. Many podcasts are listened to on iPods and other mobile devices. And because of the periodic nature of podcasts, you can develop a steady base of listeners who tune in week after week for whatever new you have to say.

Defining a Podcast

A podcast is one of a series of episodic audio files, typically distributed over the Internet via RSS feeds. Podcasts differ from the earlier webcasts in that they're downloadable files, rather than streaming audio, and thus can be downloaded for listening at any future time on just about any type of device that offers audio playback—MP3 players, smartphones, computers, you name it.

Podcasts are typically delivered via a central website or service, such as Apple's iTunes Store. Most podcasters deliver new episodes on a regular basis, often weekly and today are delivered primarily in the MP3 audio format.

You can think of podcasts as the online equivalent of radio shows, complete with host (or hosts) and various topics of discussion. In fact, some podcasts *are* radio shows—that is, terrestrial or Internet radio programs packaged in podcast format for streaming or downloading. But most podcasts are created specifically for the Internet and are delivered as such.

34

The History of Podcasting

The first podcast-like audio programs date back to 2000, when i2Go, an early manufacturer of MP3 players, introduced a digital audio news service called MyAudio2Go. This web-based service enabled users to download episodic news and entertainment programs for listening on the company's portable audio players or any personal computer.

MyAudio2Go was a short-lived service, as i2Go folded later that year. But the concept of episodic audio content was picked up by Dave Winer, the developer of the RSS feed format used by virtually all bloggers today. Winer's idea was to marry episodic audio programming with the RSS format, delivering new episodes via RSS feeds. The first demonstration of this process was made in January, 2001, although it didn't really catch on until late in 2003, when ex-VH1 VJ Adam Curry created a script to move RSS-delivered MP3 files to Apple's iTunes Store, and thus to iPod owners. In fact, it was the iPod that introduced podcasting to the big time—and gave the format its name.

Podcasting exploded during 2004 and 2005, especially when Apple integrated podcasts into its iTunes software. This brought podcasting into the mainstream and helped the format's adoption by many traditional media outlets, such as the BBC and NPR.

Podcasting Today

Today, just about every major and minor news organization makes its content available via podcasts. And it's not just radio networks; many print publications supplement their online content with podcasts from their writers and reporters.

Of course, there are a ton of "bedroom" podcasters, individuals with no network affiliation who create podcasts in their own bedrooms or basements and distribute them over the Web. These personal podcasts are more like audio blogs than they are traditional radio programs, but they offer that unique form of personal expression popular on the Internet.

Then there are marketing-oriented podcasts, in which we're interested. These are podcasts produced by companies to promote themselves or their products and are distributed as part of their web marketing strategy. The most successful of these marketing podcasts are informational rather than blatantly promotional, offering a mix of news and information of interest to current and

34

potential customers. Listeners get useful information, and the marketer establishes his company as a trusted authority on the topic in question. It's soft-sell marketing, but it can be quite effective—as long as you deliver a podcast that people really want to listen to.

Understanding Web Videos

Just as podcasts are the online equivalent of radio shows, web videos are the online equivalent of television programming—or, in some instances, television commercials.

Not that you can just upload an existing commercial to the Web and find success. In most cases, this sort of blatant self-promotion doesn't work at all. As with podcasts, the most successful online videos are those that deliver a more subtle message while providing viewers with something useful or entertaining.

The History of Web Videos

Web videos are even newer than podcasts, primarily for bandwidth reasons. That is, a web video is a big file that requires a lot of bandwidth to deliver. Until relatively recently, that sort of bandwidth simply didn't exist or was too expensive to be practical. It wasn't until broadband Internet connections supplanted dial-up connections that watching videos of any type online became feasible.

So even though streaming web video first appeared in the late 1990s, the use of videos on websites was sporadic. More telling, there was no single web depository for online videos, no place viewers could go to watch or users could use for uploading their own videos. There were a handful of sites offering web video hosting and viewing, but none really hit the radar screen—until 2005.

It's All About the YouTube

The world of web video changed in 2005 when the YouTube site was launched. YouTube was designed as a video sharing community, where users could upload their own videos and watch videos uploaded by others. It was an immediate hit.

After just 12 months in business, YouTube was attracting 38 million visitors a month. That attracted the interest of Google, who acquired the company in 2006. Growth since then has been steadily stratospheric, with the site currently recording more than 200 million video views per day from more than 100 million users.

The impact of YouTube has been both immediate and substantial. YouTube is *the* site for video viewing online and the primary place for users of all types to upload their own videos. It doesn't matter what type of video you're looking for; someone has uploaded it to YouTube. And if you want to get your video viewed, no other site comes close in offering the number of eyeballs.

Who uploads videos to YouTube? Individuals, of course, upload all sorts of videos—personal video blogs (vlogs), home movies, stupid pet tricks, you name it. Budding filmmakers also make extensive use of the YouTube site, uploading their latest experiments or independent efforts. But businesses are also starting to use YouTube to promote their companies and products, realizing that there's a huge potential bang to be had from a relatively low financial investment. (That's because YouTube videos are seldom costly professional productions; even business videos are often filmed with consumer-grade camcorders.)

Businesses use YouTube to provide additional information to their customers, show them how to use their products or complete some sort of related project, relay the latest company or industry news, or just offer a bit of entertainment. Like podcasts, YouTube videos are a bit of a soft sell, more like infomercials than commercials, that help establish your company as the resident authority—and the place to go when a related product or service needs to be purchased.

Incorporating Multimedia into Your Marketing Mix

Whether we're talking podcasts or web videos, it's important to note that subtle sells; you can't expect success from a hard-sell approach. That is, people don't listen to podcasts or watch YouTube videos that are overtly promotional in nature. You can't put up a radio or television commercial and expect to garner an online audience; people have too many other options to listen to or watch a commercial online.

To that end, you need to produce audios and videos that offer true value to your intended audience—potential customers, as it were. What kind of value that is depends to a degree on the medium as well as your company and products.

Podcasts are like little radio shows, one or two people talking into a microphone for anywhere from a few minutes to a half hour. That implies a news-type format or perhaps something akin to a talk radio show. Either the host reads the latest news and opinions, ala Paul Harvey and his ilk, or conducts

34

interviews with relevant guests. In either case, you're broadcasting interesting and useful information that somehow ties into the products or services you're selling.

The effect of a successful online video is similar. You provide information or instruction that relates to your products or services. Perhaps that's a video newscast where you talk about industry news or technical developments; perhaps it's a how-to video that shows people how to use your product to do something useful. In any case, viewers watch it because it provides valuable information. What they retain is a sense of your brand or company as a source of authority on the topic at hand.

Now, you might consider this sort of subtle sell an insidious form of corporate propaganda, and you'd be right. You're edging your way into the customer's life, hoping he'll associate your brand with the useful information he's received via your podcasts and videos. WidgetCo provided value to me, WidgetCo is good, I want to make my next purchase from WidgetCo. That's much different from a paid advertisement and ultimately more effective; you get deep into your audience's subconscious and plant your brand message in a very subtle yet long-lasting fashion.

The key is to use podcasts and videos to supplement the promotional message you impart in other online media. You don't use podcasts and videos to broadcast advertisements; instead, you build on your promotional message with the practical information in audio and video media.

And here's another thing. By giving a voice or a face to your company or brand, podcasts and videos help personalize your company and develop a direct connection to your customer base. It's not an anonymous promotional message from an ad or press release; it's John Smith talking to you in person about something that interests you. This type of personal communication is particularly effective and needs to be a part of your web marketing mix.

The Bottom Line

Multimedia on the Internet involves anything that moves or makes a sound—primarily, videos and podcasts. Web videos are like short commercials streamed online; podcasts are like radio programs, similarly streamed to online listeners.

Multimedia marketing utilizes web videos and podcasts to deliver a promotional message to online consumers. Successful video and podcast marketing delivers a subtle message and gives a face and voice to your brand or product.

THE ROLE OF OLD MEDIA IN THE NEW MEDIA WORLD

Podcasts are the online equivalent of traditional radio, and web video is the online equivalent of television. That doesn't necessarily mean that one replaces the other, but it should make you rethink the role of each in your total marketing mix.

Currently, you might think of radio and television as purely advertising media. That is, you run radio and television ads, and that's that. But there's no reason why you can't use these traditional media in the same low-key fashion as you use their online equivalents.

Consider, for example, producing your own local or syndicated radio show instead of just advertising on someone else's show. Put together a good solid hour of talk or entertainment pertaining to the topic at hand and sprinkle mentions of your brand (as a sponsor, perhaps) throughout the broadcast. It's a more subtle sell than a 30-second commercial but perhaps a more authoritative one.

This sort of approach also works across media. Your hour-long radio show can become an hour-long podcast; the same content can be used for both.

Even if you don't create cross-media content, you can still cross-promote between media. Use your radio commercials to mention your podcast; use your podcast to push your latest YouTube videos. And always, always establish the same look and feel and message across all the media you utilize. Your radio commercials should use the same voice talent and background music as your podcasts; your YouTube videos should incorporate the same images and messages you push in your television commercials. Think holistically, especially between similar media, and you'll improve the effectiveness of every medium you utilize.

34

Podcast Marketing

Podcast marketing can be an important part of your online marketing mix. The key is producing a podcast—or, more accurately, a series of podcast episodes—that current and potential customers want to listen to. That means producing a podcast that sounds professional, of course, but also one that provides value of some sort to your listeners.

You also need to find some way to let potential listeners know about your podcast and make it easy for them to subscribe to receive future episodes. And throughout the entire process, you have to ensure that you're imparting the desired promotional message—but in a subtle, barely-perceivable fashion. It's a different challenge from what you're probably used to.

Creating a Podcast: The Technical Details

Let's start with the technical stuff. What do you need to produce a podcast?

A podcast is, at its most basic, a radio show. That means you need to record one or more people speaking. You may also need to add some music (at least to bumper the spoken segments) and perhaps record remote guests who may be calling in via telephone. And assuming that you're recording this for future distribution, you may want to utilize some form of audio editing software to mix together different segments and tighten up the loose ends, as well as save the finished product to a distributable audio file.

That might sound complicated, but it really isn't. While you could rent or borrow a professional radio studio to do the work, that really isn't necessary. Instead you can get by with a few pieces of readily accessible and low-cost equipment and record your podcast from any empty (and noise-free) office.

Recording Equipment

First, you need a computer. Any computer, desktop or notebook, Windows or Mac, will do. You then need a microphone. Not the microphone built into your notebook's webcam—you're going to need something a little higher quality than that. But you don't need to invest in a $1,000 professional mic; instead, look at one of the many USB mics designed specifically for recording podcasts, most of which are in the $100–$200 range. The nice thing about a USB microphone is that it connects directly to a USB port on your computer, no fancy audio card or interface required.

Recording Software

You're also going to need an audio recording and editing program. This software not only records the input from your microphone, but it also lets you set the proper recording levels, save your program to an audio file, and even edit your audio files. (This latter feature is great for editing out mistakes and dead air or splicing together different segments recorded at different times.)

Some of the most popular such programs are free, such as Audacity (audacity.sourceforge.net) and PodProducer (www.podproducer.net). If you need more functionality, consider one of the following low-cost podcast recording programs:

- ePodcast Creator (www.industrialsoftware.com)
- Propaganda (www.makepropaganda.com)
- RecordForAll (www.recordforall.com)

In addition, any pro-level audio recording/editing program will also do the trick, although they're a bit pricier. (They also offer more functionality in terms of mixing, equalization, and sound effects.) These programs include

- Cubase (www.steinberg.net)
- Pro Tools (www.avid.com)
- Sound Forge Audio Studio (www.sonycreativesoftware.com/soundforgesoftware/)

If your podcast features guests who call in via telephone, you're going to need some way to feed the telephone audio into your computer. One solution is to simply run an audio tap from your phone to the audio input of your computer; you can find simple tap devices at Radio Shack and similar stores. You can also use Skype (a computer-based Internet phone service) as your phone service and a program like HotRecorder (www.hotrecorder.com) or Replay Recorder for Skype (www.applian.com/replay-telecorder/) to record your calls.

Recording the Podcast

That's about it in terms of equipment and software. When it comes to recording the podcast, it's a simple matter of connecting your microphone, setting your audio levels, and pressing the Record button on your audio recording program.

How long should your podcasts be? Most podcasts are in the 10–30 minute range. Anything less probably isn't worth listening too; on the other hand, if you go too long, you'll lose people's attention. While hour-long podcasts certainly exist, you'll stand a better chance of success with a 15-minute or half-hour length.

note Save your podcast as an MP3 file with a minimum bit rate of 128 kbps. You can record as high as 192 kbps, but unless the podcast includes a lot of music, you don't need the higher audio quality—which results in larger files that are slower to download.

When you're done recording, use the same program to edit your recording, if necessary, then save the final product as an MP3 file. This is what you then distribute and syndicate over the Web.

Creating a Podcast: The Marketing Strategy

More important than the technical details, however, is your podcast strategy. Just what kind of podcast do you want to create, and what content should you feature?

Remember, a podcast isn't a commercial; you can't just hit the Record button and spend the next ten minutes talking about how great your products are. It's far, far better to provide valuable information about a related topic and promote your product more obliquely.

For example, let's say your company sells medical supplies for diabetics. Instead of just talking about your latest meters and needles, you could instead talk about diabetes in general, either in terms of latest medical developments or the practical side of living with diabetes. Interview doctors, industry experts, even diabetes patients. You can then throw in references to your diabetic products or even toss in some self-produced commercials for said products. But mention of your company and products is secondary; the main focus of the podcast is on diabetes and diabetics.

35

Likewise, if you work for a company that sells musical instruments, you can structure your podcast around uses of those instruments. Maybe you interview endorsers of your products, talk about up-and-coming musicians, or even offer simple music lessons or examples. Yes, you end up talking about your products, but in an oblique fashion.

You can even use podcasts in a B2B setting. For this type of podcast, you might want to interview key customers and talk about unique solutions you offer specific market segments. This type of podcast is maybe a little more self-serving, but as long as you keep the focus on your customers, you're probably okay.

You get the point. Your podcast has to offer unique value to listeners and not just overtly promote your company and products. Your content must be useful, interesting, and unique if you want to draw a large audience. You can then use the podcast's content to establish your authority with these listeners, who at some future date will convert to paying customers.

> **note** How often should you podcast? Often enough to keep listeners from forgetting about you, but not so often as to be annoying. For most companies, that means posting a new episode every week or so. Make it regular so listeners will anticipate something new.

In other words, your podcast must be worth listening to and talking about. Only then will you attract listeners who want to share what they hear with others—which is how you grow your listener base.

Distributing Your Podcast

How do you attract listeners to your podcast? You have to make the podcast readily available, subscribeable, and sharable. And you have to promote it, to some extent.

Making It Available

In terms of availability, there are a few things you need to do.

First, you need to create a section of your website to host all your podcasts. Your most recent podcast should be featured here, but past episode should also be available for downloading. A simple "click to download" arrangement works fine.

FIGURE 35.1

The podcast page on Orvis' website (www.orvis.com).

Next, given the importance of Apple iPods to podcast success, you need to make your podcast available via Apple's iTunes Store. This is where the majority of people discover new podcasts, so it's essential for your podcasts to be available here.

Know, however, that Apple doesn't host or serve the podcast itself; it only links to the podcast's RSS feed. As such you need to submit the link for your RSS feed to iTunes by clicking the Submit a Podcast link on the Podcasts page of the iTunes Store. It's easy enough to do, and gets you listed.

You should also list your podcasts with the major web-based podcast directories. These include

- Digital Podcast (www.digitalpodcast.com)
- Podcast.com (www.podcast.com)
- Podcast Alley (www.podcastalley.com)
- Podcast Pickle (www.podcastpickle.com)

Listing with these services is free.

FIGURE 35.2
Podcasts available from Apple's iTunes Store.

Making It Subscribeable

Speaking of RSS feeds, you need one because a podcast isn't a podcast without it. Having a feed for your podcast makes it easy for loyal listeners to subscribe and automatically receive notice when new episodes are available.

The easiest way to create a feed for your podcast is to use the Feedburner service (feedburner.google.com). You can then post a button or link on your podcast web page so listeners can subscribe with a single click.

Making It Shareable

In addition to offering an RSS feed for your podcasts, you should also make it easy for listeners to share them with other people. This edges us into the social aspect of podcasts, where people share what they hear with friends, family, and co-workers.

As such, you need to include the standard assortment of social sharing buttons on your podcast page. That includes buttons for sharing via email, Twitter, Facebook, Digg, Delicious, and the like. Make it easy to share (and encourage listeners to do so), and you'll gain more listeners.

Promoting Your Podcasts

None of this subscription and sharing business matters if you don't first attract listeners to your podcast.

Obviously, the first step in promoting your podcasts is to make them publicly available, as we just discussed. That means displaying them prominently on your website, getting them listed with iTunes, and doing the listing thing with other podcast-listing services.

You can also use your other online media to promote your podcasts. Make sure you mention your podcasts on the home page of your website and on your blog. When you have a new episode posted, talk about it and link to it from your Twitter feed, Facebook page, and the like. You might even do a little online PR on launch and when you have interesting episodes to plug.

You should also aim your PR guys at other blogs and websites, especially those with active message forums, that focus on the same topic as you do in your podcasts. Get others talking about your podcasts, and you'll gain more listeners.

In other words, use all the tools at your disposal to get the word out about your podcasts. If listeners like what they hear, they'll subscribe to future episodes and share the podcast with their online friends. That's how to grow your listener base.

The Bottom Line

A regular podcast is a great way to give voice to your company or brand and establish yourself (or your company) as an authority in your field. It's a subtle sell, more like an audio infomercial; you have to mix your promotional message with real information provided in the podcast.

To create a podcast, all you need is a computer, a microphone, and an audio recording program. After you make the recording, you syndicate the podcast via RSS feed—and made sure you feed it to Apple's iTunes Store. You should distribute your podcasts on a regular schedule; weekly is a good frequency, if you can do it.

35

PODCAST FORMATS

When it comes to constructing a podcast, there are a few basic formats you can use.

First, you can go with a single host/narrator. This type of podcast is essentially you (or your designated host) sitting in front of a microphone and talking. This is probably the easiest format to produce, at least technically, but unless the host is a pro or a natural behind the mic, it can be a little boring for listeners.

You can add more interest to a podcast and relieve the burden on a single host by using multiple hosts. This involves having two or more people sitting around talking, and it's not a bad way to go. In many ways, a conversation is more interesting to listen to than a monologue. (Unless you have a champion monologist, of course.)

You can add even more variety by adding guests to the mix. Have your host (or hosts) interview one or more guests each episode. These guests should have something to do with the topic at hand, of course, so they can add perspective to the discussion. Guests can be hosted live in the "studio," or if they're more distant, they can call in via telephone.

Finally, if you're into a true conversation with your customers, you can try a call-in format, where listeners call in via phone to ask you questions or comment on the discussion. This sort of thing is a staple of talk radio but a little more difficult to pull off in a podcast, in that people are listening to a recording not a live broadcast. Still, you can post your call-in number and encourage listeners to call in at a certain time during the week. It's also tricky in that you never know what people are going to say on the air—which can be awkward or embarrassing at times.

Video Marketing

I'm a big proponent of online video marketing, specifically via YouTube. I think it's one of the most cost-effective forms of marketing available, period; you get a huge potential bang for a very small buck. In fact, if you do it right, you can start producing videos for YouTube with a minimal expenditure. What's not to like about that?

Success in video marketing, however, requires more than just getting the technical details right. It's all about what you put on the screen, producing videos that current and potential customers want to watch. If you can provide a truly valuable viewing experience, you stand the chance of your video being shared from viewer to viewer and possibly going viral. That's effective marketing!

Is Web Video Right for Your Business?

Video marketing has long been a part of many business' marketing plans. Not online video, mind you, but rather broadcast and cable television, most often in the form of television advertising. TV ads have typically been a little too expensive for smaller businesses, however, unless they could afford a late-night spot on a local channel or something on local cable.

That all changes on the Internet, however, because you can essentially post your videos for free on YouTube and similar video sharing sites. Your only cost is the expense of shooting and editing the video, which can be done with standard-issue consumer equipment. This makes online video marketing affordable for virtually any business.

But is video the right way to promote your business? If you've never produced a video or television ad, you might not be sure. But in many cases, a short video can have tremendous positive effect on your website's traffic or in orders generated via an 800-number.

Let's face it, we like to watch. The average consumer would rather watch a video than read a newspaper or magazine. Like it or not (and I'm not particularly pleased with the ongoing shift away from print), you need to be aware of and adapt your marketing efforts to this trend.

That speaks in favor of online videos, which don't limit you to the same 30-second constraint you have with ads on traditional television. You can include a lot of information in a three-minute web video and present that information in an entertaining and engaging fashion. People like to be entertained, educated, and informed, and online video can do all three of these things—and, in the process, provide a clear picture of the product or service that you're offering.

Done effectively, a web video can add a viral component to your company's online marketing strategy. When you post a video to YouTube, it takes on a life of its own. Your video will be viewed and shared by thousands of YouTube users, posted to numerous websites and blogs, emailed around the Internet—you name it. Just make sure you tailor your message to the YouTube crowd, and you can start generating traffic from the millions of people who frequent YouTube each day.

Welcome to YouTube

When it comes to web video, there's one really big dog that should be the centerpiece of your marketing plans. I'm talking about YouTube (www.youtube.com), the Internet's largest video sharing community.

If you've never heard of YouTube, you should probably be fired from your day job. More likely you're a fan of the site and use it to watch all sorts of interesting videos. That puts you in good company.

It's hard to believe, but as of this writing, YouTube has only been around for five years. Before YouTube, there really wasn't a central place on the Web to upload or view videos.

The whole thing got started by three former employees of PayPal, who had a little cash in their pockets and the suspicion that there might be a need for a service that facilitated the process of uploading, watching, and sharing videos.

The trio registered the domain name YouTube.com, worked out the necessary technology, and officially launched the site in December 2005.

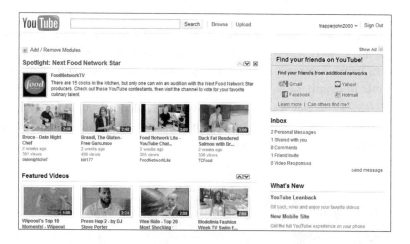

FIGURE 36.1

YouTube, the Internet's largest video sharing community.

YouTube proved immensely popular from virtually the first day in business. Site traffic that first month was 3 million visitors, which is pretty good for a startup. The number of visitors tripled by the third month (February), tripled again by July (to 30 million visitors), and reached 38 million visitors by the end of the site's first year in business. That made YouTube one of the top 10 sites on the Web, period—and one of the fastest-growing websites in history.

That kind of growth didn't go unnoticed, and the site was acquired by Google in October, 2006. Google paid $1.65 billion for YouTube—an incredible sum for such a young company and one that had yet to generate significant revenues.

That was four years ago, and YouTube has continued to experience phenomenal growth. YouTube consistently rates in the top five of all websites, with more than 100 million visitors per month. These visitors watch more than 2 billion videos every day, a number I still have trouble wrapping my head around.

With this kind of traffic, it's easy to see that YouTube is replacing traditional television viewing for many users. According to Google, an average YouTube viewer spends 164 minutes online every day; in contrast, viewers spend just 130 minutes per day watching traditional television. Where would you rather put your marketing message?

How YouTube Works

For those of you unfamiliar with YouTube, here's the short version of YouTube 101.

Anyone, individual or business, can upload videos to YouTube. These can be home movies, video blogs, old television programs (as long as copyright isn't an issue), commercials, even independent films. Videos can be up to 15 minutes in length, although most are (much) shorter.

Anyone can watch videos that have been uploaded. A video is viewed on its own video viewing page; users can leave comments and vote positively or negatively on any given video.

FIGURE 36.2
A typical YouTube video viewing page.

If a viewer likes a video, he can easily share it with others; this is how a video goes viral, by being passed around as a favorite. Viewers can post YouTube videos to Facebook or MySpace, send links to videos via email, even embed videos in their blogs or web pages. All the sharing mechanisms are right there on the video viewing page, just below the video itself.

YouTube represents an essentially free advertising channel. The site doesn't charge producers to store their videos or to serve up the bandwidth necessary to view them. It also doesn't charge viewers anything to watch those videos. (YouTube makes its money from advertising; it is part of the Google empire, after all, same as our old friend, AdWords.)

What Kinds of Videos Work Best?

There are literally millions of videos on the YouTube site. Not all of them are widely viewed; most quickly disappear into the ether.

Many, if not most, YouTube videos are uploaded by individuals. These range from simple talking head video blogs to stupid pet (and human) tricks to you name it.

Other YouTube videos are uploaded by businesses. These videos attempt to promote a company, a brand, or a product. Some of these videos are blatant commercials (including existing commercials repurposed to the YouTube site), some offer in-depth prepurchase information about a given product or service, some offer post-purchase information or support, and some use other approaches to gain viewers—and prospective customers.

What types of promotional videos get viewed on YouTube? I find that successful YouTube business videos tend to fall into three major categories: They're either informative, educational, or entertaining.

In other words, for a video to attract viewers it must offer them something of value. It must be something they want or even need to watch. If you can't provide unique value, no one will watch or share your videos.

Informative Videos

The first type of video you can produce is an informative video—that is, a video that imparts information of some sort. This most often is the YouTube equivalent of a newscast, with you (or your spokesperson) acting as reporter or anchorman. Alternately, an informative video may function as a video brochure, presenting in-depth information about you or your products.

With this type of video, what's key is the information you present. This can be information about your company, your products, or your industry. What it has to be is relevant to the viewer.

One approach is to inform the viewer about your product. This could take the form of a extended product guide or demonstration, where you use the medium of video to provide a closer look at what your product is, what it does, or how it's made. The big automakers do a good job of this, utilizing the video medium to deliver virtual test drives, product overviews, and the like.

Another approach is to talk about the latest issues in your industry. If you're a dentist, for example, you can go on camera and talk about the latest teeth whitening techniques, or how to fight plaque, or what kind of toothbrush works best. Or if you work for a clothing retailer, you can produce informational "stories" about the latest seasonal fashions and such.

And it doesn't have to be straight news. You can offer opinions on the latest developments or give advice to viewers. The key is to use the format to establish yourself or your company as the authority to turn to, so that when customers need to buy what you're selling, they'll think of you.

In this respect, an informative video is more like an infomercial than it is a commercial. It's a soft sell, not a hard one; it's the information you present that makes the video and attracts viewers.

As to how to produce a simple informative video, think "talking head." It's the same approach local television news broadcasts take: One, sometimes two people sitting in front of the camera and reading a script. Maybe you throw in some graphics to add visual interest, maybe you shoot from a couple of different camera angles, but the bottom line is it's a simple matter of talking heads.

FIGURE 36.3

A "talking head" newscast from FoodForLifeTV.

If you decide to go the video product tour route, that's a whole different process. This type of video is much more involved, with multiple shots and scenes, lots of different camera angles, inspirational background music, you name it. In fact, this is the one type of video where it might pay to engage professional production services; you have to put your best foot forward.

FIGURE 36.4

A video product tour from BMW.

Educational Videos

The next type of video you can produce is the educational video. For education, think instruction—that is, a "how to" video, where you show the viewer how to do something useful, typically in step-by-step fashion.

For example, if you're a pharmaceutical company selling asthma drugs, you might produce a video showing people how to use your latest inhaler. If you sell aquarium supplies, you might produce a video showing people how to install your latest canister filter. If you sell auto parts, you might create a series of videos showing how to change oil, replace a brake light, and so forth. If you offer custom woodworking services, you might create a video showing how to build a bookcase or install wood trim. You get the picture.

FIGURE 36.5

Cooking instruction from ChefTips.

The key here is to offer truly useful content for either pre- or post-purchase use. Present the content in a step-by-step fashion, using multiple shots and camera angles. Attack a task common enough to draw a large audience, make the steps easy to follow, and then use the video to sell other goods and services.

Producing an educational video is more complex than a simple talking-head video. You need to plan it all out in advance, scripting and storyboarding every shot you need to make. The shooting process is likewise complex, as you have to produce each of those shots. You then feed all those shots into a video editing program, stitch them together with the appropriate transitions and onscreen graphics, and produce yourself an easy-to-follow step-by-step video lesson.

Entertaining Videos

Informing and educating are important and will draw a fair number of YouTube viewers if you do it right. But everybody likes to be entertained— which is why pure entertainment videos typically show up at the top of YouTube's most viewed lists.

What's entertaining? Unfortunately, I can't tell you. What's entertaining is in the eye of the beholder; what I laugh at might leave you cold.

To that end, I really can't tell you how to produce an entertaining video. You need to be creative, that's for sure, but beyond that, either you have the spark or you don't. If you do, you create a video that people remember and want to share. If you don't, you create a video that falls flat on its face. It's a high-risk category, that's for sure.

Here's what I do know about entertaining videos: When they work, they work really well. It's the entertaining video that is most likely to go viral.

One of my favorite examples continues to be Blendtec, a blender company that produces the Will It Blend? series of videos. In each video, company president Tom Dickson puts something crazy into one of the company's blenders, and sees if it blends. I'm not talking bananas and cumquats; Tom has blended (or tried to blend) things like G.I. Joe dolls, flashlights, and iPhones. These aren't terribly informative or educational videos, but they sure are entertaining and have helped the company increase sales by several factors.

FIGURE 36.6

An entertaining "Will It Blend?" video from Blendtec.

If done right, then, an entertaining video is great for establishing and maintaining your brand image. But there's no guarantee it will work; you'll either succeed wildly or fail miserably.

Creating a YouTube Video

Just how do you create a YouTube video? It doesn't have to be hard work or expensive. You do, however, have to get the technical details right.

Professional Production—or Not?

The first choice you have to make is how professional you want to go. Obviously, the Budweisers of the world go whole-hog on professional production; their YouTube videos are spitting images of their traditional commercial work.

If you go the professional production route, expect to spend some big bucks. It's not unusual to spend $50,000 or more for a 2-3 minute video and to spend days if not weeks producing it. That's a lot of money and a lot of work for something that gets viewed on a little window on a computer screen.

For that reason, most YouTube videos, even those produced by big companies, do not feature this type of professional production. Instead, most YouTube

36

videos are shot using standard consumer-grade equipment, the kind you can find at any Best Buy or similar consumer electronics store. Go this route, and you can produce your first video for well under $1,000—and then reuse that same equipment for each subsequent video you shoot. That's a minimal investment for what could be a huge payback.

Buy the Right Equipment

If you decide to go the self-production route, you need to make an initial investment in equipment. Not a lot of equipment and not expensive equipment. Just a few things you can pick up at your local consumer electronics or photography store.

Here's the shopping list:

- **Camcorder**—I like a model with either hard drive or flash storage; that makes it easy to transfer files to your computer for editing. If you're buying, go with a model that records high definition (HD) video; YouTube accepts HD video, and some viewers expect it. Also look for a model that lets you use an external microphone; we discuss this in a moment. In any case, expect to spend between $300 and $500 on the model you choose.

- **Tripod**—You need to shoot a rock-steady picture, which you can't do by holding the camcorder in your hands. Invest in a $30–$40 tripod so you don't have to worry about the shakes.

- **Lighting**—Normal room lighting isn't good enough for a professional-quality video. Invest $150–$200 on a lighting kit with two or three photofloods on stands. Position the lights in a V, with the subject at the center of the V and the lights facing the subject at 45-degree angles. It will make a very noticeable difference in picture quality.

- **Microphone**—To improve the audio quality—that is, to make what you're saying more understandable—replace the camcorder's built-in microphone with an external model. Go with a lavaliere mic that clips onto the subject's shirt; the sound quality will be impressive. A wired mic runs $40–$50, while a wireless model runs $150–$200.

- **Seamless background**—Don't position the subject in front of a cluttered background. Instead, buy a sheet of seamless background paper, cloth, or muslin. Go with a contrasting color—lighter if the subject is wearing a dark shirt, darker if the subject is wearing light clothing.

■ **Video editing software**—You'll want to import your video files from your camcorder to your computer. From there, you can edit together different takes, add transitions between scenes, and superimpose graphics and text onscreen. You do all this with a video editing program, such as Windows Movie Maker or iMovie—included free with your Windows or Mac computer.

note You probably won't find all this equipment at Best Buy. Instead, shop at your local camera store; this is the same equipment that still photographers use.

Of course, you might have some of this equipment already. If you already have a decent camcorder you use at home, that's great; it can do double-duty. And chances are you already have a video editing program of some sort installed on your computer; you can use that, too.

In other words, you might be able to produce your first YouTube video without *any* new investment. And that's a good thing.

Get the Size Right

YouTube started out offering videos in small windows on their web pages—just 320 pixels wide by 240 pixels tall. That low resolution format has since been supplanted by true high definition videos, in either 720p (1280 x 720 pixels) or 1080p (1920 x 1080 pixels) format. That's what you need to shoot at, edit in, and save to.

Both HD formats are widescreen, meaning they're wider than the squarish picture used in standard definition television. You'll want to shoot in widescreen, of course, and take advantage of all that screen real estate.

Shoot for the Smaller Screen

Even if you provide an HD video, most viewers will be watching your video in a small window in their web browsers. As such, you need to create a video that looks good at this small size, viewed on a typical computer screen. What does this mean in terms of visual style?

Big and bright is the order of the day. You can shoot an epic with a cast of thousands, but those thousands will look like little dots in a small browser window. The best YouTube videos are visually simple, with a single main subject filling up most of the small video window. (That's your typical talking head video, folks.) Get up close and frame the subject so that he or it fills most of the screen.

36

You also want to make sure the scene you're shooting is adequately lit. Too many YouTube videos come out way too dark, which makes them hard to view. This is why I recommend you invest in a set of affordable photo floodlights.

Finally, know that the type of streaming video that YouTube provides doesn't always reproduce rapid movement well, especially over slower Internet connections. Move the camera too fast or have your subject move too fast in the frame and viewers are likely to see motion smears, pixilation, and other unacceptable video effects. Keep things slow and simple for best results.

Accentuate the Contrast

As noted previously, visual contrast is highly desirable with small-footprint videos. Put a pale or white-clad subject in front of a black background or a black-clad subject in front of a white one. And consider using brightly colored backgrounds, which really pop in YouTube thumbnails; believe it or not, hot pink really grabs the attention of casual viewers!

Shoot Professionally—Even if You're an Amateur

When you're shooting your video, embrace professional production techniques—even if you're just using a consumer-grade camcorder. Here are the things you need to keep in mind:

- Make sure the subject is well-lit; use an external lighting kit.
- Make sure the speaker can be heard; use an external microphone if your camera has an auxiliary mic input.
- Minimize background and crowd noise; keep it quiet on the set.
- Keep the camera steady; use a tripod.
- Don't move the camera around too much.
- Don't zoom in and out too much.

In other words, do everything you can to keep the focus on the main subject. Don't let the camera-work distract!

Look Professional—or Not

If you're representing a professional business, your videos need to look professional. The standard look of personal YouTube videos—an unshaven twentysomething in a t-shirt, staring intently at a web camera—just doesn't give off the professional vibe that most businesses want. Whether your video has a cast of one or of thousands, make sure that anyone on camera is well-dressed and well-groomed, that everyone is well-lit and well-mic'd, and that the whole production has a professional sheen.

Unless, that is, you want to give out a hip young vibe. In that instance, take off the suits and ties and emulate the personal look that's become ubiquitous on the YouTube site. In other words, make sure your video has a look and feel that matches your company's message.

Consider Creating a Slideshow

If you don't need full-motion video or don't have access to a video camera, consider putting together a slideshow of still photographs. Just compile the photos into a slideshow, add background music or a voiceover, and upload the whole thing to YouTube. Likewise, some topics benefit from PowerPoint presentations, which can also be converted to video for uploading to YouTube.

Break the Rules

Don't confuse these tips for creating better-looking videos with hard and fast rules. It's okay to think outside the box and do things a little different. For example, if you want to create a hip-looking video for a younger audience, it's permissible to take the camera off the tripod and go for a "shaky-cam" effect. Do whatever it takes to achieve the effect you want.

Creating Compelling Content

Even the best-looking video will fail miserably if the content isn't compelling. It's important to remember that what you're shooting is more important than how you're shooting it.

Provide Unique Value

When creating content for YouTube, you want to give viewers a reason to come back for future viewings and to share your video with others. It's this sharing that makes for a viral video—compelling content begs to be more widely viewed.

People will watch your video if it's something they're interested in and if they can't find that information anyplace else. Your video must provide a unique value to viewers, something they want or need to know or do. It's all about the content, and don't forget that.

Be Entertaining

In addition to providing unique content, your video also needs to be entertaining—even if you're producing an informative or educational video. Produce a boring video, and no one will watch it. People like to be entertained. Give the people what they want.

It doesn't matter what product your selling or what your message is. Find a way to make your product, service, brand, or company entertaining. Not necessarily funny (although that helps), but approachable and enjoyable—at least enough to keep the viewer watching for the entire length of the video.

Keep It Short

YouTube lets you upload videos up to 15 minutes in length, but I don't recommend you go that full length. One way to kill your video's entertainment value is to make it too long. Viewers today—and especially online—have a very short attention span. The YouTube audience is the post-MTV generation, which means even a three-minute video has trouble holding their attention.

It's imperative, then, that you keep your videos short enough so that viewers don't tune out mid-way. How short is short? It depends on who you ask; some experts say five minutes at the top end, some say one minute or less, some even say 20 seconds is ideal. My recommendation is to keep your video no longer than two or three minutes—and the shorter, the better. Videos any longer than three minutes or so typically don't get big viewership.

That doesn't mean you have to produce a video that's exactly three minutes long. As I said, shorter is better. If you can say what you want to say in 60 seconds, great. If you need the full three minutes, take it. But take viewers' short attention spans into account and present your message quickly and efficiently.

note If you have a message that takes more than a few minutes to present, consider chopping it up into multiple shorter videos, which can then be combined into a YouTube playlist. For example, if you want to post a ten-minute speech, edit it into four segments of two to three minutes apiece.

Keep It Simple

You don't have to spend a lot of money on a YouTube video for it to be effective. In fact, it's easy for a company to spend too much money on its videos;

the result is typically an overproduced monstrosity that looks horrible online. In many cases, a single person talking directly to a camera is all you need.

In fact, the YouTube community tends to reward simple and direct videos. YouTubers are often turned off by overtly commercial productions; they prefer the immediacy of a low-budget video.

So keep it simple and keep it focused. That lets you connect directly with your viewers—which forges a tighter bond.

Stay Focused

Part of keeping it simple is focusing on a single message. Remember, you only have a few minutes at most to communicate to the YouTube viewer. Don't spend that time trying to show your entire product line or even multiple features of a sophisticated product. Hone in on a single product and communicate its strongest feature or benefit. One video per product or feature should be your rule.

Avoid the Hard Sell

Even though your message should be simple, you don't have to hit the viewer over the head with it. On YouTube, the soft sell works better than the hard sell. That's why a how-to video showing your product in use typically works better than a straight-ahead product demonstration; the former is a soft sell that communicates a subtle message to the viewer—who will typically turn off a harder message.

In other words, infomercials and edutainment are better than straight advertisements. In fact, if a video feels like an ad, most YouTube viewers will avoid it like the plague.

Keep It Fresh

The video you create today will be forgotten a month or two from now. With thousands of new videos being posted on YouTube every day, your video will quickly become yesterday's news. This requires you to constantly update your company's video library; older videos need to be either refreshed or replaced on a regular basis. And if you go more than a few months without posting a new video, your company's channel will lose viewership.

Driving Viewers to Your Website

Creating a highly-viewed video is great, but it's ultimately meaningless unless you can convert those viewers into paying customers. How, then, do you turn views into sales? Here are a few tips that will help in the process.

Include Your URL in the Video

The key to marketing on YouTube is to lead viewers from your video on the YouTube site to your company's website—where you can then directly sell your products and services. How is this accomplished?

Unfortunately, YouTube doesn't allow live links from a video to a third-party website. (Unless you're promoting the video, that is—which we discuss later in this chapter.) You can, however, include your website address in the body of the video—and hope that viewers will remember it or write it down for future reference.

There's no point being subtle about this. Because people have trouble remembering things like 800-numbers and URLs, you need to include your address early and often in the video. I recommend starting your video with a blank title screen with the URL prominently displayed. You should also end the video with a similar blank screen with the URL highlighted. Make sure the URL is big and easily readable; high contrast colors, such as white text on a black background (or vice versa), provide the best results.

note Naturally, if your business is telephone-based instead of Internet-based, you can substitute your 800-number for the website address—or list them both, if you prefer.

You should also display your URL onscreen during the main part of your video. Use your video editing program to overlay the URL across the screen. The URL shouldn't interfere with the main content, of course, but you should be able to do it in a way that isn't overly intrusive.

note You should plug your site's URL by incorporating a subtle selling pitch in the script of your video. This is the same way that information "hosts" plug their products in their presentations.

FIGURE 36.7
A URL superimposed on the video screen.

Include Your URL in the Accompanying Text

You can't link live from within a YouTube video. Unfortunately, you also can't include a link to your website in the description that accompanies the video. You can, however, include your URL in the text description, but just not as a live link. So when you write the description for your video, make sure you include your URL or 800-number in the text.

Link from Your Channel Page

While you can't include a live link in your video or accompanying text, you can include a direct link to your website in your YouTube channel page. Anyone clicking your user name will see your channel page, with the link to your website prominently displayed. When a viewer clicks the website link, they're taken directly to your site—where you can sell them more of what you have to offer.

note Your channel page is essentially your brand home on the YouTube site. All your videos are displayed there, as is other company information you want to present. You should take the time to customize your channel page to reflect your brand identity; use the same colors and graphics here as you do on your own website.

FIGURE 36.8

A typical YouTube channel page.

Close the Sale on Your Website

Now it's time to close the sale—which you do on your own website, given that you can't sell directly from your YouTube page.

The URL you point to from your YouTube video should be a dedicated landing page. That means that you don't point to a generic page on your site or even to your site's home page; either approach requires unnecessary work on the part of the customer to place an order. Instead, link to a specific product page on your site, one that includes information only about the product shown in the video.

Why design a special landing page for viewers of your YouTube video? It's simple: You want to make it as easy as possible for them to give you their money. If you just dump potential customers on your site's home page, they could get lost. Or they might have trouble finding the product they want and give up. In any instance, you don't want them randomly browsing your site; you want them immediately responding to your specific offer.

For this reason, your product landing page should have the same look and feel of the video so that viewers sense the underlying connection. It doesn't hurt to include a screenshot or two from the video or even an embedded version of the video in the case the customer wants to rewatch it. The page should also include more detailed information about the product than was possible in the video, as well as more detailed product photos.

Promoting Your YouTube Videos—Organically

The best-made video on YouTube is a dismal failure if no one watches it. How do you attract viewers to your YouTube videos—and thus create more potential customers for your business?

With millions of videos posted on the YouTube site and 24 hours of new video being uploaded every minute, it's tough to get your content noticed. Fortunately, there are many different ways you can promote your YouTube videos to attract new viewers.

Start with Great Content...

It goes without saying that all the promotion in the world won't attract viewers to a video that doesn't offer some distinct value. Viewers who follow the promotion to a lousy video will simply click the Stop button when they begin to get bored—which will be soon enough. It all starts with great content, which can then benefit from additional promotion.

Target Your Content

Here's something else about the content of your videos; the more targeted it is, the faster it will find an audience. Yes, general videos would seem to appeal to a larger slice of the YouTube community. But general videos also get lost among the millions of other general videos; it's tough to stand out in this large a crowd.

A much better approach is to target a particular slice of the community—a distinct customer base. It's just like any other form of advertising, the more narrowly you target the message, the more appeal you have to those targeted consumers. You don't really care about getting a million viewers who aren't interested in what you're selling; better to attract a few hundred highly targeted potential customers.

In addition, when you niche-target your content, you can more easily promote via YouTube's community features, as well in the blogosphere and on social networks. When the audience is narrowly identified, it's a snap to locate those groups, blogs, forums, and the like that target the same audience. A video that is broadly focused is much more difficult to promote; there are just too many channels to choose from, none of which is an exact hit. A narrowly targeted video can be more effectively and efficiently promoted via similarly narrowly targeted channels.

Optimize Your Tags

When it comes to making viewers aware of your videos, remember the tags—those keywords that viewers use to search for videos on YouTube. Most viewers find new videos by searching for a given topic; the better optimized your video is for search, the more viewers you'll attract. Add the appropriate tags, and you make it easier for viewers to find your videos.

Optimizing the tags you apply to your videos is just like applying SEO for your website. Do some keyword research and get inside your customers' heads. When you figure out the keywords they'll most likely search for, you have the most effective tags for your video.

Write a Compelling Title and Description

The title of your video is key to attracting viewers. Not only is your title searched by YouTube when users submit queries, but it's also how most viewers determine what your video is about.

Yes, the full description is there to read, but most people skim rather than read—especially when they're browsing through a page full of search results. So your title has to not only include the most important keywords or tags, but also convey the content of the video.

That means, of course, that you have to create a concise, descriptive, and compelling title. It's copywriting at its finest, distilling the essence of what you have to offer in a very short line of copy; it takes a lot of work and no little experience to get right.

Then there's the text description that accompanies each video you upload. Don't neglect this; it's another place to seed with appropriate keywords. In addition, you use the description to lead viewers back to your website, so remember to include your URL or 800 number.

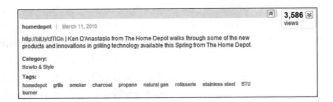

FIGURE 36.9
Description and tags for a typical YouTube video.

Pick the Best Thumbnail Image

YouTube is a visual medium, which means you can't rely on the accompanying text to completely sell your offerings. Remember what a typical YouTube search results page looks like—lots of video listings, each accompanied by a single thumbnail image. You need to attract viewers to your specific listing in the search results, which means presenting the most attractive and relevant thumbnail image possible.

FIGURE 36.10

Optimize your thumbnail image to stand out on search results pages.

When you upload a video, YouTube lets you choose from three possible images to use as the video's thumbnail image. These images are grabbed from different points in the video. You need to pick the one thumbnail that will attract the most number of clicks.

The best thumbnails are clear, not blurry, and have a dominant subject—ideally a person's face or a close-up of the product you're selling. You may also stand out from the other listings with a brightly colored or high contrast image in your thumbnail—anything to make the thumbnail "pop" on the search results page.

36

Take Advantage of YouTube's Community Features

One of the best places to promote your YouTube video is on YouTube itself. When you make the YouTube community aware of what you're doing, you'll find other viewers doing your promotion for you; "word of mouth" marketing, as it were, is alive and well on the YouTube site.

Let's start with those users who've added you to their friends list, as well as those who have subscribed to your video channel. These are your most loyal customers, the backbone of your YouTube community.

When it comes to dealing with subscribers, YouTube does the work for you. Whenever you post a new video to the YouTube site, YouTube automatically sends an email to all of your channel's subscribers informing them of the video. That's easy.

You can also share your videos with people on your friends list. The Share options under each YouTube video include an Email option; use this to send an email blast (with a link to the video) to everyone on your friends list.

In addition, you can send bulletins, via email, to your YouTube friends. A bulletin can include whatever message you like, as well as links to selected videos. These bulletins are emailed to people on your friends list and also posted to the Bulletins section of your channel page.

The point is to remember that YouTube is a video sharing *community*. Take advantage of those community features to forge a closer connection with your most loyal followers.

Upload to Other Video Sharing Sites

You shouldn't limit your videos to only YouTube. There are lots of other video sharing sites on the Web that, while smaller than the YouTube community, can help expand the reach of your videos. You already have your video produced, after all; why not distribute it as widely as you can?

Granted, none of the following sites has near the traffic as does YouTube, but they're all free to use, so you might as well get to know them. These sites include the following:

- blip.tv (www.blip.tv)
- Dailymotion (www.dailymotion.com)
- Flixya (www.flixya.com)
- GUBA (www.guba.com)
- Metacafe (www.metacafe.com)

- Revver (www.revver.com)
- Veoh (www.veoh.com)
- Vimeo (www.vimeo.com)
- Yahoo! Video (video.yahoo.com)

Promote Your Videos Socially

When you upload a video to YouTube, you should make note of it in all the social media you use. This means sharing the video as a status update on your Facebook page, tweeting a link to the video on Twitter, and the like. This is the opportunity to get all cross-media with your videos—share and share alike, as it were.

Put Your Videos on Your Own Website

Finally, you should also include your video on your own company website. Your site has lots of visitors who may never visit the YouTube site; give them the opportunity to view your videos without leaving your official site.

To this end, I recommend creating a video page on your website. Post your entire video archive here so that viewers can browse the library at will. This page should mirror your YouTube channel page in look and feel, of course; it's kind of an alternative to YouTube, but on your own site.

FIGURE 36.11

How-to videos on Lowes.com.

Advertising Your YouTube Videos

Organic promotion is fine, but what about more blatant promotion—the kind you have to pay for?

If you're jonesing to add another line to your advertising budget, good news: YouTube lets you advertise your videos on the YouTube site. These so-called Promoted Videos appear on YouTube search results pages, much like traditional PPC ads appear on the results pages for a Google search.

Understanding YouTube Promoted Videos

What, exactly, is a YouTube Promoted Video? It's an advertisement, pure and simple, for a specific YouTube video. Specifically it's a pay-per-click ad, where you're charged only when someone clicks the ad to view the video.

Promoted Video ads appear on YouTube's search results pages. When someone searches for a particular topic, ads related to that topic appear in the Promoted Videos section on the right side of the page. Each ad includes a brief text description and link, as well as a video thumbnail. When a user clicks the ad or thumbnail, they're taken to your video page—and you're charged for that click.

FIGURE 36.12

Promoted videos on a YouTube search results page.

Not surprisingly, YouTube's promoted videos work just like Google's AdWords program—with the addition of a video thumbnail to accompany the ad's text. This is a pay-per-click program, just like AdWords; you're charged only when someone clicks your ad. You bid on specific keywords and pay a certain price per click.

Creating a Promoted Videos Campaign

You can set up advertising campaigns for any video you've uploaded to the YouTube site. In fact, you have to promote each video individually; you can set up separate campaigns for different videos, but you can't set up a generic campaign for all your videos.

To get started, you select a keyword or group of keywords that best describe your video. You bid on these keywords and select how much you're willing to pay for each click. (That's your maximum bid per click.)

> **note** As with all PPC advertising, the higher the CPC you set for your YouTube ad, the more likely your ad will place high on matching search results pages. Set too low a CPC, and higher-bidding advertisers for a given keyword will have their ads appear higher and more often.

You then get to create the Promoted Video ad itself. Each ad consists of a short title and two lines of descriptive text. Your YouTube user name appears below the description, and a thumbnail image of your choice appears on the left side of the ad.

When someone searches YouTube for a keyword that you've purchased, your ad will appear on that person's search results page in the Promoted Videos section. At that point your account is charged for the click at the previously agreed-upon rate.

Of course, you also set a total budget for your campaign. This budget is YouTube-specific, independent of your AdWords budget. When your PPC charges reach this amount, your ad is disabled. You determine how much you're willing to spend each month, and your advertising charges will never exceed this amount.

To sign up for the Promoted Videos program, go to ads.youtube.com. You can then select which ad you want to promote and start creating the campaign.

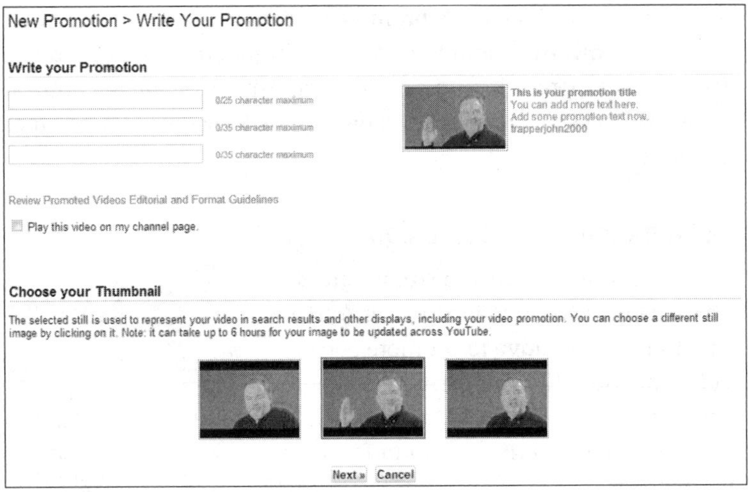

New Promotion > Write Your Promotion

Write your Promotion

0/25 character maximum

0/35 character maximum

0/35 character maximum

This is your promotion title
You can add more text here.
Add some promotion text now.
trapperjohn2000

Review Promoted Videos Editorial and Format Guidelines

☐ Play this video on my channel page.

Choose your Thumbnail

The selected still is used to represent your video in search results and other displays, including your video promotion. You can choose a different still image by clicking on it. Note: it can take up to 6 hours for your image to be updated across YouTube.

Next »   Cancel

FIGURE 36.13

Creating a YouTube Promoted Videos ad.

Tracking Performance from the Promoted Videos Dashboard

You track the performance of your promoted videos from the Promoted Videos Dashboard (ads.youtube.com). This Dashboard displays key information about your current campaigns, including impressions, clicks, click-through-rate, average CPC, total cost, and the like. You can track performance by ad, by video, by keyword, and so on.

FIGURE 36.14

Tracking performance from the Dashboard Summary page.

Adding Call-to-Action Overlays to Your Videos

There's one more advantage to promoting your YouTube videos in this fashion. Earlier, I noted that there was no way to directly link from a video to your own website. That's true, with one exception.

That exception is a Promoted Video. When you advertise a specific video on YouTube, that video can display what YouTube calls a Call-to-Action Overlay. This is a small band that runs across the bottom of the video and includes a live hyperlink. You can point this link anywhere off the YouTube site. My recommendation, of course, is to point to a special landing page on your own website so that viewers can click the link to get more information or purchase what you're selling.

FIGURE 36.15

A Call-to-Action Overlay on a YouTube video.

You add a Call-to-Action Overlay from the editing page for the promoted video. Creating the overlay is as easy as writing a short title and two lines of description and then providing display and a link-to URLs.

Savvy marketers will recognize the value of linking from their YouTube videos back to their website. Because the only way to do this is via Call-to-Action Overlays, and the only way to add an overlay is to promote the video...well, you see where I'm going with this.

The strategy, then, is to create a Promoted Video ad for each video you want to link back to your site. Set as low a daily budget as you like. The size of the budget doesn't matter; all YouTube cares about is that you're promoting the video. Go with a minimal promotional budget, get a little exposure for your videos on YouTube's search results pages, but then reap the rewards of viewers linking directly from those videos back to your website.

The Bottom Line

Video marketing can be an important component of your web marketing strategy, and YouTube is the primary site to distribute your web videos. What's nice about marketing on YouTube is that you don't to spend a ton of money producing your videos; most YouTube videos are produced using common consumer video equipment. You also don't have to pay YouTube to host and serve your videos; it's a free service, for all involved.

YouTube videos should not be blatant advertisements; they need to deliver a more subtle message, like infomercials. Viewers like to be either informed, educated, or entertained, so make sure your videos serve at least one of these functions.

To get your video noticed on the YouTube site, consider advertising it via YouTube's Promoted Videos program. This is contextual PPC advertising, similar to what Google offers through its AdWords program. You should also optimize your videos' accompanying text and tags (keywords) for search, to achieve higher placement in YouTube's organic search results.

When you advertise a YouTube video, you can place a Call-to-Action Overlay on top of the video during playback. This overlay can link back to your normal website, and is the only way to link outside of the YouTube site.

GOING VIRAL

The most successful YouTube videos are those that go *viral*. A viral video is one that becomes hugely popular, with hundreds of thousands or even millions of views, via Internet-based sharing. That is, a viewer finds a video that he likes and then shares it with his friends, either on the YouTube site or via email or social media, such as Facebook and Twitter.

Viral videos are seldom the most practical ones. Instead, it's the entertaining or humorous videos that go big time. And by big time, I mean really big; the most viral of viral videos quickly move off YouTube and get picked up by traditional media. That's exposure with a capital E, and you can't buy it; it has to come organically.

Because of this potential for huge exposure, many companies aim for creating videos that go viral. While having a video that garners millions of viewers might be good for the ego (and perhaps necessary to build a huge brand like Budweiser), that might not be the most appropriate goal for the average web marketer. For most companies, attracting a thousand targeted customers is both more profitable and more realistic than getting viewed by a million strangers with no intention of ever purchasing anything from you.

So while striving for viral status might be appealing, it's probably not the best strategy for most marketers. (It's also very difficult to do; the most embarrassing videos are those that strive to be virally entertaining and instead fall flat on their faces.) Instead of shooting for the moon with a video that might be entertaining to a broad demographic, focus on creating a video that appeals to your target audience. That's the way you achieve YouTube success in a low-key fashion.

Tracking Multimedia Marketing Performance

Companies that embrace multimedia marketing online often find that they get a big bang for their buck; the investment is typically minimal, so any response you get puts you in the plus column.

That said, you do need to track the performance of your podcasts and videos. Just what should you be looking for—and how?

Tracking Podcast Performance

Tracking the performance of your podcasts is a two-fold process. You should track the individual downloads of each podcast episode, as well as the overall number of subscriptions you get for the podcast feed.

Tracking Subscriptions

Let's start with feed tracking. Assuming that your podcast is distributed via multiple channels (your website, the iTunes Store, and so forth), you end up with multiple points where the consumer can subscribe. Ideally, you want to track the total number of subscriptions, as well as where those subscriptions originated—that is, which sites were the best sources for new subscribers.

Feed tracking is typically done through a feed subscription service, such as FeedBurner (feedburner.google.com). However, you probably won't be able to get detailed information about where subscriptions originated; aggregate numbers are more the norm.

If you want data about where subscriptions are generated, you can rely on reporting from third-party sites like the iTunes Store. You should also, of course, track clicks on the "subscribe to this feed" link on your own website. Or you can subscribe to a third-party feed monitoring service, such as Pheedo (www.pheedo.com), which will provide all manner of metrics from subscriber count to interaction and engagement.

Tracking subscribers is important because this tells you how many people found a podcast interesting or useful enough to hear more. A growing subscriber list means you're doing something right.

Tracking Downloads

You can also track the performance of individual podcast episodes. Episodes downloaded from your website can be easily tracked as part of your normal web analytics efforts.

The problem with this is that more podcasts are downloaded than listened to. That is, many RSS feed readers will automatically download a podcast's audio file to the user's computer or portable audio player and put that episode in a queue for future listening. That's the file download from your site you can measure. But you have no way of knowing whether a particular subscriber actually listened to that episode or not. That's a hole in podcast tracking, and I've yet to see an effective workaround for it.

In any case, you can work with the data you have. Tracking downloads for each episode lets you see which topics are attracting the most listener interest, at least on a relative basis. Find an episode with an exceptionally large number of downloads, and you know you've touched a nerve somewhere.

Tracking Call to Action

Assuming that your podcast includes some sort of call to action—the mention of your company website or toll-free phone number, a link to a product page, or the like—you can and should track that call to action. That means trying to track traffic to your website, or to a particular page on your site, generated from the podcast.

When it comes to website tracking, this isn't always easy to do. You're asking audio listeners to remember and then manually enter the URL you give them, and you can't track where manually entered URLs come from; that is, you can't isolate manual entry from those who listened to your podcast. You can make your job easier by mentioning a specific landing page URL in your podcast, but that's a longer URL that's going to be more difficult for listeners to remember. Like I said, this sort of tracking isn't necessarily easy to do.

Another approach is to create a special offer just for your podcast listeners. Any customer taking advantage of this podcast-only offer—for a discounted product, or free information, or whatever—is one tick in the plus column for your podcast.

Tracking phone responses is easier, of course, especially if you have a dedicated number for your podcast listeners. Track calls to this dedicated number to measure effectiveness.

Tracking Video Performance

Fortunately, it's a lot easier to track video performance than it is podcast performance—at least when it comes to YouTube videos. That's because YouTube provides its own quite sophisticated tracking tool, which tells you not only how many times a video has been viewed but also who is doing the viewing.

Tracking Views

YouTube calls its tracking tool Insight and puts some of the most important metrics right on the video viewing page. The most important of these is the *views* number—literally, how many times your video was viewed. This number appears directly beneath the video player on the video page.

Click the down-arrow next to the Views metric and you see the Insight panel for that video. This panel displays some very basic performance metrics, including views over time and with whom the video is most popular, in terms of age and gender.

When it comes to judging this basic performance, how many views is a good number? That's hard to say. Certainly, if your video gets a million views overnight, you're doing something right—that's pure viral status. But for certain types of videos and businesses, a total of 100 views might be good. (For example, if you're selling high-priced real estate.) You have to judge performance based on your own parameters and with realistic expectations.

In my mind, however, raw views is a false measurement. Just because your video has a lot of viewers doesn't mean it has accomplished the goals you set out to achieve. A video with 100,000 views is nice, but it means nothing if you wanted to boost your sales and it didn't do that. Entertaining YouTube viewers is one thing; generating sales (or establishing brand image and so on) is quite another.

note It's particularly useful to compare views for all the videos in your library. While raw numbers might not tell you much, comparative numbers will tell you which of your videos are performing best—which might need to be replaced.

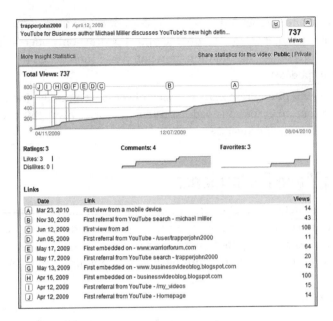

FIGURE 37.1

Viewing basic performance statistics about a YouTube video.

Tracking Demographics

If you want more detailed performance metrics, open the Insight page for a given video. This is accessed via your main video upload list; click Insight next to the video you want to analyze.

The Insight page features six individual tabs, each focusing on a particular type of data. These tabs include

- **Views**—This tab displays total views over time; you can also filter results by region or time frame.

- **Discovery**—This tab analyzes how viewers found the video—linked from other videos, searched for on the YouTube site (and with what keywords), external links, and the like.

- **Demographics**—This tab tells you the age and gender breakdown of the video's audience.

> **note** YouTube's view count data includes views of the video on the YouTube site as well as views from other sites on which the video is embedded.

■ **Community**—This tab measures so-called community engagements—ratings, comments, and number of times your video was chosen as a viewer favorite.

■ **Hot Spots**—This is an interesting one, analyzing how popular your video is over the course of the video—that is, at what point(s) viewers lose interest while watching.

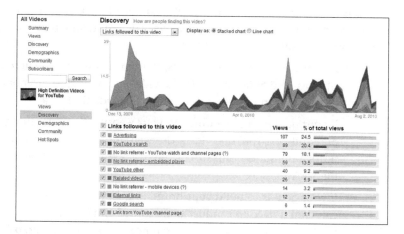

FIGURE 37.2
Viewing more detailed YouTube performance data.

Of all these more advanced metrics, I think Discovery may be the most important. It's key to determine how viewers find your videos. Until you know this information, it's impossible to determine how to promote your YouTube videos.

For example, if you find that the majority of viewers discover a video by searching on YouTube, you know that you need to optimize future videos for search. In this instance, you're further empowered by Insight's listing of what keywords were searched for; with this knowledge in hand, you can make sure to include the most popular keywords in the descriptions of subsequent YouTube videos.

Alternately, you can use the Discovery tool to determine why a particular video performs less well than others. Look at how viewers did (or more important, didn't) find a less-viewed video, and you'll find out areas where you need to improve. If, for example, a video didn't pull well via search, then you know that you need to pay more attention to keywords in future video descriptions.

The key is to determine how viewers find out about your videos—and then exploit that information.

Tracking Conversions

The final way to measure video success is to determine what kind of response you want. Is the video designed to generate direct sales, either via your website or 800-number? Is the video designed to drive traffic to your website? Is the video designed to enhance or reinforce your company or brand image? Or is the video designed to reduce customer or technical support costs?

This is key: To measure the success of your YouTube video, you have to first determine what it is you hope to achieve. Then, and only then, can you measure the results:

- If your goal is to generate sales, then measure sales. Include your website URL and 800-number in the video, along with a promotion or order code, and then track sales that include that code.

- If your goal is to drive traffic to your website, then measure your traffic pre- and post-YouTube video. Use web analytics to determine where site traffic originates from; specifically track traffic that came directly from the YouTube site.

- If your goal is to build your brand image, measurement is more difficult. You'll need to conduct some sort of market research after your YouTube campaign has had a chance to do its thing and ask customers what they think of your brand—and where they heard about it.

- If your goal is to reduce customer or technical support costs, measure the number of support requests before and after uploading the YouTube video(s). The more effective the video, the lower the subsequent calls for support.

You get the point. Know what you want to achieve and then measure that metric. You might find that a video that outperforms its siblings in terms of views doesn't actually deliver the conversions you were seeking—or vice versa.

The Bottom Line

It isn't always easy to track the effectiveness of your multimedia marketing, as it doesn't necessarily lead directly to your website for fulfillment. This is especially true with podcasts, which have no web links. Instead, with podcasts, you have to track subscriptions and downloads, to get a sense of how many people are listening.

For video marketing, YouTube offers a good selection of tools to monitor the performance of your company's videos. You can track video views, analyze the demographics of your viewers, and even track conversions on your website. It's easy to get a good feel for how effective your videos really are.

TRACKING INTERACTIVITY

One measure of a video's effectiveness is how well it involves viewers— that is, how viewers interact with the video. The level of interaction can be deduced by the number of comments and video responses left by viewers; the more viewers that are drawn into the video, the more viewers who will leave personal comments and responses.

Think of it this way. If your video is just light entertainment, viewers will likely not be inspired to leave comments. If, on the other hand, your video has proven particularly useful or educational, then viewers will be more likely to leave comments to that effect. The more comments you get, the better the video is in involving the viewer.

On a meta level, you can track the effectiveness of your all your videos in total by noting the number of subscribers you get to your YouTube channel. If your videos connect with viewers, they're more likely to subscribe to your channel to get notice of future videos. If your videos are less effective, viewers are less likely to subscribe.

37

Understanding Mobile Marketing

The future of the Internet is in the palm of your hand. Literally. Many experts, me included, believe that the next wave of web marketing is actually mobile marketing—marketing to consumers who access the Internet from their smartphones and other mobile devices.

Why is this? It's simple. The Internet is becoming less and less of a computer-specific activity; more and more people are accessing the Internet from other types of devices. As a personal example, I'm an iPhone user, and I use my iPhone several times a day to log onto the Internet and browse one or another websites. It doesn't matter to me whether I'm using my computer or my iPhone—I'm still doing the same web-related stuff.

As a web marketer, then, you need to recognize this shift away from computers to mobile devices in terms of Internet access. That means reconfiguring your marketing tools to work with mobile devices and adjusting your web marketing plan to better target mobile consumers.

What Is Mobile Marketing—and Why Is It Important?

Mobile marketing is relatively easy to define and just as easy to understand. Put simply, it's marketing on or with a mobile device, such as a mobile phone. If you want a fancier definition, try this one from the Mobile Marketing Association:

> Mobile Marketing is a set of practices that enables organizations to communicate and engage with their audience in an interactive and relevant manner through any mobile device or network.

Simple enough explanation, but what exactly does it mean?

Mobile Marketing in the Real World

For all practical purposes, mobile marketing today takes place on mobile phones. Yes, there are other mobile devices you can market to, such as Apple's iPad, but it's the lowly cell phone that is most used by consumers today.

By the way, note that I said "cell phone," not the more restrictive "smartphone." That's because any phone that can send and receive text messages is ripe for mobile marketing via text message. That's right, mobile marketing isn't limited to web-based activities; it can be done via text message, as well.

That said, we're going to focus our attention on web-related mobile marketing. (The title of this book is *The Ultimate Web Marketing Guide*, after all.) Mobile marketing via text message, then, becomes an interesting component of your overall marketing plan that you probably want to examine in more depth.

Focusing on web-related mobile marketing leads us to those consumers who own mobile phones that can connect to the Internet. These include smartphones, such as the iPhone, Android, and Blackberry, but also any cell phone with a built-in web browser and a means to connect to the Web. That's a large and growing segment of the marketplace.

Web-based mobile marketing, then, targets those activities you engage in that reach cell phone users over the mobile Web. These activities include

- **Mobile website**—That is, the mobile version of your company website. (You do have a mobile website, don't you?)

- **Mobile advertising**—These are ads you purchase on mobile websites—ads specially formatted for the mobile screen and targeted to mobile customers. Most mobile advertising, as with most web advertising, is of the PPC nature.

- **Mobile search**—This is similar to traditional web-based search marketing, but fine-tuned for users searching from their mobile phones. (The fine-tuning has a lot to do with location, as mobile searchers tend to search for local businesses while they're on the go.)

- **Mobile applications**—This is exclusively for smartphone users, specifically for users of the iPhone and Android phones. Users can install small applications on their devices; businesses are increasingly creating apps to serve their customers and promote their brands.

- **Mobile email**—Smartphone users can receive email on their devices; mobile marketers are learning to take advantage of this opportunity.

■ **Mobile social networking**—More and more Facebook and Twitter users are accessing their social networks from their mobile phones. Again, savvy mobile marketers are exploiting this new usage model.

There are probably more types of mobile marketing being experimented with than I mentioned here. But it's okay; mobile marketing is a relatively new medium for marketers, and we're all feeling our way.

Mobile Marketing: Big and Getting Bigger

So why all this attention on mobile marketing? It's because mobile Web use is fast gaining on traditional computer-based Web use. If web marketing is your thing, you have to reach consumers no matter which types of devices they use to access the Web—but then take advantage of the unique features of each device.

Let's start with some statistics. At the beginning of 2010, there are more than 4.7 billion subscribers to cellular telephone services worldwide, with 285 million of these people in the U.S;[1] fully 91% of all Americans had a cellphone subscription (as of year-end 2008). There are 1.2 billion new mobile phones sold each year, which makes it the fastest-selling item in the entire consumer electronics industry.

These raw numbers dwarf those of the personal computer industry, but it gets even more interesting when you drill down to look at mobile Internet usage. Research finds that 35% of all mobile phone users have used their phones to access the Internet;[2] that's more than a billion people worldwide and more than a hundred thousand in the U.S alone.

And these mobile users are spending money. In 2009, $1.6 billion in purchases were made from mobile devices.[3] That's big money, folks, and reason enough for most companies to embrace the mobile Web.

It should come as no surprise, then, that mobile marketing is projected to become one of the fastest-growing areas of web marketing, second only to social media marketing.[4] You can't dismiss hundreds of millions of potential customers; indeed, you want to reach Internet users no matter how they connect to the Web. A mobile phone is just another gateway to your web content.

38

---

1. Plunkett Research, Ltd.
2. Pew Research Center, "Internet, Broadband, and Cell Phone Statistics," 2009.
3. ABI Research, "Mobile Money Services and Contactless Payment Forecasts," 2009.
4. Forester Research, "U.S. Interactive Marketing Forecast, 2009 to 2014," July 2009.

It's more than just the numbers, however. Unlike connecting to the Web via computer, which can only be done while a customer is setting in front of his or her PC, a customer can connect to the Web via mobile phone anytime and anywhere. People always have their phones with them; this gives you nonstop connectivity to your customers.

The mobile Web also lets you use access location-based information about your customers. That's a nice demographic touch, being able to target customers based on location. It lets you provide more contextual information to your customers—information about shoes if they're in a shoe store, for example, or promotions for frozen food if they're in a grocery store. It's narrowcasting, as opposed to mass marketing, which should generate more effective results.

All this adds up to a channel that you can't ignore and that has some distinct advantages to savvy marketers.

How Mobile Marketing Differs from Traditional Web Marketing

What makes mobile marketing different from traditional web marketing? It's all about the size of the presentation—and the local nature of the message.

Marketing for a Smaller Screen

Let's talk size first. When it comes to mobile marketing, bigger is not better. In fact, small is all—as in, adapting your marketing to the small size of the cell phone screen.

Most web marketing is designed with traditional web browsers and the computer screen in mind. Web pages keep getting wider and wider to fill the space on widescreen monitors; we employ banner ads and full-screen graphics and fill every inch of screen space available.

That is not the tack to take with mobile marketing. What works on the big computer screen is totally useless on the small screen of a typical mobile phone. You don't have much width, you don't even have much depth if you want to avoid scrolling. Your visual message needs to be simplified and smallerized, pure and simple.

You also have to make sure your images and text are visible on the small screen. You might be surprised how small and downright unreadable some of the items you currently employ are when viewed on a mobile device. It may look fine on a 19" monitor running at 1280 x 768 pixel resolution but appear ant-like on a mobile device with a 3.5″ screen running at 240 x 320 resolution.

Then there's screen orientation. You're used to computer displays that are wider than they're tall (landscape orientation). Most cell phones displays are in a portrait orientation, taller than they're wide.

All this requires a rethinking of your visual presentation. You need to present less information on a smaller screen. It's a challenge.

Target Marketing

The information you do present needs to be tailored to the mobile market. Mobile users, while they have their phones with them all the time, aren't constantly connected as are computer users; they connect to the Internet on an as-needed basis. Your ability to communicate with them, then, depends more on them reaching out to you than the other way around.

This isn't necessarily a bad thing. When you think local marketing, think target marketing, not mass marketing. Instead of broadcasting a promotional message to thousands or hundreds of thousands of people, most of whom are wholly uninterested in what you have to say, you can send out a very targeted message to those few mobile customers who are interested in what you're promoting.

That's in part due to the local nature of mobile computing. You see, people use their mobile devices to get the information they need while they're on the go. Quite often, this information is locality-based—where's the nearest coffee shop, which store has the lowest prices, how do I get from here to there, that sort of thing. That makes mobile marketing synonymous with local marketing.

So if you have a local business, mobile marketing is the way to go. Optimize your mobile website for local search in order to rank high when local consumers search for what you're selling. Place PPC ads that are triggered in select locales only. Reach out to local mobile users with targeted email campaigns. It's an ideal situation for local businesses—even those small businesses that haven't exploited web marketing in the past.

And even if your business is more global, you can still reach out to local consumers with products and services of specific interest to people in a given location. For example, if you sell home improvement products, you can promote seeds and plants that are best for a given geographic region. If you sell athletic apparel, promote Peyton Manning jerseys to customers in Indiana and

Lebron James jerseys to customers in Miami. If you're an automobile manufacturer, push convertibles in Southern California and four-wheel drive vehicles in Minnesota. Targeted marketing is the key.

Exploiting Mobile Search

The targeted nature of mobile marketing is most apparent in the field of mobile search. Mobile search, of course, is traditional web searching conducted on mobile phones—which makes the whole process just a tad different.

One difference between mobile and traditional search is the importance of high search result rankings. Google and other search engines typically display ten results on a web search results page; you can appear anywhere in the top ten and still get a decent click-through rate. Mobile search results pages aren't that long, however; on some devices, you might only see three or four results on a screen. That makes it much more important to rank at the very top in terms of search results; lower rankings will get relegated to a subsidiary screen, with the resultant decrease in visibility and click-throughs.

The other big difference is the local nature of mobile searching. As previously noted, much mobile searching is for local businesses and events—movie times, nearby restaurants, local retailers, and the like. You need to take advantage of this by optimizing your mobile website for this mobile/local search.

How do you optimize your site for local search? We discussed this earlier in the book, but in general you need to come up with keywords that help identify the location of your business. That can include any or all of the following:

- Your store address
- Street name
- City name
- State name
- ZIP code, and nearby ZIP codes
- Neighborhood
- Region or regional nicknames—"Tri-State Region" or "Silicone Valley," for example
- Native nicknames—"Garden State," "Sunshine State," and so forth

note Learn more about SEO for local search in Chapter 12, "Advanced SEO Techniques."

Add these local keywords to your regular list of keywords and mobile customers will be able to find you when they're searching locally. This should move your site nearer the top of mobile search results pages.

Developing a Mobile Marketing Strategy

Knowing how important mobile marketing may be to your business, you need to develop a mobile marketing strategy in conjunction with your overall web marketing plan. As with all components of your larger marketing strategy, your mobile marketing strategy needs to work within your global initiatives and fully exploit the unique opportunities of the mobile medium.

First, make sure that you promote your mobile-specific initiatives in your other media. So, for example, if you have a mobile number for text messages and the like, display that number in your print ads, online ads, blog, website, press releases, and the like.

Next, determine just which components of mobile marketing you want to utilize. Mobile/local SEO is a must, especially if you have a mobile website and look to promote locally. But you can also include mobile ads, mobile email marketing, text messaging marketing, and the like. Each type of mobile marketing has its own plusses and minuses and works best in specific situations.

> **note** Of course, mobile marketing may not be important to your particular type of business, in which case you don't have to plan or budget much for it at all. Mobile marketing is particularly important to local businesses, or to those businesses that have a local component. It's less important to B2B companies, companies purely interested in brand building, and companies selling extremely high ticket products and services.

When it comes to devising specific mobile marketing initiatives, remember to keep it simple. The mobile screen is smaller, and people don't spend the same amount of time online as they do when using computers. As such, simple messages work better; promote a single idea with a distinct call to action.

Finally, how much of your budget should you devote to mobile marketing? This is a more challenging question to answer, as every situation is different. But starting out, I'd recommend allocating 2%–5% of your total marketing budget to mobile initiatives; this should be enough to get things off the ground. (And don't forget to budget for mobile/local SEO for your mobile website.)

The Bottom Line

Mobile marketing is any marketing you do via cell phones and other mobile devices. This includes mobile websites, mobile advertising, mobile search, mobile applications, mobile email, mobile social marketing, and marketing via text messages. As more and more users connect to the Internet via mobile devices, mobile marketing is becoming an increasingly important part of companies' online marketing mix.

Successful mobile marketing adjusts the marketer's message for the smaller mobile screen. It also targets users on the go; in this regard, mobile marketing is very much local marketing.

MOBILE MARKETING VIA TEXT MESSAGES

Mobile marketing isn't exclusively web-related. You can also utilize text messaging as a component of your mobile marketing strategy.

The advantage of using text messaging is that more cell phone users have access to text messaging than they do to the Internet. In fact, text messaging is fairly ubiquitous today, which makes it an ideal way to reach a broad swath of consumers.

Because of this, text message marketing one of the most popular forms of marketing activities today. This is especially so in Europe, where several hundred million marketing text messages are sent each month. It's not quite as big a deal in the U.S., which has been slower to embrace texting in general, but it's still something to consider.

Text message marketing typically starts by you encouraging customers to send you a short text message. Maybe they text you to participate in a contest or to vote in some sort of competition. You get the idea.

Whatever the motivation, this activity provides you with your customers' cell phone numbers, which you can then use (with their permission, of course; text message marketing is opt-in marketing) to send them text messages in the future. You can send out texts announcing new products, upcoming promotions, you name it. You can even send MMS messages, which incorporate both text and images, which may be more appealing to visually-oriented marketers.

There's lots of room for creativity in text message marketing. For example, you might encourage customers to text you photos they take at an event you host or text when they see an instance of your product in use. You can then use these photos or texts to feed other marketing vehicles, such as your blog or Twitter feeds. It's all interconnected if you do it right.

39

Designing a Mobile-Friendly Website

The centerpiece of your mobile marketing strategy is a mobile website—that is, a version of your website optimized for viewing on cell phones and other mobile devices.

What makes a mobile website different from a regular website? Do you really need two different websites? And how do you go about designing a mobile-friendly website? Those are the questions answered in this chapter.

Why You Need a Mobile Website

With an increasing number of consumers accessing the Web from mobile devices instead of computers, having a version of your website that works with these devices is fast becoming imperative for most businesses. You can't just assume that your current website will look good on a mobile phone; most sites simply aren't designed for small cellphone screens.

Take a test. Grab the nearest web-enabled mobile phone, fire up the web browser, and browse to your normal website. How's it look? Not too good, probably; the home page is probably too wide and the elements too small to view comfortably. What fits comfortably on a big computer screen is overkill on a mobile screen. (And if your boss questions why you need to spend the money on a mobile site, hand him your cell phone to perform this same test.)

It's not just about looks, either. Website functionality needs to be different—simplified, actually—for mobile users. That's because it's more difficult to navigate a website on a cellphone than it is on a computer; you don't have a mouse to move around with. For that reason, a mobile website has to be navigable with fewer clicks than a traditional site.

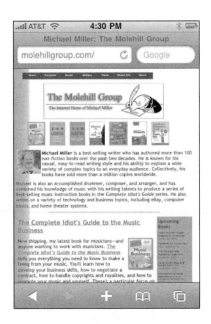

FIGURE 39.1
The author's website viewed on an iPhone—too many small elements for the mobile screen.

Speaking of functionality, know that some mobile web browsers do not display some technologies well or at all. As a prominent example, Apple's Safari browser, used on the popular iPhone, is not compatible with Flash media. If you have any Flash elements on your page, they simply won't display on an iPhone. That's a big ouch.

If you want to play on the mobile Web, then, you have to have a website that works with cell phones and other mobile devices. And playing in the mobile marketplace is fast becoming a necessity; it's estimated that mobile web usage will surpass PC-based access by 2013.[1] As a marketer, you should be somewhat indifferent as to how consumers access your web content—but you do have to make sure your content works with all devices that can access it.

note One alternative to a mobile website, at least on the iPhone and Android phones, is a mobile application that parses your content for those particular devices. Learn more about smartphone applications in Chapter 41, "Marketing via Mobile Apps."

---

1. Gartner, Inc., "Gartner's Top Predictions for IT Organizations and Users, 2010 and Beyond: A New Balance," 2010.

That said, a surprisingly low number of sites today are optimized for mobile use. Only 12% of the top 500 web retailers currently have mobile websites.[2] While this number is growing, it still provides a competitive advantage for those sites that jump on the mobile bandwagon.

Creating a Mobile Website

The good news is that it's relatively easy to create a mobile-friendly version of your website. Your IT guys should have the tools or be able to readily obtain the tools to do the job.

What do you need to do to create a great-looking and fully functional mobile website? Here are some of the elements to keep in mind.

Reduce the Number of Elements

Designing a mobile website is all about simplifying. The first thing you should simplify is the number of elements on a page. The typical cell phone screen is only so large; you can only fit a limited number of items on the screen and have them big enough to be visible.

To this end, you need to reduce the number of elements that appear on the screen at one time. Instead of displaying a dozen different elements, opt for a half dozen or fewer. It's a matter of what can fit in the limited space, and choosing those elements that are most important.

Consider, as an example, Target's home page. On the regular Web, Target presents a horizontal navigation menu that stretches the full width of the browser window, more navigation down the left side of the page, a big Flash-animated promotional graphic in the middle of the page, more product specials below that, and even more below that.

On its mobile page, however, Target simplifies things immensely. The mobile site presents a short list of important

> **note** When you're reducing the number of elements you present on your mobile site, make sure you prioritize those elements that remain. Browsing through pages on a mobile site can be quite time consuming; make sure users see the most important content at the top of the first page.

---

2. Acquity Group, "Mobile Commerce Audit 2010," 2010.

navigational categories, from Browse Products and Find a Store to Coupons and GiftCards. It's what customers need to find and nothing more.

FIGURE 39.2

Target's home page for the traditional Web.

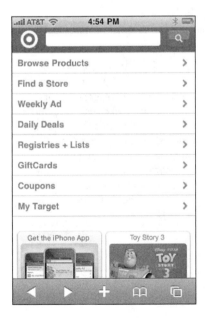

FIGURE 39.3

Target's mobile home page—simplified for mobile screens.

Add a Search Box

When you limit the content you present on your mobile page, you reduce the number of navigational avenues into your site. Because there are fewer navigation options, it's important to provide a way for users to find specific content. That argues for a site search box, placed prominently on the home page. You have to give customers a way to find what they're looking for, no matter what.

Orientation Matters

Pages on the traditional web have a landscape orientation with horizontal menu bars, as users typically have widescreen computer monitors. Cell phone screens, however, are more portrait or vertically oriented. This means you need to reorient your web pages to fit the format of the mobile screen.

Take, for example, Crutchfield's traditional home page. It has a lot of different elements, and the elements are organized to fit on a widescreen computer monitor; it's definitely a landscape orientation.

Compare that to the company's mobile page. In addition to reducing the number of elements presented, those items are presented in a vertical list to match the vertical nature of the mobile phone screen.

FIGURE 39.4

Crutchfield's traditional home page—horizontal content for widescreen viewing.

FIGURE 39.5

Crutchfield's mobile home page—fewer elements, arranged vertically.

Use Smaller Images, Fewer Images, or No Images at All

Here's something else about really good mobile websites—they don't use a lot of graphics. Space is at a premium, and you can't waste it with superfluous images. In most instances, you can present content more efficiently in text than in pictures; let that drive your mobile page design.

Compare the use of images on Victoria's Secret's regular website with that on its mobile site. The regular website is filled to overflowing with sexy photos, as you might suspect, while the mobile site offers just a single banner image before it gets straight to category navigation. This approach puts more content on the smaller screen, which makes navigation much easier for mobile users.

Using text instead of images also affects the download time for your mobile pages. Mobile web access is typically slower than you get on a computer-based connection; everything takes longer on the mobile Web. Keep this in mind and reduce the number of large elements that take a long time to download—don't make visitors suffer through an interminable download just to look at a pretty picture.

FIGURE 39.6
Victoria Secret's normal home page, full of product images.

FIGURE 39.7
Victoria Secret's mobile site; text is more important than images.

Keep It Small

With cellular data network speeds in mind (and knowing that even 3G networks aren't always speedy), you need to work hard on keeping the file size for the entire page as small as possible. You want to aim for a maximum page file size of 20KB. Smaller is better.

Add a Little White Space

When designing for the mobile screen, it's tempting to try to cram as many elements as possible into the smaller space. Resist the temptation. White space is an important element of any page design, and even more so for small screens. Too much stuff in a small space is both visually unappealing and difficult to navigate. The admonition to keep it simple applies to design as well as content.

Don't Do Tables

If you use tables on your main website, ditch them for your mobile site. Tables simply don't display well on mobile devices; if a table is too wide (which it probably is), it throws off the entire page.

Consider Color Contrast

Getting into the design side of things, know that not all mobile devices have great screens. (The iPhone shines here, but not every phone is an iPhone.) Some devices simply don't reproduce color well; some devices don't even have color screens. To that end, pay attention to the contrast on your page and make sure the text color is in sharp contrast to the background color. And when in doubt, remember that good old black text on a white background works best.

Minimize Text Entry

If you require a lot of customer interaction on your site, rethink how you get visitor input. Put simply, it's difficult to enter text on a mobile phone; you have to click here and press there and then tap an onscreen keyboard multiple times just to record a single letter. Consider accepting input via simple radio buttons or lists that visitors can select from. Require as few input keystrokes as possible.

Design for Multiple Phones

When designing a mobile website, it's tempting to focus your mobile efforts on Apple's iPhone, as it so dominates the consumer smartphone market. But the iPhone isn't the only web-enabled phone on the market; in fact, it only has a 28% share of the smartphone market, let alone the market for all web-enabled phones. If you focus on the iPhone exclusively, you'll be ignoring more than three-quarters of the potential mobile market.

This leads to the pain of making sure your site can be displayed at a variety of screen sizes, shapes, and resolutions. Some mobile screens are tall and skinny, some are short and long, some are perfectly square. And resolution varies from 128 x 160 all the way to the iPhone 4's 960 x 640 pixels. It's tough to make a single site look good on all these different displays.

note While the iPhone represents less than a third of all smartphones in use today, it accounts for close to two-thirds (65%) of all mobile web browsing, according to NetMarketShare.

The best solution, then, is probably to keep your mobile site as clean and simple as possible, to maximize the viewing experience across multiple mobile platforms. Alternatively, you can design one site for iPhones and another for other mobile devices. In any case, you have to take multiple phones into account.

Think Like the Customer

My final word of advice for designing an effective mobile website is one you've heard throughout this book. When it comes to determining what you put on a mobile page, you need to *think like the customer*. The goal is to know what your customers are looking for on your mobile site and then present that content in an easy-to-find fashion.

This is important for any website, of course, but more so for a mobile site, where you don't have a lot of screen real estate to work with. You can't present multiple tunnels into your content; you have to determine the one best way and present it front and center. That means knowing, not guessing, what the mobile customer deems important. If it's not there on that first small page, the customer won't stick around to hunt for it.

In addition, know that the mobile web surfer is more time constrained than the user sitting in front of a computer screen in his home or office. Mobile

39

users are, most often, *mobile*—that is, they're accessing the Web while they're on the go. They need to get their information quickly so they can get on with whatever it is else they're doing. (Like driving their cars or walking down the street...) They're surfing in a very directed fashion. Don't make them work for that information; give them what they need as quickly as possible.

Options: How to Host Your Mobile Site

When creating a mobile version of your website, you also have to determine exactly how that site is hosted and accessed. That is, do you want to give the mobile site its own domain name, have it reside on a subdomain on your main domain, or have it in its own subfolder on your main site? There are pros and cons to each approach.

Create a New Domain

Your first option is to create a completely new domain for your mobile site. For example, if the domain for your main site is www.yourwebsite.com, you might register the www.yourwebsite-mobile.com domain for your mobile site.

While some companies seem to like the idea of having a separate domain for their mobile sites, I've not found this the best option. Frankly, I—and most users—find this confusing. You're now trying to identify two different sites with your single brand. How many people, after all, will remember two different URLs and know when to use which?

Bottom line, while using a separate domain is possible, it's not recommended.

Use the .mobi Domain

If you want to kind of sort of keep your same domain (the *yourwebsite* part of www.yourwebite.com), consider using the same domain but with a different top-level domain. You now have available the .mobi (for "mobile") top-level domain, which you can attach to your regular domain. So you could register www.yourwebsite.mobi, continuing our example.

That said, the .mobi top-level domain isn't widely used, and you probably can't expect your customers to remember it. I find this option not much more attractive than using a separate domain.

Use a Subdomain

A better option might be to use a separate subdomain from your main domain. By this, I mean putting something other than *www.* in front of your domain name. The best examples of this are m.yourwebsite.com and mobile.yourwebsite.com.

> **note** The tech guys tell me that the subdomain option is also the easiest to set up. I know it's the cheapest, as there are no new domains to register.

This option keeps your mobile site part of your online brand without creating unnecessary confusion. It's also becoming somewhat standard, so it's something consumers are becoming accustomed to seeing. This is the option I recommend for most companies.

Use a Subfolder on Your Main Domain

A slightly different option to using a subdomain is to put your mobile website in a subfolder under your main domain. For example, you might establish your mobile site at www.yourwebsite.com/mobile/. This is less common than using the m. or mobile. subdomains, but has the same practical effect.

Utilize Server Agent Detection

Finally, you should consider letting your server serve the appropriate page based on the device accessing your site. That is, instead of forcing the user to enter a different URL for your mobile site, you use what is called *user agent detection* to determine what type of device is accessing your site. When your server determines that a mobile device is being used, it serves your mobile page instead of your normal page.

This is a nice technical solution to the whole mobile server/branding issue. It's particularly elegant from the users' point of view, as they don't have to do anything special; they enter your normal URL and get served your mobile page if they're using a mobile device.

Unfortunately, this approach doesn't always work because there are, as you might suspect, technical issues with using user agent detection. Most specifically, the technology doesn't always detect the proper device, which can be a bit embarrassing. In addition, with this option the user can't switch from the mobile version of your site to view the full version; there's only one URL involved, and manual override isn't one of the options.

39

Still, you probably should discuss this option with your tech team and see what they recommend. Done right, it certainly makes life easier for your customers.

The Bottom Line

To best reach a mobile audience, you need to develop a version of your website that works and displays well on mobile devices. That means simplifying the site, reducing the number of elements, orienting the page in portrait (rather than landscape) fashion, using smaller or no images, improving page contrast, minimizing user entry, and such.

It also means deciding how best to host the mobile site. Most common today is hosting the mobile site as a subdomain on the main website—m.mywebsite.com, for example. You may also want to consider employing user agent detection to direct mobile users to your mobile site, with no input needed on their part.

WHY A SINGLE SITE WON'T WORK

There is another serving/hosting option. You could always design a single site for both computer and mobile viewing. With this approach you don't have to worry about different URLs, and you certainly expend a lot less effort in designing the sites.

However, there are tons of issues with what I'll call the lazy marketer's approach, chief of which is that trying to serve two audiences with a single site does both of them an injustice. That is, there's no way to make a site that's ideal for all types of viewing devices.

If you make a full-featured site for traditional computer viewing, it simply won't look good on a mobile device. The orientation will be wrong, it'll be too busy, the elements will be way too small, and you'll undoubtedly use some elements that just won't work on some cell phones.

If, on the other hand, you design a site that plays well with mobile devices, you'll be leaving a lot of content on the table for computer users. Why limit yourself to what content and technology you can use just to appease the mobile segment of your audience? Your traditional site will be at a disadvantage to those competitors who optimize individual sites for both computer and mobile viewing.

An individual site is the right approach. I'm shocked, however, to see the number of big-name sites that don't yet have mobile versions available. That's a big problem but also an opening for more savvy competitors. If you're savvy, you'll invest in a separate mobile version of your site and optimize it for viewing on the most popular mobile devices. Yes, it's more work, but as more and more of your customers access the Web from their iPhones and Androids and Blackberrys, it's work that will pay dividends.

39

40

Advertising on Mobile Devices

Another key component of your mobile marketing strategy is that old standby, advertising. Mobile advertising is a bit different than traditional web advertising, however, because you have size considerations as well as audience considerations to take into account.

That's right, creating effective ads for mobile devices requires yet another set of skills beyond that of normal PPC or online display advertising. That's just the nature of dealing with evolving markets.

How Important Is Mobile Advertising?

Mobile advertising is an increasingly significant part of the overall web marketing mix. Not surprisingly, however, its importance depends to some degree on what type of business you're running.

Does It Work?

If you've never done any mobile advertising, one of your first questions no doubt concerns effectiveness—does this crazy gizmo really work?

Well, according to those who've done it, the answer is yes. Based on a recent survey, 87% of current mobile advertisers say that the medium met or exceeded their expectations.[1] That ain't bad.

---

1. Millennial Media, "State of the Industry: Mobile Advertising," 2010.

In fact, nearly a third (30%) of mobile advertisers say that it has become an indispensible part of their media mix. Another 67% dub mobile advertising "somewhat valuable;" only 2% say it's not valuable at all.

> **note** One nice thing about mobile advertising is that there's typically just one ad displayed per mobile page. That means less direct competition when you get placement on a page.

Who's Doing It?

What types of businesses are more successful with mobile advertising? Why, it's those businesses that are most targeted by mobile phone users. That is, those businesses that on-the-go consumers most frequent—businesses in the travel, restaurant, entertainment, and retail industries. (Consumer packaged goods companies are big spenders on mobile advertising, too.)

So if you rely on customers to find you while they're on the go, mobile advertising makes a lot of sense.

How Much Should You Spend?

If you want to join the mobile advertising bandwagon, how much should you spend? The largest number of mobile advertisers (31%) indicate that they spend between $100,000 and $249,000 a year. There is some competition from larger advertisers, with 15% of all advertisers saying they spend more than $1 million yearly.

Determining What Type of Advertising to Do— and Where to Do It

The mobile Web features both text-only and image ads. Text-only ads are guaranteed to work across all mobile devices, while image ads work only on smartphones that display full images onscreen.

Comparing Text and Image Ads

What does a mobile ad look like? When it comes to text-based ads, they look a lot like normal PPC text ads, but with less copy—just 24 to 36 characters of text, followed by your destination URL.

FIGURE 40.1

A mobile PPC text ad near the bottom of the screen.

A mobile image ad looks even more like a traditional banner ad, but with a very small banner that fits easily on the mobile screen. You have to upload the image for the banner, of course, which then becomes clickable.

Speaking of clickable, you have the option of what you want a click to do. By default, clicking a mobile ad takes the consumer to a landing page on the advertiser's website—one designed for mobile viewing, ideally. But you can also opt to include a "click to call" link in your ad; clicking this link initiates a phone call to a number you specify. This is a great way to connect directly with customers on the go.

note The focus here is on ads displayed on mobile web pages. Another segment of the mobile advertising industry targets advertising delivered via SMS and MMS text messages.

40

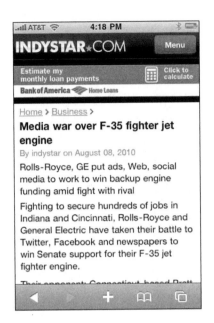

FIGURE 40.2

A mobile image ad near the top of the screen.

Comparing PPC and CPM Ads

As with traditional online advertising, you have your choice of pay-per-click (PPC) or cost-per-thousand (CPM) campaigns. PPC ads are typically keyword-driven; CPM ads on the mobile platform are more like PPC ads in appearance than typical display ads, if only because of the screen space involved.

Not surprisingly, most mobile advertisers today go the PPC route. It's what advertisers are most familiar with, and it has the advantage of being very much a "pay for play" type of approach; you only pay when you get results.

Choosing a Mobile Advertising Network

Also not surprisingly, one of the more popular mobile PPC ad networks today is Google AdWords. With AdWords, you create mobile ads the same way you create traditional PPC ads; your mobile ads are integrated into your other AdWords campaigns.

note AdWords lets you create both text and image ads; it's your choice.

AdWords, however, is not the only mobile advertising network available. (It's not even the largest.) Other popular services include the following:

- AdMob (www.admob.com)
- InMobi (www.inmobi.com)
- Jumptap (www.jumptap.com)
- MADS (www.mads.com)
- Millennial Media (www.millennialmedia.com)
- Mobclix (www.mobclix.com)
- Mojiva (www.mojiva.com)
- Microsoft adCenter (adcenter.microsoft.com)
- Quattro Wireless (www.quattrowireless.com)

> **note** AdMob was recently acquired by Google and will probably be integrated into its AdWords network.

Creating a Mobile Ad

Because mobile ads are so small, there's not much to creating one. For example, if you're using AdWords, you start the ad-creation process by specifying whether you're creating a text or an image ad. If you're building a text ad, you then enter the ad title and description and provide the destination URL. It's pretty much a by-the-book process.

If you choose to create an image ad, you get to determine what size ad you want to create. You can upload an image file in JPG, GIF, or PNG formats, in any of the following sizes: 300 x 50, 216 x 36, 168 x 28, 300 x 75, 216 x 54, 168 x 42, or 192 x 53.

> **note** Use the GIF format if you want animation in your mobile ad.

As there is no standard display size for mobile devices, it's tough to know which image size to use when every device is different. That said, the 300 x 50 pixel size is most common, especially on iPhones and other smartphone devices.

> **note** To test the effectiveness of different cell phone networks, create separate image ads for each carrier and then track the performance of each ad/carrier individually.

When you're creating an image ad, make sure the image is clearly visible on a small mobile screen. Don't get too detailed with fiddly small graphics; big and bold works best, even if you have to limit the number of items you can fit into a small mobile banner.

40

Once you've created your ad, it's a simple matter of selecting on which keywords you want to bid, setting a maximum CPC rate, and entering the ad copy. If you want to create an image ad, you have to upload an appropriately-sized image. That's really all there is to it.

Targeting the Mobile Customer

What should you advertise to mobile customers? The mobile platform is unique in many ways, especially in the immediacy it affords to consumers. They can pick up their phones and find the information they want right now, no matter where they are or what they're doing. Your advertising needs to play to that immediacy.

To that end, I wouldn't recommend using mobile advertising for straight brand or image building. Instead, it's better for more targeted promotions.

Indeed, one of the most appealing features of mobile advertising is the capability of very precise customer targeting. Depending on the ad network you use, you can target ads by any or all of the following characteristics:

- Cellular service (carrier)
- Device type (iPhone, Android, WAP phone, etc.)
- Location
- Age
- Gender
- Usage (how often they use the phone and in what context)

That kind of targeting lets you serve very specific ads to identified consumers. For example, if you run a local auto repair store, you can target your ads to mobile users who live in or near your ZIP code. Or if you're selling a service delivered via an iPhone app, you can target frequent iPhone users.

note You can also embed ads in mobile applications, such as those for the iPhone and Android phones. If you develop your own app, you can place ads for your other products in the app, or sell ad space to third parties; you can also advertise in other companies apps, if they're so inclined. Learn more about these mobile applications in Chapter 41, "Marketing via Mobile Apps."

note For best results in mobile advertising, include a clear-cut call to action, something that makes sense to the targeted mobile user. Invite the user to click to do something useful, or obtain relevant information, or generate some sort of valuable result. Don't just display your name and logo; put the mobile ad space to work.

40

In addition, you can schedule your ads only to run during specific times of the day. You might, for example, want to target commuters using public transportation, who have a bit of time on their hands as they travel to and from work; in this instance, you'd schedule yours ads to run in the pre- and post-work rush hours only.

The key is to use mobile advertising's targeting capabilities to fine-tune both the ads you serve and the people you serve them to. The goal is to achieve a much better match between message and consumer, using the unique features of the mobile medium.

The Bottom Line

Mobile advertising is a bid and apparently effective business. It's particularly useful if you have a local business, product, or service to promote; it can be a very targeted form of advertising.

Mobile ads can be either text- or image-based. Whatever type of ad you create, it's going to be relatively small, like a miniature banner ad on a mobile website. The ad should link back to a landing page on your mobile website, or include a "click to call" feature so consumers can respond directly from their cell phones.

PRIVACY ISSUES WITH MOBILE ADVERTISING

Not everyone likes mobile advertising. As you might suspect, some consumers don't like wasting valuable screen real estate on mobile ads; you can't please all the people all of the time. But a bigger groundswell of opposition concerns the privacy issues inherent with mobile advertising. The very features that make mobile advertising such a targeted opportunity also impinge on consumer's privacy.

You see, in order to target mobile ads by location and demographics, the mobile carrier has to track where specific customers are at any given time, tie that information to their account information, and then pass all that onto the mobile ad network. For some folks, that's getting way too personal. I empathize.

40

The danger, then, is if too many consumers rebel against this constant tracking and argue for better privacy protection or some sort of "do not track" list. In fact, just such a list is being discussed at the FTC. If such a list is implemented, it would apply to mobile advertising based on customer behavior.

The effect of a ban on mobile tracking won't necessarily reduce the number of ads served, however. The more likely unintended consequence will be a reduction in targeted offers and an increase in ads that simply don't make sense to the consumer. Even though tracking may appear to be a bad thing, in terms of privacy, it's a good thing in terms of creating relevant advertising.

Marketing via Mobile Apps

There's another unique way to market your company or your brand to mobile users. Some mobile devices—notably smartphones like the iPhone and Android—are actually mini-computers and run computer-like applications. Many companies are creating their own branded applications for these devices, thus getting their names in front of large numbers of mobile consumers.

Should mobile applications be a component of your mobile marketing mix? If so, what kinds of apps should you be developing? These are questions that all serious mobile marketers need to answer.

What Is a Mobile App—and Why Should You Care?

The latest big thing in web marketing is the mobile application—literally, an application that runs on a mobile phone. The biggest market for mobile apps today is for users of Apple's iPhone and iPad, with users of Android phones also representing a significant opportunity.

A mobile app is a program that a user downloads directly to his mobile device. Most apps are delivered via an "app store," such as Apple's App Store or the Android Market, which is accessed directly from the mobile device.

To give you an idea of how popular mobile apps are today, Apple's App Store hosts more than 250,000 individual applications, from close to 50,000 different publishers. More than 600 new applications are submitted to the App Store every day.

And users are embracing these apps. The average iPhone user has 37 apps installed on his phone; the average Android user, 22 apps; the average Blackberry user, 10 apps.[1] Consumers are projected to spend $6.7 billion on more than 4.5 billion app downloads in 2010, rising to $29.5 billion (on more than 21.6 billion downloads) by 2013.[2] And that's with 82% of all apps being free.

A mobile app typically performs a single duty, or multiple duties within a defined area. For example, the Weather Channel app provides current weather, forecasts, and radar. The Food Network app serves up recipes and videos from the network's television shows. The PianoSharp app turns a user's iPhone into miniature piano keyboard. And the iHandy Level app lets the iPhone function as a virtual level.

Mobile apps are also used by some content providers to access the providers' websites. Accessing a site via a custom-made app is often preferable to accessing via a mobile web browser; the app serves content in a format customized for the given device.

Apps can display advertisements alongside their other content, thus enabling a publisher to promote its website or other products or just generate some revenue by selling the space. Publisher can also use "in-app selling" to sell goods and services from within an application.

Mobile apps can be either free or paid. Free apps predominate, especially when you're using them to promote your brand and products. However, some companies generate a fair amount of revenue by selling paid apps at a buck or two apiece. That's probably not the best promotional approach, however; you'll get a lot more downloads if your app is free.

In fact, the best way to think of a mobile app is as a browser on a mobile device dedicated entirely to your brand or product. Users of your app have just one destination, and that destination is you and your content. It's another way to make a direct connection with your customers.

note If you're interested in adding in-application advertising to your app, or in advertising in someone else's app, the largest mobile app advertising networks are AdMob (www.admob.com), Apple's iAd (advertising.apple.com), and Medialets (www.medialets.com).

---

1. Nielsen, "The State of Mobile Apps," 2010.
2. Gartner, "Application Stores: The Revenue Opportunity Behind the Hype," 2009.

Building an Effective Mobile App

With billions of apps downloaded each year, it sounds like you probably should incorporate mobile apps as part of your mobile/web marketing plan. But what type of app should you do?

Your goal is to develop an app that promotes your brand or product. As such, the app needs to relate to your brand or product and engage potential customers. The app needs to be useful, not just promotional. It can't just be an advertisement; it has to provide real value to users.

That value has to be instantly obvious and sustainable over time. That is, the app needs to be something that people want or need to use on a frequent basis. You need to serve some sort of need, solve a problem, or offer information that customers have on a daily basis. If your app isn't frequently used, it'll be deleted from users' devices.

Popular App Categories

That said, it's not surprising that games are the most popular apps today. (People do like to play their games.) But the number-two category is news/weather, with apps typically provided by local and national news organizations. The third most popular type of app are maps/navigation/search; not surprising, as people are trying to find places while they're on the go. And fourth are social networking apps for those folks tweeting and accessing Facebook on the go.

The most popular app categories, then, in descending order are

- Games (used by 65% of users)
- News/weather (56%)
- Maps/navigation/search (55%)
- Social networking (54%)
- Music (46%)
- Entertainment/food (38%)
- Banking/finance (31%)
- Productivity (30%)
- Sports (30%)

41

Apps for Accessing Your Website

Some of the most popular apps are nothing more than content reformatted for a given mobile device. That is, instead of accessing your local newspaper's mobile website, you open the newspaper's app and read the news there.

This is a popular approach for a number of reasons. First, it provides a more optimized viewing experience for users; you get to format your content so that it looks as good as possible on a given phone. Second, you now have a captive audience, at least while your app is open; they stay on your site without being tempted to browse elsewhere. Third, it's good branding; you get your company or product name right there on their smartphone screen.

This approach is particularly popular if you have a website that's difficult to display or navigate on the mobile screen. For example, Amazon's website is very feature-rich, but that doesn't translate well to the small screen. In contrast, Amazon's iPhone app is perfectly sized and filtered for the mobile screen and makes shopping the site much easier than it would be otherwise.

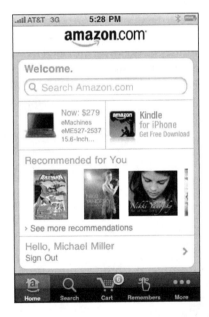

FIGURE 41.1

Amazon's iPhone app.

The key is to provide a reason for people to use your app, as opposed to just visiting your mobile website. By choosing and formatting content specifically for a given device, you give them a good reason to download and use the app on a regular basis. For example, the aforementioned Food Network application serves up seasonal recipes formatted for the iPhone screen, as well as short videos from their most popular shows, ideal for viewing on the go. It's a great app for viewers who want a constant fix from their favorite network.

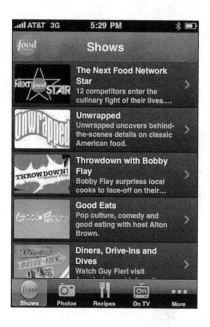

FIGURE 41.2

The Food Networks' iPhone app.

Apps for Promoting Your Brand

There are other ways to promote your brand, however, than just recycling content from your website. You can really get creative by figuring out ways to fully utilize the features of a given mobile device.

For example, users and developers have discovered that the iPhone is a great device for playing certain types of games. It's actually quite good for simple driving games, in that you can twist and turn the device to mimic the actions of a steering wheel. To that end, Volkswagen created a racing application that lets users experience the VW driving experience in a virtual fashion. It's a fun app to play and one that constantly exposes users to the VW brand—and lets them request a real test drive. Good marketing smarts behind this one.

41

FIGURE 41.3

Volkswagen's Touareg Challenge iPhone app.

I also like Benjamin Moore's Ben Color Capture app. It's a great app for a paint company, as it lets users snap a photo of room or item and then match those colors to paint shades in the company's library. If a match is found (and it probably is), the app takes advantage of the iPhone's GPS functionality to direct the customer to a local retailer.

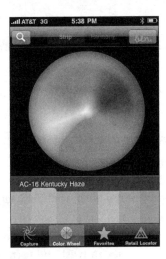

FIGURE 41.4

Benjamin Moore's Ben Color Capture iPhone app.

The key with both these examples is that they provide customers with something that they want to do over and over. In the case of VW, it's a fun experience; in the case of Benjamin Moore, it's a useful service. In both cases, the iPhone's unique features are fully exploited, product/company branding is well integrated throughout the app, and there is a distinct call-to-action that can be executed from within the app itself.

I also like the iPhone apps from Charmin and Purina. Charmin's Sit Or Squat app helps users find clean public restrooms, changing tables, and the like; Purina's Petcentric Places helps people find veterinarians, animal shelters, dog parks, and pet-friendly hotels across the nation. Both apps provide a unique public service while still promoting their brands.

When determining what type of app you want to develop, consider the types of things that your customers like or need to do. It's kind of the same approach you should be taking with YouTube videos; give the customer something useful or entertaining and make the promotional part of it somewhat of a soft sell.

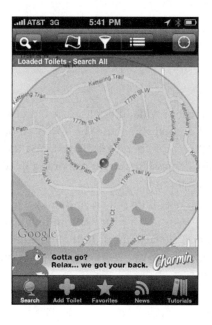

FIGURE 41.5

Charmin's Sit Or Squat iPhone app.

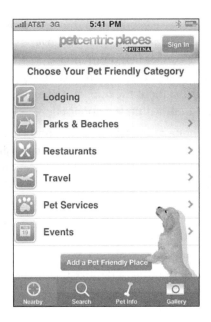

FIGURE 41.6
Purina's Petcentric Places iPhone app.

Converting Customers

A mobile app must provide utility to users but also needs, obviously, to promote the brand or product behind the app. To that end, the brand or company logo must be prominently displayed, and the app must relate to the
product promise. It wouldn't do for a sporting goods company to offer a
quilting app, for example.

So your app must be a little self-serving. It also must lead users directly back
to your (mobile) website. This isn't just an image-building effort; you want to
convert app users into customers. To that end, make it easy and worthwhile
for app users to click to your website for more information or services or to
make a purchase.

Of course, some apps are all about conversions—that is, they facilitate purchases via a mobile device. For example, Pizza Hut's iPhone app actually
makes ordering pizzas entertaining by letting customers drag and drop top-
pings onto an onscreen pizza. The order that customers create is then trans-
mitted directly to their nearest Pizza Hut location for rapid delivery. It's a fun
and functional app that generated $1 million in orders in its first six months
on the market.

41

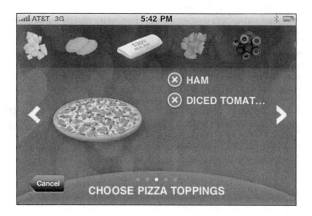

FIGURE 41.7
Pizza Hut's iPhone app.

The key to Pizza Hut's success is that it takes advantage of the features and interface to streamline the ordering process. There's not a lot of data entry via keypad, there are no separate URLs to punch in, and there's not a lot of confusing navigation required. It's a click and drag affair; build your pizza and place your order. What could be easier?

Marketing Your Mobile App

Developing your app is just the first step in the process. When you're competing with a quarter million other apps, how do you get customers to notice you?

Word of mouth is important in the app marketplace. Put simply, most people find apps through other people. Once customers find out about your app—and they like it—they're likely to tell their friends about it. It's a form of viral marketing.

Key to this, of course, is to provide an app that people really like to use. If it's just so much promotional value in app format, folks will delete it from their phones soon after downloading and definitely not recommend it to others. If you can provide an app that is useful and gets used, however, you'll benefit from the word of mouth promotion.

But you can't rely solely on word of mouth. You also have to promote the app on its own—and the most effective way to do this is by using your existing media to tell your existing customers. Promote your app on your website and blog, mention it in your print advertising, put out a press release, maybe even do a little online advertising for it. (For that matter, mobile advertising makes a lot of sense when promoting a mobile app.) Use all the tools at your disposal to persuade customers to download your app and give it a spin.

The more downloads your app receives in a given app store, the higher it ranks in the stores' bestseller lists. (These lists are often organized by category, by the way, making it easier to rank higher in a given category than in overall sales.) A high bestseller ranking results in increased visibility, which results in even more downloads. It's a goal, then to reach bestseller status; your downloads will increase geometrically from there.

The Bottom Line

Many companies are turning to mobile apps as a way to promote their wares to mobile users. These apps are a big deal, especially on the iPhone and Android platforms.

You can use a mobile app to provide better access to your mobile website, increase brand awareness, or drive sales or other conversions. The key is to provide unique value to the app's users, otherwise people won't use your app after downloading.

When it comes to promoting your app, the key is to drive up downloads so that it appears in the app store's bestseller lists. You can also promote your app on your mobile website or via mobile advertising—and don't forget to mention your mobile app as part of your online PR efforts.

DEVELOPING A MOBILE APP

You want to add a mobile app to your web marketing mix. How do you go about developing such an app?

For purpose of this conversation I'm going to assume that you're a marketing person, not a web developer. That is, you won't be developing the app yourself.

What you need to do, then, is find yourself a qualified app developer. This is actually fairly easy to do, as developers also see the opportunity and are flocking to the mobile platform (for the iPhone, especially).

And mobile app development is relatively simple, at least compared to developing traditional software applications. For one thing, mobile

41

apps are much simpler, typically single-purpose. Developers also get to take advantage of application development toolkits that make it easy to access and manipulate the common screen elements of a given device platform.

Developers can learn more about developing for the iPhone at Apple's iPhone Dev Center (developer.apple.com/iphone/). For Android development, check out the Android Developers site (developer.android.com).

Mobile app development may be easy, but it isn't cheap. Forrester Research reports that development costs for a mobile app can run anywhere from $20,000 to $150,000. It might be a little hard to swallow spending that much for something you then give away for free, but consider a form of advertising; you'd easily spend that much on a big-time ad in traditional media. If you get the downloads, and the resultant traffic to and conversions on your website, it's a good investment.

As to finding iPhone developers in your area, just do a Google search. But as with all development, including website development, make sure you drive the project from a marketing perspective; don't let the developer get carried away with the flashy technology.

41

42

Tracking Mobile Marketing Performance

Mobile marketing is every bit as diverse as more traditional web marketing. Between mobile search, mobile advertising, mobile applications, and the like, there are a lot of activities to keep track of. How do you know when your efforts are paying off?

Tracking the performance of your mobile marketing efforts means paying attention to many of the same metrics as you use for the rest of your web marketing plan, with a few new metrics thrown in for good measure. Bottom line, you need to measure the number of eyeballs you get—and how many of them convert to sales.

Tracking the Performance of Your Mobile Website

Here's the easy part: tracking the performance of your mobile website. That's because you use the same metrics to measure mobile website performance as you do to measure the performance of your regular website—and the same web analytics tools to report those metrics.

Tracking Key Metrics

Without belaboring the point, here are the metrics you want to pay attention to. They're mainly the same metrics that you measure on your main site, with one slight shift in importance:

- Unique visitors
- Pageviews
- Time on site
- Top pages

- Top landing pages
- Traffic sources
- Bounce rate
- Percent exit
- Top exit pages
- Conversions
- Geographic data
- Mobile devices
- Mobile carriers

> **note** The session duration metric for your mobile site will probably be less than on your main site. That's because mobile users get to the info they want faster and then exit a site quicker than do traditional users; the nature of mobile usage discourages leisurely browsing.

It's these last three metrics that are unique and especially important to mobile website performance.

Tracking Location

Most web analytics tools can tell you where visitors live, in terms of countries, states, and even cities. For example, Google Analytics lets you display geographic information globally, by country, and by state. From there, you filter the data (visits, pages per visit, average time on site, percent new visits, and bounce rate) by city within the state.

If you're marketing regionally or locally, this is great information. If you run a local restaurant, for example, and find out you're getting a ton of visitors from Kuala Lumpur, you might want to do a little digging and find out why; it's wasted bandwidth.

Ideally, you want the majority of visitors to come from a nearby location—your city or an adjacent community. You'll probably find that visitors from outside your local area spend much less time onsite, which can be expected; you probably weren't what they were searching for. So you'll want to filter out nonlocal destinations to get a true picture of how local visitors are using your site.

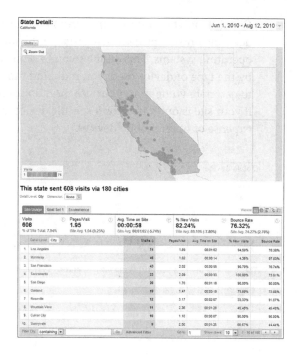

FIGURE 42.1

Tracking site performance in Google Analytics by city within the state of California.

Tracking Mobile Devices

The mobile devices metric tracks which mobile devices visitors used to access your site. This is typically reported by tracking the mobile operating system used in each device; you'll likely see entries for the following operating systems:

- iPhone
- iPad
- iPod (for the iPod Touch, not a phone but still a portable device that can be used for web browsing)
- Android
- Blackberry
- Windows Phone OS
- SymbianOS

note You may also see data for mobile operating systems from specific phone manufacturers, such as Samsung. These show up in much smaller numbers, however.

42

Google Analytics, for example, tracks number of visits, pages per visit, average time on site, percent new visits, and bounce rate for each of these mobile operating systems. This enables you to segment all aspects of site performance by the type of device used; you may find that users of one type of phone tend to get more value from your site than do users of other phones. (This is likely if your site is optimized for a specific device, such as the iPhone, at the expense of other mobile devices.)

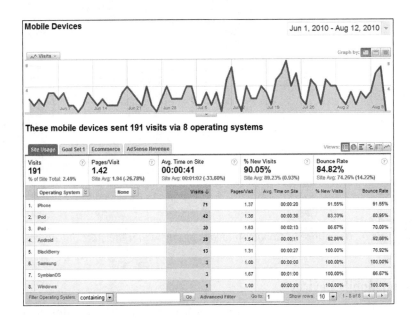

FIGURE 42.2
Tracking site performance in Google Analytics by type of mobile device.

Tracking Mobile Carriers

Likewise, most web analytics tools track site performance by mobile carriers, such as T-Mobile or Verizon. For example, Google Analytics tracks total visits, pages per visit, average time on site, percent new visits, and bounce rate by carrier. This lets you see which carrier is delivering the most traffic to your site and how that carrier's visitors are using your site.

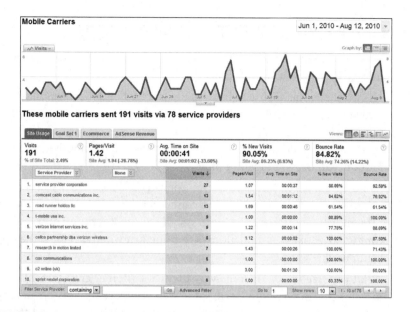

FIGURE 42.3

Tracking site performance in Google Analytics by mobile carrier.

Tracking the Performance of Your Mobile Advertising

When it comes to tracking the performance of your mobile advertising, the same metrics apply as to tracking other forms of web advertising. The key metrics include the following:

- Impressions
- Clicks
- Click-through rate
- Conversions

You probably also want to track various customer engagement metrics, such as duration of visit, frequency of visit, and percent of repeat visits. As you might suspect, your mobile advertising service should provide tools for tracking all of these metrics.

Tracking the Performance of Your Mobile Apps

Now we come to the new kid on the block. Just how do you track the effectiveness of your mobile applications?

The most obvious metric to track is the number of downloads that your app receives. While downloads don't necessarily translate into users (a person can download your app and never use it, or even delete it after installation), it is a hard, trackable data point. It's also a great way to compare your app's performance against competing apps.

As noted, however, just because an app was downloaded doesn't mean it was actually used. If your app always connects to your website to download fresh content, you can track those accesses, of course. But many apps are more self-contained, making it difficult to determine just when and how the app is being used.

What you need, then, is some way to track customer engagement for your mobile app. To serve this need, some web analytics services are adding tracking tools for mobile apps. These tools work by having you insert tracking code into the app itself; the service can then measure the app's use, often on a page-by-page basis, by tracking the embedded code.

For example, Webtrends (www.webtrends.com) offers its Mobile App Analytics service, which tracks the performance of iPhone, Android, and Blackberry apps. Metrics tracked include the following:

- Application version (useful for seeing whether users are keeping their apps upgraded)
- Connection type (3G, 2G, WiFi)
- Service provider
- OS version
- Device model
- Per-screen usage
- Event tracking
- Screen path analytics
- Conversion

> **note** Some mobile app analytics use the GPS function built into many mobile devices to track user location, as well as activity by location.

Code it right, and you can see which screens in your app people are using the most, as well as what screen path they follow through your app. Obviously, you can also track general app usage so you can better determine what percentage of people who download your app use it on a regular basis.

42

These engagement and usage metrics, then, can tell you how useful and how used your application is. This is in contrast to the raw downloads metric, which only tells you how well you're marketing your application.

Ultimately, however, you want to track how well your app turns users into customers, which means tracking conversions. This is also a bit of a coding and tracking challenge, but it can be done. While you may get some bump in brand awareness just by having a useful mobile app out in the wild, it's even better if you can document how often the users of your app return to purchase your product or service. That's a direct measurement of your app's effectiveness.

The Bottom Line

Tracking the performance of your mobile website involves many of the same metrics used to track your regular website. In addition, you want to track the location of your site's visitors (local is typically better), as well as the mobile devices and carriers used to access your site.

Tracking the performance of your mobile advertising also involves traditional metrics, such as impressions, clicks, CTR, conversions, and the like. When it comes to tracking the performance of mobile apps, however, you want to measure the number of downloads, as well as various engagement metrics, such as per-screen usage, screen path, and conversion.

MOBILE MARKETING MISTAKES

Here's the thing. While mobile marketing requires many of the same traditional skills you use for the rest of your web marketing, it's still different, in many ways, from web marketing. If you try to treat mobile marketing as nothing more than a subset of web marketing, you're bound to be disappointed in your results.

The first mistake that many marketers make is treating mobile users the same as they do computer users. Now, even though both sets of consumers are accessing content on the Web, they're doing it in much different fashions. In fact, their needs are often quite dissimilar. The mobile user, after all, is on the go, has different physical and time constraints, and typically wants or needs to do different things than does a

42

user in the home. You have to get inside the mobile user's head and deliver what it is he's looking for.

Likewise, you make a mistake by treating mobile devices the same way you treat personal computers. The experience of accessing the Web with a mobile phone is significantly different from using a PC for the same task; the screen is much smaller, there's no full-sized keyboard, there's no printer connected, and bandwidth and download speeds are typically much lower. Like I said, it's different.

The final mistake that many marketers make is not exploiting the capabilities of a given mobile devices. There are a lot of cool features present in a smartphone that don't exist on a personal computer, not the least of which is the ability to make phone calls. (Other unique features: geolocation, digital camera, and audio and video playback.) Don't overlook these features; instead, integrate them into your mobile apps and other marketing activities.

Managing Your Web Marketing Activities

Now that we've discussed all the various aspects of web marketing, it's time to put together the pieces of this puzzle to fit within your day-to-do routine. It's fine and all to consider web marketing in the abstract, but if you're in the trenches you need to turn that theory into practical application.

In other words, you need to figure out how to manage all those web marketing activities you've committed yourself and your company to. Sounds like a simple thing until you consider the sheer number of activities involved—and how much effort is needed.

Managing Your Web Marketing Mix

Let's start with the job of managing your overall marketing mix. We first looked at the mix issue way back in Chapter 3, "Balancing and Budgeting Online Activities." At that point we really hadn't had a chance to examine each component of the mix in detail, which obviously we have in the succeeding chapters. Now that you're more informed about the various web marketing activities, it makes sense to revisit the whole mix issue.

What's important to you, in terms of web marketing, may be different from that of a marketer in a different company. Every company, every brand, every product has unique marketing requirements; different companies in the same market space may even approach things differently. Thus there's no way for me or anyone else to make universal pronouncements about what you should or shouldn't be doing in terms of web marketing. Your ongoing web marketing mix will be unique to you.

That said, there are some things we know about the tools at your disposal that can influence the weight you give to each of these tools. Some components of web marketing are becoming more important and more popular; others are fading from popularity; still others remain every bit as important as they were at the beginning of the online revolution and are likely to retain their popularity as web marketing continues to evolve.

> **note** The tools of the trade are ever changing; new tools and technologies are constantly being developed and adopted. As such, it's critical to stay current with the changes in the industry, both strategically and technologically.

For instance, we know that search engine marketing is probably the most effective component of your web marketing mix; it's been this way since the advent of Google and will likely remain so for the foreseeable future. Most consumers find new websites by searching for them, which means that optimizing your site for search is, without a doubt, the most important thing you can do to attract new customers. SEO is also one of the most efficient marketing tools at your disposal; as important as it is, you don't have to devote a lot of your ongoing budget or time to this task.

Of course, few companies can rely one hundred percent on organic search results. Most businesses need to augment search engine marketing with other forms of online promotion; you need to attract customers via a variety of methods and channels. In essence, you need a presence just about everywhere online that your customers go, and you need an appropriate balance between the various means of communicating with your online customers.

What you have to manage, then, are which tools you employ and the relative importance you give to each tool. Yes, your website and corresponding SEO are primary, but this isn't the only activity you'll be undertaking. For one thing, you don't want to be over reliant on a single tool; if your SEO efforts are unsuccessful, you have no other tools lined up to promote your product or brand. (You don't want to put all your marketing eggs in one basket, in other words.) For another, not every customer finds you via search; you have to reach out to customers in all the different ways they interact online.

This means that you need to consider email marketing, blog marketing, social media marketing, multimedia marketing, mobile marketing, online PR, and the like when managing your web marketing strategy. It's important to get a mix of traffic to your site from a variety of different channels. You can't assume that all your customers do the same things online; you have to find them wherever they may be, whatever they may be doing.

And, equally important, you have to establish an ongoing conversation with your customers. It's not just about attracting new customers; it's also about maintaining and to some degree exploiting existing ones. To this end you need marketing vehicles that enable both continuous communication and two-way communication with your customer base. This argues in favor of social media, such as social networks, Twitter, blogs, and the like. These media aren't necessarily expensive to use but do require a definite time commitment and skill set.

There's also the consideration of how your customers access the Internet. We can no longer assume that consumers only access the Internet via their computers; mobile access may soon become the dominant means of accessing the Web. As such you need to make sure that all your marketing activities are compatible with mobile access and also develop tactics that directly appeal to mobile users.

If all this sounds complicated (and getting more so), that's because it is. The old days of doing print, radio, and television advertising, along with a little direct mail and general public relations stuff are long gone. You still have to maintain those traditional activities, of course, but now you have to address all the other activities made possible by the Internet and by the use of mobile devices. The number of things you can do has increased tremendously; how you fit each of these pieces together into a coherent whole is a major challenge.

It's also an ongoing challenge, as we can have absolutely no expectation that the activities mentioned will remain constant. Everything on the Internet is in constant flux, including web marketing. Hey, five years ago we really didn't have Facebook or Twitter or YouTube, at least from a marketing perspective; today, these are three of the top tools in any web marketer's toolkit. There's no reason not to expect that web marketing five years from now will look at least as different as today's marketing would have appeared five years ago.

Things have changed, things are changing, things will always change, and you have to adapt to it. That means a constant reevaluation of your web marketing activities. You need to be fearless about trying new things, as well as abandoning older, less successful activities. You won't be able to rest on your laurels or anything else; web marketing is a constant challenge for all involved.

Managing Your Staff

Speaking of who's involved, let's move on to the people part of the equation. How best should you manage the staff assigned to implement your web marketing plan?

The key here is how much staff you have. If you are it, your management task is easy—although your personal time management is a real challenge. On the other hand, if you have a staff of hundreds, you can pretty much assign a person to just about any activity you think of.

But that might not be the best approach, even if you have the resources. It's important to know that different components of your mix not only produce different results, but require different levels of attention. Some activities take up a lot of time, others not so much. And, equally important, some tasks are time-intensive at the beginning but become less so over time.

note When I say "staff," I include those outside resources you might bring in to handle various components of your marketing program. As we all know, using freelancers or consultants to manage specific campaigns or areas is quite common; you need to consider all resources when you determine how best to manage things.

Compare and contrast the activities of setting up your website with those of managing social media. Setting up a website is extremely time-intensive while you're doing it, but the effort fades to next to nothing once the site goes live. (Yes, you still need to reevaulate and fine tune your site over time, but the bulk of the effort is during the initial construction.) Doing social media marketing, on the other hand, requires relatively little start up effort but almost constant management of ongoing activities.

In addition, different activities require different skill sets. The design skills you need to create an effective website are much different from the people-oriented skills you need to manage social media, the writing skills you need to feed a daily blog, or the media savvy you need to produce YouTube videos. It's difficult to imagine a single individual being skilled enough—or having enough time—to manage all these different activities.

What you need to do, then, is apportion out the tasks based on related skills necessary. For example, it makes sense to have a dedicated person or unit doing all your social networking—Twitter, Facebook, your blog, and so forth. It also makes sense to have another dedicated person or unit handling your multimedia activities—YouTube, podcasts, and so forth. You can set up

43

another person or unit to handle your advertising, another to handle website upkeep and general SEO, another to do your PR, and so on.

Of course, you have to attract and manage people with the right skill sets for each type of web marketing activity you undertake. You then have to manage these people, within their assigned areas, to the best effect. That doesn't mean managing them equally, of course; you need to give a bit more freedom to the more creative types, put a shorter leash on those with direct revenue responsibilities, and be understanding of the amount of time your public communicators spend trolling the social media sites. It's an interesting mix of activities, with an interesting mix of people involved.

That doesn't mean, however, that your people should work in a vacuum. Quite the opposite; today's online marketing requires all the different players to interact and interface in a more cohesive and constructive fashion than most of us are accustomed to. The days of separate silos within a marketing department are long gone. Instead, your entire staff need to work with and learn from one another.

To be successful, all your different marketing activities have to fit together in a holistic fashion. Your social marketing must tie into your blog, which must tie into your email newsletter, which must tie into your PPC advertising, which must tie into your search engine marketing, which must tie into the design of your website, which must reflect the input from your social marketing...and so on. Everything you do, every item you produce, every impression you make is tied into every other activity.

For this to happen, each person on staff needs to be constantly aware of what others are doing. This requires a new kind of marketing management, one that encourages cooperation instead of competition among team members. You truly have to think of your marketing staff not as a collection of departments, but as a cohesive and collaborative team.

Managing Your Budget

Similarly, you have to consider your web marketing budget in a holistic manner. In the old days you had a handful of different line items, and you managed them separately. That's not the case anymore; everything you do is interconnected, and so must be the items in your marketing budget.

And there are a lot of items. As noted, it's not just three flavors of advertising, direct mail, and PR, like it used to be. You now have budget items for PPC advertising, online display advertising, SEO, email marketing, blog marketing,

43

social media marketing (and perhaps several line items under this one, for Facebook, Twitter, and so forth), video marketing, podcasts, mobile marketing, and, of course, online PR. That's a lot to keep track of.

What's even more challenging is that each of these items relates to each other item. You can't silo your online marketing budget; one line item affects another.

To that end, you have to consider your web marketing budget as somewhat fluid. As you move throughout the budget period, you might find that social media is becoming more important and blogging less so or maybe that your PPC advertising isn't working as well as your email marketing. You need to be able to quickly shift marketing dollars from one activity to another so that you can rapidly react to new opportunities. You just can't focus myopically on the individual line items in your budget; the lines have to blur.

This creates a bit of a management challenge, of course—especially in managing your managers, or at least those who monitor your budget. It may be difficult to convince the bean counters why it's not that important to hold the blog marketing department to its numbers when there's more opportunity in social marketing, for example, but it's something you have to do. You have to force them to focus on the big number, not on all the little ones.

Managing Results

The need to budget holistically doesn't ignore the need to track individual results. You need to know, as soon as you can, what's working and what's not so that you can readjust your plans accordingly. Is your email marketing campaign paying off? Are you getting the results you want from your company blog? Is your ROI from your PPC advertising what you expected? And how many people are following you on Twitter and Facebook?

Tracking results, then, remains an important part of your marketing management duties. You need to not only track the raw results of individual activities, you have to track results against expectations and results against expenditures. You need to know what activities are giving you the most bang for the buck.

In addition to tracking results individually, you need to break down the silos (again) and compare the results of all your activities against each other. That is, you need to develop a sense of which activities are both most important and most effective. You need to know how your activities relate to one another, whether social marketing is more or less important to you than SEO or PPC advertising or email marketing. Understanding the relative importance of each activity will help you adjust your marketing mix going forward.

That said, you also need to balance short-term versus long-term results. It's not all about short-term results; you need to invest in the future of your web marketing program. There no doubt will be some newer activities that aren't paying off big just yet but hold immense promise for the future. You have to plant the seeds of your future success, and that means nurturing those seeds that have yet to fully bloom. When it comes to embracing new technologies and activities, you need to be patient and persevere—and give the new kids a bit of a break, budget-wise.

Managing Change

This last point brings us to the topic of change, of which there is a lot in web marketing. What was hot five years ago is cooling down today; what seems cutting-edge today might be old hat five years from now.

Consider the world of web marketing five years ago. Nobody was talking about video marketing or social marketing; the staples of most marketing plans were search engine marketing, PPC advertising, and (for those on top of the curve) email marketing. Everybody was talking about how to take advantage of podcasts and blog marketing; these were the latest big things.

Today, we still have PPC advertising and SEO, of course. Email marketing is a tried and true technique. Blog marketing and podcasting have cooled off a bit, although they still matter. But the latest big things are Facebook, Twitter, and YouTube, with mobile marketing rising large on the horizon. It's a totally different mix, even if most of the old components remain.

What this means in terms of marketing management is that you need to keep on top of all developments, no matter how unimportant they may seem at the time. Unless you want your competition to get the jump on you, you need to be first out of the block in experimenting with new media and channels. You need to be fast and first and not shy about experimenting—and sometimes failing.

To do this, you personally need to be engaged with and immersed in developing online communities and technologies. You don't want to read about something new in the trade papers (or trade websites); you want to experience it firsthand. You have to be part of it to know what it's all about.

This argues, of course, for that fluidity we discussed in regard to budget management. Not only do you need to be able to shift your budget around to exploit new technologies and channels, you probably need to set aside a portion of your budget just for this eventuality. Carving out a piece of your budget (10% or so) for "new activities" just makes sense.

note We talk more about managing change in the final chapter of this book, Chapter 44, "Looking to the Future."

Managing Management

If you're fortunate, you work for a company that's young and hip and embraces new technology and techniques and everything that implies. If you're less fortunate, you work for a bunch of crusty old Luddites who can't even read their own email.

Old-line management is anathema to cutting edge web marketing. Senior management who've never blogged or tweeted, who don't have their own Facebook pages, who don't watch YouTube videos or download mobiles apps to their iPhones, simply won't understand much of what you need to do online. Not only won't they understand the technology, but they won't understand the customers and how they're using technology today.

It's this last point that's most important. Not only is it key that you and your staff *think like the customer*, but your company's management team needs to get inside your customers' heads, as well. If they don't know how customers are thinking today—and they're thinking much differently than they did in the past—your management team won't know how to reach those customers and definitely won't understand what it takes to market to them.

What you need to do, then, is get your senior managers out from behind their desks and into the virtual world. Your managers need to experience your company, your products, and, most importantly, your online presence the same way that your customers do. Only then will they be able to embrace and fully support your web marketing efforts.

What does this mean? Let's start small by encouraging your execs to visit your company website. You'd be surprised how many don't. And make sure they visit the site not from the corporate high-speed connection, but from a typical wireless home connection. Maybe you take your boss out for a coffee at Starbucks and connect from there on your laptop. The key is to make them experience your site the same way your customers do. Walk them through the experience of finding product information or making a purchase and see what they think.

From there, take your execs by the hand and get them set up with their own Facebook pages. Show them how Twitter works. Let them spend some time playing Farmville and watching stupid pet videos on YouTube. Help them experience the Web in all its glory and absurdity, just as your customers do. Once they get their feet wet, maybe then they'll understand today's online customers—and your web marketing strategy—a little bit better.

I recall talking to another marketer about a conference he attended where the CEO of a large national retailer gave the keynote speech. After giving a pretty nifty high-tech presentation, no doubt prepared by an unnamed marketing minion, the CEO opened the session for questions, the first of which was along the lines of "All this is great, we hear the drums beating, and your video was so exciting to watch, but how much time do you personally spend in the field with your customers?" The CEO's answer was honest but ultimately telling; he told the questioner, "I don't spend any time in the field. I don't have time to do that."

Management that doesn't have time to connect with their customers ultimately lose touch with them—and that's a recipe for failure. It's unfortunate that with all the opportunity for opening conversations with customers afforded by the Internet today, so few senior executives actually do so. I'm not suggesting that every senior manager in your company start answering random questions on your Facebook page, but they should at least be aware of how your customers are using the technology to interface with you.

It's your job, then, to affect the culture of your company to embrace technology, the Internet, and mobile communications. You are the voice of the customer in your company, and you must be heard.

Managing Your Time

Finally, we come to the issue of time management—in particular, the management of your own personal time. With so much happening in web marketing today, especially with the time-draining nature of social media, it's easy to get sucked in and end up spending too much time on the wrong activities—or simply too much time working in general.

It's important that you touch all the bases in your web marketing mix but also that you manage the time you spend with each activity. This argues for creating a daily schedule and sticking to it. You should block out how much

43

time you spend not just overseeing your team but also participating in each aspect of web marketing. So you give yourself 15 minutes a day to tweet, 15 minutes on Facebook, 15 minutes on YouTube, 15 minutes surfing the competition's websites, and so forth. This forces you to spend face time on those activities you might not personally like, as well as limits the amount of time you waste on activities that really light your fire. It's a balancing act.

When you're putting together your daily schedule, focus your time on those activities that have the most impact. That means doing what your customers do and going where they go. If your customers are big on Facebook and not so much on LinkedIn, you should spend more time with the former and less with the latter, even if you personally like networking with the business community.

You should also leave yourself some time for just experimenting, trying out new things. You need some nondirected "discovery" time to experience the Web like your customers do. It's the only way to stay on top of new trends and technologies.

Don't feel, however, that you have to get deeply involved in everything you do online on a personal basis. I'm assuming you have staff assigned to that. While it's important for you to know what's going on, on a general basis, it's not necessary for the VP or Director of Marketing to respond to every comment on a YouTube video or Facebook update. Don't let yourself get sucked into petty issues; focus your attention on what really matters, while still keeping abreast of general activities.

The Bottom Line

Executing your web marketing strategy involves more than just the initial planning; you also need to manage your ongoing marketing activities. That means managing the mix you employ, and changing that mix as you learn more over time—and as new opportunities emerge. It also means managing your staff and your budget, and collecting and analyzing the results of your activities.

In addition, you need to manage change. That is, you need to keep abreast of new technological and marketing developments, and embrace them as necessary in your day-to-day marketing activities. You also need to manage your company's management, so that they understand what you're doing and why—and, most importantly, how your customers are embracing new technologies and practices. If company management doesn't get how the market is changing, you face an uphill batter reacting to and taking advantage of these changes in customer behavior.

MANAGING EXCITEMENT

Web marketing is great and all that, but it isn't everything. There's no aspect of web marketing that exists in and onto itself; it's all there to serve your company and your customer. "I market, therefore I am" should not be part of your marketing philosophy.

To that end, you should never let yourself be taken in by the hype. (And in web marketing, there's a lot of hype.) It's easy, I know, to be seduced by the latest technology or approach or whatever; you won't be the first market to get all hot and bothered by what's hot this week in web marketing, whether that's social media or YouTube or whatever, and convince yourself that it's something you need to do now and big.

If you let yourself be guided by these impulses, you'll end up doing a lot of stupid things you'll regret later and scattering your efforts across too many fronts. Instead, you need to remain calm, cool, and collected and relatively unswayed by the allure of the new. Keep focused on your overall plan, while still addressing new developments. Don't let yourself be diverted by all the shiny new things; experiment judiciously, not fool heartedly.

What you don't want to do is have a web marketing strategy du jour. Yes, it's important to remain flexible and embrace important new developments, but your overall goals and strategy should remain relatively constant. Fit the new developments into your existing strategy; don't warp your strategy to embrace everything new that comes along. Consistency, a big picture viewpoint, and long-term thinking are key. With a steady hand at the oar, small course corrections are easy to make when market changes warrant.

44

Looking to the Future

We've come to the end of the line—well, to the end of the book, in any case. And after looking at all the various components of web marketing today, you might think we've covered everything that can be covered.

That's not the case, however. The Internet in general and web marketing in particular are constantly evolving, and new ways to communicate and promote are always emerging. It's not enough to get good at the promotional opportunities available today; you also have to keep on top of those opportunities that will develop in the future.

What's next, then? That's what this chapter is all about—a look forward to the immediate and not-so-immediate future of online marketing

Email Is Dying

One good way to stay on top of trends is to watch what the young people are doing. Watch college students, watch high schoolers, and observe what technologies they're using (and how), as well as those they're not. Within a few years, you'll see their behavior migrating into the general population.

College students, after all, were the first to embrace social networking; Facebook was created as a community for students, not for the general public. The same thing is true of email and instant messaging and with the public Internet in general. The kids do it first, and then the rest of us follow.

That said, I definitely notice how my step-kids are using the Internet. And what I see today is that they're not communicating online in the same way that we're used to. Specifically, they're not using email. They're instant

44

messaging and (on their phones) text messaging, they're tweeting and Facebooking, but today's youth seldom bother to check their email inboxes. It's not something they use on a regular basis.

Why is this? I think it's the immediacy, or lack of. Kids have gotten used to immediate gratification, and I really mean immediate. Instant messaging and text messaging are done in real time; email isn't. The (slightly) older generation might think that email is fast, at least when compared to postal mail, but youngsters think it takes way, way too long. They don't have the time or the patience to wait for a response, so they quit using it.

There's also the long-form nature of email. Again, older users might consider email to be a condensed version of traditional paper letters, but you're still talking sentences and paragraphs. To today's youth, a sentence is about as long as they can handle; writing or reading a paragraph is simply out of the question. It may be the attention span thing again, or maybe writing and reading skills have dramatically declined. Whatever the case, kids today don't like to read much, and they certainly don't like to write anything that's too involved.

This decreasing importance of email as a means of communication means that email marketing is likely to be less important going forward than it is today, especially if you're targeting younger consumers. If your customers never check their inboxes, there's little point in trying to reach them via email. You better find other means of contacting them, instead.

Blogs Are Fading

When you're evaluating that whole long-form versus short-form thing, you have to consider what this means for the future of blogging. Back in the day (meaning two or three years ago), everybody and their brother had a personal blog. Not so today. Most people found that they didn't have the dedication to write regular blog posts, so they just dropped it. There are a lot of abandoned blogs out there now.

That doesn't mean that people aren't posting their innermost thoughts online anymore. They are. They're just doing it in shorter tweets and Facebook status updates. Let's face it; social networks have made it much easier for folks to share their personal diaries online. There's a lot less effort involved to make a post to Facebook than there is to create and maintain a blog. If nothing else, you don't have to write as much—and people definitely don't like to write as much as they used to.

The abandonment of the personal blog doesn't necessarily mean that professional blogs are also dying; businesses still derive promotional value from their blogging activities. But the shrinking of the blogosphere is probably not a good sign for blogging in general. It's certainly something to monitor going forward.

Social Networking Is Taking Over

So if people are emailing and blogging less, what are they doing instead? If you guessed something about Facebook and Twitter, you're definitely on the right track.

Social media are the darling of web marketers today, and it doesn't look like that's going to change anytime soon. More and more people of all ages and income levels are using Facebook, Twitter, and the like; the phenomenon that started with younger users has migrated into the general population and shows no sign of abating.

This has led to a mind-boggling growth in the use of social media, especially of Facebook and Twitter. While all growth slows, I don't expect a major slow-down anytime soon, at least in Facebook. Let's face it, Facebook is addictive; it pulls you in and then it pulls in everyone around you. It's like a black hole of social communication, in a good way.

I'm not so convinced about Twitter. Twitter has also experienced significant growth but differs from Facebook in that it also has a high abandonment rate. That's not a good sign. What I think Twitter is evolving into is a one-way broadcast medium, rather than a two-way social medium. That is, celebrities, news organizations, companies, and the like will continue to broadcast their messages via tweets to their subscribers, but you won't necessarily see a corresponding influx of individual tweeters, at least not in the long term. I just don't think Twitter is social enough to compete with the full-featured community that is Facebook.

If Facebook continues to grow, then, that means a continuing opportunity for marketers. It also means more competition, as more and more marketers jump on the social networking bandwagon. If you were on Facebook in the early days you may have had your category pretty much to yourself. That won't be the case going forward. You have to prepare for increased competition for eyeballs on the Facebook site, which argues for more aggressive and creative marketing on the site. The Facebook user base may continue to grow, but it's going to be more difficult to make your presence known.

44

Mobility Matters

The biggest opportunity in the near-term future, in my opinion and in the opinion of many marketing experts, lies in the field of mobility. That is, more and more people are using their mobile phones to connect to the Internet and do web-related tasks.

The move to mobile connectivity offers two-fold opportunities. The first, and the most obvious, is the simple displacement of existing activities from the computer to the mobile phone. That is, instead of checking email or reading Facebook on a desktop or laptop computer, people do it on their phones, instead. This argues for making your website and blog and all other web-related activities mobile-friendly—and for optimizing your site and blog for mobile search.

The second opportunity concerns those activities that are new and unique to mobile browsing. The important question is, in what different ways are people using their mobile phones than they did their computers? Answer this question, and you'll discover new promotional opportunities.

One such new opportunity concerns timing, or rather availability. Even if a person uses a mobile phone to do nothing more than what she did on a computer, she has her phone with her all the time. You never lose her; you have nonstop connectivity to this person, wherever and whenever she goes. That's a 24/7 opportunity to exploit.

There's also the localized opportunity. Because you can target your mobile marketing by the user's location, you can provide more contextually relevant information. That should help you better target your marketing activities and achieve better results for doing so.

Bottom line, the market is becoming more mobile; this is a large and growing trend. You need to adapt your web marketing strategy accordingly.

Narrowcasting Gets Big

It's been said that every new technology makes customers more powerful. That's certainly true in the case of those technologies—chief of which is mobile computing—that enable narrowcasting.

The capability that mobile technologies afford for context- and location-sensitive communications is narrowcasting, pure and simple. It's not mass marketing; it's sending a specific message to a specific consumer that's relevant to what that consumer is doing and where he's located.

Your challenge, then, is to take advantage of the technology to craft messages that are uniquely relevant to each of your customers individually. It's not about broadcasting to the entire customer base; it's about reaching out with personal messages.

And here's where narrowcasting becomes even more important: As narrowcasting becomes more widespread, consumers will begin to pay attention only to advertising that's relevant to their needs. That is, they'll ignore broadcast messages in favor of narrowcast ones. It makes sense; you listen more to conversations that are about you. Broadcast messages won't be as important.

All Marketing Is Local—and Global

The narrowcasting nature of mobile computing helps you localize your marketing messages. This is great if you're a local business or have a local component to your business. You don't have to waste marketing dollars by broadcasting your message to uninterested consumers around the globe; you can target customers in a specific city or ZIP code or neighborhood.

This focus on local narrowcasting is important, but there's also a flip side to the coin. Sure, you can narrowcast to your heart's content, but the Internet also lets you cheaply and efficiently send your message anywhere on Earth.

This is one feature of all new communications technologies, from the printing press to the Internet: It reduces the importance of distance. That's certainly true with the Web, where every business is competing globally, whether they want to or not.

The global nature of the Internet is a double-edged sword. Yes, even the smallest neighborhood business can reach out to potential customers in Europe or China. But that small business is now also competing with businesses in Europe and China, too. You don't have the luxury of isolation; even if you have no interest in competing globally, your customers know what's available elsewhere in the world. If you can't provide what they need at a price that's competitive, they'll just order it online from somebody else.

Whether or not you wish to pursue global business, you still need to be aware of what's happening around the world. You're competing globally, so you better adapt to that fact.

Embracing Change

The takeaway from all this crystal ball gazing is that the only constant is change—so you better learn to embrace it. Things are going to change whether you get on board or not, so you might as well get on board and make the best of it.

This argues in favor of keeping abreast of developing trends in technology and communication. And not just keeping abreast; you need to get in front of the trends. If you're not leading, you're following somebody.

Take social networking, for example. Sure, social networks are hot today, but if you're just now jumping on the bandwagon you're already several years behind the curve. You need to extricate yourself from your day-to-day activities to look at and immerse yourself in the bigger, longer-term trends; it's the only way you'll keep your business on the cutting edge going forward.

note Here's the thing about new technology, Internet or otherwise: It doesn't always do something new. A lot of times, new technology simply does existing things a little better. Consider the rise of social networking, for example. There's really nothing new that Facebook does; it's really just a mashup of old school message boards, email, instant messaging, and photo sharing. But Facebook combines all these activities in a way that's uniquely appealing, and as such is leading to the decline of those separate activities. Facebook is something new doing old stuff a little better.

A few years back I wrote a book called *Online Marketing Heroes*, where I interviewed 25 movers and shakers in the online marketing business. My final interview was with Patrick Duparcq, a professor of marketing at the Kellogg School of Management at Northwestern University. Patrick is a bit of a visionary, definitely someone who's up on coming trends; he has to be, not just for his students but also for the many clients of his consulting business.

Patrick told me that he tries to stay five years ahead of the curve. Not six months, not a year, but *five years*. Here's how he put it:

> If you're not thinking about what's going to be important five years from now, you're going to be caught with your competitors releasing some very neat ways to interact with customers. And if only then you say, "Aha, this is something we should look at as well," by definition you're already three years behind. All of a sudden you're woken up by something you see your competitors are doing, and then you have to decide to buy it, and then you have to start training your people to start thinking about how that can be used for your company. It takes easily two to three years.

It's important then, to not just acknowledge change, but to embrace it. You need to live with the emerging technologies and communities to determine how your customers are changing, how what they do is changing, and how you need to adapt to those changes.

The technological change inherent in the Internet makes customers more powerful, reduces the importance of distance, makes it easier for you to connect one-on-one with your customers, and levels the play-ing field between larger and smaller compa-nies. These are all good things and should be embraced. Yeah, it's a lot of work—but it's fun work, it's good work, and hopefully it's work that will pay off. And that's something to be proud of.

note Read the full inter-view with Patrick in my book, *Online Marketing Heroes: Interviews with 25 Successful Online Marketing Gurus* (Michael Miller, Wiley, 2008).

44

The Bottom Line

Here's the ultimate bottom line, for this chapter and for the entire book: Everything changes. Traditional media didn't always used to be traditional; at one point in time, newspapers were the big thing, radio was brand-spanking new, and television was something only dreamed of. Today, all those media are old, and what's new is happening on the Internet.

But the Internet itself is constantly changing. What was hot five or ten years ago is much cooler today; today's big things will also cool as even newer ways of doing things evolve. As a marketing professional, you need to keep on top of everything that's changing, not necessarily to jump wholeheartedly on an unproven bandwagon, but to become aware of those developments that may change the way you reach your customers—and the way they reach you.

So whether it's the move from email and blogging to social networking, or the move from desktop computing to the mobile Internet, you need to be on top of it, constantly analyzing how it is and may in the future affect your busi-ness. That doesn't mean abandoning everything that's more than a few years old, or letting your traditional marketing skills wither and die. It simply means that you need to keep on top of developing trends, keep your skillset fresh, and be prepared to adapt your plans as necessary.

It's an ever changing world out there, and you're part of it. Get used to it—and learn to embrace change.

44

EVERYTHING OLD IS NEW AGAIN

All this talk of change argues in favor of learning the new skills necessary to manage these new technologies. I certainly won't argue in favor of learning new skills; life is a constant learning process, all the more so when you're talking technology and communications.

But no matter what new skills you may need, traditional marketing skills are still important. In fact, I think they become more important over time.

Web marketing might appear to be a new phenomenon, but it's really just a new package for a bunch of old activities. Yes, you're compiling lists of keywords and designing Flash animations and tweeting and blogging and such, but at the end of the day all you're really doing is reaching out to consumers. You're using some new tools to do so, but the task is the same as it's always been.

Online marketing is just like traditional marketing in that you identify a target audience, develop a strategy for reaching that audience, and then execute that strategy via a series of activities. It's easy to get caught up in the technology and the media and think you're doing something new and different, but you're not. Solid marketing skills still matter; in fact, when you're competing against technical people who don't necessarily have a marketing background, marketing skills can make all the difference.

My advice to you, then, is to remember what you learned back in Marketing 101 and apply that knowledge to each new technology and medium you encounter. You have to *think like the customer*, remember to present benefits instead of features, and offer unique value in everything you do.

Web marketing, then, doesn't have to be difficult. If you have the basic marketing skills and don't let yourself be dazzled by the flashing lights and pretty music, you'll know what to do. Serve the customer well, and you'll be successful.

Glossary

% exit	The percentage of users who exit from a given web page.
active time	The average amount of time that visitors spend actually interacting with content on a web page, based on mouse moves, clicks, hovers, scrolls, and so on. Also known as *engagement time*.
adware	A form of spyware perpetrated by unscrupulous advertisers, typically used to display alternate advertisements or pop-up ads.
affiliate marketing	A form of marketing where a website pays another website for sales that result from their customer referrals.
application advertising	Ads placed within mobile or social applications.
average position	The position achieved by a PPC ad, on average, on a search results page.
B2B	See *business-to-business.*
B2C	See *business-to-consumer.*
banner ad	A type of large display advertising. While banners can be any shape or size, the term often defines an ad that runs horizontally across the top of a web page.
blog	Short for "web log," a personal or professional journal on the Web.
blog marketing	Any marketing activity that involves blogs. One form of blog marketing involves the creation of a company or product blog; another form involves PR efforts directed at third-party bloggers.

blogosphere	The entire universe of blogs.
blogvertising	The act of bartering or selling product mentions in participating blogs; a form of product placement.
bounce rate	The percentage of visits to a website where the visitor enters and exits on the same page without visiting any other pages on the site in between.
business-to-business	Marketing of products and services from one business to another business. Also known as *B2B*.
business-to-consumer	Marketing of products and services to consumers. Also known as *B2C*.
call to action	That portion of an advertisement or other promotional item that urges the consumer to perform a specific action.
channel conflict	Real or potential issues that arise from multiple channels selling the same products and services.
click	A single instance of a visitor clicking a link from one page to another.
click path	The sequence of clicks that website visitors follow on a given site.
click-through rate	The percentage of people who view an item who then click it; calculated by dividing the number of clicks by the number of impressions. Also known as *CTR*.
co-registration	The use of email addresses from customers who opted in at another website.
company blog	A professional blog maintained by a business, typically used to promote the company and its brands or products.
context-sensitive ads	See *contextual advertising.*
contextual advertising	Ads that are placed in the context of the hosting web page, typically by means of matching keywords. Contextual ads are intended to be relevant to the web page's content.
conversion	When a customer converts from clicking an ad or viewing a web page to performing the desired action, such as making a purchase.
conversion rate	The number of conversions divided by the number of clicks or pageviews.
cookie	A small text file installed on a user's computer, typically used to track web browsing behavior or store user information.

cost per action	A form of online advertising where the advertiser pays only when a click results in a sale or other customer transaction. Payment is typically in the form of a commission, or percent of the final sales price. Also known as *CPA*.
cost per click	(1) A form of online advertising where the advertiser pays only when an ad is clicked. (2) The amount paid by an advertiser for each click on a PPC ad. Also known as *CPC*.
cost per conversion	The average cost of each ad conversion.
cost per lead	A form of online advertising where the advertiser pays a set amount per lead generated from a click on an ad. Also defines how much a marketer pays, on average, to acquire a lead.
cost per order	A form of online advertising where the advertiser pays a set fee for the completion of a customer order resulting from a click on an ad.
cost-per-thousand advertising	An advertising model, used in both traditional and online advertising, where the cost of the ad is determined by the number of impressions—that is, the number of people viewing the ad. Also known as *cost-per-thousand impressions advertising* and *CPM advertising*.
cost-per-thousand impressions advertising	See *cost-per-thousand advertising*.
CPA	See *cost per action*.
CPC	See *cost per click*.
CPL	See *cost per lead*.
CPM advertising	See *cost-per-thousand advertising*.
CPO	See *cost per order*.
crawler	See *spider*.
CTR	See *click-through rate*.
delivery rate	In email marketing, the percentage of recipients who received a mailing, ideally to the recipient's main inbox, and not a spam or junk email folder.
digital marketing	See *web marketing*.
direct traffic	Website traffic derived from visitors that manually enter a site's URL.

display advertising	On the Web, ads that consist of images or other media, as opposed to those that consist solely of text.
duration of visit	See *active time.*
dynamic drill-down navigation	An approach to website navigation where all the pages on the side are essentially on the same level but accessed through different virtual paths; there are no predefined paths or hierarchy, just what a user chooses dynamically. Also known as *faceted navigation.*
dynamic web page	A web page with content and URL that is generated on the fly, typically as a result of a search on the website.
ecommerce	Electronic commerce; the selling of goods or services over the Internet, typically from a website designed for that purpose.
email marketing	Online promotion delivered via electronic mail. Legitimate email marketing differs from *spam* in that is opt-in.
embedded marketing	See *product placement.*
engagement time	See *active time.*
Facebook	The Internet's largest social networking site.
faceted navigation	See *dynamic drill-down navigation.*
fan	On Facebook, someone who "likes" a company or product page.
fan page	On Facebook, a page for a company, product, or celebrity.
feed	See *site feed.*
feed subscriptions	Subscriptions to a blog's site feed.
first visit	The first visit to a website from a visitor who has not previously visited the site.
follower	On Twitter, someone who subscribes to your tweets.
frequency	A measurement of how often visitors come to a website, calculated by dividing the total number of sessions or visits by the total number of unique visitors.
friend	On a social network, a user who connects with you.
Google AdSense	Google's network for website owners that places contextual PPC ads on their sites.
Google AdWords	Google's PPC network for advertisers.
hashtag	On Twitter, a way to assign topics to given posts.

hit	A request for a file from a web server. Note that a hit is not the same as a *pageview*, as a single page can have multiple elements (images, text boxes, and so forth) that need to be individually loaded from the server.
HTML	Short for *hypertext markup language*, the coding language used to create pages on the Web.
HTML ads	Web advertisements that combine text and images with interactive HTML elements, such as pull-down lists, check boxes, forms, and the like.
impression	A single display of an advertisement on a web page.
inbound link	A link to a given web page from another website.
Internet marketing	See *web marketing.*
interstitial advertising	On the Web, ads that appear during the transition from one web page to the next.
keyword	A word or phrase entered as part of a search query. Also a word or phrase chosen by an advertiser to trigger the display of an online ad.
keyword density	The number of times a keyword appears compared to the total number of words on a page.
keyword research	The art of determining which keywords to use on a website or in PPC advertising.
keyword stuffing	A technique that inserts multiple instances of a keyword onto a page in an effort to increase the keyword density and thus increase the page's apparent relevancy of a page.
landing page	A page on your website that a visitor lands on when coming from another site or advertisement. Landing pages are typically created specifically to connect with specific referring links.
leaderboard	A large banner display ad.
like	On Facebook, how someone becomes a fan of your page, by clicking the Like button.
local search	Web search for local businesses, attractions, and events.
malware	Malicious software, such as viruses and spyware.
marketing	The act of presenting something to someone else.
microblog	A service, such as Twitter, that enables the broadcasting of short text messages to other interested users.

mobile advertising	Ads optimized or created expressly for display on smartphones and other mobile devices.
mobile application	A software application designed for use on a smartphone or other mobile device.
mobile marketing	Marketing activities performed on or with a mobile device, such as a mobile phone.
mobile search	Web search initiated by users of smartphones and other mobile devices.
mobile website	A website optimized for viewing on smartphones and other mobile devices.
multimedia marketing	Marketing activities that utilize audio and visual media, such as *podcasts* and online videos.
narrowcasting	The transmission of a message to a specific list or type of recipients.
new visitor	A visitor who has not made any previous visits to a website.
news feed	See *site feed.*
offsite analytics	Web analytics that use Internet-wide information to determine which are the most visited sites on the Web.
online advertising	Any advertising placed on web pages or other Internet-related media.
online marketing	See *web marketing.*
online payment service	A web-based service that facilitates credit card payments for ecommerce websites. Popular online payment services include PayPal, Google Checkout, and Checkout by Amazon.
online PR	Public relations activities that utilize the Internet or are directed to entities on the Internet.
online press room	A virtual media room, typically one or more pages on a website, that offer downloadable pictures, videos, and other media for the press.
onsite analytics	Web analytics that use site-specific data to track visitors to a specific website.
open rate	In email marketing, the percentage of messages that were opened by recipients.
opt-in	Advertisements or other promotions that are delivered only to consumers who proactively agree to receive such communications.

organic search results	Site listings that result from a user's web search. Organic results are in contrast to paid results from PPC advertising.
page depth	The average number of pageviews a visitor initiates before ending a session, calculated by dividing total number of pageviews by total number of sessions. Also known as *pageviews per session*.
page tagging	A technique that places a "bug," in the form of a piece of JavaScript code, in the basic HTML of a web page in order to capture data about visitors to that web page.
PageRank	Google's method of determining a web page's importance by counting the number of other pages that link to that page. The more pages that link to a page, the higher that page's PageRank—and the higher it will appear in the search results.
pageview	A display of a complete web page. One visitor looking at a single page on a site generates one pageview.
pageview duration	The average amount of time that visitors spend on each page of a website. Also known as *time on page*.
pageviews per session	See *page depth*.
pay-per-click advertising	A form of online advertising where the advertiser pays only when the ad is clicked by a consumer. Most pay-per-click ads are text ads. Also known as *PPC advertising*.
percent exit	See *% exit*.
percent of clicks served	A metric that describes which ads in an ad group are getting the most displays, calculated by dividing the number of impressions for a given ad by the total number of impressions in an ad group.
podcast	One of a series of episodic audio files, typically distributed over the Internet via RSS feeds.
pop-up ads	Advertisements that appear in new windows when a page is visited or a link is clicked.
PPC advertising	See *pay-per-click advertising*.
PR	See *public relations*.
product blog	A professional blog used to promote a company's products.
product placement	The act of arranging the appearance of mention of a product in a natural context, but not via traditional advertising. Also known as *embedded marketing*.

Promoted Tweets	Advertisements on Twitter.
Promoted Videos	PPC advertisements on YouTube.
public relations	The practice of managing communication between a company and the public.
qualitative research	Investigation and analysis that seek to explain why and how events happen.
quantitative research	Data gathering and analysis that involves hard numbers.
reactivation	In email marketing, an attempt to turn an inactive customer into an active one.
recency	In web analytics, the number of days since a visitor's most recent visit.
referring site	A website that sends traffic to another site.
remnant space	Leftover ad space on a website, typically sold at a discounted price.
repeat visitor	A visitor who has made at least one previous visit to a website.
return on investment	A measurement of effectiveness, calculated by dividing the return of a project by the project's cost. Also known as *ROI*.
retweet	On Twitter, the act of forwarding a tweet to other users.
rich media ads	On the Web, advertisements that employ multimedia features, such as audio, video, and animations.
ROI	See *return on investment*.
search engine marketing	The process of driving visitors to a website from that site's listings in search engine results. Search engine marketing typically involves *search engine optimization*. Also known as *SEM*.
search engine optimization	The process of optimizing a website so that it places higher in search engine results. Also known as *SEO*.
search engine rank	How high a page appears in the search results for a relevant keyword.
SEM	See *search engine marketing*.
SEO	See *search engine optimization*.
session	A series of pageviews from the same visitor with no more than 30 minutes between pageviews—and with no visits to other sites between pageviews.
session duration	The average amount of time that visitors spend on a website each time they visit.

shopping cart	In an ecommerce website, a system that holds customer purchases and feeds into the site's checkout system.
singleton	A visit from a visitor where only a single page is viewed.
site feed	An automatically updated stream of a blog's contents.
sitemap	A map of a website used to submit pages to a search engine.
skyscraper ad	A tall, vertical display ad format that typically runs down the side of a page.
social bookmarking service	A web-based service, such as Digg or Delicious, that enables users to save and share their favorite web pages with friends and colleagues online. Also known as a *social news service*.
social media	Those websites, services, and platforms that people use to share experiences and opinions with each other.
social media advertising	Ads running on and targeted at users of social media sites.
social media marketing	All marketing activities on or via social media.
social network	A website, such as Facebook, that lets users connect with each other (as "friends") and share what they're doing or thinking.
social news service	See *social bookmarking service*.
social plug-in	On Facebook, a *widget* that you install on your website that provides a direct connection to the Facebook site.
social sharing	The sharing online of videos, photos, and other media.
spam	Unrequested and unwanted junk email. Also known as *unwanted commercial email*.
spider	An automated software program that crawls the Web to construct an index for a search engine. Also known as a *crawler*.
spyware	Malicious software that surreptitiously captures information from an infected computer.
status update	On a social network, a short message posted to a user's friends or fans.
text advertising	On the Web, ads that consist solely of text or clickable text links.
time on page	See *pageview duration*.
traffic source	The site visited just before a visitor visits another website.
tweet	The short (140-character maximum) text messages sent via Twitter.

Twitter	The Internet's largest microblogging service.
Twitterverse	The entire universe of Twitter users.
UCE	Unwanted commercial email; see *spam*.
unique visitor	A visitor who visits a website one or more times within a given time frame, typically a single 24-hour period; a visitor can make multiple visits during that time frame but counts as just a single unique visitor.
unsubscribe rate	In email marketing, the percentage of users who remove their names from a mailing list.
unwanted commercial email	See *spam*.
video marketing	Marketing via videos produced for or distributed over the Web.
view-through conversions	The number of conversions that occur within 30 days of a customer clicking the ad.
viral	An item that becomes hugely popular, with hundreds of thousands or even millions of views, via Internet-based sharing.
virtual community	A social network that enables community via a 3D, game-like interface.
visibility time	The time (in seconds or minutes) that a single page or element is viewed by a visitor.
visit	A series of pageviews from the same visitor with no more than 30 minutes between each pageview.
visitor	A uniquely identified client that views the pages on a website; someone who visits your site.
web analytics	Tools and services that track website usage.
web marketing	The act of presenting something to someone else online. Also known as *online marketing, digital marketing,* or *Internet marketing.*
web video	A video uploaded for viewing over the Internet.
widget	A small dedicated application.
YouTube	The Internet's largest video sharing community.

Index

subfolders on main domain, 533
user agent detection, 533-534

HotWired, 239

HTML ads, 197

HTML tags
optimizing, 142
anchor text, 145-146
header tags, 145
META tags, 143-145
TITLE tags, 142-143
what search engines look for, 135

Hummingbird, 403

I

iAd, 546

IceRocket, 379

iContact, 289

iHandy Level, 546

image ads versus text ads, mobile advertising, 538-539

images
mobile websites, 528
optimizing, 152
ALT attribute, 152-153
searches, 153
TITLE attribute, 153
PPC image ads, creating, 225-226
versus text, search engines, 126
thumbnail images, YouTube, 497

importance
of blogs and bloggers, 345-346
of high rankings, 119-120

impressions
evaluating metrics, 260
web analytics, 109

improving performance, 173

inbound link tools, 170

inbound links
optimizing, 148
getting the word out, 149
link requests, 149-150
link trading, 150
links between pages on your site, 151-152
linkworthy content, 148
purchasing links, 151
tracking blog performance, 355
what search engines look for, 135-136

incorporating multimedia into your marketing mix, 465-466

independent websites, online advertising, 202

indexing dynamic pages, 125

Indianapolis Business Journal, 297

informative videos, 481-482

InfoUSA, 166

integrating efforts across multiple social media, 411
constructing compatible messages, 411-412
integration tools, 412-414

integration tools, integrating across multiple social media, 412-414

interacting with customers, company blogs, 319

interactivity, tracking, 513

Internet advertising, web analytics, 58

Internet marketing. *See* web marketing

interstitial ads, 194-195

inventory management, ecommerce websites, 100

iTunes Store, 473

J

journalists, informing of new news (online press rooms), 452

junk email, 21

JupiterMedia, 310

K

key issues, 69

key phrases, 211

Keyword Tool (Google), 213

keyword tools, 171

KEYWORDS, 144

keywords
optimizing, 139
determining density, 140-141
performing keyword research, 139-140
writing keyword-oriented copy, 141-142
PPC (pay-per-click), 206-208

Mobile Marketing
Finding Your Customers No Matter Where They Are

iPhone & iPad Apps Marketing
Secrets to Selling Your iPhone and iPad Apps

BLOGGING TO DRIVE BUSINESS
Create and Maintain Valuable Customer Connections

Social Media Marketing
Publicity through Viral Marketing

Facebook Marketing
Designing Your Next Marketing Campaign
Second Edition

que
Biz-Tech Series

Straightforward Strategies and Tactics for Business Today

The **Que Biz-Tech series** is designed for the legions of executives and marketers out there trying to come to grips with emerging technologies that can make or break their business. These books help the reader know what's important, what isn't, and provide deep inside know-how for entering the brave new world of business technology, covering topics such as mobile marketing, microblogging, and iPhone and iPad app marketing.

- Straightforward strategies and tactics for companies who are either using or will be using a new technology/product or way of thinking/ doing business

- Written by well-known industry experts in their respective fields— and designed to be an open platform for the author to teach a topic in the way he or she believes the audience will learn best

- Covers new technologies that companies must embrace to remain competitive in the marketplace and shows them how to maximize those technologies for profit

- Written with the marketing and business user in mind—these books meld solid technical know-how with corporate-savvy advice for improving the bottom line

 Visit **quepublishing.com/biztech** to learn more about the **Que Biz-Tech series**

FREE Online Edition

Your purchase of **The Ultimate Web Marketing Guide** includes access to a free online edition for 45 days through the Safari Books Online subscription service. Nearly every Que book is available online through Safari Books Online, along with more than 5,000 other technical books and videos from publishers such as Addison-Wesley Professional, Cisco Press, Exam Cram, IBM Press, O'Reilly, Prentice Hall, and Sams.

SAFARI BOOKS ONLINE allows you to search for a specific answer, cut and paste code, download chapters, and stay current with emerging technologies.

Activate your FREE Online Edition at
www.informit.com/safarifree

> **STEP 1:** Enter the coupon code: GLYEHBI.

> **STEP 2:** New Safari users, complete the brief registration form.
> Safari subscribers, just log in.

If you have difficulty registering on Safari or accessing the online edition, please e-mail customer-service@safaribooksonline.com